Israel and the Family of Nations

Can Israel be both Jewish and truly democratic? How can a nation-state, which incorporates a large national minority with a distinct identity of its own, be a state of all its citizens?

Written by two eminent Israeli scholars, a professor of constitutional law and a historian, Alexander Yakobson and Amnon Rubinstein are the first to treat Zionism and Israeli experience in light of other states' experiences and in particular of newly established states that have undergone constitutional changes and wrestled with issues of minorities. Citing various European constitutions and laws, the authors explore the concept of a Jewish state and its various meanings in the light of international law, and the current norms of human rights as applied to other democratic societies compatible with liberal democratic norms and conclude that international reality does not accord with the concept that regards a modern liberal democracy as a culturally 'neutral' and nationally colourless entity.

In light of the new political map in Israel and the prospect of future disengagement from the West Bank, *Israel and the Family of Nations* is essential reading for all those who wish to understand Israel's future challenges.

Dr Alexander Yakobson is a Senior Lecturer in the history department of the Hebrew University of Jerusalem. **Professor Amnon Rubinstein** is currently Provost and Dean of the Radzyner School of Law at the Interdisciplinary Center (IDC) in Herzlia. He is a former Minister of Education and a regular contributor to Israeli dailies.

Israeli history, politics and society
Series Editor: Efraim Karsh
King's College London

This series provides a multidisciplinary examination of all aspects of Israeli history, politics and society, and serves as a means of communication between the various communities interested in Israel: academics, policy-makers, practitioners, journalists and the informed public.

1 **Peace in the Middle East**
The challenge for Israel
Edited by Efraim Karsh

2 **The Shaping of Israeli Identity**
Myth, memory and trauma
Edited by Robert Wistrich and David Ohana

3 **Between War and Peace**
Dilemmas of Israeli security
Edited by Efraim Karsh

4 **US–Israeli Relations at the Crossroads**
Edited by Gabriel Sheffer

5 **Revisiting the Yom Kippur War**
Edited by P.R. Kumaraswamy

6 **Israel**
The dynamics of change and continuity
Edited by David Levi-Faur, Gabriel Sheffer and David Vogel

7 **In Search of Identity**
Jewish aspects in Israeli culture
Edited by Dan Urian and Efraim Karsh

8 **Israel at the Polls, 1996**
Edited by Daniel J. Elazar and Shmuel Sandler

9 **From Rabin to Netanyahu**
Israel's troubled agenda
Edited by Efraim Karsh

10 **Fabricating Israeli History**
The 'new historians', second revised edition
Efraim Karsh

11 **Divided against Zion**
Anti-Zionist opposition in Britain to a Jewish State in Palestine, 1945–1948
Rory Miller

12 **Peacemaking in a Divided Society**
Israel after Rabin
Edited by Sasson Sofer

13 **A Twenty-Year Retrospective of Egyptian–Israeli Relations**
Peace in spite of everything
Ephraim Dowek

14 **Global Politics**
Essays in honor of David Vital
Edited by Abraham Ben-Zvi and Aharon Klieman

15 **Parties, Elections and Cleavages**
Israel in comparative and theoretical perspective
Edited by Reuven Y. Hazan and Moshe Maor

16 **Israel at the Polls 1999**
Edited by Daniel J. Elazar and M. Ben Mollov

17 **Public Policy in Israel**
Edited by David Nachmias and Gila Menahem

18 **Developments in Israeli Public Administration**
Edited by Moshe Maor

19 **Israeli Diplomacy and the Quest for Peace**
Mordechai Gazit

20 **Israeli–Romanian Relations at the End of Ceaucescu's Era**
Yosef Govrin

21 **John F. Kennedy and the Politics of Arms Sales to Israel**
Abraham Ben-Zvi

22 **Green Crescent over Nazareth**
The displacement of Christians by Muslims in the Holy Land
Raphael Israeli

23 **Jerusalem Divided**
The armistice region, 1947–1967
Raphael Israeli

24 **Decision on Palestine Deferred**
America, Britain and wartime diplomacy, 1939–1945
Monty Noam Penkower

25 **A Dissenting Democracy**
The case of 'peace now', an Israeli peace movement
Magnus Norell

26 **Britain, Israel and Anglo-Jewry 1947–1957**
Natan Aridan

27 **Israeli Identity**
In search of a successor to the pioneer, tsabar and settler
Lilly Weissbrod

28 **The Israeli Palestinians**
An Arab minority in the Jewish State
Edited by Alexander Bligh

29 **Israel, the Hashemites and the Palestinians**
The fateful triangle
Edited by Efraim Karsh and P.R. Kumaraswamy

30 **Last Days in Israel**
Abraham Diskin

31 **War in Palestine, 1948**
Strategy and diplomacy
David Tal

32 **Rethinking the Middle East**
Efraim Karsh

33 **Ben-Gurion against the Knesset**
Giora Goldberg

34 **Trapped Fools**
Thirty years of Israeli policy in the territories
Schlomo Gazit

35 **Israel's Quest for Recognition and Acceptance in Asia**
Garrison state diplomacy
Jacob Abadi

36 **The Harp and Shield of David**
Ireland, Zionism and the State of Israel, 1937–1963
Eliash Shulamit

37 **H.V. Evatt and the Establishment of Israel**
The undercover Zionist
Daniel Mandel

38 **Navigating Perilous Waters**
An Israeli strategy for peace and security
Ephraim Sneh

39 **Lyndon B. Johnson and the Politics of Arms Sales to Israel**
In the shadow of the hawk
Abraham Ben-Zvi

40 **Israel at the Polls 2003**
Edited by Shmeul Sandler, Ben M. Mollov and Jonathan Rynhold

41 **Between Capital and Land**
The Jewish national fund's finances and land-purchase priorities in Palestine, 1939–1945
Eric Engel Tuten

42 **Israeli Democracy at the Crossroads**
Raphael Cohen-Almagor

43 **Israeli Institutions at the Crossroads**
Raphael Cohen-Almagor

44 **The Israeli–Palestine Peace Process Negotiations, 1999–2001**
Within reach
Gilead Sher

45 **Ben-Gurion's Political Struggles, 1963–67**
A lion in winter
Zaki Shalom

46 **Ben-Gurion, Zionism and American Jewry**
1948–1963
Ariel Feldestein

47 **The Origins of the American–Israeli Alliance**
The Jordanian factor
Abraham Ben-Zvi

48 **Israel's National Security**
Issues and challenges since the Yom Kippur War
Efraim Inbar

49 **The Rise of Israel**
A history of a revolutionary state
Jonathan Adelman

50 **Israel and the Family of Nations**
The Jewish nation-state and human rights
Alexander Yakobson and Amnon Rubinstein

Israel: The First Hundred Years (Mini Series)
Edited by Efraim Karsh

1   **Israel's Transition from
    Community to State**
    Edited by Efraim Karsh

2   **From War to Peace?**
    Edited by Efraim Karsh

3   **Politics and Society since 1948**
    Edited by Efraim Karsh

4   **Israel in the International Arena**
    Edited by Efraim Karsh

5   **Israel in the Next Century**
    Edited by Efraim Karsh

Israel and the Family of Nations

The Jewish nation-state and human rights

Alexander Yakobson and Amnon Rubinstein

Translated by Ruth Morris and Ruchie Avital

Routledge
Taylor & Francis Group

LONDON AND NEW YORK

First published 2009
Paperback edition first published 2010
by Routledge
2 Park Square, Milton Park, Abingdon, Oxon OX14 4RN

Simultaneously published in the USA and Canada
by Routledge
270 Madison Ave, New York, NY 10016

Routledge is an imprint of the Taylor & Francis Group, an informa business

Typeset in Times by Wearset Ltd, Boldon, Tyne and Wear

British Library Cataloguing in Publication Data
A catalogue record for this book is available from the British Library

Library of Congress Cataloging in Publication Data
A catalog record for this book has been requested

ISBN13: 978-0-415-46441-3 (hbk)
ISBN13: 978-0-415-78137-4 (pbk)
ISBN13: 978-0-203-89402-6 (ebk)

Contents

Introduction   1

1 The establishment of the State of Israel: the UN debates in 1947   12

The declaration of the establishment of the State of Israel 12
The debates in 1947: the UNSCOP report 15
The debates on the partition plan in the UN General Assembly 21
The right to national self-determination and its dilemmas 30
The historic connection and historic right 41
'An alien body in the Arab Middle East' 44
The validity of the principle of partition 56

2 Two arguments: Zionism as a colonialist phenomenon and the invention of Jewish nationalism   65

Colonialism and imperialist support 65
'A hope of two thousand years': modern Jewish identity and
  historical continuity 76

3 Zionism and international norms   83

It all started with Herzl 84
What would be the status of the Arab minority? 91

4 The Jewish State and Israeli democracy   97

The concept of a Jewish state in Israeli discourse 97
The Jewish state and the rights of the Arab minority 104
Israel's Arabs as a national minority 118

5   'Either Jewish or democratic'?   124

'Jewish and democratic state': oxymoron? 124
The Law of Return and international norms of civil equality 125
Europe: diasporas and repatriation laws 126
Official ties with kin-minorities 131
Israel, the Jewish Diaspora and the Law of Return 133
A Jewish state and a state of all its citizens 135
*'The Jewish-Israeli people' and the right to self-determination
    137*

6   A 'neutral state' and a democratic nation-state   141

The neutrality principle and a typology of democratic systems 141
Partition and 'neutrality' 148
*The neutrality principle, the Law of Return and the refugee
    problem 156*
Two examples of partition: India and Ireland 158
'Imperial' nations: the United Kingdom and Spain 164
*Civic nationalism in a multi-ethnic society: the United States and
    other examples 171*
Complex identities, national identity and citizenship 180

Epilogue: nowhere else   192

**Appendix 1: extracts from some contemporary
democratic constitutions**   200

**Appendix 2: Armenia and the Armenian diaspora –
Nansen's address to the League of Nations**   218

Notes   220
Bibliography   233
Index   238

Introduction

This book examines the concept of a 'Jewish state' and the principal features that determine the Jewish character of the State of Israel in the light of international law, the principle of national self-determination and the norms of human rights accepted in the modern democratic world. This discussion relates to the ongoing controversy, both in Israel and outside it, over Israel's official designation as a Jewish state. Originally, Zionism sought (in the 'Basle Programme'[1] adopted by the First Zionist Congress) to establish 'in Palestine a home for the Jewish people secured under public law'. It sought and eventually obtained international recognition of the Jewish people's right to a state, never endorsing the 'nation that dwells alone' view. Today, however, there are those that claim that the very concept of a 'Jewish state' (and everything that it implies, primarily the Law of Return[2]) runs counter to international human rights norms and discriminates, by definition, against non-Jewish citizens.

This claim, often heard outside the country, is today voiced in Israel not only by members of the radical Left or Arab nationalists. Quite a few 'mainstream' Israelis who are committed to universal humanist values raise questions about this matter. Some of them, while still clinging to the definition of Israel as a Jewish state and to the Law of Return, take an apologetic approach, viewing the Jewish state as a form of 'affirmative action' that favours the Jewish people because of the catastrophes that befell it in the past. By implication, such 'affirmative action' is meant to be merely a temporary arrangement.

On the other hand, some of those who cherish the concept of a Jewish state fear that embracing the values of universal equality will mean having to abandon this idea. Furthermore, in ultra-nationalist circles and among those who favour religious coercion, the concept of a 'Jewish state' serves as a seal of approval for undermining accepted democratic principles. From these quarters one hears that, since Israel is a Jewish state (and, according to most Israelis, should continue to preserve this character), its non-Jewish citizens cannot, by definition, enjoy full civil equality. By the same token, secular Jews are required to accept the Orthodox establishment's definition of Judaism – otherwise the state will not be truly Jewish. Thus, the ostensible contradiction between a Jewish state and liberal democracy drives some to anti-democratic conclusions, while others draw from it the conclusion that Israel's Jewish character should be rejected. Others prefer to ignore the issue and dodge the question. Few have made the effort to systematically come to grips with the question of the relationship between these two principles: Are they in fact fundamentally contradictory?

In this book, we intend to demonstrate that no such contradiction exists. On the contrary, it is the denial of the legitimacy of the concept of a Jewish state that undermines the principles of universal equality, since it denies the right of the Jewish people to self-determination and national independence. There is a considerable measure of historical irony here: at the very time that the majority of the Israeli public has accepted – on the pragmatic level at least – the right of the Arab-Palestinian people to an independent state of its own, and steps have been taken on the ground to realize this right, there are groups in the Israeli Left that have in fact repudiated the principle of 'two states for two peoples' by adopting a stance that amounts to denying the right of the Jewish people to national independence.

We shall show that it was the international community, through the UN Partition Plan of 1947, that decided in favour of setting up a 'Jewish state' – in other words, a homeland and safe haven for the Jewish people, and that everything that naturally derives from that definition, including the Law of Return, meets human rights norms as accepted by the free world today, not just those acceptable in 1947. Whatever, in the country's day-to-day reality, contradicts liberal democratic principles does not follow from Israel's definition as a Jewish state. This definition means no more and no less than that Israel was established as an expression of the Jewish people's right to a homeland and an independent state – the right of national self-determination, as it is known today. This is how it was perceived, both internationally and by the founding fathers of Zionism.

The United Nations General Assembly, which decided, by adopting the partition plan based on the principle that both peoples in the country were entitled to national independence, to establish a 'Jewish state' and an 'Arab state' in Mandatory Palestine, stipulated that both these states would be required to adopt a democratic form of governance and guarantee the rights of the national minorities (Arab and Jewish respectively) living within their borders. Thus, the international community saw no contradiction between the national definitions of the character of the two future states – Arab and Jewish – and the principle of citizens' equality before the law. Similarly, in classical Zionist thinking, a Jewish state means a homeland and refuge for the Jewish people, not a state that discriminates between Jewish and non-Jewish citizens, or a state that is dominated by the Jewish religion. It goes without saying that not all criticism, however harsh, of Israeli realities is to be interpreted as a denial of Israel's legitimacy as a Jewish state – in other words, a denial of the Jewish people's right to a state. But neither is there any justification for some people's tendency to deprecate the very idea of Jewish independence because of shortcomings in its realization. This is not how other peoples, national movements and nation-states are treated in the modern world. Even nations that do not maintain even a semblance of democracy are universally recognized as entitled to national independence, and even in such cases (not in fact wholly exceptional in the Middle East) no one claims that the very idea of national independence is an undemocratic one.

National or ethnic minorities exist in many democratic nation-states. In every such case, the country's public character is determined primarily by the majority and influenced mainly by its culture and identity, with consideration given to the rights of the minority. That is why the Jewish State necessarily has a Jewish character which is expressed in features such as the official status of the Hebrew language (although Arabic is also recognized as a second official language), the state emblems and symbols, the official weekly day of rest and holidays, as well as the character of its public education and its cultural life. Israel's national emblems and symbols are Jewish in nature. Some claim that this fact inevitably alienates the state from its non-Jewish citizens: according to those that take this view, the nation's symbols should be 'neutral' so that all of the state's citizens can identify with them in equal measure. But the sign of the cross, which appears on the national flags of the United Kingdom, Australia, New Zealand, Switzerland, Greece, Hungary and Scandinavia's exemplary democracies, as well as on coats-of-arms of many countries, is not a 'neutral' symbol, and not all the citizens of these countries can identify with it. It is, however, the symbol of the majority's historical and cultural identity. The same can be said of the ancient religious symbol that appears on the flag of secular India, which has a large Muslim minority.

Many believe that the connection between the State of Israel and Diaspora Jews, a bond attested to by the Law of Return as well as in other ways, is a unique phenomenon. Some argue that this attachment is detrimental to the principle of civil equality. The Law of Return, which is clearly fundamental to the Jewish character of the state, is targeted by much of the criticism levelled at Israel in this regard. However, we will show that here too the case of Israel is not, as conventional wisdom would often have it, unique. The contemporary democratic world provides numerous such examples of ties between nation-states and their national diasporas. These ties sometimes include provisions for national repatriation, as reflected in numerous constitutions, as well as in laws governing immigration and citizenship.

Until recently, it could have been argued that in one area – which has both symbolic and practical significance – there was in fact a contradiction between the principle of civil equality and the Jewish character of the state as interpreted by the Israeli (not necessarily right-wing) establishment. While the bulk of the country's land that is not privately owned belongs to the State (and thus, legally, to all its citizens), the Jewish National Fund (JNF), as a branch of the Zionist movement, has in the past purchased land on a wide scale explicitly for the purpose of Jewish settlement. The problem, as far as civil equality is concerned, is that the State sold some of the State land to the JNF. Clearly, this procedure amounts to circumventing the principle that all State property, including land, is the property of all citizens. However, Israel's High Court of Justice recently ruled (in what is known as the 'Kaadan case') that transferring State land to the JNF is illegal, holding that here too, as in other areas, there is no inconsistency between civil equality and the Jewish character of the state, and that this character cannot serve as an excuse for discrimination between one citizen and another. For the future, then, the practice has been outlawed; the argument now is over the status of lands handed by the State to the JNF decades ago. This argument, despite the legal complications involved, should undoubtedly be resolved in favour of the principle that guided the High Court in its decision in the case before it. In general, it may be said that the quasi-official status granted in Israel to the institutions of the Zionist movement is legitimate to the extent that it is intended to express and serve the ties between the state and Diaspora Jewry; however, it is not legitimate to use these institutions in order to create what is in effect ethnic discrimination between one citizen and another within the state.

Some make a distinction between the terms 'the state of the Jews' (*Der Judenstaat*, the title of Herzl's celebrated book) and 'a Jewish state': Whereas the former term is considered legitimate, the latter is imputed with negative associations of narrow nationalism and religious coercion. We will show that there is no justification for this distinction. The 'Jewish state' that the UN General Assembly voted to establish in 1947 is in fact a state for the Jewish people – in other words, 'the state of the Jews' of which Herzl dreamed. It should be noted that while some people find it hard to stomach the term 'Jewish state', no such difficulty has been caused by the term 'Palestinian state' – or, indeed, by the official designation of all of Israel's Arab neighbours as 'Arab states'. It is clear to all that a Palestinian state (or an Arab state in Palestine, as the UN Partition Plan put it) means nothing more than the state of the Palestinians, the state of the Arab-Palestinian people. By the same token, the Czech Republic is the republic of the Czech people, despite the fact that it also has Slovak citizens; and therefore it has both a distinctly Czech character and a duty to protect the rights of its Slovak (and any other) minority. Had the Palestinian Arabs accepted the Partition and established their independent state in 1948, that state would have included a Jewish minority. One can only hypothesize what the status of that Jewish minority might have been in such a state, ruled by the Mufti of Jerusalem. However, no one claims that the very idea of an Arab-Palestinian state is inherently illegitimate because it is inconsistent with the principles of civil equality. Similarly, even when they have substantial non-Arab minorities all of Israel's neighbours are officially defined as Arab states, and although justified criticism is levelled at them – among other things because of the way they treat their minorities – no one claims that their very definition as Arab states is illegitimate.

The arguments against defining Israel as a Jewish state are usually based on an abstract, radical and rather utopian model of liberal democracy. After presentation of this model – whose theoretical validity is also open to debate, and indeed, such a debate is taking place among experts in the field – it is claimed that Israel, as a Jewish state, does not meet its requirements. In order to refute this claim, we shall examine the situation that actually prevails today throughout the free world and analyse the constitutions and laws of many contemporary democracies. Readers of different backgrounds may be interested in hearing how liberal democracy functions in a context of nation-states throughout the world. It should be remembered that democracy and human rights are concepts that evolve over time, undergoing radicalization in certain areas. Although the basic principles have tended to remain the same, not everything that was considered legitimate in 1947 is acceptable in today's democratic world. In principle, one might have argued that while the Jewish character of the State of Israel was consistent with the norms of the late 1940s, it is inconsistent with those that are generally accepted today. Therefore, this book will relate to the democratic world's prevailing realities in the 1990s and early twenty-first century, and will try to identify the dominant trends in relevant areas. It is a given that even in the most tranquil and liberal countries issues related to religious, linguistic and national minorities prompt debates and controversies. Some of the debates on the status of the Arab minority in Israel – for example, the question of the relationship between the State's principal language and the language of the minority – are of concern to any country that has minorities. In this respect, the arrangement in Israel regarding the status of Arabic, according to which it is recognized as a second official language (although this principle is not always implemented de facto), is more liberal and far-reaching than the situation in many other democratic states. However, it is also clear that the peculiar situation of the Arab minority in Israel, which results from the prolonged Israeli–Arab and Israeli–Palestinian conflict, creates distinct and difficult problems.

A large body of research and professional literature deals with such issues as national identity and citizenship; 'civic' versus 'ethnic' nationalism; individual rights and collective rights of minorities; the nation-state and its future in an age of globalization, European integration, mass immigration and multiculturalism. Apart from a few basic references, we do not intend to deal with this literature in detail, or to take sides in the scholarly controversies on those matters. We intend to concentrate mainly on the practice, rather than the theory, of the contemporary liberal nation-state. Some scholars tend to take a positive view of this practice, while others are more critical. However, one must bear in mind that the European states that belong to the Council of Europe have for many years now been subject to the judicial review of the European Court of Human Rights, which rules in accordance with the European Convention for the Protection of Human Rights and Fundamental Freedoms. Consequently, the human rights norms prevailing in these countries – among other things, on the treatment of national and religious minorities – certainly reflect the highest international standards. This applies not only to the old, well-established West European democracies, but also to the new democracies of Central and Eastern Europe, which have become part of the European democratic community and have been required to prove their adherence to European human rights norms.

Our premise is that, irrespective of any debate on democratic theory, today's European (mostly Western) states which fall under the purview of the European Court of Human Rights should be considered genuine liberal democracies. If, for example, Finland's immigration laws grant people of Finnish ethnic extraction from the former Soviet Union preferential conditions for the purpose of immigrating to Finland, and if the government of Finland has declared that it views these people's immigration to Finland as 'repatriation' (in the sense of *re*turning to one's native land, or *patria*), even though some of the people in question are descendants of Finns who emigrated from Finland hundreds of years ago – all of this does not show that Finland is a 'second-rate' or 'ethnic' democracy. Rather, it shows that, according to the norms practised in today's democratic world, it is legitimate for a nation-state to maintain ties with its ethno-national diaspora, and, among other things, to express these ties through laws on immigration and naturalization.

It is sometimes argued that the standard Western liberal-democratic model is not necessarily – or at any rate, not entirely – appropriate for other regions of the world and their cultures. In principle, arguments based on 'cultural specificity' may have some degree of validity. On the other hand, it is obvious that these claims have often been used as a pretext for gross violations of basic human rights. In any case, we do not intend to present Israel's case as 'specific' in these terms. In our view, Israel can and should meet the highest standards of contemporary Western-style liberal democracy. Naturally, contemporary democracies themselves differ to a considerable degree over the matters to be discussed in this book. These differences reflect the historical and cultural uniqueness of every society. In this sense, every case, including the Israeli one, is unique; but at the same time, a commitment to certain basic principles is universally required. One of the specific circumstances of the Israeli case is, of course, the prolonged national conflict in which the country is engaged. But many other democracies have had to deal with threats and emergencies of various kinds, and have faced the difficult dilemma of trying to protect the safety of the nation without sacrificing its moral values. It seems that a prolonged, 'chronic' state of emergency, often considered an oxymoron, might become a feature of some contemporary democracies as a result of the threat posed by Islamist terrorism.

Israel differs from the many nation-states that have significant national minorities in that, in most cases, the name of the state (and the traditional name of the country) is commensurate with the name of the majority-people as well as with that of its language. Consequently, the question of 'the state's identity' in a national sense does not arise in the same terms in which it arises in Israel. Generally speaking, in the constitution of a democratic nation-state, the standard provisions regarding the name of a state and its official (or 'national') language represent the definition of the national identity of that state; and it should be borne in mind that national language is widely regarded as a fundamental distinctive feature of modern national identity. By definition, a national minority is a community that defines its national identity by means of a different name from that which defines the identity of the state, and in most cases, its language also differs from the state language. It is the 'national majority' which gives the state its name and its identity. No one asks if Slovakia is a Slovak state – it is simply Slovakia. It is left to the hundreds of thousands of members of the Hungarian minority in this state to decide whether to refer to themselves as 'Slovaks' (which could be perceived as a denial of their national identity). On the other hand, the statement 'I am not a Slovak' by an 'ethnic Hungarian' could be interpreted as a denial of his or her Slovak citizenship. This is a dilemma common to many minority groups. Similarly, Basques and Catalans with a pronounced national awareness often find it difficult to define themselves as 'Spanish', because they view this term as relating to the Spanish-speaking majority rather than to all the citizens and national groups (defined as 'nationalities' by the Spanish Constitution) living in Spain. Even among the Swedes (or according to the official designation, 'Swedish speakers') living in Finland – one of the best-protected minorities in the world – some hesitate to call themselves 'Finns'.

In this sense, Israel's Arab citizens are in fact better off because the term 'Israeli' is officially regarded, in the Jewish state, as an (inclusive) civic rather than a national identity (despite the unmistakable historical and cultural connection between the name 'Israel' and the Jewish people). In principle, an Arab citizen of Israel can call him- or herself 'Israeli' without giving up their own national identity or adopting that of the Jewish majority. And in fact, most of Israel's Druze citizens define themselves as 'Israelis' without any difficulty; in doing so, they are expressing their identification with the state and a civic connection with it, without adopting the national identity of the majority.

On the other hand, some democracies insist on full congruence between citizenship and national identity. The clearest example of this model of civic nationalism is France, in which no other identity except French – shared, according to the official and widely accepted view, by all the citizens of the Republic – is recognized. Consequently, France refuses to acknowledge the existence of national or ethnic minorities within its territory, and in principle does not grant official status to any language other than French. This approach has both important advantages and considerable disadvantages. When all the citizens of a state are viewed as sharing the same national identity, this strengthens the sense of partnership between them and their identification with the state. On the other hand, this model denies the distinct identity of minorities that usually exist whether or not they are officially recognized. In France, this approach has clear constitutional implications. When in 1991 the socialist government passed the *Act on the status of the territorial unit of Corsica* that referred to the 'Corsican people, a component of the French people' (an intriguing attempt to combine two notions of peoplehood), the law was thrown out by France's Constitutional Council, which ruled that the '*unicité*' of the French people was a binding constitutional norm. The government's signing of the European Charter for Regional or Minority Languages was similarly held by the Constitutional Council to be unconstitutional on the grounds that the Republic cannot officially recognize any language other than French which, according to the Constitution, is 'the language of the Republic'. Those who, basing themselves on the French model, use the slogan of 'a state of all its citizens' in order to negate the Jewish character of the state should bear in mind that adopting this model in Israel would mean denying the status of Arabs in Israel as a national minority and

▪ doing away with the official status of the Arabic language. It is highly doubtful that this is what they have in mind.

Beyond the various possible ways to define peoplehood and national identity, it should be remembered that, in an important sense, every democratic state views all its citizens, regardless of culture, ethnicity and identity, as a single people or nation, by virtue of belonging to a single civic community. We all use the term 'people' in that sense when we say, for example, that the Knesset is freely elected by the people, or that the elections are 'a people's judgement' on the government of the day, or when we discuss holding a national referendum on a particular subject. The people, in the civic sense of the term, are sovereign in a democracy. 'Democracy' means, literally, 'people's rule' – in other words, the rule of the citizen body. In this sense, every democratic country is by definition a 'state of all its citizens'. Similarly, the adjective 'national' has different meanings in different contexts. Everyone understands that the Gross National Product is not the product of a particular national group, and that the National Insurance insures all citizens regardless of their national identity. Nevertheless, it is clear that the citizens of the State of Israel are made up mainly of two national groups with two different national identities. Israel's Arab citizens are a national minority in a Jewish state; the Arab-Palestinian people, to which most of them regard themselves as belonging, has a right to a state of its own alongside Israel according to the principle of 'two states for two peoples'.

Hence it is untenable to argue that the very fact that Israel is a Jewish state – i.e. a state which embodies the Jewish people's right to national independence – makes Israel a defective democracy. In making this statement, however, we are not ignoring the very real flaws of Israeli democracy in its current form. Some of these are in fact, as is often claimed, a spin-off of the long-drawn-out national conflict in which the state is embroiled, while others have nothing to do with the conflict, or are connected with it only marginally, and in any case are not an inevitable outcome of it. We will address some of these issues in this book.

The argument that the Jewish state is a legitimate expression of the Jewish people's right to self-determination and independence can of course be met by denying the existence of a Jewish people. And indeed, this has been one of the traditional arguments of the opponents of Zionism – that the Jews are merely adherents to a religion and not a people. These arguments, which at one point appeared to have fallen by the wayside, have recently enjoyed a new lease of life in Israel with their adoption by a number of radical opponents of the Jewish State. Even in those quarters, however, one seldom hears the explicit statement that 'there is no Jewish people' – perhaps because it is too reminiscent of Golda Meir's notorious claim that 'There is no Palestinian people'.[3] Liberals and democrats have – or at least should have – a natural distaste for such arguments. It is a truism that there is no universally accepted 'objective' or 'scientific' definition of a people or nation; rather, this is first and foremost a matter of self-definition by the group in question. Historically, the establishment of the State of Israel seems to provide, as regards the genuine nature of modern Jewish peoplehood, as 'scientific' a proof as one could hope for. However, if it is a question of international legitimacy, one should bear in mind that the international community – the League of Nations in the Mandate for Palestine, followed by the United Nations in its 1947 Partition Plan and in the explanations provided for it – explicitly recognized the Jewish people, its historic connection to Israel and its rights to a national homeland and independence in it.

Some propose relinquishing or at least downplaying the Jewish character of Israel not because they view it as illegitimate, but based on what might be defined as a stance informed by post- (as opposed to anti-) Zionist 'Israeliness'. Those who endorse this view insist that the Jewish-Israeli public should define its national identity as 'Israeli' rather than 'Jewish'. To debate this issue goes beyond the scope of this book. In principle, there can be no doubt that the Hebrew-speaking Jewish public in Israel (which, naturally, often uses the term 'Israeli' in this sense) has the right to adopt this definition, or any other definition, of its identity, just as there can be no doubt that in practice, the vast majority of it does not wish to relinquish its Jewish identity or its connection with the Jewish people in the Diaspora. It is also clear that adopting this definition will not create a shared national identity for all the citizens of the state, because the Arab minority in Israel has shown no sign of a desire to give up its Arab national identity or its ties to the Palestinian people.

Since its inception, modern nationalism was identified with political freedom and social advancement. A historic and logical connection exists between the modern nation-state and the concept of the people's sovereignty. Nevertheless, the dangerous and destructive potential that lay in narrow and aggressive nationalism had become apparent in the nineteenth century. In the twentieth century – the age when the democratic nation-state flourished – fascism and Nazism, under the banner of national and racial superiority, brought about an unprecedented human catastrophe. In the last few decades, struggles for national liberation have gained broad international support, while at the same time there have been numerous examples of the danger of nationalistic 'negating of the Other' and of the bloody nature of national strife. It is vital to be aware of these dangers, from which no national movement is exempt. However, a people's desire to safeguard its identity and culture, to attain and to maintain national independence should by right – and, usually, does in fact – enjoy the support of those who cherish democratic and humanistic values (whatever their general views on the future of the nation-state in the modern world). This should also apply to the Jewish people and their nation-state. Moreover, it should apply to the two peoples in historic Palestine/land of Israel: The nationalism of both is legitimate as long as it is aimed at guaranteeing each of them independence in its own land, but not when used to deny the other people this right.

This book presents and discusses international norms and examples from around the world. It does not address the unique nature of the historic, emotional, cultural and religious bond of the Jewish people to the land of Israel. We have refrained from doing so not because we make light of these things, or out of an attempt to deny the unique nature of Jewish history. Every people have their own unique history and culture; certainly, this fully applies to the Jewish people. If one wants to describe the history of the Zionist movement, if one wants to understand what motivated its founders and their followers to become engaged in an undertaking that to many appeared utopian and hopeless, one must understand these unique factors, as well as the terrible distress of the Jewish people in the twentieth century. However, when one discusses the principles of justice, the discussion should be conducted in terms of universal norms. Many peoples have struggled for national independence. A people's right to independence is not conditional on having roots in its homeland which stretch back thousands of years, or on the fact that the story of its bond to its homeland is one of the foundations of world culture (and not only of its own national culture). Nor does this right depend on the fact that the people underwent persecution and catastrophes due to its lack of independence. In terms of universal norms, the statement in Israel's Declaration of Independence is sufficient: 'It is a natural right of the Jewish people to be masters of their own fate, like all other peoples, in their own sovereign State.'

Recently, it has become a trend in certain circles to abandon, openly and without equivocation, the principle of two states for two peoples in favour of a 'bi-national' state in all of the land between the Jordan and the Mediterranean. Thus, for example, Tony Judt writes in an article in *The New York Review of Books*: 'The very idea of a "Jewish state" – a state in which Jews and the Jewish religion have exclusive privileges from which non-Jewish citizens are forever excluded – is rooted in another time and place. Israel, in short, is an anachronism.'[4] He proposes to replace the 'anachronism' of a Jewish nation-state with a bi-national state (which he apparently considers to be a state-of-the-art model of modern statecraft, whereas it is a type of state which is very rare in the democratic world and wholly non-existent in the Middle East). This, in theory, would require both peoples to renounce full national independence – a demand that is unjustified, but whose rhetorical strength lies in that it purports to apply equally to both sides. But this equality is on paper only. In reality, it is perfectly clear that a country with an Arab-Muslim majority (as such a 'bi-national' state is bound to be, sooner rather than later), located in the heart of the Arab-Muslim world, cannot be anything but an Arab-Muslim state in all respects, regardless of any formal definitions. In order to believe that such a state would in fact be bi-national, a number of wildly implausible assumptions need to be made: that the Arab-Palestinian people would agree over the long term that its state – the only state it will have – would not have an Arab character and would not be regarded as part of the Arab world; that it would agree to be the only one among the Arab peoples whose state would not be officially Arab, would not be a member of the Arab League and would not share, by declaration, the aspirations for Arab unity; and that the Palestinian people would agree to make this concession – a declared relinquishing of Palestine's 'Arabness', something which no Arab nation has agreed to do in its own state for the sake of the non-Arab native minorities – for the sake of the Jews, widely considered 'foreign intruders' and 'colonialist invaders' in Palestine, whose very claim to constitute a nation is no more than 'Zionist propaganda'. All these assumptions are entirely unreasonable and fanciful. This much can be asserted simply on the basis of Palestinian national narrative and regional realities, without needing to raise uncomfortable questions as to the chances of such a state to be a democracy. So the true alternative to a Jewish nation-state in part of the country (alongside a Palestinian nation-state) is an Arab nation-state in all of it – one state for one people. It is somewhat ironic that such a solution is being advocated in the name of equality.

1 The establishment of the State of Israel

The UN debates in 1947

The declaration of the establishment of the State of Israel

The debate that has gained momentum in recent years over the legitimacy of Israel's definition as a Jewish state usually ignores a basic fact: The 'Jewish State' is what the international community decided to establish in 1947 (on part of Mandatory Palestine), whereas 'Israel' is merely the name that the Zionist leadership chose to give this state. From the perspective of international legitimacy, the question of whether 'Israel' is entitled to define itself as a Jewish state is, therefore, somewhat paradoxical. The Israeli Declaration of Independence[1] did not determine that Israel was to be a Jewish state, but rather that the Jewish State was 'to be called Israel'. The context in which this appears within the wording of the Declaration clearly points to the fact that the founders of the state based its international legitimacy on the partition resolution of the United Nations and on the principle of national self-determination, which the Declaration views as a universal principle, and which the establishment of the State of Israel is intended to realize for the Jewish people.

The Declaration begins with a survey of the history of the Jewish people from ancient times, with an emphasis on the unbroken connection between the Jewish people and the Land of Israel, even during the period of the Diaspora. The Jewish people 'never ceased to pray and hope for their return and the restoration of their national freedom'.

The Declaration relates to modern Zionism, which is described as a movement for the revival of Jewish independence and to the international recognition (by means of the Balfour Declaration and the Mandate of the League of Nations) of the historic connection between the Jewish people and the Land of Israel and the right of the Jewish people to re-establish its national home:

> The Nazi holocaust, which engulfed millions of Jews in Europe, proved anew the urgency of the reestablishment of the Jewish State, which would solve the problem of Jewish homelessness by opening the gates to all Jews and lifting the Jewish people to equality in the family of nations.

And the Declaration goes on to say:

On November 29, 1947, the General Assembly of the United Nations adopted a resolution for the establishment of an independent Jewish State in Palestine, and called upon the inhabitants of the country to take such steps as may be necessary on their part to put the plan into effect. This recognition by the United Nations of the right of the Jewish people to establish their independent State is irrevocable. It is a natural right of the Jewish people to be masters of their own fate, like all other peoples, in their own sovereign State. . . . Accordingly, we, the members of the People's Council, representing the Jewish people in the land of Israel and the Zionist movement, met together in solemn assembly today, the day of the termination of the British mandate for Palestine, by virtue of the natural and historic right of the Jewish people and of the Resolution of the General Assembly of the United Nations, hereby proclaim the establishment of the Jewish State in the land of Israel, to be called Israel.

The Declaration then describes the nature of the state in the making: Israel would be a state 'open to the immigration of Jews from all countries of their dispersion', but would also 'uphold the full social and political equality of all its citizens, without distinction of race, creed or sex'. Next, the Declaration calls upon 'the Arab inhabitants of the State of Israel to adhere to the ways of peace and play their part in the development of the State, with full and equal citizenship and due representation in its bodies and institutions'. These principles, it should be noted, not only conformed to the traditional position of all strands of the Zionist movement regarding the status of the Arab citizens of the future Jewish state, but were also mandated by the UN partition resolution, which demanded that both the Jewish state and the Arab state guarantee full equal rights to national minorities. The Declaration notes that, in accordance with the partition plan, Israel is

> ready to cooperate with the organs and representatives of the United Nations in the implementation of the Resolution of the Assembly of 29 November 1947, and will take steps to bring about the economic union over the entire land of Israel (Palestine).

This statement was made when the war was already being fought with the Palestinian Arabs (whose leadership had totally rejected the partition plan), and on the eve of the invasion of Arab countries into Israel with the declared objective of destroying the nascent Jewish state. In his comments before the People's Council, Ben-Gurion related to the argument held beforehand in the provisional government on the question of whether or not to determine the state's borders in the Declaration:

> We decided to *evade* (I choose this word deliberately) this question for a simple reason: If the United Nations upholds its decision and commitments and maintains the peace and prevents bombings and will enforce its own

resolutions – then for our part, we will honour all the UN resolutions. So far, the United Nations has not done this and it has been left up to us. That is why not everything is binding on us, and we have left this matter open. We did not say 'not the UN borders', but nor did we say the opposite. We left the matter open to developments.

For many years, Israel's peace camp, expressing its criticism of the policy of Israeli governments towards the Palestinians, maintained that whereas the partition borders had been erased by the war that the Arab side launched in 1947–1948, the principle of partitioning the country between its two peoples remained morally valid and binding, in the spirit of what is stated in Israel's Declaration of Independence, which views the right of national independence as 'the natural right of all peoples'. The acceptance of the principle of 'two states for two peoples' eventually became the ultimate test of one's belonging to what is known as the Israeli peace camp – the camp which embraces political moderation not only for pragmatic Israeli considerations, but also out of the belief that it is morally wrong to rule over another people and that the Palestinian people has the right to self-determination.

The voices heard in recent years which disparage the concept of the 'Jewish state', claiming that it contradicts the principle of equality, are in fact denying the principle of two states for two peoples. While one of the two peoples in the country from the Jordan to the Mediterranean defines itself, and therefore is, Arab and Palestinian, the other defines itself, and therefore is, Jewish and Israeli. No Jewish state means no state for one of the two peoples. The fact that the state is the expression of the right of the Jewish people to national independence does not mean that it is not also the state of those of its citizens that belong to the Arab national minority – that is, a democratic state or, in other words, a state of all its citizens. Israel is a democratic nation-state that contains a sizeable national minority. In that, it is by no means unique in the democratic world.[2]

The statement of principles for Israeli–Palestinian peace, as agreed upon by Ami Ayalon and the Palestinian intellectual and public figure Sari Nusseibeh in autumn 2002, spells out what should be self-evident: that the principle of two states for two peoples requires the existence of two nation-states side by side – an Arab-Palestinian state and a Jewish-Israeli state. The document also makes it clear that the existence of two nation-states also involves two national laws of return:

> Nation-state: Palestine is the only state of the Palestinian people and Israel is the only state of the Jewish people. ... Right of return: Palestinian refugees will return only to the State of Palestine; Jews will return only to the State of Israel.[3]

Seemingly, none of those that declare their support for the solution of two states for two peoples should disagree with any of this. However, strangely enough, the very idea that the Jewish people are also entitled to a state of their own has come under attack today as being anti-democratic.

The debates in 1947: the UNSCOP report

The debates that were held in the United Nations in 1947 regarding the question of Palestine make it abundantly clear what meaning the international community attributed to the term 'Jewish state', and what the rationale of those that supported the partition solution was. They supported the establishment of an independent state for the Jewish people – not just for the Jewish population of Mandatory Palestine. They viewed the establishment of this state as an act of historic justice for the Jewish people and a humanitarian solution to the problem of the displaced Jews in Europe after the war, and also, in a broader sense, as a solution for the ancient problem of the Jews as a homeless people. They recognized the historic bond between the Jewish people and the land of Israel/ Palestine as well as the actual existence of two peoples and two national movements in the land. They attached great importance to the previous international recognition of the historic connection of the Jewish people to Palestine and the need to 'reconstitute their national home in that country' – recognition that was included in the Mandate for Palestine endorsed by the Council of the League of Nations in 1922. The arguments of the opponents of the partition plan are no less instructive. Among other things, Arab representatives and their supporters repeatedly argued that the Jews were a religious community rather than a people, and that consequently they were not entitled to a state of their own. Indeed, little has changed in this debate since 1947.

The most detailed discussion of these subjects appears in a report of the UN Special Committee on Palestine, UNSCOP, the committee that investigated the situation in Palestine on behalf of the United Nations and recommended, by a majority vote, that the country be partitioned into two states. At the end of the report appears the 'Partition Plan' that was eventually endorsed (after slightly reducing the size of the territory allocated to the Jewish State) by the UN General Assembly in the famous 29 November 1947 vote. This detailed and well-argued report includes a historical analysis and assessment of the situation in the country, a presentation of the arguments of both parties to the conflict and an evaluation of the validity of these arguments by the members of the committee, and, finally, their reasoned conclusions regarding the desirable solution.[4] A minority report was also submitted proposing a different solution: a single independent state in the entire country to be established on a federative basis, made up of an 'Arab state' and a 'Jewish state'. The autonomous Jewish state that was to be part of the federation would also have included an Arab minority. This did not prevent the delegates from Yugoslavia, Iran and India from supporting this solution, demonstrating that the concept of a 'Jewish state' was, in a certain sense, accepted even by these states. They supported the establishment of a Jewish political entity – albeit not an independent one.

The majority report (of the representatives of Canada, Czechoslovakia, Guatemala, the Netherlands, Peru, Sweden and Uruguay) extensively analyses the international commitments given to the Jewish people in the Balfour Declaration and the Mandate. The members of the committee reject the claims of the

Arab nations which denied the validity of the mandate, arguing that it ran counter to the Covenant of the League of Nations (Chapter II, Article 179). The committee also conducted an in-depth discussion of the promises that the British gave to the representatives of the Arab national movement during the First World War and stated that it was impossible to unequivocally determine whether Palestine had been included within the united Arab state that had been pledged to them (Article 167 and ff.). The committee mentions the 'Weizmann–Feisal Agreement' and the willingness in principle of Emir Feisal, who represented the Arab demands at the post-First World War Paris Peace Conference, to accept the Balfour Declaration and view the encourage-ment of large-scale Jewish immigration to Palestine favourably (Articles 173–175). This agreement was conditional on the implementation of the idea of a united Arab state, an idea that never came to fruition. The Committee quotes (in Article 175) the British Peel Commission report, which noted in 1937 that:

> There was a time when Arab statesmen were willing to consider giving Palestine to the Jews, provided that the rest of Arab Asia was free. That condition was not fulfilled then, but it is on the eve of fulfilment now.

The committee analysed the meaning of the phrase 'Jewish National Home' and drew the conclusion that an independent Jewish state was a reasonable though not the sole possible interpretation of this expression.

The committee held that:

> both the Balfour Declaration and the Mandate involved international com-mitments to the Jewish people as a whole. It was obvious that these com-mitments were not limited only to the Jewish population of Palestine, since at the time there were only some 80,000 Jews there.
>
> (Chapter II, Article 146)

Thus the committee relates to the Jews of the world as a people with national aspirations, recognized as such by the international community. This is notewor-thy because many of the opponents of the 1947 partition maintained that the Jews were not a people or a national group, but merely a religious community not entitled to develop national aspirations. These opponents argued that the phrase 'the Jewish people' should be taken as a description of the collective of believers in the Jewish religion, devoid of any national and political status. Such arguments can still be heard today (though some of those voicing them are willing to concede that the Hebrew-speaking Jewish community in Israel, in contrast to world Jewry, is indeed a national entity). However, in 1947 the members of the UN committee, following what had been determined in the Mandate of the League of Nations, pursued a different premise. They viewed the Jewish people as a national entity whose existence preceded the creation of a large modern Jewish community in Palestine.

At the same time, the chief arguments in favour of partition related neither to the historic past nor to the Jewish people in the world, but rather to the reality on the ground in 1947: the actual existence of two peoples and two national movements in Mandatory Palestine. The committee's members sought to safeguard the national rights of both parties. They determined that it would not be right to ignore the national aspirations of the Palestinian Arabs and to impose Jewish rule over the entire land by continuing Jewish immigration that would eventually make the Jews into a majority that could establish its state in it.

> The basic premise underlying the partition proposal is that the claims to Palestine of the Arabs and Jews, both possessing validity, are irreconcilable, and that among all of the solutions advanced, partition will provide the most realistic and practicable settlement and is the most likely to afford a workable basis for meeting in part the claims and national aspirations of both parties.
>
> It is a fact that both of these peoples have their historic roots in Palestine, and that both make vital contributions to the economic and cultural life of the country...
>
> The basic conflict in Palestine is a clash of two intense nationalisms. Regardless of the historic origins of the conflict, the rights and wrongs of the promises and counter-promises [to both sides] and the international intervention incident to the Mandate, there are now in Palestine some 650,000 Jews and some 1,200,000 Arabs who are dissimilar in their ways of living and, for the time being, separated by political interests. ... Only by means of partition can these conflicting national aspirations find substantial expression and qualify both peoples to take their places as independent nations in the international community and in the United Nations. ... Jewish immigration is the central issue in Palestine today and is the one factor, above all others, that rules out the necessary co-operation between the Arab and Jewish communities in a single State. The creation of a Jewish State under a partition scheme is the only hope of removing this issue from the arena of conflict.
>
> It is recognized that partition has been strongly opposed by Arabs, but it is felt that that opposition would be lessened by a solution which definitively fixes the extent of territory to be allotted to the Jews with its implicit limitation on immigration.
>
> (Chapter VI, Part I, Articles 1–9)

The final comments here are especially instructive. The continued massive Jewish immigration to the Jewish State after its establishment (beyond the 150,000 Jews in displaced person (DP) camps in Europe that the Commission recommended allowing into the country even during the interim period before the granting of independence) was something that the members of the committee took as a given. Following unequivocal statements to this effect made by the Jewish representatives who appeared before them, the members of the committee noted that for the Jewish side, 'the issues of the Jewish State and unrestricted immigration are inextricably interwoven', and that (exactly as would be stated in the Israeli Declaration of Independence), 'the opening of the gates of the country to massive Jewish immigration will be a major goal of the Jewish State after its establishment' (Chapter II, Article 127). In the view of the members of the committee, the restriction on Jewish immigration after the establishment of the state would be territorial: since the state would be limited to a certain part of Palestine only, Jewish immigration would also be restricted to that part. This would allay the Palestinian Arabs' fear that the continued Jewish immigration would turn them into a minority in their own country, while imposing Jewish rule over the entire territory.[5] The establishment of a Jewish State on part of the land is intended 'to remove the issue of immigration from the arena of conflict' – in other words, to turn it into an internal matter of the Jewish State. When the report was debated in the UN General Assembly, a number of delegates commented in a similar vein. In his speech on 6 October before the Ad Hoc Committee of the General Assembly on the Palestinian Question debating the report, the Panamanian delegate spoke optimistically of the ability of the Jewish State to absorb masses of Jewish immigrants in its territory.[6] In comments made before the plenary of the General Assembly on 26 November, the delegate of Uruguay noted that the Balfour Declaration and the Mandate promised 'to create a Jewish national home in Palestine and to promote the immigration of the Jewish masses to that country in order that they might work out their destiny and build their home there'. In time, the question of Jewish immigration to Palestine, he continued, has become the bone of contention between the Jews and the Arabs; however, from the moment a Jewish state is established on part of the land, 'the problem of immigration will cease to be such a painful and bitter one' occupying the international community, as it would then become an internal issue of that country.

Moreover, the UNSCOP report explicitly confirms that in determining the size of the territory to be allotted to the Jewish State, the members of the committee took into account the need to ensure sufficient space for the absorption of Jewish immigrants. Consequently, the Jewish State was granted a territory larger than would have been justified if taking into account only the existing numerical ratios between Jews and Arabs in the country. This, naturally, increased the number of Arabs who would be included within its borders. As noted in Chapter IV, Part II, Articles 3 and 5:

> A partition scheme for Palestine must take into account both the claims of the Jews to receive immigrants and the needs of the Arab population, which is increasing rapidly by natural means. Thus, as far as possible, both partitioned States must leave some room for further land settlement . . .
>
> The proposed Jewish State leaves considerable room for further development and land settlement and, in meeting this need to the extent that it has been met in these proposals, a very substantial minority of Arabs is included in the Jewish State.

These comments are of considerable importance. The Arab delegates to the General Assembly, while opposing the very principle of partition, repeatedly maintained that the terms of the partition proposed by UNSCOP were manifestly unfair to the Arab side, because the Jews, who represented only one-third of the country's population, would receive a disproportionate part of its territory – more than 50 per cent (although most of this territory was in the Negev desert). However, the members of the committee determined the size of the territory of the Jewish State not only in accordance with the needs of the existing Jewish community in Palestine, but also in consideration of the anticipated immigration to the Jewish State after its establishment. The need to guarantee land reserves that would enable the absorption of Jewish immigrants appeared to the members of the committee important enough to justify allocating a relatively large area to this state, thus considerably increasing its proportion of Arab inhabitants, despite the fact that their guiding principle was, naturally, that people belonging to each national community should be included, as far as possible, in the area of their national state. According to the partition plan, the Arab minority within the Jewish State was intended to number close to 45 per cent of its inhabitants, although, as noted, it was assumed that the Jewish majority would grow exten-sively as a result of massive Jewish immigration. Today, Israel has a large Arab minority of around 19 per cent. Those who deny the legitimacy of defining Israel as a Jewish state, and in particular the legitimacy of the Law of Return, main-tain, among other things, that this definition and this law are inappropriate in a country that has such a large Arab minority. The approach taken by the members of the UN committee of 1947 was exactly the opposite: they were willing, as noted, to increase substantially the Arab minority included in the Jewish State in order to give the state sufficient territory to absorb large-scale Jewish immigra-tion. This naturally followed from the basic logic of partition: as we have seen, the question of continued Jewish immigration represents a major consideration in the decision by the committee members in favour of partition, after they became convinced that the dispute between the two peoples over this subject would not enable them to cooperate in a single bi-national state.

The Guatemalan delegate to the United Nations, Jorge Garcia-Granados, a member of UNSCOP and an enthusiastic supporter of partition and of a Jewish state, published a book a short time later, describing the committee's visit to Mandatory Palestine and its internal debates in preparation for the submission of its report to the General Assembly. The author expressed his sympathy for the Jewish people and their aspiration to have a national home of their own, admiration for the achievements of the Jewish community in Mandatory Palestine and deep sympathy for the displaced Holocaust survivors and the hardships suffered by them. However, when presenting the basic logic that guided the majority of committee members in adopting the concept of partition, the Latin American diplomat framed his comments in universal terms – the right of peoples to national independence:

> Given two peoples, each of whom was convinced it was fighting for its national existence in Palestine, the only solution was to separate them,

bestow upon each sovereignty and independence, and allow the natural and irresistible law of economic necessity to force them to work together economically.[7]

As Garcia-Granados describes it, the members of the committee viewed the question of continued Jewish immigration and the issue of partition as being closely related. The chairman of the committee, the Swedish delegate, enumerated the possible solutions to the Palestine problem in a meeting held in Beirut between UNSCOP and representatives of Arab countries:

> 'Let us take up the possible solutions. First a bi-national state with a limited immigration; second a federal state comprising two or more states, each having the power to determine whether immigration would take place; third, partition, involving the establishment of two independent states which would decide on immigration.' ... The replies reiterated the Arab position. They would not consider the establishment of a Jewish state in all Palestine, or in part of Palestine.... They wanted Palestine to be an Arab State with Jews as a minority group and all immigration to be determined by the Arab government of that Arab State.[8]

The establishment of a Jewish state and the assumption that the gates of such a state would be open to massive Jewish immigration did not, in the minds of the members of the UNSCOP committee, in any way contradict the need to ensure equal civil rights for the large Arab majority that would included in its borders. Recommendation 7 in Chapter V of the committee report, under the heading 'Democratic Principles and Protection of Minorities', notes that

> in view of the fact that independence is to be granted in Palestine on the recommendation and under the auspices of the United Nations, it is a proper and an important concern of the United Nations that the constitution or other fundamental law as well as the political structure of the new State or States shall be basically democratic.

Thus, contrary to the claims heard in recent years according to which a 'Jewish state' is an invalid or at least a flawed concept from the perspective of international norms of human rights and democracy, those who proposed a partition and a Jewish state in 1947 were invoking the legitimate interest of the international community in guaranteeing compliance with democratic principles. The committee determined that the constitution or basic laws of the two future states must guarantee:

> full protection for the rights and interests of minorities, including the protection of the linguistic, religious and ethnic rights of the peoples and respect for their cultures, and full equality of all citizens with regard to political, civil and religious matters.

This general rule was further expanded on in Chapter II, 'Religion and Minority Rights'. Among the rights guaranteed is the right of each community to maintain its own schools for the education of its own members in its own language. It is clear that the committee saw no contradiction between providing full civil rights to the large Arab minority in the future Jewish state while allowing it to maintain its cultural particularity, on the one hand, and the Jewish character of the state by means of which the Jewish people would 'take its place as an independent nation in the international community and in the United Nations', on the other.

The debates on the partition plan in the UN General Assembly

The question of Palestine was discussed twice in the General Assembly in 1947: once when it was decided to establish a special committee on this matter, and once again during the debate on the committee report. During these debates, an important diplomatic development occurred: the surprising support of the Soviet Union for the partition and the establishment of a Jewish state, as expressed by its ambassador, Andrei Gromyko. This support greatly contributed to the final outcome – the adoption of the partition plan by the General Assembly by the required two-thirds majority. The Soviet Union's motives are not entirely clear and were probably mixed. They certainly included a desire to weaken the British Empire and expel it from Palestine. The Soviet Union was hostile to the pro-British Arab regimes, in particular those in Transjordan and Egypt, and there was no reason for it to support the Palestinian-Arab leadership headed by the Mufti of Jerusalem, Haj Amin al-Husseini. The Soviet position favouring the Jewish side came as a surprise due to the Soviet Communist Party's long-held opposition to Zionism. This opposition began well before the Russian Revolution. Lenin and the Bolsheviks vehemently opposed Zionism, including the socialist brand of Zionism, with the claim that the idea of a Jewish state in Palestine was a 'reactionary utopia'. Within a few years after the Revolution, all Zionist activity in the Soviet Union was outlawed. The Bolsheviks opposed not just Zionism, but also non-Zionist, 'diasporic' versions of Jewish national identity – notably, that advocated by the social-democratic 'Bund' (which sought Jewish national autonomy in Russia). This was based on Lenin's explicit claim that the Jews were not a people or a 'nation', but merely a 'caste', a relic of the distant past whose continued collective existence served only the interests of anti-Semites and Jewish reactionary forces. The fate of this 'caste' was to disappear as a result of assimilation – for the benefit of the Jews themselves. This assimilation would be made possible thanks to the full equality that the socialist revolution would grant the Jews (as individuals).

In time, the Soviet regime changed its position vis-à-vis the issue of a Jewish national identity. When the official designation of all Soviet citizens by 'nationality' (i.e. belonging to a national group) was introduced as part of the regime's general policy on the national question in the multi-national Soviet state, it was no longer possible to persist in the use of the polemical designation of the Jews as a 'caste', and the Jewish citizens were registered in their identity card ('passport') as 'Nationality: Jewish'. Secular and socialist Yiddish culture was fostered by the regime until it was brutally eliminated in the late 1940s. Moreover, by establishing the 'Jewish Autonomous Region' in Birobidzhan, the Soviet regime recognized the Jews of the Soviet Union as a national group entitled to an autonomous political entity of its own – similar to many other nationalities in the Soviet Union. The Birobidzhan project failed due to the small number of Jews that moved to that remote area (although formally the 'Jewish Autonomous Region' continues to exist to this day). However, it is significant that the Soviet government recognized in principle the need for a national-territorial solution, albeit a partial one, to the Jewish problem. Nevertheless, Soviet hostility to Zionism did not let up, and all forms of Zionist activity in the Soviet Union were banned and crushed.

From the moment the Soviet government decided to support partition and the establishment of a Jewish state in Palestine, it justified its stance, as was its wont, using the most enlightened and advanced arguments known to international discourse – humanitarian considerations and adherence to the principle of national self-determination. When Andrei Gromyko gave his famous speech to the UN General Assembly on 14 May 1947, supporting partition should the two sides fail to agree on another solution (a united bi-national Arab–Jewish state), he was in fact endorsing – without mentioning the term 'Zionism' – the essence of the traditional Zionist justification for the idea of a Jewish state: The Jewish *people* (that is, not just the Jewish community in Palestine) aspires to attain national independence. This aspiration is legitimate and particularly understandable on the backdrop of Jewish suffering, whose most extreme expression was the extermination of Europe's Jews by the Nazis. Moreover, the Soviet delegate did not hesitate to use the 'reactionary' argument regarding the historic bond between the Jewish people and Palestine:

> As we know, the aspirations of a considerable part of the Jewish people are linked with the problem of Palestine and of its future administration. This fact scarcely requires proof. ...
>
> During the last war, the Jewish people underwent exceptional sorrow and suffering. Without any exaggeration, this sorrow and suffering are indescribable. It is difficult to express them in dry statistics on the Jewish victims of the fascist aggressors. The Jews in territories where the Hitlerites held sway were subjected to almost complete physical annihilation. The total number of members of the Jewish population who perished at the hands of the Nazi executioners is estimated at approximately six million. Only about a million and a half Jews in Western Europe survived the war. ...
>
> Past experience, particularly during the Second World War, shows that no Western European State was able to provide adequate assistance for the Jewish people in defending its rights and its very existence from the violence of the Hitlerites and their allies. This is an unpleasant fact, but unfortunately, like all other facts, it must be admitted. ...

The fact that no Western European State has been able to ensure the defence of the elementary rights of the Jewish people, and to safeguard it against the violence of the fascist executioners, explains the aspirations of the Jews to establish their own State. It would be unjust not to take this into consideration and to deny the right of the Jewish people to realize this aspiration. ...

It is essential to bear in mind the indisputable fact that the population of Palestine consists of two peoples, the Arabs and the Jews. Both have historical roots in Palestine. Palestine has become the homeland of both these peoples.

In his second speech in the General Assembly on 26 November, on the eve of the final authorization of the partition plan, Gromyko expressed full support, on behalf of his government, for the majority recommendation of the special committee, i.e. the two-state solution:

The logical conclusion followed that, if these two peoples that inhabit Palestine, both of which have deeply rooted historical ties with the land, cannot live together within the boundaries of a single State, there is no alternative but to create, in place of one country, two States – an Arab and a Jewish one. ...

The representatives of the Arab States claim that the partition of Palestine would be an historic injustice. But this view of the case is unacceptable, if only because, after all, the Jewish people has been closely linked with Palestine for a considerable period in history. Apart from that, we must not overlook ... the position in which the Jewish people found themselves as a result of the recent world war. ...

The delegation of the USSR maintains that the decision to partition Palestine is in keeping with the high principles and aims of the United Nations. It is in keeping with the principle of the national self-determination of peoples.

The Soviet delegate's repeated use of the term 'the Jewish people', which includes all world Jewry and not just the Jews of Palestine, is notable. This people, he said, is connected historically to Palestine; it has suffered from terrible persecutions (only in the Western capitalist nations, of course), and now it is justified in demanding the establishment of an independent nation of its own. This fundamentally deviated from the traditional Soviet approach to the 'Jewish question'. Even after recognizing its own Jewish population as one of the Soviet Union's 'nationalities', the Soviet regime, which sought to isolate this population from the Jews in the West, continued to reject what it labelled 'the Zionist concept of a worldwide Jewish nation'. It was now claimed that Jews were a national or ethnic minority in each of the countries where they lived, but there was no national connection between the various Jewish communities. Using this conceptual framework it was possible to recognize the Jewish community in

Palestine as a 'people' entitled to national independence – but, as we see, the actual arguments of the Soviet delegate went far beyond that.

Other supporters of the partition plan used similar arguments. In his speech in the General Assembly on 26 November, the Polish delegate said:

> We know that a large proportion of the Jewish people consider Palestine as their national home, where they wish to establish their own national life. In view of our own close historic association with the Jewish people, we cannot help sympathizing with these aspirations. ...
>
> The reestablishment of a Jewish State more than two thousand years after its extinction is a fact of such historic import that it should receive worldwide attention. My delegation and my Government welcome it, and are fully conscious of the great historic significance of the act. But there is sometimes overlooked, and the eloquence with which our Arab colleagues conducted their debate almost made us overlook, a no less important fact, namely, that the proposal ... establishes an Arab State in Palestine, a State which gives to the Arab people of Palestine their national political independence.

Immediately afterwards, the Syrian delegate came forward and maintained that Poland supported the establishment of a Jewish state only in order to get rid of its own Jews. He also made the false claim that according to the *Encyclopaedia Judaica*, 'The Jews of Eastern Europe are in no way connected to the Children of Israel and that they come from pure Russian-Tartar extraction.' 'Anthropological' arguments such as these, which were repeatedly voiced by Arab delegates during the debate,[9] were countered that day by the Uruguayan delegate in an emotional speech:

> The Uruguayan delegation maintained four points as fundamental: firstly, a territorial solution of the Jewish problem; secondly, the creation of independent Jewish and Arab States within the present territory of Palestine ...
>
> The Jewish people have suffered, and are suffering, their age-old fate. Speaking of the 'Jewish people' in direct connection with this problem, we are suddenly confronted with something too strange to be passed over. We are told, and it has always been proclaimed, that the Jews hang together, that a group of Jews which moves from one place to another and settles in a particular country, continues to remain Jewish above all else and is not assimilated by its environment. We are also told that the Jewish race maintains a remarkable unity among its component parts. But when one goes further into the question and tries to find a basis for the solution of this problem, one comes upon anthropological theories which will prove that the Oriental or Central European Jews are not connected with, or related to, the people of Israel at all.
>
> Race or people, race or religion, the same common denominator of persecution and suffering has characterized the fate of this section of humanity.

... We consider that the solution recommended, whereby the Jewish people will be given a territory of their own, constitutes a victory over all the acts of racial discrimination by which an attempt was made to create a superior race based upon the subjection, persecution and slavery of others. ...

Why is it necessary that there should be a Jewish State? Precisely to put an end to that form of discrimination and alienation, that persecution of a section of humanity. And what a burden of suffering they have borne! No one in our day has endured such a burden.

Similarly, the delegate of Czechoslovakia (who still represented Masaryk's democratic government, before the Communist coup in his country) spoke before the Ad Hoc Committee on 16 October:

It has been said that the Jews are not a distinct nation, but only a distinct religion, and that because of that are not entitled to a state of their own. In my view, this should be decided in light of the will of the people involved. For anyone who has seen the Jewish people at work in Palestine, there can be no doubt about their unshakable will to live as a nation with all the attributes of a nation.

However, for the authors of the UNSCOP report and most of the supporters of partition during the General Assembly debates, the existence of the Jewish people as a people having national aspirations was self-evident and they saw no need to explain it. It should be borne in mind that the international recognition of the Jewish people and its national aspirations as formulated in the League of Nations Mandate was one of the cornerstones of the debate held in 1947.

The Syrian delegate formulated his position on the question of Jewish peoplehood with great clarity in his speech of 22 September in the plenary of the General Assembly, in response to the UNSCOP report and its recommendation in favour of partition:

The Committee assumed that the Jews are a race and a nation entitled to cherish national aspirations. The Jews are not a nation. Every Jew belongs to a certain nationality. None of them in the world is now stateless or without nationality. In their entirety, they embrace all the nationalities of the world. Nor are the Jews a race. The Children of Israel today are a very small fraction of the Jewry of the world, for the Jews are composed of all races of mankind, from the Negroes to the blond, fair-skinned Scandinavians. Judaism is merely a religion and nothing else. The followers of a certain religious creed cannot be entitled to national aspirations.

Following such comments, one might expect the Syrian delegate to then proceed to express the great respect he felt towards the Jewish religion, which should not have to deal with petty, mundane matters such as the establishment and management of political entities. He was, however, unable to overcome his fierce animosity towards the nonexistent – as he claimed – Jewish people. This anti-pathy, given full expression in the next part of his speech, was unmistakably ethno-national:

> There were so many nations that contributed greatly to the civilization of the world and which were stronger and more powerful than the Jewish dynasty. Yet we find none of them in existence now. They were not exter-minated; they were assimilated by their invaders and became adapted to the environments in which they found themselves. Of the peoples of antiquity, only the Jews maintain their isolation and seclusion, to the dissatisfaction and anger of their compatriots and their neighbours, who never failed to molest and persecute them, on each occasion giving to the world a problem of refugees; a problem of displaced persons. Not a single century in history has been free from such a problem as we now face. The world has always been faced with the problem of Jewish refugees and displaced persons and Jewish persecution at some time or other. Why is that? The only reason is the special manner of life which the Jews adopt for themselves and to which they adhere in spite of all the developments and metamorphoses which have taken place all over the world for all nations. The Jews are all alone, and the United Nations now is faced with the last but not least of these problems. It is as important as any of the previous problems.

The Syrian delegate then suggested to the government of the Soviet Union that if it really wanted to resolve the problem of the displaced Jews by establishing an independent Jewish state, it should do so in Birobidzhan. This excerpt exem-plifies the argument put forward by the Uruguayan delegate – that there is a gross contradiction between the anti-Jewish hostility, its character and the way it is expressed on the one hand, and the claim that Jews are merely a religious community and nothing more. There was precious little theology in what the Syrian delegate had to say about the Jews, their history and their plight.

Had the Syrian delegate desisted from revealing the depth of his antipathy towards the Jews in favour of a more convincing presentation of the argument that they were no more than a religious community, he could have said some-thing along the lines of the remarks made by the Indian delegate on 2 May in his speech to the General Committee, which served as the presidium of the General Assembly. The latter expressed his full appreciation for the Jewish religion and for Jews as a highly gifted group of believers:

> They have a religion. If I were a Jew, I should be most proud of my reli-gion. I would stand up and look into everyone's eyes and say, 'I am a Jew and I wish to be respected, and wish to respect everyone' – reciprocal respect and reciprocal admiration.

However, the Indian delegate went on to argue that the religion of the Jews does not make them a nation: a nation is not a matter of religion or ethnicity; rather, it is identical with the aggregate of the inhabitants of a particular country. It is clear that the Indian delegate was influenced by the example of his own country and the trauma of the partition of India (which also occurred in 1947). During the struggle to establish a separate Muslim state in India, the Muslim League maintained – against stiff opposition on the part of the Congress Party – that the Muslims of the subcontinent represented a separate nation, that of Pakistan. However, this attempt to apply the Indian Congress Party's concept of nationhood (embracing all of India's religious, ethnic and linguistic communities) to Palestine led to a surprising conclusion: 'What do we find in Palestine, for instance? Christians, Muslims, Jews, and perhaps others, and I dare say, some atheists too, and political ideologists are residing together. They are all living there as one people.' And that, concludes the Indian delegate, is the 'Palestine people'; this people should be given independence. The claim that the Jews and Arabs of Palestine are members of the same 'people' (thus denying the reality of both the Jewish and the Arab national identity in the country) is, obviously, an ideological construction alien to local conditions. If there is anything that the Jews and Arabs have always agreed upon throughout the various phases of their conflict over Palestine, it is the fact that they do *not* belong to the same people. It is also clear that this 'one people' theory is inconsistent with the conclusions of the UNSCOP minority report, which the Indian delegate supported, which expressly refers to the existence of two peoples, a Jewish people and an Arab people, having opposing national aspirations, in Palestine (Chapter VII, 'Plans for a Federal State', Articles 2, 5, 7). It is similarly inconsistent with the solution of a federative state made up of an 'Arab state' and a 'Jewish state'. And indeed, according to the Guatemalan delegate to UNSCOP, during the committee's own debates when consolidating its conclusions, the Indian delegate (who was a Muslim activist in the Congress Party) expressed a view that differed fundamentally from the idea of a bi-national federative state:

> Sir Abdur interrupted here to state that he rejected the principle of basing political rights on religion, custom or tradition. He could not admit that the Jews had any claim to Palestine because of religious connection. He was against a bi-national state because he did not see two nations in Palestine. He was prepared to consider a unitary state with proportional representation in government and constitutional safeguards for everyone.

The Guatemalan representative went on to note: 'It was obvious that the root of his thinking was his refusal to see the Jews as anything but a religion, despite everything we had heard and seen to the contrary.'[10] As noted, this approach ran counter to the minority plan, which recognized the existence of two peoples and two national movements in Palestine, and recommended the establishment of a federative state made up of a Jewish state and an Arab state. Such a state would clearly be a bi-national state, although the term itself does not appear in the report – perhaps out of consideration for the sensibilities of the Indian delegate. The latter joined his voice to that of the minority position, apparently because he viewed it as the only way to prevent partition, although this ideological stance was in fact fundamentally different from the view expressed in the minority report.

It goes without saying that, throughout the General Assembly debates, the Arab delegates, who rejected the idea of partition as well as that of a bi-national federation, did not adopt the national concept offered by the Indian delegate who maintained that all the residents of Palestine comprised a single people, or nation. But this theory seems to be the inescapable conclusion if one takes seriously the argument that Jews are no more than a religious group, and that their national identity is, as the Syrian delegate maintained, identical with their citizenship in each of the countries in which they reside. In that case, Jews of Mandatory Palestine, who were Palestinian subjects, should indeed have been considered part of the Palestinian people. However, the Arab delegates, including the Palestinian-Arab delegates, did not claim that a 'state of all its citizens' should be established for the multi-ethnic and multi-denominational Palestinian people consisting of all the residents of Palestine, in accordance with the Indian model. Their express claim was that an Arab state should be established in the whole of Palestine. Jamal Husseini, vice president of the Arab Higher Committee for Palestine, spoke before the Ad Hoc Committee of the General Assembly on 29 September 1947 and presented its proposals for solving the problem. He proposed:

1   That an Arab state in the whole of Palestine be established on democratic lines.
2   That the said Arab state of Palestine would respect human rights, fundamental freedoms and equality of all persons before the law.
3   That the said Arab state of Palestine would protect the legitimate rights and interests of all minorities.

All these worthy principles were supposed to prevail in the 'Arab State of Palestine' which would, naturally, be headed by the chairman of the Arab Higher Committee, the Mufti of Jerusalem, who had supported Nazi Germany during the Second World War. Even if it is rather a moot point whether a Jewish minority would in fact have enjoyed equality and protection under such conditions and in such a state, there seems to be no good reason to argue that there is something fundamentally illegitimate about the very concept of an Arab state – or a Jewish one.

One of the three countries whose delegates subscribed to the minority report recommending a bi-national federation instead of partition was Yugoslavia. The arguments in favour of this position in the remarks made by the Yugoslavian delegate before the Ad Hoc Committee on 14 October include many of the principles espoused by those who supported partition. The Yugoslavian delegate, like the proponents of partition and unlike the Arab delegates, viewed the Jews – at least the Jews of Palestine – as having a shared national identity rather than being merely a religious community. However, he argued that the national aspirations of both peoples in Palestine should find expression in a common state, without partitioning the country:

> It must be recognized, in the first place, that Palestine was homeland of both Arabs and Jews and that both played a vital part in the economic and cultural life of the country; secondly, that both peoples, having arrived at national consciousness and being engaged in a struggle for national liberation, had a right to freedom, independence and self-government; thirdly that economic unity was in the interest of both communities and should not be called into question; fourthly, that equality of rights – individual, civil, political and religious – for all the inhabitants of Palestine was a precondition of a democratic system and, furthermore, that full equality of rights, in their common State, must be guaranteed to the Arab and Jewish peoples as a whole; and, finally, that the solution of the Palestine problem would not solve the Jewish problem in general.

The maintenance of the integrity of Palestine as a federation of two autonomous states, Arab and Jewish, appeared to the Yugoslavian delegate to be preferable to partition into two separate states, not only because of the practical difficulties that he (along with other delegates) noted – the need to draw an artificial border-line through a tiny country, poor in natural resources, populated by two communities mixed together, endangering crucial economic ties.[11] It is likely that Yugoslavia, as a multi-national federation, was particularly sensitive to the argument raised by the opponents of partition, namely that a decision to partition a country along ethno-national lines would set a dangerous precedent (we shall return to this subject later on). On the other hand, the majority in UNSCOP took the view that the conflict between the two peoples precluded cooperation in the framework of a single state – first and foremost, as we have seen, because of the dispute over Jewish immigration.

The supporters of partition proposed resolving the problem through the establishment of an independent Jewish state in part of Palestine, capable of receiving Jewish immigration without threatening to turn the Arabs of Palestine as a whole into a minority in their own land. The majority report holds, just as the Yugoslavian delegate did in his remarks, that it was incontrovertible that a solution for Palestine could not be considered a solution of the Jewish problem in general. However, it also determined, as we have seen, that a Jewish state should be allocated territory of a sufficient size to enable it to realize the desire of the Jews of Palestine to absorb Jewish immigration. That is the fundamental difference between the two proposals: It could be claimed, at least theoretically, that a federative framework would give sufficient expression to the national aspirations of both peoples; however, it is clear that the autonomous, federated Jewish state would not be able to accept immigrants of its own accord. Consequently, the practical meaning of the bi-national federative solution was the closing of gates of the country to Jewish immigration. It could therefore be viewed as a solution of sorts for the national aspirations of the Jews of Palestine, but not for the

Jewish people in the Diaspora. The Yugoslavian delegate was aware of this difficulty, and later on in his speech on 14 October he admitted that 'the most serious problem was that of the future immigration of the Jews' to Palestine. He admits that despite 'the great compassion for the Jewish people, since the people of Yugoslavia had suffered similarly at the hands of the same aggressor', he was unable to propose a solution that would 'give full satisfaction to Zionist aspirations' in this area – beyond the recommendation to enable the immediate immigration of Jews from the DP camps in Europe, and especially from the camps for illegal immigrants in Cyprus for a three-year transition period.

However, the stance taken by the Arab side turned the debate between the majority and minority opinions in UNSCOP into a theoretical one. The delegates of the Arab countries and the Palestinian Arabs, not content with rejecting the two-state solution, rejected no less resolutely the minority report with its proposal for an Arab–Jewish federation. They demanded a unitary Arab state in all of Palestine. The delegate of the Arab Higher Committee expressed this view in his remarks before the Ad Hoc Committee of the General Assembly on 29 September:

> As for the United Nations Special Committee on Palestine, Mr. Husseini declared that it could not be a basis for discussion. That report, he said, contains two schemes [partition and federation], both of which are based on considerations that are, in the view of the Arabs of Palestine, inconsistent with and repugnant to their rights, the United Nations Charter and Covenant of the League of Nations. The Arabs of Palestine are, therefore, solidly determined to oppose, with all the means at their disposal, any scheme that provides for the dissection, segregation or partition of their country, or that gives to a minority on the ground of creed, any special and preferential rights or status.

Had the Arab delegates not rejected the bi-national option, there is no way of knowing if the partition plan would have obtained the required two-thirds majority in the United Nations. The delegates of quite a few states that ultimately supported partition expressed their regret that the two peoples living in Palestine were unable to cooperate and agree on a compromise solution that would not necessitate partitioning the country.[12] The General Assembly set up a special committee to look into the possibility of finding a compromise position between the UNSCOP majority and minority views; however, because the Arab delegates rejected the minority position too, no consolidated alternative to the partition proposal was presented to the General Assembly.

The right to national self-determination and its dilemmas

The debate in the General Assembly was consequently on the sole proposal before it – the partition plan. Naturally, the arguments put forth by Arab delegates were not based only on the theory that the European Jews were the descendants of the Khazars, the denial of Jewish peoplehood, the claim that the German Jews in Palestine wanted nothing more than to return to their homeland,[13] or the proposal that the problem of the displaced Jews in Europe should be resolved by having the Holocaust survivors return to their previous places of residence, take possession of the property that had belonged to murdered Jews and thus become enriched.[14] The speeches of the Arab delegates and their supporters included more weighty arguments. Their main argument was that the Palestinian Arabs represented the indigenous majority population in Palestine and had a natural right to independence; hence, independence should be granted to Palestine as an Arab state. The Arab side too was thus invoking the right to national self-determination (a term that was frequently used by Arab delegates), as well as the democratic principle of majority rule. Thus, the representative of the Higher Arab Committee, in his speech to the Ad Hoc Committee on 24 November, accused the Soviet Union and the United States of collaborating to 'support the monstrous distortion of the principle of self-determination in Palestine', in their support for a plan to partition the country contrary to the wishes of the majority its inhabitants, instead of supporting an independent state under the rule of the Arab majority. Similarly, the Yemeni delegate, in the meeting of the Ad Hoc Committee on 15 October:

> was surprised that some delegations had based their adherence to partition on the ground of the principle of self-determination. Since the population of Palestine was predominantly Arab, the only logical and just application of that principle was that Palestine should become an independent Arab State with full protection of the rights of Palestinian Jewish minorities. If it were conceded that the principle of self-determination could justify the grant of discriminatory and preferential privileges to a minority over the will of the majority, or the division of a country against the wishes of the majority, then the world would be overwhelmed with similar problems and chaos would prevail.

In contrast to this, Moshe Shertok (Sharett), the representative of the Jewish Agency, had said in his speech at the First Committee of the General Assembly on 12 May that it would not be fair to demand the independence of Palestine as a country without ensuring the independence of the Jewish people as a nation at the same time.

The UNSCOP majority report recognized the legitimacy of the Palestinian Arabs' aspirations to independence, but sought to also take into account the Jewish national aspirations, and consequently proposed partition. The Arab delegates and their supporters in the debate maintained that this would set a dangerous precedent endangering the territorial integrity of many countries. This is a serious argument, which exemplifies the dilemmas inherent in the realization of the principle of national self-determination when it clashes with the principle of a state's territorial integrity. A single universally applicable solution has yet to be found to this dilemma, which accompanies many national conflicts in various parts of the world (the Balkans being a salient example). On the one hand, there are cases in which the 'right of secession' of a national group is recognized – particularly when it already enjoys a measure of recognition and self-government within a defined region. Thus, for example, in the United Kingdom it is a widely shared assumption, once voiced explicitly by John Major, the former Conservative Prime Minister, in a television interview explaining his opposition to Scottish devolution, that if the majority of Scots were to vote for the nationalist party, Scotland could not be prevented from seceding from the United Kingdom because, in Major's words, 'no people can rule another people against their will'. The UK government also officially recognized the right of Northern Ireland to secede if the majority of the population in that region should favour doing so. The dissolution of Czechoslovakia into the Czech Republic and the Slovak Republic (Slovakia) was carried out by mutual agreement, and the Czech side earned justified praise for not attempting to protect the country's integrity by force. Canada's Supreme Court has recognized in principle, subject to procedural qualifications, Quebec's right to secede from Canada.

On the other hand, Spain does not recognize the right of the Basques or of Catalonia to secede. As a rule, most countries in which a question of this kind could arise do not recognize any 'right of secession' at the expense of their territorial integrity. The division of British India into India and Pakistan involved terrible bloodshed and the uprooting of millions of refugees from their homes. However, it is likely that an attempt to force the Muslims of the subcontinent to live under majority Hindi rule would have led to even greater bloodshed. From a historical perspective, therefore, the Indian Congress's eventual, and highly reluctant, acceptance of partition deserves great appreciation.[15] India itself helped Bangladesh to secede from Pakistan; this step was viewed by world opinion with understanding due to the atrocities to which the people of Bangladesh had been subjected. The break-up of the Soviet Union and Yugoslavia led to bloody conflicts that illustrate the danger of separatism and, even more so, the danger of any attempt to keep a multi-national state together by force (something that was attempted by Serbia, in contrast with Russia). In most cases, violent separatist groups, such as the Tamil Tigers in Sri Lanka, do not enjoy international sympathy and support. Ethno-national separatism should certainly not be given a sweeping stamp of approval. And indeed, many of the states that opposed the partition of Palestine in 1947 explained that they feared that it would set a dangerous precedent: they preferred to see independence granted to the country as a whole.

On the other hand, the Dutch delegate, who voted in favour of partition, pointed in his speech to the General Assembly on 26 November to the historic example of his own country: the secession of Belgium, which had been part of the Netherlands up until 1830. History proves, he said, that it is impossible to hold two different peoples in a single state by force: 'The differences between Arabs and Jews now are much greater than those between Belgium and the Netherlands in 1830.' The Dutch delegate went on to note that the Dutch and

Belgians 'today' cooperated very closely within the Benelux framework, and he expressed his hope that the Jews and Arabs would succeed in attaining a similar combination of political independence and close economic cooperation (as indeed should have emerged from the partition plan, which spoke of an 'economic union' between the two states).

The danger of states shattering along ethno-national lines should certainly not be taken lightly. This type of break-up is particularly problematic in light of the fact that it often involves violent struggles, if only because in most cases there is no clear-cut, agreed-upon border that can be drawn between one national group and another. Consequently, and despite the fact that the United Nations Charter states that every people has a right to self-determination, there is in fact no international consensus on the manner in which this principle is to be implemented, beyond its application to the liberation of the peoples of Asia and Africa from colonial rule. Some view the granting of limited expression of a people's national aspirations within a framework that does not recognize its right to an independent state as the proper way to realize the principle of self-determination in non-colonial situations. Some would seek to restrict the principle of full national self-determination without completely relinquishing it, and support the 'right of secession' only when the people in question are in severe distress in the absence of independence.[16] It may perhaps be claimed, theoretically, that the establishment of an autonomous 'Jewish state' as part of an Arab–Jewish federation, as recommended by the UNSCOP minority report, would have amounted to granting self-determination to the Jews of Palestine (though not to the Jewish people as a whole). It is clear that when the international community opted for the two-state solution in 1947 over the integrity of the land under the rule of the Arab majority, it estimated, and rightly so, that the state of the relations between the two peoples living in the country could guarantee neither peace nor the fundamental rights of the Jews in the framework of a single state. It would not be far-fetched to assume that the members of UNSCOP who opted for partition were well aware of the Nazi past of the recognized leader of the Palestinian Arabs, the head of the Arab Higher Committee, the Grand Mufti of Jerusalem Haj Amin Al-Husseini, when they reached this conclusion. While the committee report refrains from making any critical remarks about either side or their leaders, the question was raised in all intensity by some of the participants in the General Assembly debate. Thus, the Guatemalan delegate says in his remarks to the Ad Hoc Committee on 10 October that:

> Several members of the Arab Higher Committee had shown Nazi leanings throughout the war. As for the Mufti of Jerusalem, he had been opposed to sparing even Jewish children. What would happen if the Jews were his subjects? ... the Jews should therefore have a country of their own ... where the Jews are masters of their own fate.

It was also clear that it would not be possible to alleviate the distress of the displaced Jews in Europe in the framework of a single state or, more generally, to solve the issue of Jewish immigration to Palestine.

Some UNSCOP members visited a number of Jewish DP camps in Europe before the writing of the final committee report. A detailed description of this visit appears in the book written by the Guatemalan delegate to the committee, Garcia-Granados. The author describes the masses of people (the overall number of 'displaced persons' was close to a quarter of a million people) who had undergone the horrors of the Holocaust and were still imprisoned, more than two years after the war had ended, in overcrowded camps, mostly in Germany. An American officer that had been placed in charge of issues related to Jewish DPs reported to the members of the committee that the presence of large concentrations of foreign Jews on German soil was reawakening anti-Semitism in Germany. 'Gentlemen, if the American army were to withdraw tomorrow, there would be pogroms on the following day. ... In fact, anti-Semitism is growing. The Germans hate the displaced persons.'[17] The members of the committee asked many of the camp inmates where they wanted to build their future, and everywhere 'the results ... were the same. No matter to whom we spoke, in whatever language – German, Russian, Polish, Rumanian, Hungarian, Yiddish – the desire was one: to go to Palestine and only to Palestine.'[18] The woman in charge of Kloster Indersdorf, a UN orphanage established in Germany, told the UNSCOP members: 'These children ... feel they are surrounded in Germany by hatred – and you must remember that their parents were starved, gassed, burned to death by the Germans. Discipline,' she said, was a major problem. 'The most effective weapon we have is to say to them, "We won't send you to Palestine." That is the most awful, the most terrifying threat we hold over them.'[19]

At a meeting with senior American and British officers from the military government in Germany and those responsible for the DP camps, the members of UNSCOP heard their assessment that 95–98 per cent of the displaced Jews wanted to go to Palestine. While the officers were of the view that most of the Jewish DPs would have been willing to settle for another solution if offered to them – in other words, they would have preferred to immigrate to other countries rather than remain in the camps in Germany – this had been the case in the past. However, as time passed, the refugees' determination to reject any solution other than immigration to Palestine grew stronger.[20] But the question of their immigration to other countries was in any case academic, as explained by the head of the United Nations International Organization for Refugee Affairs to the UNSCOP plenary. When asked if, in his opinion, there was any chance for a 'mass settlement of Jewish refugees outside of Palestine in the near future', he responded:

Taking into account all available information, I see no possibility of any country in the world accepting Jewish immigration on a large scale. That is understandable enough. In some quarters, Jews are unpopular and governments are anxious to avert the situations which prevailed for many centuries in Europe. In other countries, where anti-Semitism is unknown, economic conditions are such that they require an agricultural or labouring type of immigration that is not easily found among the professional men, craftsmen and specialized workmen in the refugee camps.[21]

Thus the very same claim – that the arrival of these refugees in large numbers could spark anti-Semitism, and anti-Semitism was of course an undesirable phenomenon in the eyes of any enlightened government – that had been voiced in various countries before the Holocaust in order to justify the closing of the gates to Jewish refugees fleeing from the Nazis was being made two years after the Holocaust as well, this time regarding the survivors in the DP camps. Consequently, the Holocaust survivors found themselves imprisoned on German soil, with the Western countries having no interest in taking them in. The Jewish world of Eastern Europe, the world from which most of them had come, had been annihilated in the Holocaust. The efforts of survivors to return to their homes and properties, which in many cases had already been distributed among their neighbours, repeatedly ended in murder (especially in Poland). The members of UNSCOP might well get the impression that the description of the Jews as a 'homeless people' was no mere metaphor.

The members of the Anglo-American committee who visited the DP camps in Germany and Austria in 1946, and who recommended that 100,000 of the DPs be permitted to immigrate to Palestine without delay, received a similar impression. British Labour MP Richard Crossman describes in his book the 'neurotic' fear, as he describes it, that the survivors in the DP camps felt about their German surroundings; their feeling that they had nowhere to go back to; their knowledge that they were not wanted in any of the Western countries; and the determined desire of the vast majority of them to reach Palestine.[22]

As we have seen, the Soviet Union's Andrei Gromyko, in his speech to the General Assembly on 14 May, presented the Jewish people's suffering in the absence of a state as one of the principal arguments in favour of the establishment of a Jewish state.

> The fact that no West-European State has been able to ensure the defence of the elementary rights of the Jewish people, and to safeguard it against the violence of the fascist executioners, explains the aspirations of the Jews to establish their own State.

As the Soviet delegate would have it, the problem of anti-Semitism – which reached new heights in the Holocaust – existed only in the capitalist states of Western Europe. Other delegates admitted the existence of the problem and its severity, and in particular the magnitude of the disaster that befell the Jewish people in the Second World War. The general recognition of the enormity of the Jewish tragedy clearly constituted the backdrop to the entire debate. However, the distress of world Jewry as an argument in favour of establishing a Jewish state was a delicate subject, not easy to deal with for delegates of countries containing a sizeable Jewish population. To say that the Jewish people needed a state of their own because in the absence of a state they were vulnerable to hatred, discrimination and persecution would imply an admission that many countries of the world had been unable to protect their citizens from anti-Semitism. Western delegates were not always more candid than Andrei

Gromyko in admitting the existence of a 'Jewish problem' – i.e. of anti-Semitism – in their countries, in the present or in the past. Thus, for example, the Belgian delegate said in his speech to the General Assembly plenary on 26 November:

> The Palestinian question is particularly disturbing for the Belgians. They have to make an effort to understand the motives of Zionism. The national home of our Jewish compatriots is in Belgium. No one has ever treated them in such a way as to make them want to find another home in Palestine.

Nevertheless, conceded the Belgian delegate, the problem does exist – i.e. it exists elsewhere. The Dutch delegate said in his speech to the General Assembly that same day: 'There has, moreover, never been any Jewish problem in the Netherlands.' The delegate of France (which ultimately, like Belgium and the Netherlands, decided to support partition) said in his speech to the General Assembly plenary on 28 November:

> As my Belgian colleague has declared on behalf of his country, I can say of mine that it has never made any distinction between Jews and non-Jews. … In France, anti-Semitism has never been anything but an ideological adventure on the part of certain intellectuals.

Similarly, the Peruvian delegate, in his speech to the Ad Hoc Committee on 14 October, referred to the 'Jewish problem, which incidentally, does not exist in Peru'. He nevertheless went on to stress the gravity of the problem and the urgent need to solve it.

Despite the tendency of various delegates to embellish the situation of the Jews in their countries, the suffering of the Jewish people was widely acknowledged. This was viewed as a major argument in favour of setting up an independent Jewish state – even at the cost of partition. Of course, in modern Jewish and Zionist history, the 'Jewish distress' and the rise of a modern national movement aspiring to a territorial solution in the land of Israel 'in this time' have been linked so closely that it is virtually impossible to separate the two. Consequently, there is little point in asking to what extent the aspiration to establish a state in Palestine would have been justified – even at the cost of a confrontation with the Arab majority in the land – if the Jewish people had 'felt at home' in the countries in which they lived. Had they felt at home, they would not have been a people seeking a homeland of their own.

To return to the issue of partition versus territorial integrity – the partition of Mandatory Palestine was of course different from ordinary cases of 'secession' in that it did not involve the partition of a sovereign state. This fact did not make the partition legitimate in the eyes of its opponents, who repeatedly emphasized the need to grant Palestine independence while maintaining its territorial integrity. They viewed this as the realization of the principle of self-determination. And indeed, at the very stage of transition to independence, many countries – those that were members of the United Nations at the time of the debate in 1947, as well as many of those that shook off colonial rule in the years that followed – were facing attempts at secession that threatened their territorial integrity. Consequently, the demand to maintain the territorial integrity of Mandatory Palestine was carefully heeded by some of the delegations.[23] On the other hand, the delegate of Uruguay noted in his speech on 26 September in the plenary that, in fact, the partition of Mandatory Palestine was nothing new: The original territory of the Mandate had already been partitioned in the past, when an Arab state – Transjordan – had been established on most of it; this state had been recognized by the international community and no one claimed that it was illegitimate because it had been created by partitioning the original Mandatory Palestine.

Moreover, what distinguished the case of Mandatory Palestine was the fact that, as a modern political entity, it had been created from the outset with the declared goal of establishing a national home for the Jewish people in it. It was for this purpose, and entirely against the wishes of Arab nationalists, that the League of Nations granted the United Kingdom a Mandate over a part of 'Greater Syria' to be known as 'Palestine'. The Ottoman Empire had never contained a sub-unit bearing the name of Palestine. Naturally, the United Kingdom had interests and reasons of its own for wishing to control this area, but the international legitimacy was given to this rule based on the promise that it had made to the Jewish people – a promise that was enshrined in the Mandate.

The delegate of Cuba, who opposed partition, warned in his speech to the plenary of the General Assembly on 28 November: 'The plan of partition for Palestine implies the establishment by this Assembly of the principle that any racial or other minority may ask to secede from the political community of which it forms part.' The subject of the right of secession is, as noted, a complex issue in many ways. However, one may ask to what degree and in what sense the Arabs and Jews of Mandatory Palestine ever belonged to the same 'political community'. These two national groups never joined in a political partnership – such as by voting in elections to the same legislature, or (informally) by participating in the same struggle for independence against the Imperial power. The shared territorial entity in which they found themselves had been set up from the outset, controversially, in order to provide a national home for one group, over the objections of the other. Due to the circumstances in which the Mandate was created and because of the continuous national strife between the two communities, no common 'Palestinian' identity shared by both Jews and Arabs could possibly develop in this territory. This situation is the opposite of what happened in a number of colonial countries, within which there developed, to a greater or lesser extent, a shared territorial identity that went beyond the various ethnic ones – notwithstanding the fact that their borders had been drawn by the colonial powers based on their own interests, without taking the ethnic and cultural make-up of the indigenous populations into account. In a situation such as that which prevailed in the territory of the British Mandate in Palestine – two peoples with opposing political national aspirations that had no loyalty to any shared territorial–political framework – the only viable solution was, indeed, the two-state solution.

When the Lebanese delegate spoke of a 'land shaped by geography and history' that must not be partitioned, he refrained from noting why and for what purpose that land had been shaped into a political entity after the First World War. However, other Arab delegates freely admitted that Palestine, as a separate political entity, owed its very existence to the intention to establish a national home for the Jewish people in it. As the Syrian delegate said in his speech to the General Assembly on 14 May:

> I think most of you, if not all, know that Palestine used to be a Syrian province. Geographical, historical, racial and religious links exist there. There is no distinction whatever between the Palestinians and the Syrians and, had it not been for the Balfour Declaration and the terms of the mandate, Palestine would now be a Syrian province, as it used to be.

On 9 October, the Syrian delegate returned to this subject before the Ad Hoc Committee and noted that the fact that Palestine had originally been part of southern Syria was attested to by the fact that 'Palestine had formed the southern section of Syria, and even under the British military government from 1918 to 1920, representatives from Palestine had been freely elected and had sat in the Syrian Constituent Assembly'. Unsurprisingly, this subject of Palestine being part of southern Syria was particularly close to the Syrian delegate's heart. However, the delegate of the Higher Arab Committee of Palestinian Arabs noted in his speech to the 'First Committee' (on political affairs) of the General Assembly of 9 May that before the First World War 'Palestine had been included in the Ottoman Empire as part of Syria', and he related to the promises that had been given to the Arabs by the British regarding support for Arab independence at the end of the First World War, maintaining that these promises applied to 'that part of Syria known today as Palestine'.

Article 166 of Chapter II of the UNSCOP report ('The Elements of the Conflict') states:

> The desire of the Arab people of Palestine to safeguard their national existence is a very natural desire. However, Palestinian nationalism, as distinct from Arab nationalism, is itself a relatively new phenomenon, which appeared only after the division of the 'Arab rectangle' by the settlement of the First World War. The National Home policy, and the vigorous policy of immigration pursued by the Jewish leadership, has sharpened the Arab fear of danger from the intruding Jewish population.

These remarks are reminiscent of a question that was once hotly debated in Israel: Whether, and since when, the Palestinian Arabs are to be considered a distinct 'Palestinian people'? This is obviously a futile debate. Just as it is impossible to provide a precise 'scientific' definition of a people, it is similarly impossible to point to the exact moment when a certain people 'came into being'. The general outlines of the historical development in this matter are fairly clear, and in this sense, the analysis of the UN committee in 1947 is no different from what prominent Palestinian intellectuals have to say:[24] The Palestinian national identity developed during, and under the influence of, the Palestinian Arabs' confrontation with Zionism as a reaction to the Zionist enterprise under the auspices of the British Mandate. At the same time, this process occurred in tandem with the development of other 'local' Arab national identities, which came into being as a result of the division of the area by the Western powers at the end of the First World War. That this division was strongly opposed at the time by the Arab nationalists who aspired to Arab unity does not make the identities that developed as a result of it any less real. Mandatory Palestine might perhaps never have come into being if not for the intention to establish a Jewish national home in it; however, if such an entity had emerged under different circumstances – ones related solely to the interests of the British Empire – a distinct Palestinian identity (conceived of as one of the Arab peoples that make up the 'Arab nation') would, no doubt, eventually have developed in its context. Just as it is absurd to cast doubt on the authenticity and strength of Palestinian nationalism today, it is similarly absurd and anachronistic to accuse the Zionist movement in its early days of 'ignoring the existence of the Palestinian people'.

All this is in no way intended to obfuscate the real difficulty and the problematic nature involved in both the Zionist enterprise and the Mandate regime that was intended to advance it, from the perspective of the Arabs of Palestine. When one takes a particular region, which is populated for the most part by people of a certain identity, and establishes in it a regime whose declared goal is to change the character of the region by means of mass immigration by members of a different people to enable them to establish their national home there, this is a very problematic act from the point of view of the inhabitants of that region, whether or not they had viewed themselves, until then, as 'a people' distinct from the population of neighbouring regions. It should be borne in mind that, in contrast with 1947, at the time the Mandate was approved one could not speak of two peoples actually living in Palestine, since the Jews were then but a small minority of the population. Consequently, and despite the fact that the idea of a Jewish national home in Palestine clearly conformed to the prevailing trend immediately following the First World War that gave weight to the national aspirations of various peoples,[25] there is a measure of truth in the words of the authors of the UNSCOP report, that the principle of self-determination 'was not applied to Palestine' at the time of the approval of the Palestine Mandate 'because of the intention to make possible the creation of the Jewish National Home there. Actually, it may well be said that the Jewish National Home and the sui generis Mandate for Palestine run counter to that principle' (Article 176). They ran counter to that principle in the sense that a regime was imposed on Palestine that was opposed to the national aspirations of the great majority of its inhabitants.

The principle of national self-determination gained general recognition in the aftermath of the First World War, under the influence, among other things, of the ideas of US President Woodrow Wilson. It was accepted as a major (though not exclusive) guiding principle at a time when the Allies determined the political future of various countries and territories whose status had to be settled in the wake of war. This principle was formulated in terms of the need to consider in the first place, when such determinations were made, the desires of the inhabitants of the territory involved. However, unlike other peoples that won independence or self-rule by virtue of this principle at that time, the Jews were a people in diaspora that lacked a territorial base. There was no concentration of Jews that could serve as a basis for a Jewish national home, either in the whole of Palestine or in a part of it. Inevitably, in this case, there was a contrast between the desire to grant the Jewish people a national home of its own, which was fundamentally consistent with the principle of national self-determination, and the commonly accepted mode of implementing this principle.

This is the issue that must be faced and grappled with if one wishes to examine whether the Jews' aspiration for a state of their own was, at that time, morally justified. The question does not arise as regards the establishment of the State of Israel in 1948, in the wake of the international decision to partition Palestine between the two peoples that actually lived there at that time. Rather, it relates to the aspiration for statehood at the outset of Zionism. Is it right to deny the Zionist movement the legitimacy usually accorded to a national movement striving to attain independence for its people on the grounds that this people did not live naturally and normally, like other peoples, in the land in which it sought independence, but rather was 'brought' to it, largely by the Zionist movement itself? The opponents of Zionism answer this question, explicitly or implicitly, in the affirmative. Moreover, many of them depict Zionism as a colonialist enterprise, basing themselves on the fact that the Jews came to Palestine from outside, from various countries, mainly (though not exclusively) from Europe.[26]

The moral significance of this position is that the Jewish people are being punished for the Jewish tragedy – for seeking to establish a state in the absence not only of national independence, but also of a home; for seeking a home in a situation where large parts of that people were denied the most fundamental human rights, including, in extreme cases, elementary human dignity and life itself. Whereas the Jewish aspiration to national independence was no different in essence from the national aspirations of other peoples, the way in which the Jewish people attained independence was indeed unique – because the Jewish tragedy was unique. Does it mean that it was less justified for that? Those who say so are voiding the principle of national self-determination of its essential moral content. It should be borne in mind that the whole concept of group rights, especially national rights, is problematic in many ways. It is problematic primarily because, quite often, defining the group and its borders presents a considerable difficulty, and also because the collective rights of one group often clash with those of another – as indeed happened in the course of the Jewish–Arab conflict over Palestine. Nevertheless, there is a clear tendency in the modern world to go beyond the traditional and more easily defined individual rights and recognize group rights as well, while making an effort to maintain a proper balance when various collective rights clash.[27] The reason for this is that when group rights fail to be recognized and protected, many individuals are denied the ability to realize major aspects of their personality and identity; in the case of national rights – of their national identity and culture.[28] In extreme cases, denying a group's national rights prevents its members from enjoying their right to human dignity and physical security. Those who maintain that the Jewish people should have been denied the right of self-determination – a right that it needed in the twentieth century more desperately than any other people – are making a claim that is patently immoral. If one were to weigh the moral cost involved in the realization of Zionism against the will of the majority of the inhabitants of historical Palestine against the moral cost involved in the denial of Zionism, that is, denial of the Jewish hope to, in the words of the Israeli national anthem, 'live as a free people in our land'; and if one were to attempt to balance the rights and needs of the two groups involved in this clash of interests, the most equitable solution would appear to be – from the outset, and not only after the fact – that of two states for two peoples.

The historic connection and historic right

The connection to the land of Israel is one of the foundations of Jewish identity. This is a basic difference between Zionism and numerous other settlement phenomena – colonialist or non-colonialist – throughout history. It is also clear that the notion of the Return to Zion captured the imaginations of many supporters of Zionism in the Christian world. Loyalty to the land of Israel as the ancient homeland of the Jewish people was expressed most dramatically in the refusal of the majority of the Zionist movement to adopt Uganda as an alternative homeland – notwithstanding Herzl's pledge that this would be no more than a temporary shelter for Jews in distress from Eastern Europe, and that adopting the plan would not imply an abandonment of the ultimate goal: a Jewish national centre in the land of Israel.

The League of Nations Mandate[29] granted international recognition to the 'historic connection of the Jewish people with Palestine' as one of the grounds for 'reconstituting their national home in that country'. The UNSCOP report also relates to this connection and holds that:

> The Jewish assurance that no political injustice would be done to the Arabs by the creation of a Jewish State in Palestine ... gains some support from the fact that not since the existence of the ancient Jewish kingdom has Palestine been an independent State.

On the other hand, the committee hastens to add, 'the fact remains that today in Palestine there are over 1,200,000 Arabs, two-thirds of the population, who oppose a Jewish State and who are intent on establishing an independent Arab State' (Chapter II, Article 154). In general, a great deal of caution is evident in the committee's treatment of the historical connection and the possibility of using it as a basis for modern political claims. The committee took care not to turn this argument into the principal foundation of its decision to support an independent Jewish state:

> Aside from contentions based on biblical and historical sources as to this right, the Jewish case rests on the Balfour Declaration of 1917 and on the Mandate for Palestine, which incorporated the Declaration in its preamble and recognized the historic connection of the Jewish people with Palestine and the grounds for reconstituting the Jewish National Home there.
>
> (Article 128)

> The Committee was fully aware that both Arabs and Jews advance strong claims to rights and interests in Palestine, the Arabs by virtue of being for centuries the indigenous and preponderant people there, and the Jews by virtue of historical association with the country and international pledges made to them respecting their rights in it. But the Committee also realized that the crux of the Palestine problem is to be found in the fact that two sizeable groups, an Arab population of over 1,200,000 and a Jewish population of over 600,000, with intense nationalist aspirations, are diffused throughout the country.
>
> (Chapter V, Introductory Statement, Paragraph 3)

The members of the committee clearly recognized the historical connection between the Jews and Palestine.[30] However, it would appear that the question as to the weight of this historical argument compared to the Arab claims belonged in itself, in the committee's view, largely to history, due to the fact that two peoples with contrasting and legitimate national aspirations actually lived in the country. Even the delegate of Guatemala, who wholeheartedly supported the right of the Jews to a state of their own, stressed in his book that the case for the establishment of a modern Jewish state could not be based on historical claims alone: 'I realized that the mere fact that a Hebrew kingdom had once existed in Palestine did not give valid title for the creation of a new Jewish state – if the Jewish claim were to rest only on that title.'[31]

The caution exercised by the UNSCOP members on this subject is understandable. The stability of existing borders is a vital interest of the international community and a basic principle of modern international law. A territorial claim based, exclusively or mainly, on a 'historical right' going back hundreds or thousands of years could indeed be viewed as a threat to this principle and as a dangerous precedent. Naturally, there is a great difference between a state demanding the sovereign territory of a neighbouring state based on a claim of historical right, on the one hand, and a homeless people trying to return to its ancient homeland, not at the expense of the sovereign territory of any state, but rather in a territorial framework defined from the outset with the aim of enabling the establishment of a national home for this people. Nevertheless, the very fact that a territorial claim based on historical arguments was being raised, against the wishes of the majority of the inhabitants of the territory involved, was problematic for the international community. During the debate in the General Assembly, the Arab representatives and other opponents of partition repeatedly stressed this point. The representative of the Arab Higher Committee warned in his speech before the First Committee of the General Assembly on 9 May that accepting the Jewish claim over Palestine on the grounds that there had been a Jewish kingdom in it 2,000 years earlier would create a precedent that would require a 'redrawing of the map of the world'. Another representative of the Arab Higher Committee stated in his speech before the Ad Hoc Committee on 29 September that if the Jewish claim over Palestine were accepted based on 'the association of the Jews with Palestine 2,000 years ago', the Arabs could have a better and stronger claim over Spain and parts of France, Turkey, Persia and Afghanistan and even parts of India, Russia and China.

The UNSCOP report and the supporters of partition in the General Assembly related, as we have seen, to the Jewish people's historical roots in the land of Israel, but their principal arguments in favour of a Jewish state were different: On the one hand, the fact that two peoples existed Palestine, and on the other, the suffering and distress of the Jewish people in the world and their legitimate aspiration to gain an independent state.[32]

Judging by the manner in which 'historical right' appears in Israel's Declaration of Independence, it would appear that its framers distinguished between the enormous importance of the 'historic and traditional attachment' to the land of Israel from the perspective of Jewish identity and sentiment and the possibility of relying on the historical argument as the chief basis for the international legitimacy of the new state. Following a historical survey that emphasizes the connection of the Jewish people with the land of Israel, the Declaration mentions the UN General Assembly resolution that recognized the 'the right of the Jewish people to establish its State'; this is followed by a statement regarding 'the natural right of the Jewish people ... like all other peoples' to national independence. This is immediately followed by the operative statement, which declares the establishment of the state 'by virtue of our natural and historic right and on the strength of the resolution of the United Nations General Assembly'. The historical right is thus 'sandwiched' between the natural right of the Jewish people to national independence – which is, as is underscored, a universal right – and the decision by the international community to support the establishment of a Jewish state on the basis of this right. For all their awareness of the importance of the Jewish people's historical bond with their ancient homeland, the framers of the Declaration refrained from turning this claim into the exclusive or chief basis for the legitimacy of the Jewish State. There is a world of difference between their approach and the ideology that emerged among the Israeli public following the Six Day War, according to which Israel – a sovereign state, not a homeless people – was entitled to hold onto territories without granting civil rights to their inhabitants, while ignoring their wishes and the international norms in the name of the historical right of the Jewish people to these territories.

'An alien body in the Arab Middle East'

One of the arguments often put forward by the Arab delegates in the General Assembly debate was that the establishment of a Jewish state would mean the introduction of an alien body into the Arab Middle East. In resorting to this argument, they made no pretence of relying on some universal principle. Rather, they gave warning to the international community that partitioning Palestine between its two peoples would undermine the stability of the region due to the determination of the entire Arab world not to accept the presence of an alien, i.e. non-Arab, entity in its midst. The Syrian delegate ended his speech before the General Assembly on 22 September with these words:

> I must solemnly state that the peace-loving Syrian and Arab peoples squarely oppose the recommendations of the Special Committee [UNSCOP], and will never allow a wedge or a foreign hostile bridgehead to be driven into the heart of their fatherland. They expect that this great Organization, which was created to maintain peace, may be reminded that justice is the only safeguard of peace. They also earnestly hope and wish that they shall not be compelled by acts of injustice to have no other course but to resort to the sacred right of self-defence.

The Iraqi delegate said in his speech to the General Assembly on 28 November:

> Palestine is the heart of the Arab world. The Arab world, through the [Arab] League, is trying to achieve unity. ... A Jewish State breaks that unity and endangers the peace and security of the Arab States. The Arab States cannot tolerate this break in their unity and this menace to their political and economic life. They are entitled to have a decisive voice in all matters which affect their regional interests. Therefore, they oppose the creation of a Jewish State in Palestine now or at any future time.

This argument, that the very existence of Israel would break up the territorial continuity of the Arab world and prevent the Arab countries from attaining unity, would be often repeated in the years to come – notably by Egypt's Pan-Arabist president Gamal Abdul Nasser. Given the modern means of communication and transportation and Israel's minuscule geographic dimensions, it is difficult to take this claim seriously. What lies behind these statements is simply an Arab unwillingness to accept the existence of a non-Arab entity in the region. The representative of the Arab Higher Committee told the Ad Hoc Committee on 29 September (quoted in indirect speech):

> One other consideration of fundamental importance to the Arab world was that of racial homogeneity. The Arabs lived in a vast territory stretching from the Mediterranean to the Indian Ocean, spoke one language, had the same history, tradition and aspirations. Their unity was a solid foundation

for peace in one of the most central and sensitive areas of the world. It was illogical, therefore, that the United Nations should associate itself with the introduction of an alien body into that established homogeneity, a course which could only produce new Balkans.[33]

The expression 'racial homogeneity', however jarring it is to our ears today, should not be taken too seriously. Clearly, what is meant is Arab national homogeneity, which refuses to accept the existence of a non-Arab entity in its midst. This aspect of the Arab opposition to a Jewish state emerged very powerfully in the partition debates in 1947; it is notable that in this case, the argument was voiced by Palestinian Arabs. Similar arguments would be heard repeatedly throughout the years of the conflict.

It must always be borne in mind that the Jewish people of Israel face not just the Palestinian-Arab people. While constituting a majority in Israel, Israeli Jews are but a tiny minority in the Arab-Muslim Middle East. It is generally recognized that a minority feels a stronger need than a majority to express its identity; the efforts of the minority to maintain its identity and avoid being assimilated into the 'homogeneity' of the majority are generally viewed with sympathy. The Arab majority in the Middle East emphasizes in every way possible the Arab identity of the region, as well as the Arab identity of its states – including those states that have large non-Arab minorities – and no one denies its right to do so. All the Arab states are officially Arab by virtue of belonging to the League of Arab States; all emphasize, in various ways, their 'Arabness' in their constitutions, and some even note this fact in their names ('Arab Republic', 'Arab Emirates'). Syria, which has hundreds of thousands of Kurds and other ethno-national minorities, is officially known as the 'Syrian Arab Republic'. Algeria, which has millions of Berbers, is, as noted in the preamble to its constitution, 'an Arab country'. Morocco, in which Berbers represent a very large proportion of the population, is, according to its constitution, 'part of the greater Arab Maghreb'. The Iraqi Kurds, following the American invasion and occupation of Iraq, emerged as influential power brokers in the new political system. While giving up, for the time being, their dream of independence, they strove both to enhance their self-government in Kurdistan and to downplay the Arab character of Iraq as a whole. Even so, they had to accept the compromise under which Iraq's 'Arabness' was enshrined in the provisional constitution by making the country's membership in the Arab League a constitutional norm. The Palestinian state planned to arise alongside Israel will be, officially, an Arab state. The Palestinian Declaration of Independence,[34] adopted by the Palestine Liberation Organization (PLO) in Algiers in 1988, states, immediately after proclaiming that the Palestinian state will guarantee complete equality of rights for all its citizens, regardless of religion, race or gender, that 'The State of Palestine is an Arab state, an integral and indivisible part of the Arab nation, at one with that nation in heritage and civilization.' That is the typical formulation that can be found in the constitutions of Arab states, declaring the Arab character of the state along with its being part of the

Arab nation or Arab homeland. A similar form of words appears in the Palestinian Basic Law adopted in 1997.

It should be noted that all this cannot be attributed to the undemocratic regimes in the Arab world. These definitions enjoy broad support among Arab public opinion – first and foremost among the Arab Left, which, traditionally, raises the banner of Arab nationalism and unity. The leaders of Israel's Arab minority, who complain that the 'Jewish state' is a discriminatory and exclusionary definition, take pride in the 'Arabness' of the Arab world and in the Arab solidarity between its peoples. Although there is considerable international criticism of the abysmal human rights record of the Arab regimes, the 'Arabness' of the Arab states is taken for granted. The principle of equality needs to be interpreted in a very creative way indeed if it is to allow the official designation of 20 Arab-majority states as Arab while disallowing the definition of a Jewish-majority state as Jewish.

Moreover, the constitutions of the Arab countries, with the exception of Lebanon, declare Islam to be the state religion, and bestow, using different formulations, an official status on the Islamic Shari'a. The Syrian constitution is content to determine only that Islam is the religion of the head of state, although it does add that the Islamic Shari'a is a principal source of legislation. Since the term 'Jewish state' relates, as we have argued, to the national independence of the Jewish people rather than to the status of the Jewish religion in the state, it is a parallel to the term 'Arab state' rather than 'Muslim state'. However, it is a fact that the Arab states have an official Muslim character. Although, notoriously, freedom of religion is violated in many of these states, their official definition as Muslim is not per se a target of international criticism, and it is notable that some Western European democracies are legally designated as having an 'official', 'established' or 'state' church, which does not impair the freedom of religion of the members of other religions. Consequently, the Arab world is, legally as well as in fact, an Arab-Muslim world; in this world, the Israeli Jews represent a small minority striving to preserve its own identity.

The words of the prominent Palestinian intellectual Professor Edward Said can exemplify the duality in the status of the Israeli Jews, a people that is on the one hand the majority nation in its state, while at the same time is a minority in the Middle East, with all that this implies. When asked, in an interview in *Ha'aretz* in August 2000,[35] if he would have accepted the partition plan of 1947, had he been involved in public life at the time, Said replied: 'My instinct is to say no. It was an unfair plan based on the minority getting equal rights to those of the majority.' Thus, according to Said, the Jews did not deserve 'equal rights' – i.e. national rights, national independence alongside a Palestinian-Arab state – because they were a minority in the country. This was, as we have seen, one of the main arguments used by the Arab delegates during the UN debates of 1947. Said, however, went on to present a thesis according to which the status of a minority is the natural state of the Jews – a status to which they are ultimately destined to return. Said rejects the solution of two states for two peoples and expresses his support for a single bi-national state. But, remarks the interviewer, 'in a bi-national state, we Jews will quickly become a minority.' Said replies:

> Yes, but you're going to be a minority anyway. In about 10 years, there will be demographic parity between Jews and Palestinians, and the process will go on. The Jews are a minority everywhere. They are a minority in America. They can certainly be a minority in Israel.

To the interviewer's question 'Knowing the region and given the history of the conflict, do you think such a Jewish minority would be treated fairly?', Said responds:

> I worry about that. The history of minorities in the Middle East has not been as bad as in Europe, but I wonder what would happen. It worries me a great deal. The question of what is going to be the fate of the Jews is very difficult for me. I really don't know. It worries me.

Said's concern for the fate of the Jews in the context of a settlement that he supports does not prevent him proposing that the Jewish people relinquish their national independence in favour of a minority status in what he calls a 'bi-national state', which would be an inseparable part of the Arab-Muslim Middle East. This, in the eyes of the Palestinian intellectual, would be a just solution to the Jewish–Arab conflict. One might say that the Jewish public in Israel shares Said's concern for its fate should the Jewish State be abolished and its Jewish population turned into a minority. However, this concern does not lead it to draw the 'bi-national' conclusion; on the contrary, it bolsters its desire to preserve the independence of the Jewish people in their own nation-state. This may be attributed in part to the Jewish people's natural assumption that in the circumstances that prevail in this region, a state with an Arab-Muslim majority and a Jewish minority (widely considered to be an 'alien' element) at the heart of the Arab Middle East would in fact be a fully fledged Arab state (similarly to all other Arab-majority states in the area), rather than a bi-national one, even if it is formally designated as bi-national. That is why no real bi-national option exists now; nor should one assume that it existed in 1947 (even had it not been explicitly rejected by the Palestinian and Arab leadership).

From time to time, public figures representing the Arab minority in Israel refer to the fact that the Jewish majority in the state is a minority in a largely Arab region. Few, however, have dealt with this issue quite as bluntly as attorney Mohammed Dahle, a prominent public activist and one of the founders of Adallah, the Legal Centre for Arab Minority Rights in Israel. In an interview with *Ha'aretz* in January 2003,[36] Dahle says, 'In the end, the solution will take a bi-national form – one state, democratic, between the river and the sea.' However, his support for a bi-national state is not based on the recognition of the principle of equal national rights for the two peoples (as those who offered the federative bi-national solution in 1947 saw it). The Israeli Jews, according to

Dahle, are fundamentally an alien element in the country, and thus are not entitled to an equal standing:

> One must understand that there is no balance of rights here. There is no balance of our right versus your right. ... At the end of the day, it is the natives, not the immigrants, who have a supreme right to the country. Those who have lived here for hundreds of years have become part of the land, just as the land has become part of them. We are not like you. We are not strangers, we are not wanderers and we are not migrants.

This alien element ('it's as though some kind of invasion force emerged from the sea and landed on the beach. ... As though the immigrants who arrived don't feel the land and its past'), stresses Dahle, constitutes only a small minority in the Arab-Muslim Middle East, something it must not forget. His words are directed at the interviewer and, through him, at the Jewish public in Israel:

> Like it or not, you are a minority in the Middle East. ... If you open an atlas and look at the map for a minute, this is what you will see: 300 million Arabs all around, a billion-and-a-half Muslims. So do you really think that you can go on hiding in this crooked structure of a Jewish state? ... The world will change, the balance of forces will change, demography will change. In fact, demography is already changing. Your only guarantee is me; your only way to survive in the Arab-Muslim world is to strike an alliance with me. Because if you don't do it, tomorrow it will be too late. When you become a minority, you will look for me, but you won't be able to find me. ... I know that we Israeli Arabs are not really a minority. The concept of being a minority is alien to Islam. It suits Judaism but is alien to Islam. And when you look around, you see that we are not really a minority. In Israel, there is a majority that is really a minority and a minority that is really a majority.

These outspoken remarks should not be attributed to the entire Arab public. Moreover, the fact that Israeli Arabs are part of the Arab majority in the region does not mean that it is not necessary to guarantee their rights as a national minority in Israel. However, in these circumstances, nothing could be more natural than for the Jewish majority in Israel to underscore the fact that the state is indeed the expression of its right to national independence – and survival.

It is sometimes argued that the issue of self-determination is relevant during the struggle for independence, but not after that independent state has already been established. The establishment of a state is the realization of a people's right to self-determination; after its realization, it would be proper, according to this view, not to emphasize the fact that the state represents an expression of the self-determination of a certain national group, but rather that it represents, in equal measure, all its citizens regardless of national extraction.[37] In fact, democratic states established in the wake of a struggle for independence tend to emphasize, in varying degrees, both aspects: the national and general civic one. As we shall see in the following chapters, the national character of a state is typically expressed, beyond the state's name, in the way it often relates to its national history and the national struggle in its declaration of independence and/or in the preamble to its constitution; in the designation of the national language, in the official emblems and symbols, in the national holidays, in the nature of its state education, and, in certain cases, in official links with its national diaspora. Sometimes, when a strong traditional connection exists between a national culture and identity and a certain religion, this finds expression in the country's constitution (Greece being a conspicuous example). At the same time, the constitutions of all democracies, old and new, underscore the principle of equality of all the country's citizens as the foundation of their system of governments. In some cases, the constitution includes explicit recognition of national minorities and their rights. This recognition expresses both the civic character of the state (from the perspective of its commitment to guarantee full civil equality for the minorities) and its specifically national character, because the recognition of a national minority also emphasizes the existence of a national majority whose national identity is expressed by the state. On the other hand, a state (such as France) that views all its citizens as sharing the same national identity, that regards national identity as being fully synonymous with citizenship, does not, naturally, recognize national minorities. The precise manner and degree to which these aspects, the civic and the national-cultural (where a distinction between the two is acknowledged), are officially expressed is a legitimate subject of debate in each country in accordance with its specific circumstances. However, in the Israeli case, it cannot be argued that the official designation of the state as Jewish is superfluous because it is self-evident, since the right of the Jewish people to self-determination, even dozens of years after its realization, is one of the least self-evident matters in the Middle East. This stems not only from the conflict and the strident voices heard from among the Arab public opinion denying the legitimacy of Jewish self-determination, but also from the very fact that the Jewish population of Israel constitutes a minority in the Arab-Muslim Middle East. This does not mean that in the Israeli circumstances there is no need to find a proper balance between the specifically national aspect and the generally civic aspect in the official definitions. The term 'a Jewish and democratic state', which was adopted in the 'Basic Law: Human Dignity and Freedom' as a fundamental definition of the state's character, represents an effort to attain this kind of balance. This should be supplemented by an explicit constitutional recognition of the Arab minority in Israel as a national minority that is an integral part of the state and its citizenry.[38]

The fact that Arab nationalism is the nationalism of the majority in the Middle East was also reflected in the way the Arab delegates related to the Jewish minorities in Arab countries during the UN debates in 1947. These delegates made it quite clear that should the United Nations resolve to partition Palestine, the Jewish communities in the Arab and Muslim world would be made to pay the price. The representative of the Arab Higher Committee of the

Palestinian Arabs stated at a meeting of the Ad Hoc Committee on 24 October (quoted in indirect speech):

> In those circumstances, it was idle to think that the creation of a Jewish State would not arouse a general uprising in the Arab world, and it should be remembered that there were as many Jews in the Arab world as there were in Palestine, whose positions might become very precarious, even though the Arab States did their best to protect them. If partition were forced upon Palestine, it would have little chance of permanence in the midst of a strongly aroused and genuinely apprehensive Middle East. The fight would continue, as it had in the case of the Crusades, until the injustice was completely removed. By imposing partition, the United Nations would virtually precipitate Palestine into a bloodbath. That was not meant to be a threat, but to draw attention to the reactions to a policy for which the United Nations would be responsible.

The Egyptian delegate was even more explicit when he spoke before the Ad Hoc Committee on 24 November:

> Mr. Heykal Pasha (Egypt) said that if the question were considered from the point of view not of a lawyer but of a statesman, it was clear that the proposed partition might lead to bloodshed. There was no animosity against the Jews or racial discrimination of any kind in Egypt any more than in any of the other Moslem states. A million Jews [sic] lived in peace in Egypt and enjoyed all rights of citizenship. They had no desire to emigrate to Palestine. However, if a Jewish State were established, nobody could prevent disorder. Riots would break out in Palestine, would spread through all the Arab States and might lead to a war between two races. Even certain pro-Zionist newspapers, such as the *New York Post*, feared that the partition of Palestine might imperil the Jews resident in Moslem countries and create hatreds that might last for centuries. It was not always possible for a government to maintain order when a people saw its blood brothers massacred in a neighbouring country. If the aim of the United Nations was to find a humane solution to the problem of the refugees and displaced persons, it should not lose sight of the fact that the proposed solution might endanger a million Jews living in the Moslem countries. Partition of Palestine might create in those countries an anti-Semitism which the Allies were trying to eradicate in Germany. ... If the United Nations decided to partition Palestine, it might be responsible for very grave disorders and for the massacre of a large number of Jews.

The Iraqi delegate in his speech to the plenary of the General Assembly on 28 November declared that:

> Partition imposed against the will of the majority of the people will jeopardize peace and harmony in the Middle East. Not only the uprising of the

Arabs of Palestine is to be expected, but the masses in the Arab world cannot be restrained. The Arab–Jewish relationship in the Arab world will greatly deteriorate.

There are more Jews in the Arab world outside Palestine than there are in Palestine. In Iraq alone, we have about one hundred and fifty thousand Jews who share with Moslems and Christians all the advantages of political and economic rights. Harmony prevails among Moslems, Christians and Jews. But any injustice imposed upon the Arabs of Palestine will disturb the harmony among Jews and non-Jews in Iraq; it will breed inter-religious prejudice and hatred.

Thus, with this pretence of warning against the uncontrollable fury of the Arab masses, the Arab delegates made an unveiled threat against the defenceless Jewish minorities in Arab countries, making them hostages of the Jewish–Arab conflict in Palestine. By doing so, they provided a powerful testimony to the shared Jewish destiny, to the fact that Jews residing in different parts of the world were, in a significant sense, members of the same people, and of the urgent need that this people be given a national home of its own. Why, actually, did it appear so natural to the Arab delegates that the Jews of Iraq or Egypt should suffer because of an alleged injustice to the Arabs of Palestine? After all, not only were these peaceful communities that had deep roots in their countries of residence and took no part in the conflict, but according to the arguments voiced by the Arab delegates themselves, there was no national connection at all between the Jews of Arab countries and the (mostly) European 'invaders', i.e. the Zionists, in Palestine. Of course, even on the assumption that there was a national or ethnic connection between the Jews living in Arab countries and the European Jews in Palestine, this would not mean that anyone had a right to imperil the lives and safety of the Jewish communities in the Arab world in revenge for the acts of the Zionists in Palestine. True, national conflicts sometimes turn into a 'contagious disease' that does not heed political borders. Even populations that are not directly involved in a conflict can be hurt by it due to their ethnicity and culture – not necessarily a result of malice or negligence on the part of the state authorities. However, the words of the Arab delegates to the United Nations in 1947 can hardly be interpreted as a warning in good faith of what might possibly occur. For the sake of comparison: It is no secret that the Arab population in Israel has been affected unfavourably in various ways by the Israeli–Arab and Israeli–Palestinian conflict. However, it is hard to imagine an Israeli delegate to the United Nations declaring that Israel's Arab citizens could expect to be 'massacred in large numbers' in case of some hostile action on the part of Arab states or of the Palestinian Authority, while at the same time maintaining that there is no national connection whatever between these citizens and Israel's neighbours.

Moreover, if the Jews are regarded merely as a religious community and not a people, then the Jews of Egypt and Iraq should be viewed as Egyptian or Iraqi Arabs (of 'Mosaic persuasion'). And indeed, on various occasions, it has been claimed that the Jews of the Arab countries are in fact 'Jewish Arabs'. However, the Iraqi delegate, as we have seen, did not refrain from threatening a serious deterioration in the relations in the 'Arab-Jewish relationship in the Arab world', and the Egyptian delegate threatened a 'a war between two races', and the development of serious 'anti-Semitism' in the Arab world (a term that is always angrily rejected by Arab spokesmen, whenever reference is made to Arab displays of hostility to Jews). It is clear that the 'races' mentioned by the Egyptian delegate were in fact ethno-national groups, just as the representative of the Palestinian Arabs spoke of the 'racial homogeneity' of the Arabs in the Middle East when he was in fact referring to Arab national homogeneity. The Egyptian delegate therefore viewed the Jews and Arabs as two distinctly different ethno-national communities; and it is notable that even though the Arab delegates also emphasized the religious aspect of the expected confrontation between Arabs and Jews throughout the Arab world, they did not threaten that mass riots against Christians in the Arab world would break out due to the support shown by their 'co-religionists' in the West for the establishment of a Jewish state.

This is not just a question of terminology. The very claim that the Jews of the Arab countries can expect to be attacked due to the conflict in Palestine clearly proves that the Arab delegates denied the existence of a Jewish peoplehood only in order to deny the right of the Jewish people to a state of its own, but accepted it as a given for the purpose of imposing 'collective responsibility' on all the Jewish communities throughout the world. In his speech to the Ad Hoc Committee on 16 October, the Egyptian delegate explained why, in his view, the Balfour Declaration ran counter to international law. He stated that the Declaration, which promised a national home for the Jewish people, should be re-examined in light of Article 13 of the UN Charter. He went on to explain that the Jewish people, whether viewed as a race or a religious group, had no claim to an international status, since this article of the Charter forbids any distinction based on race or religion.

The establishment of a national home for the Jewish people would thus, according to the Egyptian delegate, represent an improper distinction based on race or religion. At the same time, he saw nothing wrong in making just such a distinction between Jews and their neighbours in order to threaten 'the massacre of a large number of Jews' throughout the Arab world should the United Nations resolve to partition Palestine between its two peoples. Similarly, the representative of the Palestinian Arabs claimed, as we have seen, that the Jews of Europe were not the descendents of the ancient Children of Israel, and afterwards declared that Moshe Shertok (Sharett), who had expressed criticism of the Mufti of Jerusalem, was the representative of the same people that crucified the founder of the Christian religion (meeting of the First Committee of the General Assembly, 12 May). All these remarks share a common denominator, well known in Jewish history: The Jews are not recognized as a distinct people with national rights, but are hated in a way that is unmistakably 'national'. In the face of this reality – which, as we have seen, is not limited to Europe – it is hard to take seriously the various 'scientific' attempts to dispute the notion of Jewish peoplehood. By treating their Jewish citizens as hostages in the conflict over Palestine, the delegates of the Arab countries irrefutably proved that they viewed these Jews neither as a group belonging to their people nor as equal citizens of their countries – and truth be told, not even as *dhimmis* (protected minorities under Islamic law) entitled to protection.

The delegates of the Arab countries knew what they were talking about. Iraq was the first to severely persecute its Jews even before the partition resolution and the war that followed in its wake. After the partition plan was approved by the UN General Assembly, riots against Jews did indeed break out in Egypt, Syria, Iraq and other Arab countries. True, it was not the wholesale massacre with which the Egyptian delegate had threatened the Jews of the Middle East, but this was only the beginning. Ultimately, the Arab–Israeli conflict did make the lives of the Jews in Arab countries intolerable, and emptied the Arab world of the Jewish communities that had lived in the region for hundreds and thousands of years. On 30 March 1949, the communist Arab Knesset member Tawfiq Toubi referred to the persecution of Jews in Arab countries in his speech to the Knesset:

> Clearly, the Jews of Arab countries, like the other minorities in those countries, live under difficult social conditions and are victims of abominable racial persecution. And we the communists here and in those countries will oppose such a situation with all our might, and we will support any proper step taken in order to put an end to the suffering of large numbers of Jews in Arab countries from nationalist persecution. ... Saving the Jews in the Arab countries from the racist persecution organized by the reactionary forces that are in power there is consequently dependent on the elimination of the rule of those forces.

In his speech on 19 March 1951, MK Toubi stated that:

> the decision by the Iraqi government regarding the confiscation of the property belonging to Iraqi Jews who have expressed their desire to emigrate to Israel is a reactionary, racist and arbitrary step ... part of a campaign of racial persecution ... a fascist step.

He stressed again that the persecution of Jews in Arab countries would only cease with the toppling of the 'reactionary regimes' there.[39] During the 1950s, reactionary regimes did fall in a number of Arab states, only to be replaced by 'progressive' nationalist dictatorships supported by the Soviet Union (which subsequently changed its position towards Israel, taking a negative approach). 'The abominable racial persecutions' of the Jews continued in these countries with an even greater intensity (although they ceased to interest the Israeli Communist Party). The Jewish community in Egypt, for example, was oppressed during the rule of the reactionary King Farouq, but it was only during Nasser's 'progressive' regime that it ceased to exist.

Even the Egyptian Communist party (which was persecuted by Nasser during most of the years of his regime) eventually toed the line in the late 1950s with the dominant nationalist trend and officially removed the Jews from its ranks, despite the fact that many of its founders were Jews who were of course Egyptian patriots and firm opponents of Zionism. The leftist Jewish writer Albert Memmi in Tunisia, who was active in the Tunisian political struggle against French colonial rule and emigrated to France some time after Tunisia gained its independence, describes the reasons for the disappearance of the Jewish community in independent Tunisia (one of the most moderate countries in the Arab world) as follows:

> We were Tunisian citizens and decided in all sincerity to 'play the game'.... But what did the Tunisians do? Just like the Moroccans and Algerians, they liquidated their Jewish communities in a clever and flexible way. They did not indulge in open brutalities as in other Arab lands – that would anyhow have been difficult after the services which had been rendered [in the anti-colonial struggle], the help given by a large number of our intellectuals, because of world public opinion, which was following events in our region closely; and also because of American aid which they needed urgently. Nonetheless they strangled the Jewish population economically. This was easy with the merchants: it was enough not to renew their licenses, to decline to grant them import permits and, at the same time, to give preference to their Moslem competitors. In the civil service, it was hardly more complicated: Jews were not taken on, or veteran Jewish officials were confronted with insurmountable language difficulties, which were rarely imposed upon Moslems. Periodically, a Jewish engineer or a senior official would be put in jail on mysterious, Kafkaesque charges, which panicked everyone else. Beyond this, there was the impact of the relative proximity of the Arab-Israel conflict. At each crisis, with every incident of any importance, the mob would go wild, setting fire to Jewish shops. This happened during the Yom Kippur War too. [Tunisia's President] Habib Bourguiba was probably never hostile to the Jews, but there was always that notorious 'delay', which meant that the police arrived on the scene only after the shops had been pillaged and burnt. Is it any wonder that the exodus to France and Israel continued and even increased?[40]

One might say that the Arab delegates predicted the 'delays' of the Tunisian police in their speeches in 1947. However, as stated, the Tunisian case is a very moderate version of the process that took place, lacking 'open brutalities'. Immigrants from Arab countries represent about half of Israel's Jewish population. This fact does not prevent the opponents of Zionism from declaring Israel to be the handiwork of Western imperialism and colonialism and from accusing Zionism of ruining the relationship between Arabs and Jews in the Arab world. At the same time, these opponents claim that the majority of Jews in the Arab countries did not support the Zionist movement or its claims. If so, then an especially harsh condemnation of the treatment of the Jews by the Arab majority in the Arab countries seems to be in order. The Arab world regards the tragedy of the Palestinian refugees in 1947–1948 as proof of the cruel and racist nature of the Zionist movement. However, whereas the price paid by Palestinian Arabs that lived in the actual combat areas during the terrible war between the two peoples living in the same land is taken as proof of the cruelty of the Jewish side, the price paid by Jews, who, whatever their identity or sympathies, were located hundreds of kilometres from the scene of the confrontation and could not possibly have taken any part in it, does not seem awaken any emotion whatever. This price is apparently viewed as the natural outcome, an inevitable side effect of the Jewish–Arab conflict over Palestine; consequently, the sole responsibility for it is placed on the Zionist side. This is how, for example, Muhammad Hassanein Heikal, the celebrated Egyptian journalist and politician and a close associate of President Nasser, described the fate of the Jewish community in Egypt after the Sinai War in 1956, in his book on the history of the Israeli–Arab conflict. Heikal sums up the matter in a short footnote:

> Another outcome of the Suez affair was the fact that the situation of the Jewish community in Egypt became untenable. If not for the invasion, the Jews of Egypt might have returned to their status from before 1948. ... By the end of 1957, almost all had left Egypt.[41]

This appeared to Heikal to provide a satisfactory explanation for the termination of the history of Egypt's Jews. He feels no need to explain why it was necessary for the situation of Egypt's Jews to become untenable in the wake of the Sinai War; although, after all, no street fighting took place during that war in the streets of Cairo or Alexandria involving the active participation of Egyptian Jewish militias. Earlier in his book, Heikal claims that only a small part of Egypt's Jews had supported the establishment of the Jewish State. As for the Palestinian refugees, he writes that their plight awakened deep feelings of bitterness in Arab public opinion, and that these feelings made the idea of peace with Israel a 'taboo'.

There seems here to be more than a mere case of a double standard (a trait from which, perhaps, no party to a national conflict can be wholly free). The matter-of-fact manner in which Arab public opinion viewed the fate of the Jews of the Arab world apparently testifies to the fact that these Jews, too, were actually perceived as 'aliens in the Arab Middle East'. This attitude to Jewish communities with deep roots in their countries of residence is reminiscent of Herzl's memorable words on the fate of the Jews of Europe in his preface to *Der Judenstaat* [The Jewish State]:

> In countries where we have lived for centuries, we are still cried down as strangers, and often by those whose ancestors were not yet domiciled in the land when the Jews had already had experience of suffering. It is the majority that decides which are the strangers.

The validity of the principle of partition

Obviously, the UN vote in favour of partition in 1947 was not a decision based solely or mainly on the moral and legal considerations that we have examined above. As in all decisions related to international politics, political and diplomatic considerations took first priority. However, it would be a mistake to dismiss the importance of the moral factor altogether – especially due to the influence of public opinion in the Western democracies. These debates were being held in the shadow of the Holocaust and against the background of the suffering of large numbers of Jews, Holocaust survivors, in the DP camps of Europe. These subjects came up frequently during the debates. Moreover, it is evident that many of the participants felt that they were facing an ancient problem of a homeless and persecuted people. It appears that the members of the UN committee who recommended partition were personally affected by what they had seen on their visit to Palestine and by what they heard from the Jewish representatives. Among other things, they witnessed the expulsion of the illegal refugee ship *Exodus* by the British from the port of Haifa and were able to obtain a first-hand impression of the distress experienced by the displaced Holocaust survivors. Whatever the reasons that motivated the various states to support the establishment of a Jewish state, the delegates of these countries explained and justified this decision in terms of the norms accepted – or at least proclaimed – by the modern international community: the right of peoples to self-determination, humanitarian considerations, democratic principles, civil equality and the guarantee of minority rights.

It is sometimes suggested that the partition resolution was only passed by the General Assembly because in 1947 it was still dominated by Western countries. In fact, the Western countries alone never represented a majority in the General Assembly, and certainly never enjoyed the two-thirds majority that was required in order to endorse the resolution. The international coalition behind this majority included most of the Western countries (although the United Kingdom abstained and Greece voted nay), the Soviet Union and the Eastern Bloc countries, many Latin American republics as well as Liberia and the Philippines. From the perspective of the representatives of the Jewish Agency at the UN, the problem was that whereas the Jewish people did not, by the very nature of the situation, have a vote in the General Assembly, the Arab and Muslim countries, which vehemently opposed partition, had a considerable contingent. Another difficulty stemmed from the fact that the US State Department (in contrast to the White House) opposed the idea of partition for fear that that its implementation would undermine US relations with the Arab and Muslim world. Consequently, American diplomacy did not mobilize to convince other countries to support partition.[42] Of the countries whose delegates signed the UNSCOP minority report, Iran and India voted against partition, whereas Yugoslavia abstained (along with China, Ethiopia and a number of Latin American countries).[43]

As for the question of the partition resolution's validity – as a rule, a resolution of the UN General Assembly is, under the Charter, merely a recommendation. Consequently, there is no basis for regarding every General Assembly resolution as binding from the point of view of 'international legitimacy' – in the spirit of the rhetoric popular in the Arab world since it has been able to count on a guaranteed majority in the General Assembly for its positions in the conflict with Israel. The question of the legal validity of the partition plan was discussed at length in the UN Security Council during the months that passed between its adoption and the proclamation of Israel's independence. The Jewish Agency representatives repeatedly urged the Security Council to act to implement the partition plan. They requested that the committee charged by the General Assembly with overseeing this implementation (with which the United Kingdom refused to cooperate, not allowing it to come to Palestine before the termination of the Mandate), be given 'teeth' and provided with an international military force under the authority of the Security Council.[44] This proposal is hardly consistent with the claims voiced from time to time that the Zionist leadership was certain of victory in the coming war[45] and never seriously intended to implement the partition plan and make do with the Jewish State's proposed borders. In any case, it is clear that if the Jewish Agency's position had been accepted by the Security Council, the refugee problem would never have been created. The UN mission charged with implementing the partition, and the international forces supporting it that the Jewish Agency insisted should come to Palestine, would have prevented any possibility of harm coming to the Palestinian population, as well as any expansion of the Jewish State at the expense of the Arab one.

The Soviet Union supported the Jewish position, according to which the Security Council was responsible for seeing the partition plan implemented, whereas the United States hesitated, and ultimately initiated an 'international trusteeship regime plan', claiming that since it was impossible to implement the partition plan peacefully, the international community should continue its mediation and reconciliation efforts. The position taken by the Arab delegates (with the United Kingdom's support) was that since General Assembly resolutions were no more than recommendations, the partition plan did not represent a binding norm according to international law, and the power of the Security Council could not be exercised in order to enforce it. The Palestinian-Arab representatives openly insisted on their right to forcibly prevent the implementation of this recommendation, which they viewed as neither legally binding nor just. At the session of the Security Council held on 16 April 1948, the representative of the Arab Higher Committee said:

> The representatives of the Jewish Agency told us yesterday that they were not attackers, not aggressors; that the Arabs had begun the fight and that once the Arabs stopped shooting, they would stop shooting also. As a matter of fact, we do not deny this fact. We told the world, during the last session of the General Assembly that we could not accept our country being torn to pieces, that we could not accept that little Palestine should be divided into three different States. We told the whole world that this was a

flagrant aggression against our country and against our interests and rights, and that we were going to fight it.[46]

However, it is precisely the fact that the Arab side was openly using force in order to prevent the implementation of partition that gave the Security Council legal grounds to exercise its authority. According to the UN Charter (Article 7), the Security Council is entitled to use enforcement action, including military force, if it determines that there is a breach of the peace or a threat to the peace. Consequently, the fact that such an action was not taken in this case was due to political rather than legal considerations.

Moreover, the case of the partition plan was different from other resolutions of the General Assembly: The legal sovereignty in Palestine as a Mandatory territory was in fact in the hands of the international community – that is, in the hands of the United Nations as the successor to the League of Nations, which had conferred the Mandate on the United Kingdom. Consequently, it would appear that the international validity of the resolution regarding the future of Palestine was greater than that of 'conventional' resolutions of the Assembly, which are no more than a recommendation made to sovereign states.[47] In this spirit, the US delegate argued in his speech before the General Assembly on 26 November, in response to Arab delegates' claims that the Assembly lacked legal authority to partition the country, that 'Palestine, as a territory under mandate, is not a State. It is not an international person, but is in a sense a ward of the international community', and consequently, the UN General Assembly has the right to adopt the partition plan on behalf of the international community. Of course, the legitimacy of partition stems above all from the very existence of two peoples having two distinct national identities and two opposing national aspirations within the same country – Palestine/land of Israel. This is the basic reality eloquently described in the 1947 UNSCOP report and existing to this day, and it is this reality that has made the partition of the country between its two peoples the only just and practicable solution.

'The tragedy of Palestine lay in the fact that the claims of both sides were legitimate, which made it necessary to reach a compromise', said the Swedish delegate, the chairman of UNSCOP, when he presented the committee's report at a meeting of the Ad Hoc Committee on 26 September. These words are reminiscent of the famous saying by Chaim Weizmann that the Jewish–Arab conflict in Palestine is a clash between two just claims. And indeed, beyond the pragmatic attempts at compromise that were made during the years of the Mandate by the Zionist leadership, not a few in the Zionist movement were willing to admit that there was justice in the national aspirations of the other side too. Of course, the attitude of the Zionist side towards its Arab-Palestinian rival should not be idealized. As usually happens in national conflicts, the willingness of the Zionist movement to compromise stemmed primarily from pragmatic considerations. The possibilities of political compromise with the other side were at the centre of intense controversy in the Zionist camp, including within the Labour movement. Some demanded a Jewish state in the whole of the country, others expressed willingness to compromise; some (especially in the more left-wing circles) favoured far-reaching compromises as a matter of principle; a radical minority suggested a bi-national state.

At the moment of historic decision, the vast majority of the Zionist movement was willing to accept the partition proposed by the international community. But such willingness did not exist on the other side, which rejected any form of practical compromise and utterly denied the legitimacy of Jewish claims. While the Zionist leadership (the Jewish Agency executive) in a memorandum submitted to UNSCOP, and David Ben-Gurion in his appearance before the committee, presented a demand of a Jewish state in all of the land – something that enabled the committee to present the partition plan as a compromise between the conflicting demands of the two sides – at the same time, they made it clear that they would be willing to discuss practical proposals for partition and for a Jewish state in only part of the country.[48] Chaim Weizmann, the veteran Zionist leader who appeared before UNSCOP and apparently felt able to express himself more freely because he did not serve in any official capacity, strongly supported the idea of partition and urged the committee to adopt it. Behind the scenes, Zionist diplomacy worked for partition; once adopted by UNSCOP, the partition plan was officially accepted by the Zionist movement. Ben-Gurion had adopted the idea of partition as early as 1937, when he supported the acceptance of the partition plan proposed by the British Peel Commission. To a large extent, the decision of the Zionist Executive in August 1946 in favour of a 'viable Jewish state' in part of the country may be viewed as the dawn of the process that eventually led to the partition resolution and the establishment of the state. US President Harry Truman, who was favourably disposed to the Zionist aspirations, needed a reasonable compromise proposal in order to counter the rigid British position, which was, at that point, strongly hostile to Zionism. The idea of partition as adopted by the Zionist Executive enabled him to take this step, and in October 1946 he declared, to the considerable chagrin of the British Government, that the United States welcomed the initiative of the Zionist Executive and endorsed the idea of partition. This US step was one of the main reasons behind the British government's decision to pass the question of the future of Palestine on to the United Nations. During the debates on the establishment of a committee on the Palestine question, the delegate of the Soviet Union gave surprising support to the idea of partition. The support of the two superpowers turned partition into a realistic political option, and this, no doubt, made it much easier for the members of UNSCOP to adopt it.

The UN Partition Plan was doomed to failure by the Arab-Palestinian leadership and the countries of the Arab League, who rejected it and went to war. However, by the end of Israel's War of Independence, the territory of the former British Mandate was partitioned along the armistice lines, not between two independent states, but rather between Israel on the one hand and the territories occupied by Transjordan and Egypt – the West Bank and the Gaza Strip – on the other. Transjordan annexed the West Bank and made it part of the Hashemite Kingdom, while Egypt maintained a military occupation in Gaza. After the Six

Day War, when the debate over an independent Palestinian state arose, the claim was often heard in Israel that 'the Arabs' had been occupying these lands for 19 years but did not establish a Palestinian state in them. This is of course true with regard to the governments of Jordan and Egypt, but not with regard to the Palestinian Arabs in these territories, who were unable to determine their own fate freely. On the other hand, one also hears the claim that Israel encouraged Transjordan to annex the West Bank, because it was opposed in principle to Palestinian independence. However, the question of annexing the West Bank to Transjordan was not ultimately dependent on what Israel wanted. Moreover, there is evidence that the Israeli leadership viewed the annexation as a problematic step in terms of Israel's interests. Israel's official position when the battles of the War of Independence died down was that a referendum should be held in these territories in order to determine their future. During a political debate held in the Knesset on 20 June 1949, the country's foreign minister Moshe Sharett explained Israel's position on this subject as follows:

> The question that is perhaps the most complex, intricate and crucial of questions in the context of the desire for peace with our neighbours is the one that is related to the future of the Arab part of the land of Israel – what is now [i.e. in the wake of the war] the Arab part. And indeed, we have said on more than one occasion, and I will reiterate it here, that if we were to be asked what is most desirable for us regarding this part, in the context of the existing conditions, the most desirable thing, that which we are most interested in, is that this part be a separate political entity by itself. ... We proposed to the Conciliation Committee [in Lausanne, which, under the auspices of the United Nations, discussed the possibilities for resolving the conflict] to conduct a referendum in this part of the country and we insist on it. A referendum will be held and the people living in this part will express their will, what they choose.[49]

Later in his remarks, Sharett explained that the signing of the armistice between Israel and Transjordan did not imply Israel's recognition of the legality of Transjordan's control of the Arab areas west of the Jordan; however, Israel could not declare war on Transjordan in order to drive its army out of these territories and establish an independent state in it. Thus, Israel's official position at this stage accepted the principle of self-determination of the Palestinian Arabs. The representatives of Herut, Mapam and the Communist Party charged, in the course of this debate, that the government was in fact interested, despite its declared position, in the annexation of these territories by Transjordan. And indeed, at this stage, secret contacts were taking place between the two governments in advance of a possible peace agreement based on the assumption that the West Bank would remain in Jordanian hands.[50] However, internal Israeli government documents testify that this was preceded by much hesitation and debate, including thoughts in the direction of the Palestinian option. On 8 August 1948, Moshe Sharett sent a cable to the minister of minorities, Bechor Shalom Sheetrit, stating that:

Jordanian option, unofficially accepting Jordan's annexation of the West Bank, and even tried to reach a peace settlement with the Hashemite kingdom – an effort that was cut short with the assassination of King Abdullah in 1951. No 'ideological' explanation for this is needed, beyond the simple fact that the Jordanian monarch was, for obvious reasons, viewed by the Israeli government as the lesser of two evils compared with the Mufti. The Israeli leadership mistrusted the Hashemite king, who, despite his many contacts with the Zionist leadership and the promises given in the past, sent his army to fight against Israel immediately after its establishment; who suggested to Golda Meir during their celebrated meeting on the eve of the outbreak of the war that the Jews give up the idea of independence and accept an autonomous Jewish republic as part of the Hashemite kingdom; and who was under the influence of the United Kingdom, which at the time was hostile to Israel. Ben-Gurion feared British plans to take over the Negev, viewed by the United Kingdom as strategically important, with the help of Abdullah; he also feared the possibility of having to face a strong and hostile neighbour in case of a unification between Jordan and Iraq (which at the time was controlled by a Hashemite dynasty and was extreme in its hostility to Israel), and was reluctant to take a step that would antagonize the Soviet Union, which at that time supported Israel and viewed Abdullah as a British agent. However, with the Mufti and his people, the official Palestinian leadership recognized by the Arab League that was totally opposed to partition, no compromise of any kind was conceivable. There were no real forces in Palestinian society that could form an alternative leadership and take the risk of making peace with Israel – in opposition to the Arab consensus.[52] The Palestinian communists, who supported the partition and peace with Israel, were a tiny minority lacking any influence. It is true that the Mufti and his people were very far from complete control over Palestinian-Arab society, whose internal rifts greatly undermined its ability to conduct an effective war against the Jews of Palestine. However, no other leadership emerged as an alternative to that of the Arab Higher Committee. The occasional contacts between Zionist representatives and Palestinian public figures considered as personal or political rivals of the Mufti came to nought. This was the situation throughout the entire period from the time of the partition resolution and the outbreak of hostilities with the Palestinians until the final battles of the War of Independence. Obviously the occupation of the West Bank by Abdullah's Arab Legion did not encourage the development of a Palestinian leadership independent of both Abdullah and the Mufti.

In the occupied Gaza Strip in September 1948, the Egyptians established the 'Government of all of Palestine', whose name is indicative of its position regarding the idea of partition, and a 'Constituent Assembly' headed by the Mufti. This government (which the Egyptians did not allow even to rule in Gaza) received recognition from the Arab countries (except for Jordan) and remained in force, symbolically at least, until it was officially dismantled in 1952. From Israel's perspective, the ultimate choice would be, exactly as presented by the UN mediator, between Abdullah and the Mufti, and the choice of

An effort should be made to strive for contact and mutual understan
with people and circles in the camp of our opponents, who carry w
among the Arab public and are currently willing to cooperate with us, ε
on the basis of recognition of the State of Israel within its borders,
order to establish a self-government in the Arab part of western Eretz]
[Palestine west of the Jordan]. While we cannot completely remove
the agenda the possibility of the Arab part of western Eretz Israel]
annexed to the State of Transjordan, we must give preference to the ε
lishment of an independent Arab state in western Eretz Israel. In any
we must strive to examine this possibility and to underscore the fact th
consider it desirable and preferable for us compared with the annex
proposal.[51]

At a meeting with his foreign affairs advisors held on 18 December 1948,
Gurion said:

There is an excess of intoxication with victory. *Aliya* [Jewish immigr
requires an end to the war; our future requires peace and friendship wi
Arabs. And so I am in favour of talking with Abdullah, although I
doubts as to whether the British will permit us [Israel and Transjord
make peace. But it must be made clear from the outset of the meetin
apart from a cease-fire, there is not yet any agreement between us, a
talks are to be held on a tabula rasa basis. The annexation of parts of
Israel by Transjordan is not something to which we can agree r
because of 1. Israeli security: An Arab state west of the Jordan is les
gerous than a state that is connected with Transjordan, and perhaps t
row with Iraq; 2. Why should we anger the Russians for nothing? 3
should we act [i.e. agree to annexation] differently from the other
countries? This does not mean that we will not agree to it under any c
stances – but only as part of a comprehensive settlement.

Despite the strong arguments from the perspective of Israel's interests a
merated by Ben-Gurion in his remarks, it is evident from this very text t
position was not final and that he left his options open. There is also indir
timony – also from December 1948 – regarding a change in Israel's sta
this matter. Ralph Bunche, the UN mediator for Palestine, maintained in
versation with the British ambassador to Amman that:

The Jews have practically abandoned their original idea of insisting
Arab areas of Palestine being formed into an independent state beca
Bunche, had convinced them that it was as likely to fall under the in
of Haj Amin al-Husseini and be an endless source of friction and diso

Whether or not it was significantly influenced by the UN mediator's
ments, the final result is eminently clear: The Israeli government did ad

the former was inevitable. The Zionist–Hashemite connection, which has been given far-reaching ideological interpretations and described as a collision between two pro-imperialist forces against the Palestinian people, was based, as far as the Zionist side was concerned, on the simple fact that with the existing Palestinian leadership no ties of any kind could be maintained.

To a great extent, the same could be said regarding the preference for the Jordanian option and the broad opposition to an independent Palestinian state in the West Bank and Gaza following the Six Day War. In the aftermath of the war, the Israeli leadership was angry with King Hussein for entering it on Nasser's side, despite Israeli warnings. During internal discussions in the Israeli Cabinet and the General Staff, ideas were raised regarding self-rule for the Palestinians and even a Palestinian state.[53] However, the overtures made to local leaders in the territories regarding their willingness to take responsibility for a solution of this kind came to nought. Within a short time, contacts with the Jordanian king in an effort to reach a peace settlement – which proved unsuccessful – were renewed. At the same time, the option of an independent Palestinian state was rejected by the majority of the Israeli political establishment. The main reason for this – at least as far as the Labour Party was concerned, which did not espouse the idea of the 'undivided land of Israel' and supported a territorial compromise – was the position of the Palestinian organizations (the PLO with its various offshoots and the Fatah, which became the central force in the PLO in 1969), which opposed, at that time, any peace settlement or peace talks with Israel.

This is of course not the whole story. The picture is more complex. The military victory and the conquest of the territories, and especially the encounter with the expanses of the historical land of Israel, awakened among the Israeli leadership and public – not only on the Right but among large portions of the Centre too – a territorial appetite and passion for settlement. 'The intoxication with victory' that Ben-Gurion warned against in 1948 left its mark. Too many ignored the dangers and moral problems involved in a military occupation rule – avowedly provisional but continuing one year after the next – over another people, over a hostile population lacking basic civil rights. Some preferred the Jordanian option because they deluded themselves into thinking that as part of a peace settlement with Jordan, it would be possible to have a considerable portion of the territories annexed to Israel. Some Israeli leaders took it upon themselves to define the Palestinian Arabs' national identity for them, asserting that they belonged to the Arab people 'which already has twenty states' rather than to the Palestinian people (while no one ventured to claim that there existed no distinct Egyptian people because the Arabs of Egypt belonged to the greater Arab nation and only to it). Finally, following the victory of the Likud in the 1977 election, the Israeli government adopted the view that the historical right of the Jewish people to the territories of Judea and Samaria took precedence over any other consideration and gave Israel the right to rule permanently over these areas, without offering political rights to their inhabitants.

Thus there is much to criticize in Israel's policy on this matter. Nevertheless, when asking why even those political circles in Israel that favoured far-reaching territorial concessions in return for peace, largely ruled out, at that stage, the option of an independent Palestinian state, the answer is that the PLO rejected the very existence of the State of Israel, at a time when no alternative Palestinian leadership in the territories had arisen, or appeared likely to arise.

The 1970s saw initial signs of a change in the position of the PLO towards the possibility of peace with Israel. This was a long process that involved steps both forward and back, hints and denials. It ended in 1988, when Yasser Arafat, in a speech to the UN General Assembly, officially and explicitly announced that the PLO agreed to make peace with the State of Israel in return for a Palestinian state on the 1967 territories. Parallel to this process, the voices in Israel grew louder in favour of talks with the PLO and the adoption of 'the Palestinian option' (or a combination of the Palestinian and Jordanian options by means of a confederation – a solution that was not officially ruled out by the Palestinians). The intifada and Jordan's official severing of its ties with the West Bank turned a Palestinian state into the only possible solution to the conflict. The Oslo agreements between Israel and the PLO signed in 1993 triggered intense controversy in Israel. However, during the years of the Oslo process, despite the difficulties and crises, the idea of a Palestinian state gained currency among the vast majority of the Israeli public. This broad consensus held fast even after the grave events that occurred in the wake of the failure of the Camp David talks. The violence and terror (including suicide bombings) resorted to by Palestinians (including armed groups within the Fatah) and the raising of the issue of the Palestinian 'right of return' to Israel (as opposed to the West Bank and Gaza) in a manner that awakened serious doubt as to the Palestinian willingness to accept the solution of two states for two people – all this changed the mood in Israel and severely undermined the Israeli public's belief in the chances for peace in the foreseeable future. Nevertheless, a clear majority accepts that if and when a political settlement is reached, it will be based on this principle. Thus, the idea of partition remained relevant, and in fact gained ground, throughout the turbulent years.

We can sum up at this point and say that the ideological debate regarding the principle of partition that split the Jewish public in Israel for decades has culminated in recent years with the vast majority of the people, including most of the right-wing camp, accepting this principle. This was formalized by Ariel Sharon's government accepting the international 'Road Map' for peace in the Middle East, which called for the establishment of a 'viable' independent Palestine state.

Paradoxically, however, certain circles on the Left, both in Israel and abroad, have in the meantime started to challenge the principle of two states for two peoples by attacking the concept of a 'Jewish state', allegedly in the name of universal democratic principles. As we have attempted to demonstrate in this chapter, this approach runs counter to the fundamental logic upon which the international decision in favour of partition was based.

2 Two arguments

Zionism as a colonialist phenomenon
and the invention of Jewish
nationalism

As we have seen, the arguments advanced by supporters of the 1947 partition resolution echo the main arguments used by the Zionist movement in establishing its claim for a Jewish state in the land of Israel/Palestine: the fact that the Jews are a people with national aspirations; the Jewish people's historical connection with the country; the right of the Jewish people, like other peoples, to national independence; and humanitarian considerations which made urgent the establishment of a Jewish national home – in this case, the distress of the Holocaust survivors in Europe. In this chapter we will discuss in greater detail two key arguments that have been voiced by the opponents of Zionism, from its beginnings, at the time of the 1947 UN debates and since then to the present day, for the purpose of denying its status as a national movement that is struggling to obtain independence for its people: the argument that Zionism is not a legitimate national movement but a colonialist phenomenon, and the argument that denies the historical continuity of the Jewish people.

Colonialism and imperialist support

The claim that from the outset Zionism was a colonialist movement whose godfather was British imperialism is an argument of paramount importance in anti-Zionist discourse. It goes without saying that in the modern world, and when referring to an ongoing national conflict, to label something 'colonialist' is to imply that it lacks all legitimacy. In addition, the accusation has the advantage of suggesting that the Zionist enterprise, like the other manifestations of modern colonialism in the Third World, is destined to disappear. Obviously, this line of reasoning does not apply to the countries of Latin America, the United States or Australia, which owe their emergence, originally, to what must indeed be called European 'colonization' in earlier periods. However, in twentieth-century terms, all colonial phenomena are considered illegitimate, and all anti-colonialist national struggles are regarded a priori as legitimate and deserving of support. If the Israeli–Arab conflict is analysed in these terms, then the details, the parties' respective rights and the merits of their case are largely irrelevant.

According to historian Ilan Pappe, a leading figure among Israel's 'new historians', who refers to Zionism as colonialism, this explains and justifies the

Palestinian Arabs' opposition to allowing Jewish refugees from Europe, who were fleeing Nazi persecution, to enter Palestine in the 1930s and 1940s:

> Zionism arrived here as a colonialist movement at the end of the 19th century. When European refugees arrived, the conflict between the foreign invaders and the locals was at its height, and hence [their arrival] looked, quite rightly, like part of the attempt by the local Jewish community (*Yishuv*) to prevail in the struggle being waged here far more than to save their Jewish brethren.[1]

Pappe does not specify the identity of the colonial power represented by these 'foreign invaders' who arrived in Palestine. His account wholly ignores the Jewish distress in the late nineteenth and early twentieth centuries – distress of which ethnic and religious discrimination was only the mildest form, and which included persecutions and pogroms whose memory in Jewish history has been blurred only by the more recent memory of the horrors of the Holocaust. Naturally, the Jewish aspirations to cultural autonomy and national independence are absent from this account as well.

The charge of 'Zionist colonialism' needs therefore to be scrutinized more closely. Modern colonialism, as distinguished from many other instances of conquest and migration in history, was a process by which European powers appropriated broad swathes of what today is known as the 'Third World', in some instances settling (colonizing) them with their own nationals. In sending their citizens to these countries, the European states in question sought both to strengthen their own hold on the countries concerned, and to improve the settlers' lot. If, then, Zionism is to be defined as a colonial phenomenon, on the grounds that the Jews came to Palestine mostly from European countries and settled there, the following question naturally arises: which colonial mother country sent its Jewish citizens to Palestine for their own good, in order to exploit, through them, its resources, and to ensure its rule over it? Given the origins of the great majority of those who came to Palestine, the inescapable conclusion is that initially the Zionist settlers served as the colonial 'long arm' of Tsarist Russia; subsequently they acted primarily on behalf of the Polish Republic; and in the 1930s they were on assignment for Nazi Germany. This is hardly the most convincing explanation for Zionism as a historical phenomenon.

Those who consider Zionism a form of colonialism are sometimes willing to admit the differences that exist between it and the usual model of European colonialism. However, they hold that none of these differences are of decisive importance for defining the nature of the phenomenon. Thus, Oren Yiftachel, Professor of Geography at Ben-Gurion University in Beersheba, writes that 'despite the salient differences compared with other colonial movements, the actual process of European settlement [in Palestine] enables Zionism to be classified (both pre- and post-1948) as a "pure" colonial settlement movement'. For the sake of proper disclosure, he lists these 'salient differences' in a footnote, where the discerning reader quickly discovers just how superficial and artificial Zionism's identification with colonialism is. The differences listed by Yiftachel are:

> Zionism's nature as an ethnic and national rather than an economic project; the refugee status of most of the Jews [who came to Palestine]; the loose organization of the Diaspora Jewish communities as opposed to well-organized [colonial] mother countries; and lastly, the ideal of the 'return to Zion' which is grounded in Jewish tradition.[2]

In other words, Zionism was a colonialist phenomenon in all respects and fully resembled other examples of modern colonialism – apart from the fact that it was a national movement, that it was not motivated by a desire for economic gain, that it arose out of Jewish suffering and was realized by people who may be defined as refugees, that the settlers had no colonial mother country, and that the bond with the Land of Israel was part of the traditional historical identity of the Jewish people.

The support that the Zionist movement received from British imperialism has often been cited as proof of its fundamentally colonialist character. It is obviously true that the British colonial power supported the Zionist movement during some of the crucial phases in its history. The Balfour Declaration made it possible to lay the foundations of the Jewish national home. Without British patronage at this point, the Zionist project could not have succeeded. Undoubtedly, this support was influenced by imperial considerations (though not exclusively by them). However, it is also true that, as time went by, the British government came to the conclusion that its support for the Jewish 'national home' was seriously harming its own imperial interests (by provoking widespread Arab and Muslim resentment). As a result, it gradually withdrew its support from Zionism, adopting a policy – particularly with the 1939 White Paper – which would have led in a straight line to the creation of an Arab state in the whole of Palestine (and hence the elimination of the Jewish national home). It imposed severe restrictions on Jewish immigration to Palestine – on the eve of the Holocaust, during the actual destruction of Europe's Jewry, and later, when survivors were trying to reach the country. As a result of this policy, the British came into a political confrontation with the entire Zionist movement, and a military confrontation with parts of it. They would eventually oppose partition and the establishment of a Jewish state, and refuse to cooperate in the implementation of the UN Partition Plan.

However important it was to the Zionist undertaking at the time, the United Kingdom's support for Zionism did not make it a colonialist movement or phenomenon. National movements, as a rule, have sought international support – if possible, from Great Powers – and have not been particular about its origin, when offered. It is true that a national movement of a diaspora people can be said to have a particularly great need of international support. But the Arab national movement itself was happy to cooperate with the British Empire during the First World War, in return receiving political promises which later were said to be in contradiction with the Balfour Declaration. At that time, it was clear that in order for the aspirations of the two national movements – Jewish and Arab – which would soon confront each other, to be attained, the Ottoman Empire had to be broken up; accordingly, both of them cooperated with the British. Earlier, Theodor Herzl had tried in vain to obtain a 'charter' for Palestine from the Ottoman sultan, and since during that period Germany was a close ally of Turkey, Herzl had made major efforts to secure Germany's backing for the Zionist movement – to no avail.

The bonds that a national movement establishes with a foreign power – even if these sometimes involve an element of sympathy and ideological affinity – are always primarily designed to generate maximum political and diplomatic support for its own goals. Trying to ascribe far-reaching ideological significance to a national movement's use of foreign support in its struggle to obtain independence is likely to lead to rather strange conclusions. At one of the critical moments of the struggle to establish the Jewish state, after the United Kingdom had adopted a hostile stance to Zionism and with the US Administration showing hesitation (leading to US State Department support for the 'international trusteeship' plan for Palestine, and consequently intense pressure being brought to bear on Palestine's Jewish leadership to refrain from declaring the Jewish state), the Zionist movement received invaluable support from Stalin's Soviet Union. The Soviet Union, which together with its satellites had played a very considerable part in the adoption of the partition plan, not only spoke out at the United Nations, denouncing British hostility and American hesitations alike; during a decisive phase in the War of Independence it also supplied the fledgling Jewish state with vitally needed arms via Czechoslovakia (while the United States was maintaining the arms embargo). Without this assistance, it is very unlikely that the state would have survived. In the case of Stalin, at least, moral considerations and the influence of public opinion can safely be ruled out as a motivation – more safely than in the case of Western democracies. His stance was dictated by Soviet imperial considerations, and perhaps also by a hope that the socialist wing of the Zionist movement, dominant at the time, would set up a pro-Soviet or, at the very least, a neutralist regime in the future Jewish state. But this support did not make Zionism a communist or pro-communist movement, despite the fact that this was one of the many charges levelled at it by Arab representatives at the time. For example, the Syrian delegate to the UN General Assembly complained on 26 November 1947 that Palestine was being swamped by communists as a result of Zionist immigration, and claimed that there were already 150,000 Jewish communists in the country. The Arab Higher Committee representative, in his address to the Ad Hoc Commission on 24 November, similarly accused the Soviet Union of supporting the establishment of the Jewish state with the goal of flooding the country with hordes of immigrants 'who will disseminate its theories and further its political goals'; while the Iraqi delegate declared to the General Assembly on 28 November that the trial of a clandestine communist group which had recently been held in Baghdad had proved that these communists were financed by the Zionists in Palestine.

Egyptian journalist and politician Mohamed Hassanein Heikal offers another interesting account of the events of the time:

> When in May 1948 Britain withdrew from Palestine and the first Arab–Israeli war broke out, one of the reasons Nokrashy Pasha, the Prime Minister [of Egypt] gave in parliament when asking for a declaration of war was that Israel was the vanguard of world communism. He cited the kibbutz movement to press his point. Both houses of parliament, in fact, voted for war against Israel 'in defence of Arab rights and against Communist atheism and nihilism'. Some support for this point of view was to be found in the speed with which the Soviet Union hastened to recognize the new state of Israel and the way in which the Israeli forces were enabled to regroup with Czechoslovak arms during the first truce in the fighting. It seems probable that the Soviet Union believed at this time that Israel could become a progressive, and therefore sympathetic, element in an area of generally reactionary and unsympathetic governments.[3]

As for the attitude of the British at the time, Heikal describes it as follows:

> The British government had refused a request by the king [of Egypt] for arms. This was the unofficial response; unofficially, British arms somehow found their way to the Egyptian front. At the same time correspondence flew between different British ministers about the 'theft' of military stores from the canal base. About 20,000 Egyptian civilians worked at the base, but they were tightly controlled. The quantities taken were so great that convoys of Lorries would have been needed to move them. It seems likely that the 'thefts' were ordered by the British themselves, the better to tempt Egypt into battle with the Zionists. London stood to gain in two ways: Zionists would be punished by terrorist attacks against the British army, and Egyptians would be absorbed in a goal other than the British withdrawal from the Suez base.[4]

According to Heikal, British military circles may have acted, in this instance, independently and without coordination with the Foreign Office. But the position of the Foreign Office itself and the British government as a whole was clearly hostile to the Zionist cause at that stage. In September 1947, after UNSCOP had recommended partitioning Palestine into two states, British Foreign Secretary Ernest Bevin, presented the Cabinet with a memorandum recommending that the country should not cooperate in applying the partition plan – advice which would in fact be followed. The document revealed Bevin's profound animosity in the face of the prospect of a Jewish state, as well as the weight of the United Kingdom's imperial interests in the Middle East:

> The majority proposal is so manifestly unjust to the Arabs that it is difficult to see how, in Sir Alexander Cadogan's words 'we could reconcile it with

our conscience'. There are also strong reasons of expediency for declining the responsibility for giving effect to this proposal. The attempt to do so would precipitate an Arab rising in Palestine which would have the moral approval of the entire Moslem world and would be more or less actively supported by the neighbouring Arab states. The Chiefs of Staff state that, in this situation, reinforcements amounting to not less than one division would have to be sent to the Middle East.

The long-term political and strategic consequences would be more serious than the immediate military problem. We should be engaged in suppressing Arab resistance in Palestine, and thus antagonizing the independent Arab states, at a time when our whole political and strategic system in the Middle East must be funded on co-operation with those States. The treaty rights which would probably be accorded to us by the Jewish state would be poor compensation for the loss of Arab goodwill and with it our prospect of establishing that firm strategic hold on the Middle East which is an indispensable part of Commonwealth defence policy.[5]

Clearly the background to all of this is the confrontation between two peoples, two national movements, each trying to the best of its abilities to enlist 'Great Power' support for its own cause. The Arab governments which sent their armed forces to fight in Palestine following Israel's declaration of independence were motivated by considerations of self-interest, but at the same time they were also sensitive to the powerful national and nationalist sentiments at work among Arab public opinion. Both the pro-Zionist and anti-Zionist stages of British policy were dictated primarily, and naturally, by Britain's foreign-policy and imperial considerations; it is futile to draw far-reaching ideological conclusions from them.

A leading proponent of defining Zionism as colonialism in present-day Israeli discourse is Ilan Pappe. He attaches great importance to the link between Zionism and British colonialism. In his public pronouncements, as we have seen, Zionism is defined unhesitatingly as colonialism, but in his academic writings he is somewhat less categorical. Thus Zionism becomes 'an admixture of colonialism and nationalism'. Illustrating this he states that 'Zionism is a national movement which has used and continues to use colonialist instruments to realize its goals.'[5] But as described by him, ultimately these 'instruments' boil down to the fact that the Zionists came from Europe to live in a part of the Middle East. He ignores the fact that a substantial number of Jews came to Palestine, even before Israel came into being, from countries of the Muslim Middle East; and of course, they came in huge numbers after 1948. Zionism always regarded itself as the national movement of the Jewish people as a whole, and not only of Europe's Jews. According to Pappe's definition, 'colonialism was already present in the very idea of Jews from Europe settling in a backwater of the Ottoman Empire'. If this is the case, if colonialism boils down to 'a physical movement of people from one place to another', then, naturally, there is no need to enquire as to the identity and culture of these people who 'moved from one place to another', as to their history, the way they defined

themselves and were perceived by others, their status and situation in their countries of origin, and their motives. Nor is it important to examine the way they
behaved in the country to which they came, the extent of their readiness to make
compromises with a local population which opposed their coming, the dynamics
of the conflict, or the dangers to which they were exposed as a result of it. This,
obviously, is no way to analyse a historical phenomenon, but it is clear that the
colonialist terminology here is introduced for the purpose of passing judgement,
not analysing.

Keenly aware that the absence of a colonial mother country adversely affects
Zionism's classification as colonialism, Pappe tries to overcome this difficulty
by making the United Kingdom a kind of 'surrogate mother' of the Zionist
movement. He makes the point that Zionist colonialism is marked out by the
complex fabric of its ties with the United Kingdom. 'The Jewish National Home
came into existence at the point of British bayonets', he argues:

> and particularly on the basis of the goodwill of London. Had Britain so
> wished, the Jewish state could have come into existence as early as 1917:
> had it not so wished, it would not have come into existence at all.

But the Jewish state could not, realistically, have been established in 1917,
because the Zionist national project was not sufficiently advanced at that stage.
Among other things, it should be noted that all the strands of the Zionist movement consistently held that the Jewish state, which they conceived as a democracy, could only be established on the basis of a Jewish majority, either in the
country as a whole or at least in a part of it – as was accepted by the mainstream
Zionist leadership after it adopted the idea of partition.

It was not by chance that the state was eventually proclaimed despite the
United Kingdom's wishes. Confronted by growing antagonism between the
Arab and Jewish national movements, the British, out of strategic and imperial
calculations and rightly fearing that they might alienate themselves from the
Arab-Muslim world on the eve of the Second World War, eventually opted for
the Arab cause. Considerations of *raison d'état* proved, unsurprisingly, stronger
than any feelings of sympathy towards the Jewish people and their plight in
British ruling circles and public opinion. This choice, which would have sealed
the fate of the Zionist undertaking within a decade (by bringing about an
independent state with an Arab majority), came at a particularly dark moment in
Jewish history. It closed the country's gates first to those who were trying to
escape the approaching catastrophe in Europe, then to those who fled the actual
Holocaust (in many cases sealing their fate, since no other country was willing
to take them), then to survivors. This would hardly have happened had the
United Kingdom considered itself, in some sense, the mother country of the
Jews, rather than a Great Power supporting – and then ceasing to support, out of
strategic considerations – a foreign national movement.

It also goes without saying that the Zionists – including those who were not
only grateful to the United Kingdom for its earlier assistance but also admired

many things British – did not consider themselves the United Kingdom's 'children' in national, cultural or ideological terms. The cultural and emotional gaps between the mostly East European Jews in Palestine and their British rulers were very considerable, infrequently leading to expressions of mutual hostility and disdain on the part of the latter that today, at any rate, would certainly be regarded as anti-Semitic. No real similarity exists between the Zionist–British clash and the classic case of Britain's colonial 'children' turning against their mother country – its conflict with the North American colonies. The American colonists considered themselves Englishmen, and it was as such that they demanded self-rule. It was only when the imperial government refused, as they saw it, to respect their traditional English freedom that they took up the struggle for independence. This is very different from the situation in which Palestine's Jews found themselves. Coming from a whole range of countries (but next to none of them from the United Kingdom), they found themselves confronted by a British power which, at the most critical moment for them, washed its hands of their future, abandoned them to the far from tender mercies of the Mufti and stood in the way of rescuing their brethren from the clutches of the Nazis in Europe.

Moreover, British support for the Zionist undertaking was based from the outset on the intention, as stated in the Balfour Declaration, of facilitating 'the establishment in Palestine of a national home for the Jewish people'. This is essentially different from any colonial enterprise, modern or pre-modern, whose aim never was, and could never have been, to establish a 'national home' of any kind – although, over time, the settlers who came from the mother country might indeed develop a national identity of their own, and come into conflict with it.

The case of South Africa is a well-known example of conflict between a colonial power and European settlers. This example is sometimes adduced to demonstrate that a conflict of this kind is quite compatible with the originally colonialist nature of the settlement (which, by itself, is quite true). But in the seventeenth century, the Dutch settlers in South Africa (the forefathers of today's Afrikaners) had in the Netherlands a mother country that was a major colonial power. The settlement of Dutch colonists in South Africa came about as a result of a policy decision by the Dutch East India Company, to which the Dutch authorities ceded responsibility for their Dutch colonies in India. The first colonies were set up in the area of the Cape of Good Hope as trading posts in order to service Dutch shipping to and from India. However, towards the end of the eighteenth century, the British gained control over this part of South Africa, and in 1814 the Netherlands officially ceded it to the United Kingdom. This was a case of one colonial power ceding its control of the colony – and the colonists – to another (as happened also in Quebec). The arrival of British settlers led to tensions with the Dutch colonists, some of whom migrated to the interior where they set up independent Boer Republics. Towards the end of the nineteenth century, the discovery of major deposits of gold and diamonds triggered intense competition between the Boers and the British settlers over their exploitation, followed by a war between the United Kingdom, supporting its own colonists, and the Boer Republics. At this stage, one can indeed speak of a national struggle. But throughout all the stages of their struggle against the British, the Boers were never bothered by the question of majority versus minority, since they had no intention of giving the right to vote to the black population under their control.

Palestine had neither gold nor diamonds. This did not prevent the representative of the Arab Higher Committee in Palestine, in his address to the Ad Hoc Commission, from declaring on 18 October 1947: 'Perhaps the Zionists' love for Palestine is more for the treasures of the Dead Sea than for the Promised Land.'[7] But even the most intractable opponents of the Zionist movement have rarely stooped so low when discussing its motives.

In the article referred to earlier, Ilan Pappe acknowledges that Zionism was 'not exactly an ordinary colonial movement, acting according to economic profit and loss considerations'. But then he goes on to state that the 'colonialist mechanism' also determined the settlers' economic policy with regard to the local population. The standard charge levelled at Zionism in this context is that the policies of acquiring land and setting up an agricultural and industrial economy based on 'Hebrew labour' (rather than on hired Arab labour) were expressions of an arrogant isolationism and adversely affected the Arab population.[6] This policy was dictated by the national and social outlooks of the dominant trends in the Zionist movement – first and foremost, of the Zionist Left. Of course, had the Zionists chosen the opposite strategy – as European settlers regularly did in colonial settings – and employed cheap Arab labour on a wide scale (something which would have been the natural result of allowing the market forces to operate freely), they would have been accused of exploiting the natives' cheap labour, and this would have provided convincing evidence that theirs was an 'ordinary colonial movement'.

Nevertheless, despite the Zionist policy (first and foremost, that of the Zionist Labour movement) of encouraging the creation of a Jewish working class in Palestine, and relying on it, rather than on Arab labour, for the building-up of the national home, there is no doubt that the rapid economic development of the country greatly benefited its Arab population as well, and raised its standard of living far above that prevailing in the neighbouring Arab countries. Within the Zionist movement, many hoped that the progress it was bringing to the land, in various fields, would eventually persuade the Arabs of Palestine that it was in their interests to accept the establishment of the Jewish national home in the country (or at least in part of it). This hope was clearly unrealistic – it is well known that economic and social improvements do not solve a national conflict.

According to Pappe, 'The discourse of the early Jewish settlers was more colonialist than national, and this affected the way they saw themselves: as immigrants making the desert bloom, agents of modernization vis-à-vis the local population, and promoters of western culture.' In practice, however, not only was this self-image of disseminating Western culture among the Arab inhabitants never the focus of the Zionist settlers' intellectual world, but from the cultural point of view no single, consistent approach to West and East can be identified among the Zionist movement's different strands. Some did indeed underscore their affinities with Western culture, and saw themselves as its representatives in the Orient; others, in contrast, considered Zionism to be a movement that was bringing the Jewish people back to its Eastern roots, its sources, not just geographical but cultural and spiritual as well. The adoption, by the Jewish community in Palestine, of the Sephardi (i.e. Middle Eastern) pronunciation of Hebrew, rather than the Ashkenazi (European) variant, at a time when most Jews in the country were European immigrants, reflected this notion of return to (Oriental) roots; the same holds true for the fairly widespread fashion of imitating local Arab customs.[7] Many thought in terms of a blend of Western and Eastern elements. Politically speaking, there were those who, until the end of the 1930s, underscored the alliance and the shared interests between Zionism and the British Empire; at the same time, outlooks also developed which sought to encourage a Jewish–Arab anti-imperialist struggle in Palestine and in the region.

Among its opponents in European Jewish circles, Zionism was regularly accused of 'inciting' Jews not just to leave Europe – their home for centuries – but also to turn their backs on European culture – above all, by adopting Hebrew as the Jewish community's language in Palestine. The most eloquent representative of this approach was the novelist Arthur Koestler. At one point, Koestler was an enthusiastic Zionist, but later became disillusioned with the Zionist enterprise. Nevertheless, he would eventually support the establishment of the state as a refuge for persecuted Jews (but no longer as a project of Jewish cultural revival). After leaving Palestine in 1929, he described his abandoning of Zionism as an act of preserving his European identity, and as a homecoming to Europe – in cultural no less than physical terms. Koestler felt that the adoption of Hebrew as the national language of Jewish society in Palestine cut off the country's Jews from both European culture in general and from their own past. He speaks of recovering from the romanticism of the Orient, which had characterized his Zionist years, as well as from his hopes for a cultural and spiritual revival by the Jewish people in their ancient homeland.[8] And indeed, in the entire history of Europeans settling outside the continent's borders, there is no comparable phenomenon to the way that Hebrew – a non-European Semitic language – was adopted in Palestine by the Jews from Europe and made into the focal element of their cultural and national identity.

Naturally, Arab hostility to Zionism and the customary dynamics of a national conflict negatively affected the Jews' cultural attitudes to their neighbours. Nevertheless, however divided they were on many other issues, all the main strands of the Zionist movement agreed on one point: there could be no Jewish entity in Palestine which did not grant full equality to its Arab citizens.

Pappe argues that the Zionists used colonial terminology as standard from the end of the nineteenth century up to the First World War, for as long as it was considered legitimate and identification with it was not problematic: 'subsequently, negative connotations would come to be associated with the term "colonialism" and the historians of Zionism in Israel would refuse to acknowledge

Zionism's colonialist nature.' In this context, however, it must be remembered that in the various European languages, 'colonization' is – or rather, used to be – the usual term for settling people on the land. In the nineteenth and early twentieth centuries (and in certain cases after this period also), it was natural to define a settlement project – even if it was unrelated to colonialism in the sense in which it is understood today, not part of any conflict, and undertaken inside the state doing the settling, not outside its borders – as 'colonization'. Hence the term used for the various places where settlers established themselves was 'colonies' and the homesteaders were known as 'colonists'. When in the nineteenth century the authorities of Tsarist Russia encouraged the country's Jews to become farmers in a number of areas in southern Russia, as part of a policy of making this population more 'productive', this was known as 'colonization' and those concerned were called 'colonists'. The same terms were used when Jews were resettled in Argentina in a project organized by the Jewish Colonization Association, financed by Baron Maurice de Hirsch of Paris. The Argentine government had given the project its blessing; only Argentina's anti-Semites refer to it as a sinister 'colonialist' undertaking. In 1924 a group of pro-Soviet left-wing New York Jews set up a body known as IKOR, from Idishe Kolonizatsie Organizatsie or the Jewish Colonization Association in the Soviet Union. Using funds raised among American Jewry, for years this organization gave considerable financial assistance to Jewish settlement projects initiated by the government of the Soviet Union – first in the Crimea and Ukraine, and later in the Autonomous Jewish Region of Birobidzhan. A similar organization with a similar name was also set up among the Jews of Argentina. Thus it is obvious that while Zionist spokesmen, speaking in European languages, can indeed be quoted as referring to Jewish 'colonization', 'colonies' and 'colonists' in Palestine, this is no proof that the Zionist movement was 'colonialist' in the present-day sense of the word.

The comparison between Zionism and colonialism is thus of little, if any, analytical value. Far from helping to understand Zionism as a historical phenomenon, it contributes to a blurring of its main attributes – although in analysing the Palestinian Arabs' reaction to Zionism, it must be borne in mind that they did see it as a colonial phenomenon and as part of the colonialist activities in the area. Ultimately, efforts to describe and hence discredit Zionism as a colonialist phenomenon are based on a fairly clear (although generally not explicitly expressed) ideological view. This view may be formulated as follows: since the Jewish people, at the outset of their national movement, were lacking a home, and not just national independence, they should have remained in this condition. Their very aspiration to a national home of their own was 'colonialist' and hence unacceptable, since by definition it required 'a physical movement of people from one place to another'. Fortunately for the Jewish people, this view was not adopted by the international community.

'A hope of two thousand years': modern Jewish identity and historical continuity

During the UN partition debates in 1947, Arab representatives repeatedly claimed, as we have seen, that there was no genuine continuity between the ancient Jews – or the Children of Israel – whose home was Judea, and the modern Jews who were seeking to set up their national home in the region. This was part of their effort to demonstrate that modern-day Jews are merely a religious community whose members come from a whole range of nationalities, with no national bond between them. Some Arab delegates argued that only a small number of modern Jews could be considered to be the descendants of the Children of Israel, or resuscitated the theory of European Jews' alleged Khazar origins. These claims, rather dubious in themselves, reflect, to the extent that they can be treated seriously, a simplistic, racial view of what constitutes a national identity in the modern sense. Common ethnic origin is not considered to be a vital component of such an identity. In contrast, a tradition about a common origin, a shared foundation myth about the distant past are important components of many national cultures, whatever the 'objective' historical basis for those traditions.[9] Even modern French nationalism, which is considered a non-ethnic, civic nationalism par excellence, is not devoid of such an element. In the French Republic, whole generations of schoolchildren have been brought up on the expression 'our ancestors the Gauls' – an expression which, biologically speaking, certainly does not apply to many of them; and yet this image has become part of French national identity. The use of biological and 'anthropological' arguments in an attempt to deny the existence of modern Jewish peoplehood does not stand up to scrutiny. Moshe Shertok, representing the Jewish Agency, countered them before the Ad Hoc Committee of the General Assembly on 17 October 1947: the claims that European Jews were descendants of a Mongol tribe were 'simply fantastic. The Encyclopaedia Judaica, on which the Arab representatives frequently rely in this connection, provides no corroboration of any such argument. This pseudo-scientific discussion is completely irrelevant.'

Those responsible for drawing up the UNSCOP report ignored these claims altogether, and did not bother to produce any 'scientific' proofs for the existence of the Jewish people or for its historic continuity. As we have seen, they referred to ancient Jewish history as, self-evidently, the ancient history of the people who wanted to set up their independent state in Palestine. The supporters of partition at the UN debates followed suit. Arab speakers themselves spoke occasionally – albeit always in a negative context – in terms of a direct link between the historical Jewish people and present-day Jews. Here the following excerpt from the Syrian delegate's address to the General Assembly plenary session on 22 September 1947 is instructive:

> There were so many nations that contributed greatly to the civilization of the world and which were stronger and more powerful than the Jewish

dynasty. Yet we find none of them in existence now. They were not exterminated; they were assimilated by their invaders and became adapted to the environments in which they found themselves. Of the peoples of antiquity, only the Jews maintain their isolation and seclusion, to the dissatisfaction and anger of their compatriots and their neighbours, who never failed to molest and persecute them, on each occasion giving to the world a problem of refugees; a problem of displaced persons. ... Why is that? The only reason is the special manner of life which the Jews adopt for themselves and to which they adhere in spite of all the developments and metamorphoses which have taken place all over the world for all nations. The Jews are all alone, and the United Nations now is faced with the last but not least of these problems.

After Moshe Shertok (Sharett) had referred to the Mufti's pro-Nazi past during his 12 May speech at the meeting of the General Assembly's First Committee, at the same session the Arab Higher Committee representative Emile Al-Ghury came out with a retort similar in spirit to that of his Syrian colleague: 'The Jews are questioning the record of an Arab spiritual leader. Does that properly come from the mouth of a people who have crucified the founder of Christianity?' The Arab representatives' efforts during the partition debates (as well as on other occasions) to shed doubt on the Jewish people's historical continuity are thus not exactly credible.

On the other hand, the Zionist claims as to this continuity can be questioned from a different point of view. Many scholars of nationalism view it as a distinctly modern phenomenon. They consider that, in the sense in which we understand nations, national identities and nationalism today, they date back – like the nation-state – to late eighteenth- and nineteenth-century Europe, i.e. the period of the French Revolution and its aftermath. The emergence of this phenomenon was, it is argued, linked to a particular stage of economic, social and political development reached by European countries, and to the needs of capitalist modernization. This process is often said to have come about sooner in a number of the continent's economically most developed countries which had achieved a greater degree of centralized power earlier than their counterparts. It was, however, the nineteenth century that provided the most fertile soil for the growth of nationalism. The crystallization of modern national identities is frequently described as a process led by elites which were devoted to a 'nation-building' project and managed to inculcate the masses with a national ideology by didactic and sometimes manipulative means. To this end, they made use of folk traditions and ancient myths, bringing them up to date and applying them to the promotion of their modern political goals. In order to produce a national consciousness among the people, these traditions were given contemporary interpretations, as they were reworked and adapted to suit present-day needs. This process is often referred to as the 'invention of tradition', and the modern nation is often described as an 'imagined community'.[10] These terms are often used in order to make the point that a modern nation is not an 'objective' fact, a direct continuation of ethno-linguistic groups that existed before the modern era, but rather a concept that was shaped by a national movement (or in the case of old-established countries like France, by the nation-state) in a particular historical period and accepted by the population in question.

If this approach is applied to Israel, then it is political Zionism, influenced by nineteenth-century European nationalism, which created the Jewish national identity oriented towards the establishment of a nation-state in Palestine. This involved reworking and providing a contemporary political-cum-secular inter-pretation of the Jews' traditional religious bond with the Land of Israel and their messianic hopes. In this respect, of course, Zionism was no different from any other national movement: from this point of view, all modern national identities are according to this view, 'invented' and 'imagined'. There is no room for selective and manipulative use of this terminology in order to 'deconstruct' the Jewish national identity, of all others – as is often done. Thus, for example, the Palestinian scholar Nur Masalha, in his book *Imperial Israel and the Palestini-ans*, adopts the discourse that regards nationalism as a modern 'invention' in order to attack the Zionist view of historical continuity between the ancient and the modern Jewish people. He claims that the Zionist concept of Jewish people-hood is based on a '(mythical) continuity between the ancient and the modern'. In particular he takes exception to the name used by the Zionists for Palestine – Land of Israel ('Eretz Israel'; although in fact all the founding fathers of Zionism regularly used the name 'Palestine' when speaking in European lan-guages, without suspecting that there was anything 'un-Jewish' about it). In this way, he argues, the Zionists are trying to determine the character of the country on the basis of dubious myths whose origins are lost in the mists of time.[11] He appears to believe that while 'Eretz Israel' (which is in fact the traditional Hebrew name of the country, used by Jews since ancient times) is a mythologi-cal and ideological name employed by the Zionists in an attempt to shape a modern reality on the basis of a tendentious interpretation of the past, 'Pales-tine', in contrast, has since time immemorial always been the country's natural and sole name. Masalha does not suggest calling the country by its oldest known name – Canaan. Such arguments are couched in the language of the most advanced and up-to-date liberal discourse, but what lies behind them is nothing other than the nationalist instinct to 'deny the Other'.

However, while other peoples lived in a particular territory at the time that they were being shaped as modern nations, and hence there was no need to 'invent' the bond between them and their homeland (although the borders of the homeland were not infrequently 'invented' or 'imagined' in the national con-sciousness), in the Jewish case things were different. Eric Hobsbawm, one of the leading scholars on modern nationalism, writes as follows:

> [W]hile the Jews, scattered throughout the world for some millennia, never
> ceased to identity themselves, wherever they were, as members of a special
> people quite distinct from the various brands of non-believers among whom
> they lived, at no stage, at least since the return from the Babylonian captiv-

ity, does this seem to have implied a serious desire for a Jewish political state, let alone a territorial state, until a Jewish nationalism was invented at the very end of the nineteenth century by analogy with the newfangled western nationalism. It is entirely illegitimate to identify the Jewish links with the ancestral land of Israel, the merit deriving from pilgrimages there, or the hope for a return when the Messiah came … with the desire to gather all Jews into a modern territorial state situated in the ancient Holy Land. One might as well argue that good Muslims, whose highest ambition is to make the pilgrimage to Mecca, in doing so really intend to declare themselves citizens of what has now become Saudi Arabia.[12]

Clearly the comparison is highly artificial. No group of Muslims has ever cherished the vision of a massive 'return', whether near or distant, to Mecca with the goal of establishing a kingdom there in the Arabian Peninsula, nor has it based its collective identity – whether it be defined as religious, ethnic or national – on any such aspiration. In the Jewish case, it is true that those who depict modern Zionism as a direct continuation of the traditional yearning for Zion are oversimplifying things; but those who insist that there is no connection at all between the two are obviously sacrificing common sense on the altar of ideology. Israel's Declaration of Independence speaks, indeed, of the Jewish people, having been exiled from the Land, as 'never ceas[ing] to pray and hope for their return to it and for the restoration in it of their political freedom'. It may be argued that the expression 'political freedom' is a modern term, and that it is not the most accurate way of describing the content of traditional Jewish 'prayer and hope'. But it is far from obvious, *pace* Hobsbawm, that the traditional vision of returning to Zion and restoring the Jewish kingdom was wholly lacking a territorial and a political dimension (in a sense befitting pre-modern conditions).

Scholars of nationalism are in fact far from unanimous in drawing a sharp distinction between modern national identities and pre-modern ethnic and cultural ones. Thus, for instance, an eminent researcher in the field, Anthony Smith, presents a different perspective on this question. According to him, while national ideologies and national movements are a modern phenomenon, the picture is far more complex when it comes to social structures of nationhood, as well as national sentiments and symbols. These elements, according to Smith, can be identified to varying extents in European countries, from England and France to Poland and Russia, from the late Middle Ages onwards; moreover, social structures that approximate, in many respects, modern definitions of a 'nation' can be found among various peoples through the ages, 'notably among the ancient Jews and Armenians, but also to some extent among the ancient Egyptians, and perhaps the medieval Japanese and Koreans'.[13] Smith is critical of the tendency on the part of a number of scholars to interpret concepts such as 'invention' or 'imagining' when applied to modern national identities as indicating that they have been 'fabricated' or created *ex nihilo*. He points out that Anderson himself, who coined the term 'imagined communities', rejected this interpretation (which is actually closer to Hobsbawm's ideas about the invention of tradition). Smith emphasizes that it is impossible to 'imagine' or 'invent' a modern identity and to inculcate it in a given people if it has no roots in its culture. The idea of a 'national revival' based on the hankering after a glorious national past, which of course does not mean that the past is reproduced in its original form, reflects a genuine and widely shared perception of continuity, and cannot be ascribed to mere manipulation. For example, the Polish Republic which was established following the First World War, while not being a 'reborn' old Poland – the aristocratic kingdom that was divided up between its neighbours at the end of the eighteenth century – was also not an 'invention' of something entirely new, without links with the past.

When it comes to the Jewish case and the question of the link between the Jews' modern identity and their ancient identity (and homeland), Smith sees Zionism as an expression of a special type of nationalism which he calls 'Diaspora nationalism'. The two other peoples who clearly fall into this category are the Armenians and the Greeks.[14] In his view, Zionism is a less exceptional phenomenon than both its supporters and its critics generally tend to assume. Smith identifies numerous common attributes shared by these three ancient diaspora peoples:

> Greeks, Jews and Armenians claimed an ancient homeland and kingdom, looked back nostalgically to a golden age or ages of great kings, saints, sages and poets, yearned to return to ancient capitals with sacred sites and buildings, took with them wherever they went their ancient scriptures, sacred scripts and separate liturgies, founded in every city congregations with churches, clergy and religious schools ... and used their wealth, education and economic skills to offset their political powerlessness. But the parallels go further. Greeks, Jews and Armenians after their subordination to others and emigration or expulsion from their original homelands, became diaspora ethno-religious communities cultivating the particular virtues and aptitudes of their traditions. These included a respect for scholarship and learning, derived from constant study of religious texts ...; and hence a generally high status accorded to religious scholars and clergy within each enclave. Allied to this was a marked aptitude for literary expression – poetic, philosophical, legal, liturgical, linguistic and historical. The resulting fund of documentary records encoding shared memories and interpretations increased in particularly every generation, enriching the ethno-heritage of these communities.[15]

Smith goes on to refer to the contribution of the ethno-religious autonomy enjoyed by the diaspora communities to the preservation of their common cultural heritage. He notes the belief in being a 'chosen people' that was characteristic of the Jews, the Greeks, and the Armenians; the memory of the historical catastrophes which brought them together (in the case of the Orthodox Greeks, the fall of Constantinople); and the impact on their collective consciousness of the persecutions and massacres that took place in the diaspora (more so in the case of the Jews and the Armenians). Smith analyses and compares the growth of the modern national movements of these three peoples. These were influenced by European nationalism, but also inspired by their own peoples' ancient traditions and historical memory. He underscores the pioneering role played by diaspora intellectuals and militants in the struggle for Greek independence at the beginning of the nineteenth century, and in the Armenian national movement in the nineteenth and twentieth centuries. In the case of the Jews, the entire people were in the Diaspora, a fact that determined the nature of its national movement. While neither the Holocaust of European Jewry nor the Armenian genocide led to these peoples' demands for national independence, they did strengthen these demands and helped win them international sympathy.

The states created by these peoples maintain, in all three cases, a special connection between their national and religious identities, and strong official links with their respective diasporas. All three have passed 'laws of return' for this purpose. It goes without saying that the State of Israel is not the direct successor of the kingdoms of the First and Second Temple periods, just as modern Greece is not the direct successor of Classical Greece or of the Greek-speaking Byzantine Empire, nor is the Armenian Republic the direct heir of the ancient Armenian kingdoms. Nevertheless, the sense of historic continuity, which played such an important role in the struggle for independence, continues to put its stamp on these societies and their cultures.

Many peoples throughout the world have a profound sense of historical continuity. The Greeks and the Armenians, the Spaniards and the Basques, the Poles and the Hungarians, the peoples of Scandinavia, the Russians, the Arabs, the Chinese, the Indians, the Japanese and the Koreans – do not start their peoples' story from the late eighteenth century, according to the theories on the emergence of modern nationalism. Whether one accepts those theories or not, the historical consciousness of these peoples is an integral part of their modern culture and identity. National movements struggling for independence appeal to this consciousness. Inevitably, they interpret their people's past in light of their current notions, sentiments and goals; often enough they are not above subjecting national history to obviously biased and manipulative interpretations. But they do not 'fabricate' their people's historic memory out of thin air; they are shaped by it no less than they shape it.

The historic consciousness of a people is often reflected in modern declarations of independence and constitutions (typically, in a preamble). The preamble to the Irish Constitution reads:

> In the name of the Most Holy Trinity...
> We, the people of Ireland, humbly acknowledging all our obligations to our Divine Lord, Jesus Christ, Who sustained our fathers through centuries of trial,
> Gratefully remembering their heroic and unremitting struggle to regain the rightful independence of our Nation...
> Do hereby adopt, enact, and give to ourselves this Constitution.

Many modern scholars of nationalism would argue that describing eight centuries of Irish history in terms of a struggle 'to regain the independence of the Nation' is anachronistic. Nevertheless, the text of the Constitution gives official expression to the historic memory and cultural identity of the modern Irish people.

The historical consciousness of the Jewish people and their ties with the land of Israel are cornerstones of Jewish identity. The international community acknowledged this bond – one which forms part of the world's cultural heritage – in the 1922 League of Nations Mandate,[18] which gave 'recognition ... to the historical connection of the Jewish people with Palestine and to the grounds for reconstituting their national home in that country'; and again when the United Nations adopted the plan to partition Palestine into an Arab state and a Jewish state. Those who reject the idea of the Jewish national home cannot do so with the help of learned debates on the nature of Jewish historical continuity. They should face the moral implications of the stance that would have insisted on leaving the Jewish people in the twentieth century without a national home of its own.

3 Zionism and international norms

As far as the democratic character of the future state was concerned, all main strands of Zionism agreed with the principles on which the UN General Assembly partition resolution was based. The leadership of the Zionist movement and of the Jewish community in Palestine had no difficulty in accepting the Assembly's resolution and its principles when it came to establishing a democratic Jewish state respecting the rights of the large Arab minority within its borders. These principles fully corresponded with the traditional Zionist vision of a future Jewish state.

It is true that the War of Independence, in which the Arabs of Palestine (in the part allotted to the Jewish state as well as outside it) took an active part in the war against the fledgling state, would harden the prevailing attitudes to the state's future Arab citizens. This would result in harsh measures being taken against them – measures which in some cases went beyond what was justified, even during a conflict. Some have argued that Zionist leaders intended from the outset to expel a considerable portion of the Palestinian-Arab population from the area earmarked for the Jewish state, because without such expulsions, Israel Arabs would have made up more than 40 per cent of the country's population. There is no concrete evidence to support this claim, and it must be remembered that the Zionist leadership, like the authors of the UNSCOP report, anticipated hundreds of thousands of Jews immigrating to the new country – a state of affairs which would considerably strengthen its Jewish majority. However, even a 'plot' like this could only have been put into practice in wartime conditions. Without the Arabs' rejection of the UN Partition Plan, without the Palestinian Arabs fighting the plan's implementation tooth and nail throughout the entire country, including in the mixed cities, and without the invasion by the Arab armies which threatened the very survival of the Jewish state and of the Jewish community in the country – no one would have fled and no one would have been expelled. Hence, the refugee problem, created by both the fleeing of Palestinian Arabs and expulsions from the war zones, would not have come about. David Ben-Gurion always declared that a clear Jewish majority in the future Israel would be ensured, not through the expulsion of Arabs but through the massive immigration of Jews. In a speech after the adoption of the partition plan, he said:

There can be no stable and viable Jewish state as long as it has a Jewish majority of only 60 per cent, and this majority comprises only 600,000 Jews. The Jewish State will [really] come about [only] after the immigration of a million and a half Jews. Therefore the creation of the State is not the formal establishment of the State and its institutions ... This implementation will require only some 10 months or so – if the UN Assembly's decision is not sabotaged by the Mandatory government or other elements .. . But from the Jewish point of view, on their own these formal stages are not sufficient. In order to ensure that the Jewish State will not only be established but will survive and be able to carry out its mission – it is necessary to bring a million and a half Jews to live and put down roots here. Only when we have at least two million Jews in the country will the State be really founded. This immigration and settlement undertaking may perhaps require 10 years – and we must view these 10 years as a period of building up the state and establishing it in concrete terms. A Jewish government whose primary concern is not to achieve immigration and settlement which will increase our numbers in Israel to two million in a very short time will be failing to meet its primary and main responsibility and will endanger our generation's great historical achievement.[1]

In the same speech Ben-Gurion makes the point that the future state will 'also be their State' – 'their' meaning Arab citizens of Israel.

It all started with Herzl

Everything started with Herzl and it all comes back to him. The idea that the Jews 'are a people – one people' formed the bedrock of the Zionist revolution, as Herzl wrote in his introduction to his book *Der Judenstaat*, 'The Jewish State'.[2] But on its own, this idea would not have set the Jewish imagination on fire, nor does it explain the enormous success of the First Zionist Congress, held in Basle in 1897. As Herzl himself pointed out, the idea was not at all new. As he wrote, 'whether we desire it or not, we are and shall remain a historical group of unmistakable solidarity.' Not a few Jews, seeking integration in European society, disputed this definition of Jewish peoplehood in Herzl's time, but it was borne out fully by Jewish history in the twentieth century. The history of the State of Israel, which was established after the Holocaust and in its first half-century, despite wars, blockades, terror and boycotts, took in close to three million immigrants, is the history of a people in search of a national home.

That the Jews are a people who need a state is an idea which, having previously been taken on board by Jews and the non-Jewish supporters of Zionism, eventually convinced the international community. However, it was not a new idea: 'The idea I have developed in this pamphlet is an ancient one,' writes Herzl at the beginning of the prologue to *Der Judenstaat*. What was new, however, in what Herzl said was the combination of this ancient idea with the search for international support (crucial for making the Jewish state into a fact) on the one hand, and Jewish commitment to modern international norms on the other. Herzl fired the Jewish imagination because he translated an ancient emotion into a programme for action through a modern political mechanism, and sought to obtain international endorsement as a crucial element in the realization of the Jewish national idea. In so doing he also forced his movement to adopt universal standards. Herzl was responsible for showing that the 'Jewish Question', as he put it, is a national question 'which can only be solved by making it a political world-question to be discussed and settled by the civilized nations of the world in council'. In other words, Herzl needed international legitimacy in order to help the Jews leave Europe and set up their state, as well as to rid the world of the scourge of anti-Semitism.

Today, Herzl's ideas appear far more natural and normal than they did at the turn of the nineteenth century. As a scattered people, the Jews stuck out like a sore thumb in a Europe of nation-states, of which the most advanced example was the French Republic. There was precious little understanding of the very idea of a diaspora. In the multi-national Austro-Hungarian Empire, whose impending fall was sensed by Herzl, the different peoples were concentrated in defined areas, sometimes enjoying territorial autonomy. In the contemporary world, however – with its vast waves of migration, the right of asylum for refugees recognized in the wake of the Second World War, workers in search of employment moving to rich countries, the progressive opening of borders within the European Union, as well as the border changes in Europe during the twentieth century – the phenomenon of diasporas has become widespread and normal. While the Jews are undeniably a diaspora people, all their other characteristics are indicative of the emergence and existence of a modern national identity. Zionism was by no means the only stream of Jewish opinion that accepted this fact. The Bund, an East European Jewish Social-Democratic movement which enjoyed wide support and was a strong rival to Zionism, sought to obtain national autonomy for the Yiddish-speaking Jewish people in Eastern Europe. Other, non-socialist, 'autonomist' Jewish groups supported this idea. Even the staunchest opponents of Zionism, the Soviet Bolsheviks, would come to accept that the Soviet Union's Jews were a people (a 'nationality') who needed their own autonomous territory – Birobidzhan – as part of the Soviet Union. The fact that many Jews, having abandoned the traditional way of life prescribed by Halacha (Jewish religious law), continued to consider themselves Jewish constituted the first proof of the power of national emotion. True, this feeling was, in large measure, also a reaction to modern anti-Semitism. But it is quite usual for modern national identities and movements to emerge and grow in the face of adversity. And Jews who wanted to escape anti-Semitism by sacrificing their Jewish identity still had – or thought they had – the option of achieving this aim by converting to Christianity. The national option (whether Zionist or non-Zionist) was certainly not 'forced' on them.

The strength of Jewish national identity varied considerably. It was strongest in Eastern Europe, where the great majority of the world's Jews lived when the Zionist movement emerged. Millions of Jews there still spoke their own distinct language (Yiddish), were heavily concentrated in certain areas and constituted a close-knit ethnic, linguistic and cultural group – perhaps closer to the Far Eastern than to the European model. These Jews, like the Chinese and Japanese, preserved their national identity even after they had abandoned the traditional religious culture in which they had grown up. Willingly or not, they remained Jews.

Much has been said about Jewishness – a combination of religion, national identity and a connection to a country – being unique or exceptional. However, this is true only to the extent that it is evaluated according to European criteria and the icons of the modern era, particularly those of the French Revolution; though as we shall see, even in contemporary Western Europe it is not wholly true either. In other contexts, the situation is entirely different. It is not exceptional for a country's national religion to be bound up with its mother country. Can India, even though according to its constitution it is a secular country, be imagined without Hinduism, and the latter without the Ganges and all its other holy places? Can Tibetan national identity be conceived of without its specifically Tibetan Buddhism, complete with its texts, temples, monks, prayer wheels, prayer flags, as well as the leadership of the Dalai Lama? And how could Japanese or Chinese identities be thought of stripped of the religious and cultural traditions which shaped them? Nineteenth-century Eastern Europe was not a region of secular republics. Most states, from the Russian Empire down, were religious, with a national Church headed by the tsar or king, and venerating Christianity's holy places. Even in the West, religions and Churches sported the national colours – particularly in England, the Scandinavian countries and Germany's Protestant denominations.

What has happened is that since the Second World War, viewed in a modern light, the presence of a Jewish Diaspora that holds dear the memory of its ancient homeland and its historical sites is no longer a matter of surprise, whether in North America or in Western Europe. What was unique about the Jews was that their Diaspora had no territorial base, no ability to organize a system of defending themselves against their persecutors and tormentors. What was exceptional about Jewish nationalism was that it turned the natural order of things on its head, undertaking the construction of a territorial centre *after* the Diaspora had put down roots outside the land of Israel; then returning to the country to which the Jews had directed their prayers, but from which they had been absent – and finally, at a subsequent stage, reviving Hebrew as an everyday language. But while scholars and experts have long mulled over what is unique to the Jewish national movement, they are now increasingly examining what is common to this movement and other national movements whose roots lie in a diaspora and not in a historical homeland, such as the Armenian and Greek national movements. True, unlike the land of Israel and the Jews, Armenia and Greece maintained significant Armenian and Greek populations. But in both cases, as Anthony Smith emphasizes, the national movement was heavily dependent on engaging the diaspora and drawing on its resources.[3]

This shifting of the emphasis to diaspora nationalism fits in with the contemporary reality, and in particular the atmosphere in Europe that followed the establishment of the European Union and the dismantling of the Soviet bloc. The gradual abolition of political and economic borders that divide countries is occurring hand in hand with the resurgence of local national and cultural identities. Although apparently contradictory phenomena, both of them draw on the same sources: the unravelling of the unitary national ethos and the re-emergence of linguistic and cultural identities superseded by the modern nation-state. The United Kingdom, Spain and Belgium have grown both more European and more 'national' on the sub-state level. In addition, the two European phenomena – the curtailing of state sovereignty and the return to ethnic and cultural nationalism in the regions – are crossing old borders: witness the Basques and the Catalans. The new Europe is a tissue of nations, nationalities, languages and diasporas. The Kurdish diaspora demonstrates against Turkey; the Armenian diaspora calls for international recognition of the genocide perpetrated against the Armenian people; the Hungarian minorities of Slovakia and Romania consider Hungary their homeland from the cultural point of view, asking it for assistance and protection.

In such a world, the Zionist claims on behalf of the Jewish people sound more natural and legitimate than they did in the world of the nineteenth century. One of the harshest criticisms that used to be directed at Zionism was that it would produce 'double loyalty' among Diaspora Jews. However, nowadays this charge sounds hollow. In a world where preserving one's distinct culture and identity is the norm rather than the exception, the idea of Jewish peoplehood is not regarded as detracting in any way from loyalty to the State – a loyalty that is derived from the obligations arising from citizenship.

This was far from the case at Zionism's beginnings, i.e. the end of the nineteenth century. Calling for a state to be set up for the Jews in an Ottoman province which had no sizeable Jewish population seemed like complete madness. Since this was more or less an exercise in making something out of nothing, the only way to turn it into a legitimate undertaking was to secure international recognition for it. To this end, Herzl moved heaven and earth and managed to strengthen the movement that he had founded, and to increase the popularity of Zionism among the Jews of Western Europe and North America.

In 1897, the First Zionist Congress adopted the Basle Programme, as proposed by Herzl. This combination of a renewed, reinvigorated definition of Jewish peoplehood and international recognition spoke to the two conflicting mindsets that split the Jewish world: the wish to remain Jewish despite the religious crisis, and the desire to be part of the progressive, modern world. This duality was reflected in the personalities of both Herzl and Nordau.[4] Despite their eminence in non-Jewish circles, the two men returned to involvement in things Jewish. The importance attached by Zionism to the need for the recognition of its claims by the 'civilized peoples' is extraordinary by the standards of modern national movements. Generally speaking, such national-territorial movements, in order to gain independence, have preferred to mobilize their forces either in the political fray, or in wars of national liberation – without, of course, turning their backs on the support of foreign powers hostile to the power against which they were fighting. Zionism chose – in fact, had little alternative but to choose – the opposite approach: to bring together in Palestine a sufficiently large Jewish community in order to set up an independent state, and to try at least to do so without war and with the approval and support of the international community.

The First Zionist Congress adopted the Basle Programme, which in the compromise formula proposed by Herzl declared: 'Zionism seeks to establish a home for the Jewish people in Palestine secured under public law.' Herzl's efforts to obtain a charter from the Turkish Sultan that would enable a Jewish centre to be established in Palestine under the protection of the Ottoman Empire ended in failure. The Balfour Declaration that was issued in 1917 satisfied this wish, announcing that: 'His Majesty's Government view with favour the establishment in Palestine of a national home for the Jewish people.' In this way, the United Kingdom recognized both the existence of the Jews as a people, and also their right to a 'national home' in Palestine.

The League of Nations, the international body which was set up after the First World War in order to bring about peace in the world and grant the right of self-determination to those peoples to whom it had been denied, adopted the Balfour Declaration as part of the Mandate given to the United Kingdom over Palestine. The Palestine Mandate recognized the Jewish people's 'historical connection' with Palestine; moreover, it recognized the 'World Zionist organization' as a 'Jewish agency' whose mission was to facilitate the Jews' return to their country. Hebrew, having only recently become an everyday language once again, was recognized as one of the three official languages of Mandatory Palestine. As shown in Chapter 2, a direct line connects the League of Nations' decisions with the decision of the UN Special Committee on Palestine (UNSCOP), which was adopted by the General Assembly in May 1947: Palestine was to be partitioned into two states, one Jewish and one Arab, with separate status for Jerusalem, with an economic union between all three parts.

The Zionist movement and the leadership of the Jewish community in Palestine accepted the provisions of the partition plan, and the authors of Israel's Declaration of Independence drafted their document accordingly. The Declaration proclaims the establishment of a Jewish State, to be called Israel, as well as the principles on which this state is to be based. Thus the new state's 'birth certificate' is accompanied by an impressive portfolio of documents attesting to its international legitimacy. It was only after Israel had become firmly established that critics emerged within Israeli society challenging this right of the Jewish people to a national home – an eloquent testimony to Israel becoming a 'normal' liberal democracy, complete with the radical excesses that accompany contemporary Western liberalism, despite the abnormal conditions of prolonged conflict. Those who take this stance base their challenge on grievances, whether real, exaggerated or imagined, about injustices committed by the State in the past or in the present – as if criticism, however justified, of a policy pursued by a nation-state undermines a people's right to independence.

Classical Zionist ideology, from Herzl's time up to Israel's Declaration of Independence, was unequivocal: in the State of the Jews, there would be real democracy, and full rights would be granted to a non-Jewish minority – the same rights for which the Jews had struggled, often without success, in the countries where they had lived in the Diaspora. This is the kind of society that is described in the Zionist utopias, especially Herzl's *Altneuland* – 'An Old-New Land'.[5] Although Herzl's depiction of the Arab character, Rashid Bey, may bring a smile to the contemporary reader's lips, the words that the author puts in his mouth show a genuine desire: that in the 'Old-New Land' there should be no discrimination whatsoever between the status of the Jews and that of non-Jews. In terms of late-nineteenth-century European thinking, the application of the principles of equality to Muslim Arabs in a future Jewish Palestine was definitely not something that could be taken for granted. At that time, French socialists had yet to suggest that voting rights be given to Muslims in Algeria, nor did French women have the vote that Herzl took care to bestow on Muslim women in his utopia. Viewed in retrospect, Rashid Bey is perhaps a naive figure, but given the time and place that the book was written, Herzl's description has pioneering overtones in terms of equal rights for the 'Other', to use modern terminology.

Herzl had his precursors. There was Moses Hess, who developed the thesis that 'the path of the Messianic social order and of world peace passes from Moses and the Prophets to Spinoza, and from the latter to the Jewish national revival, which is the prerequisite for the implementation of this vision'.[6] Herzl was not familiar with Moses Hess's writings, which would come to influence socialist-Zionist ideology. But his dream was that the Jews would have a state which would be 'a copy of an ideal European country'.[7] Max Nordau, who before his conversion to Zionism was a noted secular thinker, also saw no contradiction between Jewishness and universalism: in the country of their ancestors, the Jews should be 'a people of noble spirit ..., an instrument of progress and of wisdom, pursuing justice'. It is also worth remembering the words with which Herzl concluded his book about the Jewish state. To today's ears, they may sound a little flowery, but at the time they conveyed a revolutionary message: 'The world will be liberated by our freedom, enriched by our wealth, magnified by our greatness. And whatever we attempt there for our own benefit will redound mightily and beneficially to the good of all mankind.'[8]

There is no ignoring the fact that neither Herzl nor the first Zionist leaders had any idea of the magnitude of Arab nationalism and the opposition that mass Jewish immigration would arouse among the Arabs of Palestine. Had they foreseen this, perhaps they would eventually have despaired of the idea of Jews settling in an Arab-Muslim Middle East. But it is not true to say that they saw the future Jewish state as a country without Arabs, as it is fashionable to argue today. Israeli journalist and writer, Uri Avnery, writes: 'Zionism entirely ignored the population living in Palestine. It envisaged a homogeneous nation-state, according to the late 19th century European model, with as few non-Jews as possible.'[9] There is not the slightest factual basis for this assertion. In no way does this quotation correspond to the ideas of Herzl and his colleagues. Non-Jews play a very important role in his utopia, *Altneuland*, so much so that most of the propaganda of the xenophobic opposition party represented by Dr Geyer is directed at them. Herzl's audacious response is expressed through the figure of Steineck, the liberal architect, especially during a political gathering in Neudorf, a village near the Jezreel Valley:

> We stand and fall by the principle that whoever has given two years' service to the New Society as prescribed by our rules, and has conducted himself properly, is eligible to membership no matter what his race or creed. I say to you, therefore, that you must hold fast to the things that have made us great: to liberalism, tolerance, love of mankind. Only then is Zion truly Zion!

Who are these non-Jews? It is not stated clearly, but the text leaves no doubt that they include the Arabs in Palestine. Over and over again Rashid Bey explains to Kingscourt, the tourist, the great benefits enjoyed by the Arab peasants as a result of the Jewish settlers' activities, how their income has increased, and how everything has prospered as a result of the Jewish immigration: 'The Jews have enriched us. Why should we be angry with them?' And then he adds: 'Our houses of worship stand side by side, and I always believe that our prayers, when they rise, mingle somewhere up above, and then continue on their way together until they appear before Our Father.' Moreover, in order to make it quite clear that the Arabs really do feel that they are the object of Dr Geyer's propaganda, Herzl has Rashid Bey say, 'So long as the Geyer policy does not win the upper hand, all will be well with our common fatherland.'

Thus not only is *Altneuland* society emphatically not presented as a homogeneous Jewish society, but the question of minorities and their treatment occupies a prominent place in the political process of the future Jewish state. Dr Geyer's party is opposed by a coalition which defends non-Jews' rights and regards the question of their treatment by the Jewish majority as the touchstone of Zionism's commitment to humanistic principles. This coalition's motto is quite simply, 'As a human being, you are my brother.' Unsurprisingly, given the fact that his book is a utopia, Herzl displays a considerable degree of naivety, and he thinks – in the form of Rashid Bey's words – that the economic benefit that the Arabs derive from the Jewish settlers will override national sentiments and the anticipated opposition to Jewish settlement.

Herzl showed the same naivety in the reply he gave to Yussef Diya'uddin Al-Khalidi, at the time (1899) Mayor of Jerusalem and a former member of the Ottoman Parliament. Al-Khalidi sent Herzl a letter via the Chief Rabbi of France, Zadok Kahn, in which, although acknowledging the Jews' rights to Palestine, he warned Herzl not to put the Zionist idea into practice: 'The idea is fine and just. Who can doubt the Jews' rights to Palestine?' Nevertheless, he opposed its implementation. Even if the Sultan in Constantinople were agreeable, it would be a mistake to assume that one day Herzl would be able to attain Palestine:

Zionism, in its present geographical sense, must necessarily come to an end
... otherwise the Jews of Turkey will be in great danger. ... Somewhere else
must be found for this unfortunate people. This would be the fairest and
most just undertaking. But, in the name of God, the world is big enough,
there are still uninhabited areas ... let Palestine be left alone.[10]

Herzl replies to him, in the manner of Rashid Bey, by lauding the major advantages that the Jews' settlement in Palestine will bring about. He addresses the sole
point raised by Al-Khalidi in objection to Zionism: the question of the future of
the non-Jewish population in the proposed Jewish state. He dismisses any possibility of non-Jews being expelled from the future State (and this appears in
French in the text): 'Mais qui donc songerait à les en éloigner?' – 'But who
would think of sending them away from there?'[11] Clearly, in Herzl's view,
Zionism's attitude to non-Jews, or in contemporary terms the 'Other', is to some
extent the ethical core of Zionism. In one of the last chapters of *Altneuland*, he
shows his hero and double, Frédéric Loewenberg, deep in thought in Jerusalem's
Temple which has been rebuilt (not on the Temple Mount):

> Jews had prayed in many temples, splendid and simple, in all the languages
> of the Diaspora. The invisible God, the Omnipresent, must have been
> equally near to them everywhere. Yet only here was the true Temple. Why?
>   Because only here had the Jews built up a free commonwealth in which
> they could strive for the loftiest human aims. They had had their own
> communities in the Ghettoes, to be sure; but there they lived under oppres-
> sion. In the *Judengasse*, they had been without honour and without rights;
> and when they left it, they ceased to be Jews. Freedom and a sense of broth-
> erhood were both needed. Only then could the Jews erect a House to the
> Almighty God Whom children envision thus and wise men so, but who is
> everywhere present as the Will-to-Good.[12]

Despite the archaic tone of these thoughts, there is nothing old-fashioned about
them, and they remain as valid today – if not even more so – as when Herzl
expressed them more than a century ago.

What would be the status of the Arab minority?

The status of the Arab minority in the future Jewish state greatly exercised the
minds of the Zionist leadership and the heads of Palestine's Jewish community.
In the early years of Zionist settlement, the question largely lay dormant.
However, following the 1905 Young Turks revolution, which led to an upsurge
in national Arab opposition to Jewish settlement activities, it came to occupy a
prominent place in Zionist writing and thought. The partition solution, which
was endorsed by Ben-Gurion in the 1930s and accepted by the overwhelming
majority of the Zionist movement following the Second World War, made it
clear that the Jewish community in Palestine and the Zionists alike understood

that there was no alternative to a territorial compromise in order to enable the two peoples to live side by side. Certainly, nothing in the Zionists' thinking or actions could have prevented their acceptance of the UN General Assembly resolution, and when this received majority approval at Lake Success in 1947, a spontaneous outbreak of jubilation erupted among the Jews of Palestine, paralleled by equally intense Arab opposition to the very idea of partitioning the country.

All parts of the Zionist movement held that the Arab minority in the Jewish State would enjoy equal rights. Ben-Gurion made repeated efforts to reach an agreement with the heads of the Arab community, as he indicates in detail in his book on the subject,[13] but these came to an abrupt end in 1936 with the outbreak of the Great Arab Revolt. In light of the ensuing rioting and attacks on Jewish localities, Ben-Gurion came to believe that what was taking place was a clash between two national movements, rather than a clash of economic interests along the lines of workers versus 'effendis'. Earlier, in his talks with Arab leaders Moussa Alami, Georges Antonios and Riad al-Solh, Ben-Gurion had accepted the existence of a national Arab (Palestinian) movement in the country. Independent of the political aspect of partition, his view of the world required him to respect the rights of non-Jews. In *Our Neighbours and Us* he wrote:

> We must remember that these rights [the Jews' rights to develop the country and make a livelihood from it] are also enjoyed by the rights of those already living there – and they must not be infringed. The vision of social justice and equality between peoples that the Jewish people have cherished for three thousand years, together with the vital interests of the Jewish people in the Diaspora and even more so in the Land of Israel – absolutely and unconditionally require the rights and interests of the country's non-Jewish residents to be scrupulously preserved and respected.[14]

Zeev Jabotinsky, leader of the Revisionists – the Zionist Right that opposed partition – entirely agreed with this position. In his eyes, a Jewish state was one which had a Jewish majority. However, he went on to accept not only the principle of equal rights, which he considered to be self-evident, but also the principle that a Jewish state would have non-Jewish cultures, religious and national groups: in other words, in contemporary terms, a multicultural or multi-ethnic state. In his characteristically succinct fashion, he formulated his idea of the system of government which he envisaged for the future Jewish state as follows:

> We consider it a duty of honour and justice to demand for the Arab minority of the future Jewish state no less than what we demand for the Jewish minorities in the countries of the Diaspora. The law of the Land of Israel must guarantee the equality of citizens, languages, religions and a very large degree of 'personal autonomy' for every group of citizens who wish for it.[15]

Jabotinsky's positions are of special interest. In the 8 November 1923 issue of the Jewish Zionist weekly *Razviet* (published in Paris in Russian), in an introduction to his article 'The Iron Wall' he counter-attacks his left-wing foes who were accusing him of being 'the Arabs' enemy'. In defending himself, he clearly and incisively presents the basis of the conflict between Zionism and the Arab world. He refers respectfully to the Arabs' national aspirations, and rejects any idea of driving them out of Palestine. He declares himself willing to swear 'on our behalf and on behalf of our descendants' that 'we will never upset the balance of these equal rights, we will never expel anyone'. In his opinion, after the establishment of a Jewish force as a result of the 'iron wall', which he considers a prerequisite for any Arab accommodation with the Zionist movement, the two peoples 'will be able to co-exist peacefully and as good neighbours'.[16] In his book *The War and the Jew* (originally entitled *The Jewish War Front*), he proposes a draft constitution for what he calls a 'Hebrew Palestine', intended to assuage the fears of those who 'are truly and sincerely worried about the rights of the country's Arabs'. In it, Jabotinsky proves himself both a humanist and a realist, as well as a nationalist Jew. He does not deny that the presence of an Arab national minority in the nascent Jewish state is problematic: 'It is more pleasant to be a majority than a minority, even in the best circumstances imaginable,' he admits, but then goes on to say: 'The Jews, because of their very great distress, must absolutely have their own State.' The first chapter of the proposed constitution naturally addresses civil equality:

> 1. The principle must be established of equal rights for all citizens, irrespective of race, religion, language or class, without any restriction, in all walks of the country's public life – on the sole condition that nothing must be done to prevent any Jew from returning to his homeland, and automatically becoming a citizen there. 2. In any Cabinet headed by a Jew, the deputy head of the government shall be an Arab and vice versa. 3. There shall be proportional representation of Jews and Arabs in the duties imposed by the State as well as the benefits that it grants. 4. This rule shall apply to parliamentary elections, civil and military service, and budgetary allocations. It shall also apply to municipalities or mixed regional authorities.[17]

The draft provides that Arabic shall be an official language on the same footing as Hebrew, and that the two national groups, Jewish and Arab, 'shall be considered autonomous public bodies with identical legal status'.[18] The author does not rule out the possibility that the Arabs might choose to emigrate, but he envisages this only if they prefer this option over being part of a minority enjoying equal rights in the Jewish State. These are very modern, not to say postmodern views. Jabotinsky introduces into the Jewish State elements of bi-nationalism. He makes a distinction between 'nationality' and 'citizenship', and is prepared to recognize the national rights of each community, including Jerusalem's 300 Armenians and Transjordan's handful of Circassians. For the leader of the nationalist Right of the time, the Land of Israel existed on both sides of the Jordan, which also provides a partial explanation for his magnanimous approach and the generosity of the constitutional arrangements that he envisages for minorities.

In the same visionary spirit as Jabotinsky, the Arab minority's status and equality of civil rights are also to be found throughout the writings of David Ben-Gurion, as in the following example:

> How the Jewish State behaves towards its citizens will be an important factor – although not the only one – in our relationships with the Arab countries. To the extent that Arab citizens feel at home in our State ... and their status in no way differs from that of their Jewish counterparts, and is perhaps better than that of an Arab in an Arab country, and as long as the State honestly and consistently helps [the Arab sector] to catch up with the Jewish population's standard of living in economic, social and cultural terms, then Arab suspicions will shrink and a bridge will be built to a Jewish-Arab Semitic pact in the Near East.[19]

In complete contrast to the often-voiced claim that the Zionists ignored the existence of Palestine's Arabs, Ben-Gurion wrote, one year before the 1917 Balfour Declaration, that Palestine, on both banks of the Jordan, had an Arab population of more than one million, of whom three-quarters were in the West Bank alone:

> Their rights must not in any way and in any circumstances be infringed. It is just as unthinkable as well as impracticable to dispossess them of their land. This is not Zionism's goal. Its true goal and its real possibilities are not to conquer that which is already inhabited, but simply to establish ourselves where the country's present-day inhabitants have not yet settled.[20]

Ben-Gurion considered the Arab question fundamental to Zionism. In February 1937, at the height of the Great Arab Revolt, he was not afraid to declare: 'Obviously the country's Arab population has the right to self-determination and autonomy. We have no intention of depriving them of these rights or limiting them.'[21] Based on this approach – dictated by pragmatism and democratic principles alike – Ben-Gurion came to support the idea of dividing the country between the two rival national movements. But while nothing came of the vehement controversy which in 1937 followed the Peel Commission's recommendations to partition Palestine,[22] post-Holocaust realities and UN debates eased the way to achieving a pro-partition consensus. And so when the General Assembly passed its resolution on 29 November 1947, the Zionists supported the two-state solution. The Arab countries and the Palestinian leadership under the Mufti of Jerusalem rejected the resolution out of hand and declared war on Palestine's Jews. Caught up in the struggle for their existence, the heads of the Zionist movement and the Jewish community had scarcely taken the time to consider in depth the kind of system of government they wanted for the future Jewish state, but they were unanimous in their acceptance of the democratic principles on which the partition plan was based. Thus the Declaration of Independence, in a spirit of faithfulness to the UN Charter, guarantees complete equality of social and political rights to all the citizens of the State of Israel, irrespective of religion, race or sex, and extends its 'hand to all neighbouring states and their peoples in an offer of peace and good neighbourliness'. It also calls upon the 'Arab inhabitants of the State of Israel to preserve peace and participate in the upbuilding of the State on the basis of full and equal citizenship and due representation in all its provisional and permanent institutions'.

The critics of Zionism stress the gaps between Zionistic rhetoric and the actual practice of the Jewish state. But rhetoric itself is of significance and influences reality. Other national movements, including the Palestinian one, have maintained a discourse of a very different kind. On the other hand, a gap between the idea and its actual implementation is not an unknown phenomenon, particularly when this idea has to be implemented under conditions of a protracted, violent struggle. In fact, it is remarkable that despite the prolonged Arab–Israeli conflict, universalist ideals voiced round the turn of the century – well before the Holocaust – by such individuals as Moses Hess, Theodor Herzl and Max Nordau, have maintained a strong hold on the Zionist movement.

When the state was established and independence declared, hostilities were already raging and many of those who would become Palestinian refugees had already left the territory of the future Jewish state. The Etzion Bloc settlements near Jerusalem had fallen to the Jordanian Arab legion the day before the declaration of Israel's independence, and this reversal did not augur well for the ability of the ill-equipped Jewish community to confront the regular Arab armies. It comes as no surprise that doubts should have arisen in the minds of the future leaders of the nascent state concerning the status of the Arab population. Nevertheless, a promise of citizenship and full civil equality to the Arab population was included in Israel's Declaration of Independence. Shortly thereafter, on the eve of elections to the Constituent Assembly (later the First Knesset), Ben-Gurion ruled against the sceptics who were arguing that the war was not over and that Israeli Arabs had to be viewed as 'enemy aliens'. He came out in favour of granting citizenship and the vote to Arabs who were residing in the territory of the State, on the grounds that 'we must not start out with national discrimination'.

None of this is to deny the injustices perpetrated vis-à-vis the Arabs, particularly in Israel's early years, which included expulsions of the residents of a number of localities even after the end of actual hostilities, the imposition of a military administration in areas with an Arab population, and the massive expropriation of land – sometimes by means of military ordinances and without equitable compensation. Without the conflict and its harmful consequences, Israel's history, including its relations with the Arab minority, would obviously have been very different.

It is worth pointing out that while a substantial Arab minority remained in the Jewish State on the conclusion of Israel's War of Independence, not a single Jew was allowed to remain in the part of Mandatory Palestine which came under the control of the Arab armies during the war. The Jordanian army expelled even the population of the Jewish Quarter of the Old City of Jerusalem, most of them ultra-Orthodox Jews and non-Zionists who had refused to take part in the fighting. It is often and rightly argued that Israel's behaviour should be judged not by comparing it to that of neighbouring, non-democratic Arab states but by the standards of Western democracies. But notoriously, these standards too are not always respected in times of conflict and danger.

Undeniably, significant and painful deviations have occurred during Israel's history from Zionism's liberal rhetoric and from the text of the Declaration of Independence. But Zionism's two-part goal remains unchanged: a homeland for the Jewish people, and a democratic state that respects the principles of freedom and equality. However difficult the circumstances, these are things well worth striving for.

4 The Jewish State and Israeli democracy

The concept of a Jewish state in Israeli discourse

In the 1947 UN partition resolution on Palestine, in Israel's Declaration of Independence and also, as we shall see, in the rulings of Israel's Supreme Court, the term 'Jewish State' denotes a political entity within which the Jewish people exercises its right to self-determination. It does not suggest giving the Jewish religion dominant status or denying rights to the country's non-Jewish citizens. Hence the only way to deny legitimacy to the concept of the Jewish State is to deny the Jewish people the right to statehood. This is exactly what the Arab representatives and their supporters did in 1947 and have continued to do on numerous occasions since then.

However, in addition to the expression's original meaning, we must bear in mind how it has been used since the State of Israel came into being. It is important to properly understand the context of the reservations generated by Israel's definition as a Jewish state – not only by those who oppose this idea a priori, but also by some of those who are sincerely convinced that it would be better to drop this definition, or to downplay it because it is used as a pretext for a variety of injustices. Israel's religious parties and the Orthodox establishment have consistently argued that a Jewish state must have a Jewish character: by which they primarily mean the imposition in public life, to the greatest extent possible, of the standards of Orthodox Judaism (Halacha), as interpreted by them. Their favourite domain is that of personal status: marriage and divorce. The Jewish character of the state has thus become the central issue in Orthodox discourse as voiced in the ongoing public debates in Israel on questions of religion and state.

Some of those who oppose religious coercion tend to distance themselves from the very concept of a Jewish state. In doing so they are in fact accepting, quite wrongly, the Orthodox establishment's definition of what a Jewish state should mean. Many secular Israelis favour the full separation of Synagogue and State, or, as this demand is usually formulated, separating religious and governmental institutions. It is sometimes said that without this separation, the State cannot lay claim to being democratic. Some, accepting the religious establishment's argument that such separation would be incompatible with the State's declared Jewish character, draw the conclusion that it is that very Jewishness which is preventing Israel from developing into a genuinely liberal democracy. The mistake made here is a double one. On the one hand, if Israel were to decide to separate religion from the State – and it must be borne in mind that this principle is variously interpreted in those democracies which have adopted it – it would nevertheless not cease to be a Jewish nation-state, since this attribute is not dependent on religion being given official status. On the other hand, it is not true that full separation is the only democratic model of relations between religion and state. As we will see, there exist liberal democracies in which there is no such separation, and in some of these there is an official Church established by law. It must be stressed, however, that those democracies which do not separate religion and State nevertheless guarantee religious freedom for all and equality of citizens regardless of religious affiliation. In this area, there is no denying that the present-day situation in Israel is far from perfect, first and foremost with regard to matters of personal status, and that it fails to comply with international democratic standards. Moreover, although these standards do not require the separation of religion and State, nevertheless, given the state of affairs in Israel, substantial arguments can be advanced in support of such a separation (or of loosening the official connection between the two), including the fact that, unlike its counterparts in the United Kingdom and the Scandinavian countries, Israel's religious establishment is involved in politics in a problematic and controversial fashion.

Since the coalition of right-wing and religious parties first came to power in 1977, many of its opponents have argued that the increased influence of the religious establishment in Israel is at odds with the basically secular tradition of the Zionist movement. Some radical critics have reached the conclusion that the potential for this negative development lay in the Zionist idea itself, in the very concept of the 'Jewish state' which lends itself to religious interpretations. Zionism, according to these critics, never fully 'divorced' itself from traditional Jewish culture and thus could never be quite true to its self-image of a secular and modernizing national movement. However, this story, for all its Jewish and Israeli peculiarities, is in fact rather less unique than many would assume. The complicated and often uneasy history of the relationship between the Jewish national movement and traditional Judaism bears great similarities to the relations between other modern national movements and the traditional religions of their peoples.

A modern national movement is typically driven by a powerful desire for modernization; one of the important aspects of modernity is secularization. Since the French Revolution, such movements have typically been initiated and led by intellectuals who espoused the most progressive contemporary Western ideas and wished to give their people not only national liberation but also progress, modernity and enlightenment. Such a movement is often highly critical (not to say hostile) towards the religious establishment, considering it backward and responsible for stagnation. In turn, the establishment sets out to combat these tendencies, seeing in them a challenge to its spiritual and cultural control over society. However, over time, the national movement becomes more aware of religious tradition's hold over the people. This hold is typically stronger among the common people than among the elite, something which presents a particular challenge to the left-wing and socialist parties that have played a leading role in many modern national movements (including Zionism). The effect of this is often that the movement tends to make a compromise with organized religion – due not only to political considerations and a desire to harness religious sentiment to the national struggle, but often also because it has come to appreciate religion's contribution to national and popular culture.[1] When independence is gained, the State often strikes a balance of sorts between the national movement's initial vision, which was modern and secular, and the religious and traditional forces of society. The details of such an arrangement vary from country to country and are not set in stone. The balance is apt to shift, over time, in favour of the more religious or the more secular forces in society, as the case may be.

Thus, for example, the Irish national movement drew inspiration from the ideas of the French Revolution and struggled for a secular and non-confessional (i.e. uninfluenced by the Catholic–Protestant divide) republic. Many of its leaders initially belonged to the Protestant minority. Eventually, however, when the Irish Free State was established in 1922 after a partition which left Ulster's largely Protestant population outside the borders of Eire, it had a pronounced Catholic identity. The Constitution recognized the Roman Catholic Church as the country's national Church; divorce, abortion and birth control were banned, education was largely under Church control, and strict 'moral' censorship was imposed on art and literature. This state of affairs continued for several decades; then liberalizing and secularizing tendencies started gathering strength. At the end of the 1970s, the Church lost its official status (although the Irish Constitution still begins with the words: 'In the Name of the Most Holy Trinity'); censorship has been considerably reduced (but not wholly abolished); divorce was allowed in the wake of a constitutional amendment approved by a referendum (but abortion is still illegal); the Church has lost a great deal (though not all) of its influence in schools and on school curricula. Today Ireland is in every respect a modern European democracy which follows European human rights standards and is answerable to the European Court of Human Rights for upholding those standards. However, even before these reforms, and despite the criticism of the hold that the Church had over the State, no one doubted Ireland being part of the Western democratic world.

The Greek national movement – which emerged at the end of the eighteenth century and the beginning of the nineteenth mainly in the circles of intellectuals from the Greek diaspora (in Western European countries) under the influence of the Enlightenment – was originally a secular, Western-oriented and modernist movement. Nevertheless, in the independent Greek State the Orthodox Church was to attain official status and immense social and political influence. Its power was often deeply controversial. The 1975 Constitution, adopted after the collapse of the colonels' regime, retains the official status of the Church, with Greek Orthodoxy being defined as 'the prevailing religion'. Its clergy are paid by the State, which is required to provide Greek children with 'national and religious education' in the spirit of Orthodoxy. One and the same ministry is in charge of public education and Church matters, while the President swears allegiance in the name of the Holy Trinity. Only in 1988 was a law enacted authorizing teachers not affiliated with the Orthodox Church to teach in primary schools. Civil marriage was introduced in 1982. The concessions made to the religious establishment in the Greek case have been considerable but not irreversible, as shown in recent decades by the socialist governments which have considerably curbed Church influence in a number of areas, particularly State education. An example of this is the removal in the 1990s of the reference to religion from Greek identity cards, notwithstanding the protests of the Church. Greece's membership of the European Union has also contributed to better protection of human rights. Proselytizing is still forbidden by the Constitution, but, following a ruling by the European Court of Human Rights, can now be punished only in cases of 'undue influence', as opposed to merely seeking to persuade people to change their religion.

In Turkey, Atatürk's strict model of secular nationalism, on which the Turkish Republic was originally based, has been considerably softened over time. It was precisely the emergence of competitive democratic politics, and later the influence of liberal European norms, that increased the political influence of Islam and led to the abolition of some of the restrictions imposed on it. The state that the founder of Pakistan, Muhammad Ali Jinnah, had originally planned to establish for the Muslims of the Indian subcontinent was conceived by him as a pluralistic modern democracy. Over time, Pakistan has grown more and more Islamic; throughout this process, Islamist parties have not lacked wide popular support. Popular support for religious and fundamentalist parties is, of course, a well-known phenomenon in the contemporary Arab world, wherever a measure of free choice is afforded to the voters. Yet Arab nationalism, too, started as a predominantly modernist and secular movement, some of whose most prominent leaders and intellectuals belonged to the Christian minority. Since then, the steady 'Islamization' of Arab nationalism has caused many secularists, including Christians, to accept that Islamic culture is an important component of Arab national identity.

Zionism, which emerged as a modern national and overwhelmingly secular movement, was opposed by most of the Orthodox sector of Jewish society. The compromises that it has had to make with organized religion, both before and after the establishment of the state, are not a unique phenomenon. Moreover, when what is known as the 'status quo in matters of religion and state' in Israel was shaped, during the first years of Israel's independence (and to some extent even earlier, within the elected institutions of the Jewish community in Mandatory Palestine), there was no 'Atatürk' here who could impose a secular modernist vision on society from above, by authoritarian methods. Instead, David Ben-Gurion and other leaders of Labour Zionism had to operate within a multiparty parliamentary system with proportional representation, which denied their party (Mapai) a parliamentary majority and constantly forced it into coalitions, often with religious parties. In the 1950s, a massive influx of immigrants (who were given the vote immediately upon arrival), many of them from more traditional Jewish communities, changed the composition of the electorate considerably in favour of religious and traditional elements. This was reflected in the 'status quo' arrangements. In 1977, the coalition of Likud and religious parties, supported by the majority of those who came in the 1950s, ousted Labour and formed a government with a stronger religious component. But it must not be imagined that the 'status quo' in this field is a cut-and-dried state of affairs. It is perfectly possible to oppose religious coercion, chauvinism and xenophobia on the basis of Zionism's democratic and liberal tradition. In fact, no better ideological footing can be found if broad sectors of the Jewish population are to be rallied to this cause.

As the experience of past decades shows, fears that the nation is being 'engulfed' by Orthodox power have been greatly exaggerated. True, since the first coalition between the Right and the religious parties in 1977, the Orthodox establishment has made gains in several fields. The number of young men from ultra-Orthodox backgrounds who use their studies at religious seminaries (*yeshivot*) in order to legally evade military service has increased considerably, together with the number of students at ultra-Orthodox schools who do not receive a general education which would enable them to fit into a modern economy. There have been and continue to be grave instances of coercion, fanaticism and misuse of public funds. Nevertheless, there is no doubt that, looking at the overall picture, Israeli society today is in many respects more liberal and more secular than it was in the 1970s. The social, economic, cultural and technological developments which have brought about the country's modernization and its integration into the world of a global economy and global communications have proved stronger than the coalition politics which have repeatedly put the religious parties in a position of strength. The concepts of liberal democracy and human rights are now more solidly entrenched in public and political debate. The Supreme Court, which since the founding of the state has consistently defended civil rights against religious coercion, has over time, as part of its growing judicial activism, increased its readiness to interfere and overrule official decisions that infringe, directly or indirectly, religious freedom and civil equality.

Sabbath observance in public life (as opposed to the private sphere) has retreated very considerably. For example, when Israeli state television – the sole channel at the time – was inaugurated in 1968, Golda Meir's Labour government ruled that broadcasts should be interrupted for the duration of the Jewish Sabbath. The decision was appealed and the Supreme Court overturned it. With today's multi-channel TV, such a debate would be pointless, and no one thinks of trying to impose Sabbath observance in this field. Who in the 1970s could have imagined that 20 or 30 years later, calls for a compromise would be coming from Orthodox public figures, suggesting that the shopping centres should be closed on the Sabbath in return for agreeing to the opening of places of culture and leisure on that day? Faced with this proposal, secular circles pointed out that the compromise was irrelevant, because these places were opening in any case, with or without rabbinical agreement; there was therefore no need, on the part of the secular public, to agree to the closing of shopping centres that have opened in recent years. The law restricting the import of non-kosher meat is clearly in breach of democratic norms, but it has not prevented large numbers of non-kosher restaurants and food shops – far more numerous than in the 1970s – from operating throughout the country, including Jerusalem.

Furthermore, the Orthodox camp has lost the drawn-out 'who is a Jew?' debate (which had great symbolic, though only limited practical significance): it has failed to obtain – and has in fact ceased to press for – an amendment of the Law of Return which would have the State recognize Orthodox conversions only. Conversions to Judaism performed abroad by Reform and Conservative rabbis are recognized by the State for the purpose of the Law of Return and the argument now is over the status of non-Orthodox conversions performed in Israel.

While the Orthodox Rabbinate's monopoly in the area of personal status law, explicitly enshrined in a statute, remains untouched on a formal level, it has nevertheless been considerably dented and various ways have evolved of working round it, the chief of which is the legal recognition, in Israel, of civil marriages contracted by Israeli couples abroad. The 'Cyprus marriage' – a widely affordable option to which thousands of Israelis routinely resort – is the most popular way to circumvent the absence of civil marriage within Israel. Israel has become in recent decades, as part of a Western (but far from universal) trend, far more liberal in its attitude to gays and same-sex couples; its military is more liberal in this field than the US one. The status of religion in the state, which is far from satisfactory from the liberal viewpoint, will continue to be controversial in the future. But contrary to various alarmist predictions which have been voiced, the Jewish State does not resemble the Iran of the ayatollahs, nor is it moving in this direction. In principle, opposing religious coercion does not call for abandoning the notion of a Jewish state; as a matter of practical politics, such an approach can only harm this struggle.

The debate on religion and state has often been linked, since 1967, to the main political divide in Israeli society – the one that touches on the Arab–Israeli conflict and the Palestinian problem. In the major debate that has taken place in Israeli society since the Six Day War about the future of the West Bank and the Gaza Strip (which was evacuated in the summer of 2005 together with part of the northern West Bank), a close alliance has evolved between the Right and the religious parties. Maintaining permanent Israeli control over these territories has been justified on national and religious grounds, while giving up this control for the sake of peace and a refusal to dominate another people was regularly described, for many years, as 'un-Jewish and anti-Zionist'. During the intense public controversy in the wake of the Oslo Accords (1993 and 1995), some (though not all) of the opponents invoked the Jewish character of the state in order to argue that the approval of the accords by a slim parliamentary majority which included Arab members of the Knesset was illegitimate; instead, they demanded a 'Jewish majority'. This implied that a Jewish state, by definition, is a state in which only Jews can enjoy full citizenship, and the political rights of non-Jews, as such, should be limited. For some, the fact that this concept was repeatedly put to such reprehensible use undermined its legitimacy.

Furthermore, while Israel's establishment, morally as well as in terms of international legitimacy, was based first and foremost on the Jewish people's right to self-determination and independence in its homeland, for many years both the Right and a considerable proportion of the Centre were unwilling to acknowledge any right to self-determination on the part of the Palestinian people. Golda Meir, heading a Labour government, notoriously claimed that there was no such thing as the Palestinian people; the Palestinian Arabs, according to this logic, were not a distinct people entitled to self-determination but only a part of the 'Arab people', who had already established more than 20 independent states and thus had no need of another one. While this deplorable attempt to define the national identity of the Palestinian Arabs 'from outside', in accordance with Israeli interests, was fairly rapidly abandoned by the Labour Party, the Right took it over when Likud came to power in 1977 and clung to it for many years.

Over and above the security and political arguments against withdrawing from the occupied territories, and even beyond the historical and religious arguments advanced in justification of the right to keep them under Israeli control, right-wing governments have been strikingly unwilling to face up to the grave moral significance of the prolonged military rule imposed on a Palestinian population lacking basic civil rights. These governments have of course ruled out any possibility of Palestinian self-determination. The autonomy plan, which sought to give the Palestinians only a limited degree of self-administration, remained on paper. Over this period, the Israeli grip on the occupied territories tightened, primarily because of the Jewish settlements that were being implanted in increasing numbers. The reality which has come about on the ground is in breach of all democratic principles. Not only has it placed the Arab population under a military administration – supposedly temporary, but in fact lasting for decades – but it has also created two populations living in the same area under two different legal systems.

The advocates of this policy have defended it by pointing out the dangers to which Israel would be exposed if it left the territories, but also by portraying Israeli rule over the territories as a natural and legitimate continuation of the Zionist enterprise. However, there is a crucial difference between the two situations. Classical Zionism sought to establish a democratic state in which Jews would be the majority and the Arab population would enjoy equal rights. Within the Zionist movement there were different views on the idea of partition, but no disagreement on the principle of civil equality within the future Jewish state. No one in the Zionist mainstream (including the Revisionist Right and the religious Zionists) envisaged Jewish rule over Arab inhabitants deprived of political rights.

The ideology of the Right called for permanent control over the entire area between the Mediterranean and the Jordan. This would have required the extension of Israeli sovereignty (rather than the imposition of military rule) over the occupied territories and the granting of citizenship to everyone living there. However, this never came about, both because the annexation of the territories by Israel was not politically feasible due to international opposition, and because it was obvious that granting Israeli citizenship to the Arab inhabitants would turn Israel into a bi-national state. It is true that the autonomy plan worked out by Prime Minister Menachem Begin did include a provision which would enable all the Arab residents of the territories to opt for Israeli citizenship after the establishment of the Palestinian autonomy (while leaving the question of sovereignty in the territories open). Here, as on other important issues, Begin proved himself faithful to democratic principles, and to the liberal tradition of Revisionist Zionism. However, in the absence of agreement on autonomy, the military occupation regime became a permanent fact of life. Although right-wing and national unity governments during that period continued to be officially committed to Palestinian autonomy, declaring their readiness to resume negotiations to achieve a political settlement, there were good reasons to think that this was merely a façade that hid the desire to maintain the occupation indefinitely and to go on establishing settlements. Meanwhile, the idea of Israeli citizenship for the Palestinian inhabitants of the territories, which appeared in Begin's autonomy plan, vanished from Israeli official discourse.

The years of Yitzhak Shamir as prime minister were characterized by political stalemate and an ever firmer entrenchment of the occupation. Jewish settlement expanded throughout the territories, with the obvious intention of making a new partition impracticable, and at the same time ruling out, in practice, the possibility of genuine Palestinian autonomy. This deplorable process was presented by its supporters as the full and genuine realization of the Zionist dream. A large part of the Israeli public always opposed it, and, among a radical minority within the left-liberal camp, it certainly contributed to a growing disenchantment with Zionism itself. Some of those who adopted a critical or downright negative attitude towards the Jewish national movement and the idea of Jewish statehood have unfortunately failed to apply their critical faculties to Arab and Palestinian nationalism. Instead they practise a form of 'reverse discrimination' in favour of those subject to the occupation and fighting it. This has in some cases gone so far as 'understanding' and even condoning, explicitly or implicitly, cruel and inhumane methods of fighting. It has often been overlooked that the Palestinian national movement, well before the 1967 war, had fought the State of Israel with the declared aim of bringing about its destruction and, moreover, deliberately targeted civilians – no less so than after the occupation of the West Bank and Gaza. Moreover, not everyone has bothered to enquire too closely whether this movement, while undertaking the struggle for Palestinian independence, is even today genuinely prepared to accept Jewish independence.

The Jewish state and the rights of the Arab minority

The concept of a Jewish state has also been used in connection with the Arab minority's civil rights in order to justify discrimination between citizens according to their national identity. This has had the same effect as the use and abuse of this concept in justifying religious coercion and the desire to perpetuate the occupation: some of those for whom democracy and human rights are paramount have reached the conclusion that the Jewish character of the state is indeed incompatible with democratic values.

It must be remembered, however, that, for all the justified criticism that can be directed at it, the state has had to face serious objective difficulties, which its critics often tend to ignore. The first Zionist leaders dreamed of a state which would live in peace with its neighbours. In such a state they envisaged complete civil equality for the Arab population. But the Jewish State came into being, and has existed, under very different circumstances. No democracy in the world, when facing an emergency – whether a war, or threats of terrorism and major violence – will fail to take measures which deviate, sometimes to a great extent, from the rules which prevail in peacetime. This is not merely a matter of official legal measures. The public mood that is created by a state of tension and conflict, and the way it affects the actual behaviour of public officials and security forces, are often of even greater practical significance.

A notorious and extreme example is the Second World War incarceration in detention camps of the entire American civilian population of Japanese descent living on the West Coast of the United States, a large part of them US citizens, totalling more than 100,000 people, including entire families, for years on end. Security considerations were cited in justifying this decision, approved by the US Supreme Court, although in fact there was not a single instance of a hostile act committed by a person of Japanese descent in that area. Such a measure is scarcely conceivable today in any democracy, even in wartime. But the United States' 'war on terror' following 9/11, though it cannot of course be compared to the Second World War, has certainly created dilemmas and given rise to various criticisms in the field of human rights. The means used by Germany and Italy, mainly in the 1970s, or later by democratic Spain, in combating terrorism (sometimes including the suppression of supporters and sympathizers of terrorists) have also been controversial. France's war in Algeria generated both official emergency measures and egregious human rights abuses – not just in Algeria but in France itself. In Paris on 17 October 1961, when General de Gaulle was President, French police forces massacred scores (according to unofficial sources, between 200 and 300) Algerian demonstrators supporting the Front de Libération Nationale (FLN), drowning some of them in the River Seine. The facts were confirmed decades later by the publication of the police records. The French authorities failed to launch an enquiry following this frightful event, and no steps against those responsible were taken. The national and sectarian conflict in Northern Ireland, where for years on end in practice the Catholic population was deprived of genuine equality, has also given rise to numerous instances of official and unofficial wrongdoing incompatible with peacetime liberal-democratic practice and inconceivable in a non-conflict setting.

Israel declared a state of emergency immediately after its establishment, as the War of Independence raged. It has never been revoked. Both legally and as a matter of fact, the state of emergency in Israel is not a passing phenomenon in the context of an acute crisis, but rather a 'chronic disease' which is an integral part of the state's existence, with varying degrees of severity (as was the case for the Jewish community of Palestine in pre-state times also). It would be obviously wrong to tackle an emergency of this kind by applying the drastic measures to which democratic states resort in wartime. Precisely because the state of emergency in Israel is a continuous phenomenon, it is vital to try to limit its negative consequences as far as possible. On the other hand, the risks to which the state has been and continues to be exposed cannot be underestimated, nor can their cumulative effect on Israeli society be ignored. This remains true even if, as happens in situations of this kind, the threat to the country's security has sometimes been exaggerated, or used in order to justify unacceptable policies. Israel has known both more turbulent and relatively tranquil times, but it has not had one single day of real peace since its establishment. This state of affairs could not fail to exert a negative influence on the status of the Arab minority.

Israel was born out of a bitter and drawn-out ethnic civil war between the country's two peoples, which had started months before the state was proclaimed and invaded by the armies of the neighbouring Arab countries. At the end of hostilities, within Israel's borders there remained only a relatively small Arab population which had lost most of its leadership and was traumatized by the defeat. It did not constitute a threat. A wiser and more generous policy towards it would probably have contributed to a better integration of this minority in the new state. But the conflict with the neighbouring Arab states had not been resolved. They refused to recognize Israel's existence, encouraging or at least not preventing terrorist raids launched from their territory. They obstructed Israel's freedom of navigation (in the Suez Canal and the Gulf of Aqaba), stating that they remained in a state of war with an eye to a 'second round' with the goal of liberating Palestine. During the state's early years, it encountered particular difficulties trying to defend its long and permeable border with Jordan. In the territories on the other side of the ceasefire line, in the West Bank and the Gaza Strip there were other Palestinian Arabs, often with family ties in Israel, many of them eking out a precarious existence in the refugee camps. Gradually, these became hotbeds of cross-border terrorism. Israel had to protect itself against constant infiltration. Often it was a case of refugees trying to go home, but there were also armed and deadly infiltrations, which occurred in increasing numbers under the banner of a 'people's war of liberation' against the Jewish State, with Palestinian paramilitary groups established for this purpose on the other side of the border. It was felt necessary to impose strict controls over border areas, chiefly in order to prevent Arab villagers in those areas from cooperating with infiltrators. Such cases occurred – unsurprisingly, if only because in many cases members of the same family were involved on both sides.

This was the context in which the decision was taken to maintain, after the War of Independence ended, a military administration in 'border areas', subjecting the freedom of movement of their inhabitants to a system of military permits. In and of itself, this decision made sense in light of Israel's situation at the time, and parallels can readily be found. One example is Greece, which for years (under a democratic government) maintained military restrictions on the Turkish-origin population close to the border with Turkey, even though the border was quiet. In theory, the Israeli military administration did not discriminate against its Arab citizens as such. It did not apply to Haifa, or Jaffa, cities on the Mediterranean coast with sizeable Arab populations. Formally speaking, it applied to all border area residents. In practice, the restrictions affected Arabs only, while Jewish residents received 'general permits'. Israel's geography, its compactness and its snaking borders, resulted in most of the Arab population having to live under these restrictions, although in time they were gradually eased and the area subject to the military administration was progressively narrowed. The system was finally abolished in 1966, under Prime Minister Levy Eshkol's government, as part of its policy of liberalization in various fields.

This protracted chapter, with the inherently arbitrary nature of the military administration, largely shaped the climate of relations between the Jewish majority and the Arab minority. Inevitably, the outcome was resentment and bitterness. The wide-ranging powers available to the military governors were apt to be sometimes abused. In addition, this system remained in place well beyond the initial few years during which it was arguably justified. This is the period during which the Kafr Qassem massacre took place – an event which traumatized the entire Arab population, and shocked many Jewish citizens.[2] The border policemen who perpetrated this carnage were indicted and given prison sentences, only to be granted pardons and released after an unduly short period. It cannot be said that justice was done in this case. The military administration was also used and abused for ends which had little or nothing to do with security, and in particular, it would appear, in order to help provide Mapai (the Labour party which was in power at the time) with Arab votes at election time. Because of the permits system in force at the time, many villagers depended for their jobs and livelihoods on the good (or bad) will of the governors, who favoured some and penalized others. The imposition of military administration made it easier to carry out massive expropriations of Arab land, particularly in the 1950s. These were carried out on the basis of laws that allowed the expropriation of private land 'for public use', with compensation to the owners. Undeniably, the absorption of the massive influx of Jewish immigration during this decade, in numbers which far exceeded the entire Jewish population of Mandatory Palestine, made it necessary to build new housing on a large scale; land expropriations were thus inevitable. But while the 'public use' in question was mainly (though not exclusively) for the benefit of the Jewish population, most of the lands expropriated were taken from Arabs – so much so that that many a village lost most of its land. This was a major blow to a traditional peasant society, whose attachment to the soil goes far beyond its economic value only. The authorities countered charges of discrimination by asserting that the development projects benefited the Arab population as well in various ways. There was some truth in this, especially as regards the infrastructure that is used by both populations, and it should be pointed out that not a few Arab citizens are today living in the new towns, such as Upper Nazareth and Carmiel, that were constructed on land expropriated from Arabs. Nevertheless, it cannot be seriously maintained that in all this the interests of both communities were taken into account in equal measure. All in all, there is no denying that Israeli governments failed in their duty to look after the interests of all of the state's citizens equally – as regards both land expropriations and development projects.

When it comes to political rights and freedoms, ever since Israel's first parliamentary elections the Arab citizens have made active use of the parliamentary, public and legal instruments provided by Israeli democracy – though it should be noted that while the military administration existed 'in border areas', it adversely affected the degree of political freedom enjoyed by the Arab population living there. However, Knesset records as well as the Arabic-language press of the time bear witness to the fact that already during this period Arab parliamentarians and journalists did not hesitate to challenge the government and subject it to bitter criticism, including over the most sensitive issues, such as the military administration itself, the refugee problem, and Israel's relations with neighbouring Arab countries. In Israel's early years, the Arab protest vote benefited mainly Maki, the Israeli Communist Party – a party with mixed Jewish and Arab membership whose main support came from the Arab electorate. The positive aspect of this vote was that the party, while strongly critical of the government and opposed to the Zionist ideology, remained faithful to its support for the idea of partition and the existence of Israel, adopted in 1947 in conformity with the Soviet 'line'. During Israel's War of Independence, the Arab as well as Jewish communists condemned what they called the 'war of aggression' waged by the 'fascist' leadership of the Mufti of Jerusalem and the invading armies of the 'reactionary' Arab regimes against the State of Israel. They showed great steadfastness in defending this unpopular position, which naturally resulted in them being vilified as traitors. Maki was thus a relatively moderate party, basically loyal to the State.

As long as 'reactionary regimes' were in power in the countries surrounding Israel, Israeli communists attacked them as 'agents of imperialism' and dissociated themselves from their hostility toward Israel. However, with the reversal in Soviet foreign policy, marked by the anti-Zionist and anti-Semitic line of Stalin's last years, and as 'progressive' nationalist and anti-Western regimes came to power in the Arab world, Maki changed direction – a change that was obviously not unwelcome to its Arab activists and voters. From the mid-1950s on, it demonstrated solidarity with Egypt's president, Gamal Abdel Nasser, who had become Israel's No. 1 enemy in the region. Because of the party's considerable influence in the Arab sector, this political about-turn gave rise to acrimonious comments, particularly during the 1956 Suez crisis, which did nothing to improve relations between the State and the Arab minority. The party's solidarity with countries that rejected Israel's right to exist further strengthened the Israeli leadership's suspicions with regard to the Arab population in general – despite the fact that most Arab votes at the time still went to Zionist parties (many of them to Mapam, a left-socialist party which, more than any other

Zionist party, integrated Arab citizens in its ranks and supported their rights). The military administration and emergency laws were sometimes used against communist militants and, more often, against more radical (i.e. more openly supportive of Nasser) nationalist groups. However, on the whole, given the country's situation, political freedom was maintained at a relatively high level, even during the 1950s, and even more so after the abolition of the military administration. It must be remembered that all of this took place during the Cold War, at a time when the Communist Party was being hounded in the United States and banned in the Federal Republic of Germany. In contrast, speeches were made from the Knesset's rostrum and articles published in the press supporting not only the Soviet Union and its anti-Israeli policies, but also its regional allies in open conflict and in an official state of war with Israel.

The personality and policies of President Nasser triggered a wave of enthusiasm throughout the Arab world, for a number of reasons that went far beyond the Arab–Israeli conflict. Israel's Arab community, naturally, did not remain unaffected. Nasserite ideology was a blend of pan-Arab nationalism, a desire for modernization, socialism, and opposition to Western colonialism and imperialism (particularly British colonialism, which in the early 1950s was still solidly established in the Middle East, especially in the Suez Canal Zone). Nasser denounced Israel as an illegitimate entity, a bastion of Western imperialism at the heart of the Arab world, and a geographical obstacle to Arab unity. He made public pronouncements to the effect that armed confrontation with Israel was unavoidable. In the future, he promised, once the construction of a new, modern and progressive Egyptian society had made the country strong enough, the time would come for the liberation of Palestine. There was undoubtedly an element of delaying tactic in this rhetoric, enabling Nasser to repel the calls of radical circles in the Arab world for an immediate showdown with Israel.

Israeli communists' support for the Nasserite regime, perceived as a progressive force in the Arab world, grew with the development of its ever closer ties to the Soviet Union. There was an obvious contradiction between the party's continuing affirmation of Israel's right to exist and its declared support for a peaceful solution of the conflict, and its support for an Arab leader who openly declared his desire to destroy Israel and encouraged terrorist Palestinian raids mounted from the Gaza Strip. This problem was solved by the Israeli communists with the help of their movement's accustomed dialectical ingenuity. They managed to give consistent support for the Egyptian president's 'progressive' and 'anti-imperialist' stance, without acknowledging his and his regime's bellicose statements about the liberation of Palestine and destruction of Israel. Sometimes the point was made that the party remained in favour of a peaceful solution to the conflict and was opposed to (usually unspecified) 'extremist rhetoric'.[3] But it was the Israeli leadership, allegedly in collusion with imperialist forces against the 'progressive' regimes of the Arab world, which was systematically accused of being responsible for all the tensions in the region, and for the danger of war. Since these regimes were part of the anti-imperialist camp led by the Soviet Union, the question of their implacable hostility to Israel was of no importance.

As for the content of the peace settlement which was to be aspired to, Maki declared that it must guarantee the respect of the rights of the Palestinian people, including the right of self-determination, as well as the respect of Israel's right to exist. It supported the 'right of return' of Palestinian refugees to Israel in accordance with UN Resolution 194. Since the tragedy of the refugees split many families in the Arab community, this stance was only natural for a party which increasingly drew its constituency from the Arab population. No less naturally, this demand was always perceived by the Israeli establishment and Jewish public opinion as a threat to the country's very survival. The Communist Party's attitude to Israel's borders was not quite clear, all the way up to the Six Day War. It did not recognize the 'Green Line' (the 1949 armistice line) as Israel's definitive border. Some militant figures called for an Israeli withdrawal to the borders of the 1947 partition plan. The official line, however, was that the border would have to be negotiated between the parties, a formula which at least hinted at the need for Israel to make territorial concessions.[4] These formulae masked very real differences of opinion within the party, which would eventually result in its 1965 split.

During the 1960s, the Syrian Ba'ath Party regime, which was even more implacable than Nasser's Egypt in its hostility to Israel and its support for the 'people's war of liberation' waged by the Palestinian organizations, became a major client-state of the Soviet Union. Maki supported this regime too. In February 1966, a military coup brought the leftist wing of the Ba'ath Party to power. The new regime's leaders wasted no time in openly calling for Israel to be wiped off the map by force, and stepped up their support for the sabotage and terror operations launched from Syrian territory by members of the Palestinian Fatah movement. This policy, and the resultant Syrian–Israeli clashes, greatly contributed to the tensions that eventually paved the way to the June 1967 war. As the situation along the Israeli–Syrian border (where disputes over water resources also played a role) continued to deteriorate, in addition to the repeated declarations by Arab leaders denying Israel's right to exist, tensions developed within the Communist Party. Some of its Jewish leaders came to the conclusion that it was no long possible to close their eyes to the threats uttered by Arab nationalists. After the split, the Jewish wing retained the name Maki, while the mainly Arab wing adopted the name Rakah (New Communist List). The latter, with its overwhelmingly Arab membership and electorate, carried on the Israeli communist tradition. For many years it was headed by Meir Vilner, a Jewish parliamentarian who unconditionally supported the Soviet line. The party nevertheless condemned the cross-border attacks carried out by the Fatah (without acknowledging their Syrian sponsorship) and denounced the PLO, set up in 1964 by the Arab League under Ahmed Shukeiri, as an extremist and maverick organization prejudicial to the Palestinian cause.[5] All this mirrored the Soviet policy of the time: hostility to Israel while still acknowledging its right to exist; support for 'progressive' Arab regimes that vociferously denied this right without adopting their view on this particular point (and usually ignoring it); blaming Israel for the military tension in the area with occasional half-hearted acknowledgement of the fact that 'Arab extremists' also contributed to it. Such a stance by a party representing a large part of the Arab minority was problematic from the viewpoint of the Israeli government and Jewish public opinion, but came to be accepted as part of an uneasy status quo.

The Communist Party (Rakah) took an unambiguously anti-Israeli stance during, and on the eve of, the June 1967 war. It did not waver as the Arab world mobilized on the eve of the Six Day War, in the face of repeated threats to wipe Israel off the map, nor after the closing of the Gulf of Aqaba at the Straits of Tiran and the blockade against the Jewish State ordered by Nasser. Rakah defined the war as an act of aggression by Israel (unlike Maki, which considered it a war of self-defence). In the aftermath of the war, Rakah called for Israel's withdrawal from the occupied territories – first unconditionally, then as part of a political settlement, while ignoring the refusal of the Arab states, at that stage, to negotiate or to make peace with Israel. It now adopted the Green Line – the 'June 1967 borders' – as the legitimate borders of the State of Israel.

During the 1973 Yom Kippur war, Rakah fully identified with Egypt and Syria. It should, however, be noted that there were quite a few manifestations of identification with Israel among the country's Arab population, during both the Six Day War and the Yom Kippur war. As might be expected, in the wake of the new situation, Israeli Arabs came to identify more closely with the population of the occupied territories; the Palestinian dimension of their identity was strengthened. The first *intifada*, which broke out in 1987, was openly supported by the Communist Party and by the even more radical nationalist and Islamist forces which had entered the Arab public arena. The *intifada* was largely an unarmed popular uprising, albeit not without its lethal terrorist attacks. Those who identified with it did not always take the trouble to make clear precisely what it was that they identified with, and with what they were not prepared to identify.

Since the beginning of the second *intifada* in September 2000, statements by most of the elected representatives of the Arab population have become more virulent, and not infrequently they can be heard endorsing the armed struggle against the State – both by the Palestinians and by the Lebanese Hizbollah movement whose praises have been sung by several Arab Knesset members, even when this organization continued its cross-border incursions after Israel's withdrawal from Lebanon in 2000. Some of the most open displays of political support for those fighting the state occurred during the armed conflict between Israel and Hizbollah in the summer of 2006. These expressions – sometimes going well beyond the bounds of free expression in a democracy, even in peacetime – have outraged the Jewish public, increasing its mistrust and harming the struggle for the rights of Arab citizens. Israel has to face a situation for which few, if any, precedents can be found in the history of modern democracies: a large national minority, most of whose elected leaders express open solidarity with the enemy during actual armed conflict. It would not be easy to find a parallel, in the history of majority–minority relations in the free world, to the poem entitled 'The Great Crossing' published soon after the Yom Kippur War by the Arab Communist Member of the Knesset Tawfik Zayad, in which he wrote that his heart was full of joy when he saw the Syrian tanks liberate the Golan Heights and the Egyptian army cross the Suez Canal. The hostile rhetoric of Arab politicians and public figures, and the Jewish public's predictable reactions to it, tend to obscure the fact that only a tiny proportion of Israel's Arab minority has over the years taken part in terrorist violence – a state of affairs which is not self-evident in the context of the bitter national conflict pitting the two peoples against each other (with Israel's Arab citizens considering themselves part of the Palestinian people).

One of Israeli democracy's deficiencies is the fact that for decades there has been no Cabinet minister representing the Arab community. The fact that the voice of this community could not be heard in the Cabinet during debates about political matters and the allocation of budgetary resources has obviously affected its status in a negative way, both practically and symbolically. Among other things, this has contributed to its manifest under-representation in the various administrative and public bodies appointed, wholly or partly, by the government, including those that deal with matters directly affecting this community. No ministerial portfolio was given to a representative of the country's Arab population until the appointment in spring 2007 of Raleb Majadele, an Arab Labour Party MK, to the post of Minister of Science, Culture and Sport in Ehud Olmert's Cabinet. This is a significant step in advancing the civic status of the Arab minority, which clearly should have been taken much earlier.

Admittedly, political circumstances did not, through much of Israel's history, facilitate the inclusion of Arab ministers in Israel's Cabinets, but it must also be said that no particular awareness of the problem, or eagerness to solve it, was displayed by the Israeli political establishment. Throughout the years of Labour ascendancy, i.e. up to 1977, when this party and its allies had Arab deputies who could have been promoted to Cabinet level (and some of whom served as deputy ministers), the explanation given was that since Israel's Cabinet had to take operational security decisions, Arab representatives should not participate in these discussions, just as Arab citizens are not required to serve in the army (a somewhat dubious parallel). The Likud-led coalitions which came to power next had no Arab parliamentarians (although the Likud Party itself regularly had an MK belonging to the small Druze community). Under the second Rabin government, from 1992 onwards, some of the Arab members of the Knesset, particularly those from the 'Democratic Front for Peace and Equality', centred around the Communist Party, formed part of the parliamentary majority that sustained the government by its votes, without belonging formally to the ruling coalition or taking seats in the Cabinet. It became possible to put this informal coalition together both in the wake of the Oslo Accords, and as a result of the major efforts made by Rabin's government to improve the circumstances of the Arab minority. Members of the Knesset from Arab or Arab-majority parties were thus, for the first time, able to bring considerable influence to bear on governmental policy.

In 1999, Labour's Ehud Barak became prime minister as a result of a direct election in which he garnered a large majority of Arab votes. Arab factions in the Knesset, which, over and above offering full political support for Arafat's Palestinian Authority, did not flinch from occasionally justifying Palestinian violence during the peace process, were not invited to join his coalition; in fact most of them had made it known beforehand that they were not interested in sharing governmental collective responsibility. Undoubtedly, Barak made a deplorable mistake by failing to offer a ministerial portfolio to the Arab Labour MK Nawaf Massalha (who was appointed deputy foreign minister instead), thereby missing the opportunity to redress a long-established inequality in Israeli politics. Not until 2001 did a non-Jewish parliamentarian join Ariel Sharon's national unity government, in the form of Labour's Salah Tarif, who became minister without portfolio. Mr Tarif, a member of the Druze community, declared that he would defend the interests of the entire Arab population.

All in all, it is obvious that the status of Israel's Arab minority falls short of the standards that have come, in recent decades, to be expected of a liberal democracy – always bearing in mind that these are, naturally, peacetime standards. It should be remembered that in a modern state, where the individual is required to use public services and have dealings with public officials ranging over many aspects of everyday life, the formal legal equality of a minority, be it national, linguistic or religious, will be of limited value only unless it is underpinned by genuinely equal treatment on the part of public and quasi-public functionaries, high and low. Discrimination and prejudice towards the minority are not necessarily the result of deliberate decisions 'from above' – although this too has happened. Often, they are the consequence of neglect, a lack of sensitivity to the minority's specific needs, the absence of adequate representation in decision-making settings and, generally speaking, the negative and suspicious attitude of public officials as well as on the part of the general public. The Arab citizens' exemption from military service dates back to Israel's earliest days and was probably the only option available at the time. However, for a broad section of the Jewish population, this exemption from what is considered a fundamental civic duty, and which the Druze community, for example, willingly undertakes, weakens the validity of the claim to completely equal rights. However, this attitude is unjustified, given that the Arab citizens are not required to serve and thus cannot be said to 'dodge' their obligations in this respect. In fact, the Arab citizen is not offered the option of serving by the State – though small numbers of Muslim and Christian Arab youngsters do volunteer.

On the assets side of this balance sheet, it must be pointed out that the Israeli-Arab population has made vast strides in all areas since the state has been in existence – not only measured absolutely, which after all is a natural result of Israel's overall development and progress, but also in relative terms, compared with the Jewish population. There is no justification for the usual practice, on the part of many civil rights organizations, of blaming the various gaps and disparities between the two populations – economic, social and educational – solely on the State and its policies. In many areas, the gap between Jews and Arabs was far greater in 1948. Hence it may be said that rather than creating the gaps or widening them, the net impact of the Jewish State has been to narrow them –

though not in sufficient measure. By way of comparison, it should be noted that the gap between the immigrant Muslim minority and majority society in Western European countries is greater, in many respects (even for the second and third generations), than its equivalent in Israel. It should also be noted that the Christian Arab community, which had achieved a relatively high level of development and modernization before the State of Israel came into being, is today very close to the average level of the Jewish majority and in some respects, even exceeds it.[6] Thus the gaps are in fact not between Jews and Arabs as such, but rather between Jews and Muslims (though the latter are, of course, the great majority of Israeli Arabs).

Great progress toward effective equality of rights took place in the 1990s, when the second Rabin government, among other things, put an end to the discrimination in the realm of family allowances from which the Arab population had suffered for two decades. A law from the 1970s gave the families of those who had served in the military far larger allowances than those given to families which did not have anyone who had been in the armed services. If the State exempts a national minority from doing military service (without offering it alternative national service), it is unfair to make a welfare benefit dependent on meeting unrealistic military obligations.[7] Since the 1990s, the Arab public has also benefited from the general trend of increasing judicial activism on the part of Israel's Supreme Court in its capacity as the High Court of Justice (which hears petitions against public authorities). This trend has resulted, among other things, in greater readiness to scrutinize any official act that allegedly infringes, directly or indirectly, the principle of civil equality. In 1992 the Knesset passed two basic laws dealing with human rights: the Basic Law on human dignity and liberty, and the Basic Law on the freedom of occupation. The then President of the Supreme Court, Aharon Barak, described these laws as a 'constitutional revolution', since they allowed the Court to apply judicial review on human rights issues to Knesset legislation as well. Since the Court has interpreted the term 'human dignity' broadly, so as to include various rights not explicitly mentioned in the law, including the right to equality, this right is now recognized as a constitutional principle that can be defended in the Supreme Court against any alleged violation, administrative or legislative.

In 1998, the Knesset passed two bills, one amending the law on State corporations, and another concerned with civil service appointments. For the first time, these introduced the notion of 'adequate representation of the Arab population' on the boards of State corporations and in the civil service, if necessary by giving preference to candidates from the Arab minority. The Supreme Court interpreted them as indicative of the legislature's adoption of the principle of 'affirmative action' wherever the Arab population is either not represented or under-represented. This is clearly the case in the two areas covered by the laws: in the civil service the Arab community, which comprises almost a fifth of the population, is represented by only 5 per cent of the employees, and among the senior grades, the under-representation is still greater. But the Court also extended the application of this principle to other State and public bodies, such as the Israel

(State) Lands Authority. In its reply to the petition submitted to the Court by civil rights organizations, the government's attorney declared that the government viewed the one existing Arab member of the Authority's governing Council (out of 24) as sufficient, and that it did not consider that it had any legal obligation to add other Arab members to this body. The High Court justices disagreed with this view. The judgment in HC 6924/98 stresses the fact that the decisions of the Authority are of paramount importance to the Arab population, who for a very protracted period had been completely unrepresented on its Council. The justices held that according to the norms of Israeli law as these have developed recently – inter alia following the adoption of the two laws on affirmative action – it is not sufficient merely to relate to equality as a 'passive concept', i.e. the prohibition of discriminating against someone on the grounds of religion or national origin. The authorities must adopt active measures in order to ensure adequate representation of the Arab population. This ruling demonstrates how the Court's 'judicial activism' has transformed its role from the traditional protection of legal rights in response to petitions by aggrieved individuals to scrutinizing official policy from the viewpoint of general legal principles, which in this case means, in fact, protecting the collective rights of a national minority.

In the landmark Kaadan ruling, the Court dealt with the issue of allocation of State-owned land. Adel Kaadan, an Arab citizen, had made an application to buy a plot of land in the Jewish communal village of Katzir in the Galilee. His application was turned down on the grounds that the land, which was State land, on which the part of the village in question was built had been transferred to the Jewish Agency and the Jewish National Fund, two Zionist movement paragovernmental institutions. The Court, in response to a petition, ruled that when allocating public land the State was not authorized to discriminate between citizens on the basis of national origin, just as it is not allowed, by transferring land to third-party organizations, to shirk its obligation to treat all citizens equally. This decision constitutes an important precedent with regard to the status of the Zionist movement's institutions in Israel. It means that they cannot be used in order to circumvent the principle of equality between citizens, which is binding on all State institutions. The High Court ruling notes that when it comes to land allocation, the Arab public has been discriminated against for years: 'In practice, the State of Israel allocates land to Jewish community settlements only', the judgment states. 'It has been established that the Administration's policy today in practice treats Arabs separately and unequally' (Section 30).[8] The court held that no legal support can be provided for a policy which is designed to prevent an Arab citizen from buying a house in such a locality. The judgment contains an in-depth analysis of the relationship between Israel's democratic system, based on equality of civil rights, and its nature as a Jewish State. With regard to charges of a supposed clash between the Jewish nature of the state and the principle of equality, the judgment reads as follows:

> The answer is that there is no such clash. We do not accept that the values of the State of Israel as a Jewish state can justify ... discrimination by the

state between the citizens of the state on the basis of religion or national origin ... The values of the State of Israel as a Jewish and democratic state, inter alia, are based on the Jewish people's right to exist independently as a sovereign state ... Indeed, the Jewish people's return to its homeland derives from the State of Israel's values as both a Jewish and a democratic state ... Those values which characterize the State of Israel give rise to several conclusions: for example, one conclusion is that Hebrew should be the country's primary official language, and national days and official holidays must reflect the national rebirth of the Jewish people; a further conclusion is that the Jewish heritage shall constitute a key element in Israel's religious and cultural heritage, as well as additional conclusions that there is no need for us to stress. But the values of the State of Israel in no way imply that the state should discriminate between its citizens. True, 'the Jewish people established the Jewish state, this is the beginning and from there we set out on our path' (Justice M. Heshin in *Isaacson*, p. 548). But once the state has been established, it must treat its citizens equally ... Every member of the minorities who live in Israel enjoys complete equality of rights. True, a special key to enter the house is given to the members of the Jewish people (see *Law of Return*–1950). But once somebody is in the house as a citizen under the law, he enjoys equal rights, just like all the other members of the household ... Hence there is no contradiction whatsoever between the values of the State of Israel as a Jewish and democratic state, and complete equality between all of its citizens.[9]

Another landmark decision, adopted by the Supreme Court in December 2001, reflects its willingness to interfere in policy decisions so as to protect a minority's collective rights against a discriminatory policy. In response to a petition filed by Arab local authority heads, the Court instructed the State to take steps to ensure that the budget allocated to the Arab sector by way of Project Renewal financing for the nationwide upgrading of existing housing projects should not be less than that due to it pro rata to its proportion of the population.[10] The government attorney acknowledged that for a long time the Arab population had not been getting its fair share as part of this project. The project in question was initially financed jointly by official bodies, the Jewish Agency, and Diaspora Jewish communities. This explains why at first only a small number of Arab neighbourhoods benefited from it. In 1990, after the government had shouldered the lion's share of the financing, the undertaking was gradually extended to the Arab sector, although still, as the Court held, not to a sufficient degree, considering the needs of this large population. The Supreme Court's ruling stipulated that 'the parameters which govern the distribution of the public cake must be equitable ... and furthermore based on objective criteria'. The justices went into the details of budgetary policy in order to make sure that the principle of equality should not remain mere lip service. They found that in some areas the Arab population was already getting its fair share of the project's budget, but not in others, and this had to be corrected. Their decision cites an earlier Supreme Court judgment concerning a different budgetary discrimination question:

> The principle of equality is binding on all of the country's public bodies. It is binding, above all, on the State itself. The principle of equality applies to all areas in which the State operates. It applies, first and foremost, to the allocation of the State's resources. The State's resources, whether land or money or other resources, belong to all citizens; and all citizens are entitled to enjoy them according to the principle of equality, without discrimination on the grounds of religion, race, sex or any other improper consideration.... Discrimination on the basis of religion or national affiliation in the allocation of the country's resources is forbidden even if it is done indirectly, and, *a fortiori*, if it is done directly.[11]

Thus it is an established principle of Israeli law, enforceable by the country's judiciary, that the State is required to act toward its citizens without religious or national discrimination and in an egalitarian fashion when allocating resources, especially budgetary and financial ones, as well as when making appointments to public positions of employment. In practice, the State can be compelled, if necessary, to meet its obligations by means of a petition to the High Court of Justice. But apart from the lengthy nature of the procedure, clearly this is not sufficient. It is difficult to see how the gaps between the two communities, which pre-dated the establishment of the state and were not satisfactorily dealt with for a long time due to neglect and discrimination, can be done away with unless a policy of affirmative action on a wide-ranging scale is adopted. This would require the adoption of far-reaching budgetary and administrative measures, and would naturally have to come at a cost, from the viewpoint of other pressing needs and priorities – and thus politically. For this to happen, many Jewish politicians will have to be willing to invest political capital. Cooperation on the part of Arab politicians would also help.

For the moment, from the point of view of budgets, development programmes, the use of State land, Arab representation in public institutions or State-owned corporations, as well as government jobs, Arab citizens have yet to achieve the full civil equality that is promised by Israel's Declaration of Independence, and is required by the country's constitutional and administrative law. There are good reasons for criticizing the policy of Israeli governments, with the exception of the 1992–1996 Rabin government, which the spokesmen for the Arab community themselves acknowledge to have been exceptionally positive. But the standard comparison that critics of Israeli policy make between the situation of Israel's Arab minority and that of minorities in developed democratic countries living in a state of peace is a superficial one that fails to take account of the Israeli reality. True, there are few cases of discrimination directly resulting from security considerations – for example, access to jobs in the arms industry. However, the context of the national conflict cannot but negatively affect the Arab minority's status. Of course, the Jewish public and the State establishment have their share of prejudices, and sometimes racist attitudes. But only once peace prevails will it be possible to evaluate, fully and fairly, Israel society's ability to guarantee the minorities living in its midst the same rights that enlightened societies today guarantee their minorities – including their Jewish minority. Unsurprisingly, there is a widespread view among the Arab population that Israel's official definition as a Jewish State is the real bedrock of ethnically motivated discrimination and injustice, and that doing away with this definition is the only way to bring about genuine equality of rights between Jews and Arabs. Some left-wing Jewish circles have come to hold the same belief, or tend to agree that 'the root of the evil' is to be found in this definition, both with regard to religious coercion and with respect to discrimination against the country's Arab population. There is no justification for this view. The definition of Israel as a Jewish State implies neither religious coercion nor ethno-national discrimination. As we will show below, everything which naturally arises from this definition, and in particular the Law of Return, is fully compatible with the current standards of liberal democracy. There is no justification for seeing the shortcomings of Israeli democracy as proof that a Jewish State is by definition contrary to democratic principles – any more than for regarding the undemocratic nature of the Arab regimes, including that of the Palestinian Authority, as proof that the very idea of an Arab state is inherently undemocratic. Not all those who object to the official definition of Israel as a Jewish State do so because they consciously deny the right of the Jewish people to a state of their own. Sometimes this stance is taken by people who sincerely (and mistakenly) believe that removing this definition would help make Israel a better and a fairer place. Thus, defending the idea of the Jewish State should mean not only refuting the arguments of its opponents, but also trying to ensure that its realization is fair and just.

Israel's Arabs as a national minority

Israeli Arabs are citizens whose national identity is different from that of the majority people in the state. They are therefore a national minority. Their demand to be recognized as such is justified. In fact, though there is no explicit recognition of this status of the Arab community in any official document, the State regularly refers to its Arab citizens in a way that clearly reflects recognition of the fact that this minority has a distinct national (as opposed to merely 'ethnic' or 'linguistic') identity of its own. The text of the Declaration of Independence appeals to:

> the members of the Arab people who are inhabitants of the State of Israel to preserve peace and participate in the upbuilding of the State on the basis of full and equal citizenship and due representation in all its provisional and permanent institutions.[12]

The term 'people' (in Hebrew, '*am*') is used quite consistently in the Declaration: it speaks of 'the Jewish people' and its national independence, and refers to the state's future Arab citizens as belonging to 'the Arab people'. This language clearly presents the Arab community in Israel as a national minority.

The Administration of Rule and Justice Ordinance setting up the basic structures of government, which was promulgated as the War of Independence continued to be fought, refers to the integration in the provisional government institutions of the 'Arab inhabitants who recognize the State of Israel'. It does not call them 'Arabic-speaking' rather than 'Arab', as is done by countries which make a point of not defining the minorities living in them as 'national' minorities (Greece, for example, insists that its citizens include Turkish-speaking Muslims, but not Turks). Two laws enacted by the Knesset in 1998 contain the principle of 'adequate representation of the Arab population' on the boards of government corporations and in the civil service. Similar language is used in various executive directives and regulations. The directive on state education in Arabic-speaking schools dating back to 1996 undertakes to 'guarantee equality of status for Israel's Arab citizens, while respecting the linguistic and cultural characteristics of their heritage'; school curricula must 'meet the needs and culture of the Arab population'. The identity of those belonging to the Arabic-speaking minority is thus, routinely and uncontroversially, recognized by the State as 'Arab'.

When it comes to language, education and culture, the collective rights of Israel's Arab minority are, as we shall presently see, wide and far-reaching by international standards. Professor Sammy Smooha, one of the leading sociologists in Israel who studies the Arab community and who is, in general, highly critical of the State's policies towards it, describes the situation as follows:

> The Arabs ... are recognized as a minority, and they are granted all the collective rights which are vital to the maintenance of separate existence: the free use of their language, a separate educational system in their language, media in their language (radio, television, press), cultural institutions in their language (art, literature, theatre), and separate religious institutions and separate religious courts guaranteeing endogamy. These institutional arrangements are financed in part or in full by the State. Furthermore, there is recognition of their right to be different, they are allowed to live in separate communities, and no pressure is brought to bear on them to assimilate.

And yet, Smooha goes on to say, 'the Arabs in Israel are not recognized as a Palestinian national minority, their national leadership is not recognized, nor is their right to autonomy and their ties with the Palestinian people.'[12] However, it should be noted that international norms on minority rights do not require either explicit official recognition of a national minority as such, or official recognition of the minority's leadership, or granting it autonomy. The most relevant document reflecting current liberal-democratic standards is this field is the Council of Europe's Framework Convention for the Protection of National Minorities, signed in 1995.[13] It requires neither official recognition nor autonomy. In practice, however, Israeli ministers and officials engage in dialogue with the Supreme Arab Monitoring Committee as well as the National Committee of Arab Mayors over topics of interest to their population (despite fierce political disagreements between the government and these bodies). In the last few decades, there has also developed increasing recognition of the ties between Israel's Arab minority and the Palestinian people – a sensitive subject, of course, because of the Israeli–Palestinian conflict and its ramifications.

Nothing in the norms laid down by the European Convention is incompatible with Israel's character as a Jewish state. Nor do its provisions contain anything which would allow a national minority to demand the status of a 'state within the state', encroaching on the competence of state institutions, as is feared by some of those who object to official recognition of the Arab community as a national minority. Article 4 (2) of the Convention stipulates:

> The Parties undertake to adopt, where necessary, adequate measures in order to promote, in all areas of economic, social, political and cultural life, full and effective equality between persons belonging to a national minority and those belonging to the majority.

Article 15 states that: 'The Parties shall create the conditions necessary for the effective participation of persons belonging to national minorities in cultural, social and economic life and in public affairs, in particular those affecting them.' As we have seen, unequal distribution of budgetary resources and under-representation of the Arab minority in public bodies cannot be reconciled with these norms – nor with Israeli law as interpreted by the High Court of Justice.

Most of the Convention's articles relate to the minority's right to preserve its linguistic, cultural and religious specificity. In this sphere, the rights of the Arab minority in Israel go further, in important respects, than the minimum requirements laid down in this document – as well as the practice of some democracies. Language is a crucial issue. The Convention insists that members of a minority must be able to use their language freely, but not that it be given the status of a second official language, as has been done in Israel. In their education system, according to Article 13, the Parties recognize that the minority is entitled to manage its own private educational and training establishments, but without this right entailing any financial obligation for the parties. In Article 14, the Parties undertake to recognize that all members of a national minority have the right to learn their minority language:

> In areas inhabited by persons belonging to national minorities traditionally or in substantial numbers, if there is sufficient demand, the Parties shall endeavour to ensure, as far as possible and within the framework of their education systems, that persons belonging to those minorities have adequate opportunities for being taught the minority language or for receiving instruction in this language ... without prejudice to the learning of the official language or the teaching in this language.

In other words, the State reserves its right to require that minority students not only learn the language of the majority, but also be taught in this language. The official Explanatory Report which comments on the Convention's provisions underscores the very flexible wording of Article 14, which leaves the Parties considerable latitude. The words 'as far as possible' indicate that the teaching in question depends on the available resources of the Party in question. The Report makes the point that Article 14 imposes no obligation upon States to provide teaching *in* the minority language (as opposed to allowing the minority language to be taught as one of the subjects). It also suggests that bilingual instruction may be one of the means of achieving the objective of this provision. The commentary on Paragraph 3 of Article 14 notes that knowledge of the official language is a factor of social cohesion and integration.

Comparing these provisions to the Israeli education system, in which Arab students attend state-financed schools where instruction is given entirely in Arabic, it is clear that in this field the State offers its national minority a collective right which goes far beyond the minimum requirements of the Convention. Nothing in the Convention lends support to the demand, often voiced by Arab public figures in Israel, that Arab school curricula should be drawn up by minority representatives not under State control. It would undoubtedly be desirable to involve the latter more closely in programme design, and significant progress has been made along these lines. It should also be noted that the State Education Law in Israel authorizes the pupils' parents at any public school to determine 25 per cent of curriculum content. Presently, not much use is made of this provision in the Arab sector, but potentially it gives parents a fairly significant degree of influence in the Arab minority's public schools.

The Explanatory Report (paragraph 13) makes a point of noting that the provisions of the Convention do not 'imply the recognition of collective rights' the rights and freedoms under the Convention may be exercised by 'persons belonging to national minorities individually or in community with others' (Section 1, Article 3.2), something which is distinct from the notion of collective rights. This clarification is intended to counter the reservations that many in Europe continue to have about the concept of collective rights, fearing that it might give rise to excessive demands at the expense of individual rights or social cohesion. But when it comes to linguistic, cultural and educational rights, the distinction between collective rights and individual ones that are exercised 'in community with others' becomes largely semantic.[14]

Article 16 of the Convention states:

> The Parties shall refrain from measures which alter the proportions of the population in areas inhabited by persons belonging to national minorities and are aimed at restricting the rights and freedoms flowing from the principles enshrined in the present framework Convention.

Changes in demographic balance are thus not banned as such, but only when they are aimed at restricting the minority's rights and freedoms under the

Convention. As examples of such practices the Explanatory Report cites expropriation, evictions and expulsions, or redrawing administrative borders with a view to restricting the enjoyment of such rights and freedoms ('gerrymandering'). Hence, expropriation (with compensation paid) of private land belonging to Arab citizens in the name of public needs, when the aim (or at least the main aim) is to change the demographic balance in a particular area in favour of Jews, would appear to be in breach of the Convention. The Explanatory Report notes that it was considered impossible to extend the prohibition to measures having the effect of restricting such rights and freedoms (as opposed to being deliberately aimed at such restriction), since such measures may sometimes be entirely justified and legitimate (such as resettling villagers in order to build a dam). However, when such public needs are of relevance solely or mainly to one particular national group, expropriation of land from people belonging to another national group would appear to run counter to the spirit, if not the letter, of Article 16, as well as to the general obligation that the Convention imposes on the authorities to ensure equal treatment for members of a national minority. In Israel's situation, given the wide scale of expropriations of Arab land which took place in the past, no additional land expropriations for public use (even when these are legitimate under international standards) should be carried out in the Arab sector except in cases of vital necessity; this appears in fact to have been the official policy for quite some time. In the rare cases where such an expropriation may be inevitable, land of equal value should be offered by way of compensation (as has been done as part of the Trans-Israel Highway project). Beyond the issue of expropriations, the Convention's provisions do not authorize any development, construction or housing policies in any region of the country which fail to take account of the rights and interests of the national-minority members who live there. This is a principle which is also to be found in Israel's Declaration of Independence, which refers to promoting 'the development of the country for the benefit of all its inhabitants'.

As for readjusting electoral boundaries in order to marginalize the minority, it is important to note that Israel's existing electoral system, though problematic in other respects, is undoubtedly the most favourable one to a national minority. The entire country is a single constituency, and the allotment of seats in the Knesset is strictly proportional, with a low qualifying threshold. This leaves no room for gerrymandering: parliamentary representation faithfully reflects the minority vote. Hence there is no need, in Israel, for special arrangements in order to ensure a minimum level of parliamentary representation of the minority – a measure resorted to in some other democracies with a more majoritarian electoral system. In all the discussions that have taken place about changing the present-day electoral system (which does have major drawbacks and is subject to harsh criticism), it is agreed that under any future election reform introducing constituencies, their boundaries will be drawn by the country's judiciary, thereby avoiding political influences (not a rare occurrence in democratic countries) and discrimination along ethnic lines.

The Framework Convention for the Protection of National Minorities is open to signature by countries which are not members of the Council of Europe. There is no reason why Israel should not do so. The Convention does not require its signatories to pass laws recognizing specific groups as 'national minorities'. Some countries have done so, while others have not, or have used different terms in their legal texts. But although the official recognition of a national minority is not required under the international norms on the protection of minorities, including the European Convention,[14] in the Israeli context there are good reasons for doing so. It is appropriate that a country that officially defines itself, in its Basic Laws, as a Jewish state, should also officially recognize the existence, within its citizen body, of a large community with a distinct national identity of its own. The authors of Israel's Declaration of Independence showed the way: not content with proclaiming the general principle of equal rights for all the citizens of the future state, irrespective of religion and national origin, they addressed themselves to the Arab population directly, referring to it as a national group ('members of the Arab people'), and guaranteed them full and equal citizenship. The country's Basic Laws and its future constitution should therefore include an explicit recognition of Israel's Arab community as a national minority.

5   'Either Jewish or democratic'?

'Jewish and democratic state': oxymoron?

> A Jewish and democratic [state] – there can be no such thing. Either it is
> 'Jewish' or it is democratic. Otherwise this is just an attempt to evade the
> requirements of liberal democracy by using a worn-out gimmick: 'Israel is a
> special case'. Israel can be a democratic state where most of its residents
> have some awareness and some connection to their Judaism, but any other
> interpretation serves to discriminate against the rights of the Arab minority.[1]

This is how radical Israeli journalist Chaim Bar'am in his column in Jerusalem's
local newspaper, *Kol Ha'ir*, summed up the case against the democratic legitimacy of Israel's definition as a Jewish state. Such a definition, Bar'am and
others in Israel and beyond tell us, contradicts the universal 'requirements of
liberal democracy' that override any plea of local specificity. This view is regularly presented as if it were a self-evident truth requiring no detailed argumenta-
tion. The precise reasons for which liberal democracy, international legitimacy
and the principle of equality are supposed to rule out a nation-state for one of the
two peoples in the land between the Jordan and the Mediterranean while
simultaneously requiring it for the other remain a mystery.

The denial of Israel's legitimacy as a Jewish state is not confined to a few
radical activists. A significant group of Israeli academics have adopted this
outlook and express it in publications in Israel and overseas. Over the last few
years, the theory that there is an irreconcilable and fundamental contradiction
between democratic values and the definition of Israel as a Jewish state has
enjoyed expressions of support from representatives of different academic disci-
plines including sociology, political science, law, philosophy, geography and
history.

The alleged contradiction between the Jewish character of the state and the
principles of democracy is described by the people in question as a fundamental
incompatibility – not as a tension between two legitimate values. Tension
between values, in and of itself, is no indication that one of the competing values
is illegitimate and ought to be given up. For example, much of modern democratic politics centres on the tension between individual liberty and equality.

Every free society grapples with the conflict between civil liberties and the need to protect public safety. Educational systems struggle with the need to provide equal opportunity and close social gaps without giving up on competition, achievement and excellence. The tension between economic development and protection of the environment is one of the important characteristics of developed modern societies. Between multiculturalism and many of the other values of modern liberalism – for example, gender equality – there is often considerable tension (not always acknowledged with sufficient candour).

In all of these cases there are tensions that create difficult dilemmas and legitimate arguments between people who prioritize different values, or interpret one value in a way that minimizes the tension with another. However, we do not hear that a person cannot believe both in liberty and in equality and that he or she must make an unequivocal choice between the two. It is obvious that these two principles (liberty and equality) complement and reinforce each other to a greater extent than they contradict each other. In the same way, the Jewish and democratic character of the state can create tensions and practical dilemmas. But this does not mean that we must choose one of these two values and reject the other. Those who reject the Jewish state do a disservice to democratic principles by failing to respect the democratically expressed will of the majority of Israel's citizens. It is true that the principle of majority rule must, in a liberal democracy, sometimes yield to the need to protect minority rights. However, in this case it is not a matter of protecting minorities according to internationally recognized democratic norms, but of denying the right of the Jewish people to national independence. This denial is in itself an assault on the principle of equality.

The Law of Return and international norms of civil equality

The Law of Return is certainly one of the most important, and most controversial, aspects of the issue at hand. Its critics claim that it is discriminatory and antidemocratic, and regard it as something of a 'smoking gun' for the purpose of proving that a Jewish state and liberal democracy are fundamentally incompatible. Thus, for example, Baruch Kimmerling, Professor of Sociology at the Hebrew University of Jerusalem, describes the Law of Return not only as a violation of civil equality, but also as the central obstacle to the transformation of Israel into a properly functioning democracy:

> The most substantial step toward normalization and democratization of the state, and toward granting equal civil liberties to all, will be the reform of the laws governing immigration. It is not possible to exaggerate the importance of such a step: a basic political and social inequality is inherent in the Law of Return.[2]

Kimmerling sees no need to explain precisely how the Law of Return violates the principle of civil equality. But the Law of Return does not discriminate between different categories of citizens within the country. It does not make the citizenship of non-Jews in any way inferior. Rather it is directed outward, to the Jews of the world. Those who condemn the Law of Return hold that Israel has no right to treat foreign citizens who are Jewish preferentially in its laws on immigration and naturalization. However, there is no basis in international law, or in the actual practice of contemporary democracies, for such a claim.

In international law, a sovereign state has wide latitude as regards its policies on immigration and naturalization. This principle is specifically enshrined in the International Convention on the Elimination of All Forms of Racial Discrimination (1965), which broadly forbids any discrimination based on race, ethnicity or religion. Article 1 (3) of the Convention states that '[n]othing in this Convention may be interpreted as affecting in any way the legal provisions of States Parties concerning nationality, citizenship or naturalization, provided that such provisions do not discriminate against any particular nationality'.

This provision, which should of course be understood as relating to the citizenship being conferred on immigrants, rather than to other aspects of citizenship, allows the state to give foreign citizens preferential treatment as regards naturalization at its discretion, but forbids it to single out a certain group (based on ethnicity or religion) placing it in an inferior position in this respect. True, not every kind of preference in this field is compatible with current standards of human rights. Australia's 'whites only' immigration policy was still considered legitimate in the 1970s; today it would surely be regarded as discriminatory, i.e. directed in practice against non-whites rather than in favour of any specific group with a genuine connection to Australia. But for a state established as a national home for the Jewish people it is not only legitimate but natural to open its gates to members of that people – precisely as was envisaged by those who supported partition in 1947. In adopting this principle, Israel is much less unique than is often supposed by both its critics and its supporters.

Europe: diasporas and repatriation laws

It is a recognized European norm that a nation-state can maintain official ties with its 'kin' outside its borders and treat them preferentially in certain areas, including immigration and naturalization. This norm is expressed in the October 2001 decision of the European Commission for Democracy through Law – an advisory body of the Council of Europe. Better known as the 'Venice Commission', this committee of legal experts was established to assist countries in adopting constitutional laws 'that conform to the standards of Europe's constitutional heritage'. The commission dealt with the question of the connection between ethno-national groups in Europe and their 'kin-states', the countries to which they are connected by virtue of ethnic and cultural ties.

The catalyst for the discussion was a law passed by Hungary that conferred certain economic privileges on ethnic Hungarians who are citizens of neighbouring states. Romania complained to the Venice Commission, asserting that this law infringed Romanian sovereignty since it conferred privileges on certain

citizens of Romania without prior agreement by the Romanian state and created inequality between Romanian citizens.

The Commission's detailed report in response to this complaint, submitted in October 2001,[3] recognizes the relationship between ethnic and cultural minorities and their kin-states as legitimate and desirable.

> The concern of the 'kin-States' for the fate of the persons belonging to their national communities (hereinafter referred to as 'kin-minorities') who are citizens of other countries ('the home-States') and reside abroad is not a new phenomenon in international law (A).

The report notes favourably the growing tendency of kin-states to concern themselves with the protection of the rights of 'kin-minorities' – mainly by means of bilateral agreements with home-states. The report cites the 1969 agreements between Italy and Austria, signed with international support, which secured the rights of the German-speaking minority in Tyrol. The Commission also cites the agreements signed in recent years between various Eastern European countries and between those countries and Germany.

Various European normative documents, including the Framework Convention for the Protection of National Minorities, encourage countries to negotiate arrangements regarding protection of the status of national minorities. One might add, as an additional example, the 1955 Bonn and Copenhagen agreement between Germany and Denmark that protects the cultural and language rights of Danes living in northern Germany and Germans living in southern Denmark. All these international agreements are based on the assumption that a nation-state may have a legitimate interest in the fate of those it regards as its 'kin' who live outside its borders.

While bilateral arrangements dealing with the status of 'kin minorities' are a well-established European norm, the Venice Commission rules that when states confer benefits on their 'kin' in a foreign country unilaterally, care should be taken not to infringe that country's sovereignty and not to create economic inequalities among its citizens. Hence, while benefits in the field of education and culture are legitimate, benefits in other fields should be restricted to exceptional cases when the aim is genuinely to foster the bond between the state and its 'kin-minority' (rather than simply improving its material conditions).

Preference in immigration and naturalization, which has up to now not been challenged in European institutions, is mentioned briefly as an example of legitimate preference: 'Indeed, the ethnic targeting is commonly done, for example, in laws on citizenship' (Dd). By way of illustration, the Commission refers to Article 116 of the German Constitution. Germany does indeed provide a well-known example. In the 1950s it expanded the right to automatic citizenship, which its Constitution provides for refugees and displaced persons of German ethnic origin ('a refugee or expellee of German ethnic origin or the spouse or descendant of such person'), to all ethnic Germans from the Soviet Union and Eastern Europe. This applied to a large population of ethnic Germans that had lived in those areas for hundreds of years, without any civic or geographic connection with the modern German state. Following the collapse of the Soviet Union, the law was revised so that the eligibility for citizenship was limited to emigrants of German extraction from the former Soviet Union. Germany's current policy toward ethnic Germans in other Eastern European states is to encourage them to remain where they are and to assist them in preserving their German culture and identity.

Those who criticize Israel's Law of Return are usually aware of the German case. Sometimes they point to the 'irony' of the similarity between the Jewish State and Germany on this matter. Of course, the Federal Republic of Germany is indisputably a liberal democracy. The attempt to find fault with the Law of Return because of its similarity to the repatriation laws of the Federal Republic, hinting at Germany's dark past, is nothing but demagoguery. Moreover, during all the period since its enactment half a century ago, the German repatriation legislation under which citizenship was granted (along with considerable financial benefits) to millions of immigrants of ethnic German extraction has never been challenged in the European Court of Human Rights.

But the truth of the matter is that the German case is not unique. There is no need to compare Israel's Law of Return only with Germany. Privileged access to rights of residence and immigration for ethno-cultural kin groups exists in varying ways and through various legal mechanisms, in long-standing Western European democracies – Ireland, Finland and Greece – as well as in a number of new European democracies, such as Poland, Hungary, Bulgaria, Slovakia, the Czech Republic, Slovenia and Croatia.

Among the republics of the former Soviet Union, repatriation laws were enacted in Russia, Ukraine and Armenia. In all of these countries, these legal arrangements are seen as an expression of the natural and legitimate connection between a nation-state and its diaspora, whether far away or living in neighbouring countries (where they became national minorities when boundaries shifted). This phenomenon is obviously not some unique product of German nationalism, nor is confined to Eastern Europe, where notions of national identity are sometimes described as 'ethnic' as opposed to 'civic'. It is a product of Europe's history of migrating populations and shifting borders. A bond between a state and its 'kin' who are citizens of a foreign country and have lived there for generations is in the nature of things ethnic or ethno-cultural. The Venice Commission does not shy away from speaking of ethnicity in this context, while affirming that such bonds are fully consistent with European norms of civic democracy. Those who find this objectionable and insist on full congruence of national identity and citizenship as the only legitimate democratic norm, have to reject the prevailing European norms as regards both kin-minorities abroad and national minorities at home (largely two sides of the same coin).

When speaking of repatriation laws, one should distinguish between what may be termed personal repatriation, where the immigrant is a former citizen, or at least a descendant of citizens, of the country to which he or she is immigrating, and national repatriation, where people are considered as returnees by virtue of belonging to an ethno-national group. The Israeli Law of Return obviously belongs to the second category. In Europe, the same laws sometimes include provisions of both kinds. The provisions that are akin to the Law of Return are those dealing with members of diaspora communities or kin-minorities that have lived outside the borders of the homeland for generations. Indeed, in some cases, the diaspora community was already ancient when the modern state was created. In these cases, only ethnic and cultural connections tie members of these communities to the kin-state willing to define their immigration as repatriation.

Thus in section 6 of the Greek Law of Citizenship we find: 'If a foreign citizen is not of Greek ethnic extraction, he must have resided in Greece for eight years' before he can apply for Greek citizenship'. This is not a grant of an automatic right to citizenship. Rather, it privileges ethnic Greeks who immigrate to Greece by exempting them from the requirement of eight years of residence demanded of all other foreign citizens who seek naturalization. In addition, sections 12 and 13 of the law confer automatic Greek citizenship on ethnic overseas Greeks who volunteer for military service in the Greek armed forces. In practice, the various Greek governments have bestowed Greek citizenship on ethnic Greeks in what amounts to an automatic fashion. Since the collapse of the Soviet Union and the opening of its successor republics to emigration, some 200,000 ethnic Greeks have arrived in Greece and received citizenship. The Greek government officially defines their immigration as a return to the homeland – repatriation. Whereas most of the Greek communities in Western countries are second- or third-generation descendants of emigrants from Greece, the Pontic Greeks (as the 'returnees' from the former Soviet Union are called) have no direct connection with the modern Greek state. Their ancestors emigrated mostly from what is now Turkey rather than from what is now Greece. Even the Greek that they speak, a dialect combining modern and ancient Greek, is very different from the modern Greek spoken in Greece.

The massive project of resettling and absorbing these people in Greece, so far from being considered as contrary to European norms, has in large measure been financed by the European Union. Many of the Pontic Greeks were settled by the Greek government in Western Thrace, where the largest concentration of Greek citizens of the ethnically Turkish minority live; this fact did not deter the European Union from financially supporting their settlement, even though certain aspects of Greek government policy toward the Turkish minority have incurred criticism in Europe.

Finland, too, defines as 'repatriation' the immigration of ethnic Finns from the former Soviet Union. In November 1997 the government of Finland presented the United Nations with a report on the way in which it was carrying out the International Convention on the Elimination of All Forms of Racial Discrimination. The report deals mainly with the securing of civil rights for immigrants in Finland. A chapter in the report is devoted to 'Finnish repatriates' from Russia and Estonia; these, according to the document, are 'descendants of Finns who emigrated to Ingria and St. Petersburg in the seventeenth, eighteenth and nineteenth centuries and are customarily called "Ingrian Finns" '.[4]

The Finnish government reported that in 1996 the 'Foreigners' Law' was changed to confer residency status on ethnic Finns who come to Finland from the former Soviet Union.[5] This is not a large group: as of 1997, about 15,000 Ingrian Finns were repatriated and granted a status facilitating their naturalization. It should be noted that Finland, in addition to being a long-standing Western liberal democracy, has adopted what is usually defined as a civic model of national identity, i.e. one which is presumed to be shared by all of the country's citizens. Thus, Swedish speakers in the country are not regarded as a national minority; rather, the Finnish people are considered to consist of two components – Finnish-speaking and Swedish-speaking. Nevertheless, the country regards itself as responsible for the fate of ethnic Finns who live in Russia and Estonia, descendants of seventeenth- and eighteenth-century emigrants from the land which only generations later became the Finnish Republic.[6] Finland both assists the Ingrian Finns in preserving their ethno-cultural identity in their countries of residence and defines their immigration as a return to the homeland. The example of Finland shows that an inclusive civic concept of national identity within the country is compatible with maintaining official ties with an ethno-cultural diaspora.

As for Poland, Article 52 of the post-Soviet Constitution declares: 'Anyone whose Polish origin has been confirmed in accordance with statute may settle permanently in Poland'. The Polish diaspora numbers in the millions, the result of both emigration and exile, as well as the drastic changes in the borders of the Polish state in the course of history. The government of the Polish Republic cultivates its connections with the diaspora, which official rhetoric defines as an integral part of the Polish people. Article 6 of the Constitution states that the Republic 'shall provide assistance to Poles living abroad to maintain their links with the national cultural heritage'. In January 2000 the Polish parliament enacted a 'Repatriation Law' directed mainly at people of Polish origin living in the former Soviet Union, some of them the children or grandchildren of Polish citizens who went or were sent to distant regions in the course of the turbulent twentieth century. Others are descendants of Polish emigrants or Polish minorities from earlier periods (before the existence of the modern Polish state). Both categories are entitled to citizenship on condition that they have preserved their Polish cultural identity. The law grants such 'returnees' Polish citizenship and requires the government to assist them in their integration into Polish society.

Section 16 of the Irish Nationality and Citizenship Act empowers the Minister for Justice to grant an exemption from the ordinary prerequisites for naturalization 'where the applicant is of Irish descent or Irish associations'. In practice, Irish policy has been to confer citizenship upon applicants of Irish descent without delay. In recent decades, as the Irish economy improved, quite a few people have acquired citizenship through the provisions of this section of the law. Generally, these were descendants of Irish citizens who emigrated in the course of the twentieth century due to harsh economic conditions in the country. However, a 'person of Irish descent' may also be the descendant of someone who left Ireland before the modern Irish state came into being in 1921, or someone who emigrated from Northern Ireland, which is not a part of the Republic. Hence a person 'of Irish descent' who receives citizenship under privileged conditions is not necessarily a descendant of Irish citizens. Moreover, those born in Northern Ireland are entitled under the Act to Irish citizenship – a provision that reflects the official notion of Irish nationhood which is not congruous with the legal boundaries of the Republic.

Armenia provides a significant example of repatriation that is disconnected from prior citizenship. Section 14 of the Armenian Constitution determines that a 'person of Armenian descent will obtain citizenship through a shortened procedure'.[7] The Armenian diaspora numbers in the millions, more than the population of the Republic of Armenia. Most of them are not descendants of emigrants from the areas that now constitute the Republic. The connection between these people and Armenia is the same kind of ethno-cultural tie (often with a religious element) that connects Diaspora Jews with the State of Israel. It is the policy of the Armenian Republic to award citizenship to any person of Armenian descent who requests it. Today, there is no significant demand for Armenian citizenship, other than among Armenian refugees from Nagorno-Karabakh. In the past, however, there was a wave of repatriation to Soviet Armenia. The government of the Soviet Union engaged in considerable public relations work over several decades in order to encourage overseas Armenians to immigrate to the Soviet Armenian Republic, which it declared to be the national home of the entire Armenian people. Around 250,000 individuals responded and settled there.

Official ties with kin-minorities

Repatriation laws are part of a broader phenomenon. The ties between European countries and their kin beyond the border are multifaceted. Numerous European constitutions mention these ties – in various East European countries, in Ireland and in Greece (see Appendix). In most cases, the kin-state's policy is to encourage kin-minorities to stay in their countries of residence while preserving their language, culture and identity and maintaining ties with the national homeland.

The Venice Commission's report refers to a number of existing laws in European countries, apart from the Hungarian case which gave rise to the report: an Austrian law from 1979 that deals with the rights of South Tyrolese (i.e. the German-speaking minority in Northern Italy); Italian legislation from 2000 called the 'Law on the Measures in Favour of the Italian Minority in Slovenia and Croatia'; as well as legislation from Russia, Slovakia, Romania, Bulgaria, Slovenia and Greece.

The Commission's decision also surveys benefits conferred under these laws, including financial support for educational and cultural institutions, access to educational institutions in the kin-state, support for minority members' travel to and within the kin-state, the right to work and to own property within the kin-state, matters of medical insurance, pension rights, special certification, preferential treatment in receiving visas, rights of residence and acquiring citizenship.[8]

The autonomous administration of the Basque Region is not authorized to deal with questions of immigration and citizenship, which are reserved for Spain's central government. However, in 1994 the Basque parliament enacted special legislation regarding the ties between the autonomous region and ethnic Basque communities and organizations outside the region. This included areas in Spain and France that Basque nationalists consider part of the Basque homeland, as well as regions to which Basque expatriates have migrated.[9] The government of the autonomous region provides funds for cultural and educational work among Basques outside its borders. It raises the money by taxing residents of the region (including, of course, those whose identity is not Basque).

The trend exists outside Europe as well. China has maintained institutionalized connections with its diaspora for decades.[10] South Korea does likewise. India recently began to develop its ties with the Indian diaspora, mainly in the sphere of economics. In January 2002 a High Level Committee on the Indian Diaspora presented a formal report to the government in which it gave detailed recommendations for tightening the connections with the diaspora in a long list of fields. Among other things, it suggested that India allow foreign citizens of Indian descent living in certain countries to hold dual citizenship, i.e. to receive Indian citizenship alongside their present foreign nationality, and to create a standing committee in the Indian parliament with the remit of overseeing relations with the diaspora.[11] In 1999, South Korea enacted a law that provides for the conferring of dual citizenship (without the right to vote) on members of Korean diaspora communities who remain where they are, including members of the large ethnic Korean community in Japan created during the Japanese rule.

Since the days of Mustafa Kemal Atatürk, founder of the Turkish Republic, Turkey maintains a strict version of civic nationalism based on full congruence of citizenship and national identity. Every citizen of the state, regardless of ethnic origin, is regarded as belonging to the Turkish nation. At the same time, Turkey has a long-standing history (from the nineteenth century) of providing sanctuary for refugees of Turkish origin. The 'Settlement Law' adopted by the Republic in 1934 lays down ethno-national criteria for the acquisition of citizenship by immigrants. It confers upon refugees 'of Turkish descent and Turkish cultural identity' the right (subject to governmental approval) to immigrate to Turkey, to settle there permanently and ultimately to receive citizenship. In 1992 Turkey enacted a special law that allowed for the immigration and acquisition of citizenship by a group of ethnic Turks from the former Soviet Union who had been exiled by Stalin to Georgia and denied the right to return to their former homes. This was not a case of refugees fleeing persecution. Rather, this was a response occasioned by the new conditions that prevailed in the 1990s. It expressed ethno-cultural solidarity on the part of the Turkish state with a kin-community against which the Soviet Union had in the past perpetrated a historical injustice – even though they had no geographic or civil ties with the Turkish Republic and the homeland from which they had been driven lay elsewhere.

It is clear that official ties between nation-states and kin-communities abroad are not only legitimate under current international standards, but represent a widespread and growing phenomenon, driven by some major contemporary trends. Among these are the growing recognition of the legitimacy of multiple identities and of the minorities' right and need to preserve their unique cultural heritage. Many countries also take note of the economic advantages that accrue to nations which remain in touch with their kin in foreign countries, especially in an era of globalization. Ultimately, the phenomenon of the kin-state flows from the fact that in many cases the borders of modern states do not fully coincide with the borders of national, ethnic and cultural groups. The natural result of this is the existence of national minorities in many countries and the ties of some of them with their kin-states.

Israel, the Jewish Diaspora and the Law of Return

For obvious historical reasons, the borders of the Jewish nation-state are not congruent with the Jewish people's places of residence. The contention, often heard from opponents of Zionism, that there is something anomalous and illegitimate about Israel's official ties with the Jewish Diaspora is wholly baseless. The strength and intensity of this connection stem from Jewish history and cultural traditions and reflect the wishes of both sides.

Whoever supports the creation of an independent state for a people with a diaspora must assume that this state will maintain strong ties with its kin abroad, inter alia through laws on immigration and naturalization. As we have seen, this was fully appreciated by the supporters of partition in 1947. Clearly, this is also true of the Palestinian case: anyone who agrees to the establishment of an independent state for the Palestinian people agrees to the Palestinian 'right of return' to this state (not to Israel). This has long been accepted, internationally, as part of any future 'two-state solution' – notably, in US President Clinton's 'parameters' for an Israeli–Palestinian settlement in 2000. The principle that any Palestinian Arab, wherever he or she may be, is entitled to Palestinian citizenship (without having to demonstrate a personal tie to the areas in which the Palestinian state is to come into being) is enshrined in the draft constitution of the future Palestinian state, drawn up by a committee of the Palestinian parliament.

Some Palestinian spokespersons have declared from time to time that they would be prepared to have Israeli Jews live in their state – as loyal citizens abiding by Palestinian law. If this comes to pass, it is clear that the Palestinian 'Law of Return' will still apply specifically to Palestinians. It will not allow members of the Jewish minority to enjoy unlimited free immigration of their people to the Palestinian state, and this fact will violate neither the principle of civil equality nor international democratic norms. More generally, one hopes that no minority in a future Palestinian state will have grievances more serious than its definition as an Arab state, its symbols, the official status of Islam and the Islamic Shari'a (enshrined in the Palestinian Basic Law of 1997) and its Law of Return.

To sum up this issue, the international standards of human rights, which forbid discrimination between citizens of the same state on the basis of ethnic origin and identity, do not prevent a state from considering itself to be committed and connected to groups of citizens of other countries through ties of ethnicity, national identity and culture. An attachment of this kind is quite common and may be expressed in various ways; one of them concerns laws on immigration and naturalization.

Another argument against the Law of Return contends that it guarantees a privileged position for the Orthodox rabbinical establishment. More generally, the argument suggests that the definition of Israel as a Jewish state prevents Israel from becoming a truly 'liberal state', which would require that Israel separate religion and state. The problem with this argument is twofold. First, there are several examples of undoubtedly liberal states in which there is an official Church established by law (while the religious freedom and equality of all citizens regardless of religion is effectively protected). No one can seriously maintain that Denmark, Norway or England are not liberal. Moreover, a separation of religion and state in Israel would in no way preclude it from being a Jewish nation-state as envisaged in the country's Declaration of Independence. It would certainly not preclude it from continuing to open its gates to Jewish immigration. The Law of Return was passed in 1950 with the support of staunchly secular Marxists from the Mapam Party as well as of the Israeli Communist Party. They would have been surprised to hear that they were voting for a measure strengthening the Orthodox establishment (or discriminating against the Arab minority).

The Law touches on religious matters only marginally – by recognizing converts to Judaism as Jews for its purposes. The Orthodox establishment tried repeatedly in the past to have the law amended so that only Orthodox conversion would be recognized. These attempts failed. The whole issue is of very limited practical importance (only a small minority of newcomers to Israel are converts, and most of them would have been entitled to all the privileges under the Law in any case, as spouses of Jews), but it is important symbolically. The Law of Return is thus an area in which the Orthodox establishment has notably failed to have its way. The limited degree to which the state needs to concern itself with religious questions in order to accept converts (Orthodox or not) as newcomers certainly does not contradict any democratic norm.

It should be noted that the term 'separation of religion and state' has very different interpretations in the countries that have adopted it. India, for instance, which under its Constitution is a secular republic, frames its laws of personal status around the religious communities to which most of its citizens belong (while allowing for civil marriage between members of different communities).[12] There is no doubt that the monopoly of religious courts over questions of personal status in Israel does contradict democratic norms. This can, and should, be changed without affecting in any way the Jewish character of the state. Moreover, precisely in this most problematic area from the standpoint of civil rights as they relate to religion and state in Israel, the Jewish religion enjoys no preference: the system of religious courts with powers bestowed by the State operates in all religious communities. The status quo in this field has certainly been shaped under the influence of Jewish religious parties. However, it is worth noting that Arab-Muslim Members of the Knesset regularly oppose, for their own reasons, attempts to do away with the exclusive jurisdiction of religious courts in matters of personal status.

Jewish history is marked by a profound connection between religion and people-hood. But this does not necessarily mean that the modern nation-state of the Jewish people must confer an official status on the institutions of the Jewish religion. Indeed, this is one of the most hotly debated topics in Israeli public life.

A Jewish state and a state of all its citizens

Is it true that a Jewish state is, by definition, not 'a state of all its citizens', as is often claimed or assumed?[13] There is no justification for this view. The phrase itself, 'a state of all its citizens', does not appear in any official definition in Israel; the same applies to most of the world's democracies. Israel's Basic Laws define Israel as a 'Jewish and democratic state'. What is a democratic state, if not the state of all of its citizens? Indeed, the Israeli Supreme Court has ruled that there is no contradiction between a 'Jewish and democratic state' and 'a state of all its citizens', since 'every democratic state is, in an important sense, a state of all its citizens'.[14] Democracy is the 'rule of the people'; in this context 'the people' means the entire citizen body of the state and excludes non-citizens. This is precisely the legal situation in Israel. Sovereignty rests with the citizens of the state, including the Arab minority, and is implemented through institutions elected by the Israeli civic community, and only by it. The phrase 'the State of the Jewish people', sometimes applied to Israel, signifies that the State embodies the right of the Jewish people to a state of their own, but contrary to what is sometimes claimed, does not confer, either in theory or in practice, any political rights within the state on Jews who are not Israeli citizens. It should be noted that unlike many democracies, Israel does not allow its citizens living abroad to vote. One of the results of this is that the Law of Return cannot be used by a Jew living abroad in order to obtain Israeli citizenship automatically and then enjoy the right of suffrage in Israel while continuing to live abroad.

Of course, democracy is much more than universal and equal suffrage and free elections. A state is more or less democratic – i.e. more or less a state of all its citizens – depending on many other factors, first and foremost of which is the practical application of the principle of civil equality (which, in the language of Israel's Supreme Court, is 'the soul of democracy'[15]) in the various spheres of public life. As we have seen in Chapter 4, this principle is part of Israel's constitutional law enforced by the Court. Where its application is flawed, this means that the state does not live up to the idea that it is a state of all its citizens.

It is worth examining how the expression 'a state of all its citizens' is understood in the country which has in fact recently included it in its constitution. The country in question is Slovenia, one of the new democracies of Eastern Europe and now a member of the European Union. Article 3 of the country's Constitution states that '(1) Slovenia is a state of all its citizens and is founded on the permanent and inalienable right of the Slovenian nation to self-determination.' and '(2) In Slovenia, supreme power is vested in the people.' The Slovenian nation whose right to self-determination is embodied by the State is referred to in the preamble to the Constitution: 'Proceeding from ... the fundamental and permanent right of the Slovene nation to self-determination; and from the historical fact that in a centuries-long struggle for national liberation we Slovenes have established our national identity and asserted our statehood...' This clearly refers to the identity of the Slovenian-speaking majority. The Constitution recognizes that there are Slovenian citizens who have a different national identity: the Republic undertakes 'to protect and guarantee the rights of the autochthonous Italian and Hungarian national communities' (Article 5.1). Thus the Slovenian national identity does not include all citizens of the state; on the other hand, it includes (in Article 5.1–2) those who are not citizens:

> Slovenia ... shall maintain concern for autochthonous Slovene national minorities in neighbouring countries ... Slovenes not holding Slovene citizenship may enjoy special rights and privileges in Slovenia. The nature and extent of such rights and privileges shall be regulated by law.

It is clear, then, that Slovenia, while defining itself as a state of all its citizens, distinguishes between citizenship and national identity. The state is based on the right to self-determination of the Slovenian nation – the nation whose historical identity and national struggles are mentioned in the preamble, that speaks Slovenian (the official language according to Article 11) and maintains official ties with fellow-Slovenes outside the country (ties that include a preferential right to settle in Slovenia). Those who do not belong to this majority nation (more than 10 per cent of the population), are part, in the civic sense, of the Slovene people to whom the supreme power in the state is declared to belong. Their right to preserve their distinct identity is guaranteed, with an emphasis on the special status of the two 'autochthonous communities'; but Article 61 states, in general terms, that 'everyone has the right to freely express affiliation with his nation or national community'. If the term 'a state of all its citizens' applies to this arrangement, then it is certainly compatible with a Jewish state.

Despite the oft-repeated assertion that only one concept of nationhood is legitimate in a civic democracy – the one that fully identifies national affiliation with citizenship – it is obvious than in contemporary democratic practice, the terms 'nation' and 'people' quite often have different meanings in different contexts. The Parliamentary Assembly of the Council of Europe, in a resolution adopted on 26 January 2006 (Recommendation 1735, *The concept of 'nation'*), presents a complicated and realistic picture in this respect:

> 4. The term 'nation' is deeply rooted in peoples' culture and history and incorporates fundamental elements of their identity. It is also closely linked

to political ideologies, which have exploited it and adulterated its original meaning. Furthermore, in view of the diversity of languages spoken in European countries, a concept such as 'nation' is quite simply untranslatable in many countries where, at best, only rough translations are to be found in national languages. Conversely, the words used in national languages have no adequate translation in English or French, the two official languages of the Council of Europe.

5. The Assembly has acknowledged that in some Council of Europe member states, the concept of 'nation' is used to indicate citizenship, which is a legal link (relation) between a state and an individual, irrespective of the latter's ethno-cultural origin, while in some other member states the same term is used in order to indicate an organic community speaking a certain language and characterized by a set of similar cultural and historic traditions, by similar perceptions of its past, similar aspirations for its present and similar visions of its future. In some member states both understandings are used simultaneously to indicate citizenship and national (ethno-cultural) origin respectively. To this end, the term 'nation' is sometimes used with a double meaning, and at other times two different words are used to express each of those meanings.

For all the complexity involved in different notions and terminologies of national identity, some basic principles are clear enough: a modern democratic state can, and frequently does, embody a national identity that does not include all its citizens; sometimes this identity may be shared by people who are citizens of other states; but the political sovereignty in the state belongs in any case to all its citizens, and to them alone; and the state should in any case endeavour to make all its citizens feel at home.

'The Jewish-Israeli people' and the right to self-determination

When those who attack the concept of a Jewish state are faced with arguments based on the principle of national self-determination, they sometimes deny that the Jews are 'a people' for the purposes of this principle. Former member of the Knesset Azmi Bishara, representing the traditional Arab nationalist perspective, has repeatedly employed this argument. To him, the Jews of the world are not a people; there was no Jewish national identity before the Zionist movement; the Jews were – and still are – simply a collection of religious communities with no national connection between them:

> I do not recognize the existence of one Jewish people around the world. I think that Judaism is a religion and not a nationality and that the Jewish public in the world does not have any national status. I do not think that this group has any right to self-determination. I also do not think that there was a Jewish national identity in Europe before the appearance of Zionism.

Judaism of that time was not even a unitary Jewish community. It was a series of Jewish communities that Zionism sought to convert into a People through the creation of this state.[16]

Bishara does recognize, however, the existence of the 'Jewish-Israeli people created here by Zionism' – a national and territorial entity 'based upon the Hebrew language', created in Mandatory Palestine by the Zionist enterprise and developed after the establishment of the state. Indeed, the Israeli Jews are clearly a national group according to all the usual uncontroversial criteria of modern nationalism, since they share a common territory, language and citizenship. Bishara acknowledges that this Jewish-Israeli people has a right to self-determination; this term, however much the reader may be tired of it by now, is a *sine qua non* in (ostensibly) progressive discourse. This right, according to Bishara, lends some legitimacy to the existence of the State of Israel, even though its creation was at the time, in his view, an act of colonialist injustice. Having recognized this right, Bishara empties it of content by advocating the realization of a Palestinian right of return to Israel: 'The right of self-determination is not absolute' and the Palestinian right of return – to Israel, and not to a Palestinian state, he stresses – overrides it; for that reason, 'a bi-national framework' will eventually have to be created in the entire territory between the River Jordan and the Mediterranean.

Having thus explained to the Jews, both in Israel and in the world at large, who they are, were and ought to be, Bishara, however, fails in his main purpose: proving that the Jewish character of Israel is illegitimate. Let us assume for the sake of argument that the Jews of Israel belong, not to the Jewish people with an ancient history and culture – as they believe – but rather to the Jewish-Israeli people created illegitimately by Zionism in the twentieth century. In any event, if there is such a people, if it has a right to self-determination, and if Israel is the expression of that right, this inevitably means that Israel is, by rights, a Jewish-Israeli state, even if not, as Bishara insists, a (merely) Jewish one. It is hardly worth the effort to have built such an elaborate and dubious theoretical-terminological edifice just in order to achieve these meagre results. That Israel is Israeli was of course never in doubt; the question was whether it had also a right to be Jewish, and the expression 'Jewish-Israeli people' can only signify a positive answer to this question.

How the identity of Israeli Jews is related to that of the Jews in Diaspora and what exact label should be put on the ties between them – this question, as all questions of this kind, is best left to the two sides involved. It is clear that the great majority of the Hebrew-speaking Jewish population in Israel views itself as part of the Jewish people and sees no contradiction between its Israeli identity, with its specifically Israeli characteristics, and its connection to the Jews in other countries. But even if this connection should be defined as ethno-cultural rather than national, this will not make it, or the Law of Return, any less legitimate.

Most kin-states (to borrow the language of the Venice Commission) define their bond with their kin-minorities abroad in national terms: they speak of

Greeks or Poles or Italians or Hungarians or Germans or Finns or Koreans abroad, frequently describe them as part of the 'nation' and refer to their ties with the 'motherland'. The language used in Irish Constitution is more cautious: 'the Irish nation cherishes its special affinity with people of Irish ancestry living abroad who share its cultural identity and heritage.' As for the 'host-states', these naturally regard the people in question according to their own notions of national identity. The large Armenian community in France is viewed by Armenia as part of the Armenian diaspora – i.e. as one of the communities belonging to the Armenian nation situated outside the homeland. In France, on the other hand, where there are officially 'no minorities', the people in question are regarded as belonging to the French nation and only to it, and are not even viewed, at least officially, as a distinct ethnic community. For all that, no one claims that their attachment to Armenia, or Armenia's attachment to them, is illegitimate; and in fact, French politicians were probably well aware of the importance of the Armenian element in these people's identity when they were dealing with the question of recognizing the massacre of Armenians in Turkey as a case of genocide.

The same people living in the United States who are considered by the Greek Republic as Greeks, i.e. members of the Greek nation whose 'links with the Motherland' are to be fostered by the State according to its Constitution, are considered in the United States as Greek-Americans, i.e. members of one of the numerous ethnic communities that comprise the American nation. Whether defined as national or as ethno-cultural, the links between many of these people and Greece are significant, long-established and uncontroversial. They include, on the Greek-Americans' part, using their influence within the US political system in order to advance issues of importance for Greece and for the Greek Cypriots (similarly to the practice of numerous other ethnic communities in the United States, notably the Irish, the Poles, the Jews and the Arabs[17]). The Greek government, on its part, works through a special 'General Secretariat for the Hellenic Diaspora' (an official institution the likes of which exist in most countries with an acknowledged kin-minority abroad) both in order to assist overseas Greeks in such areas as language, culture and education and in order to mobilize their political support when needed (for example, during the conflict with Macedonia).

Among scholars, some prefer to define such diasporic identities as ethnic rather than national in the full sense, stressing that one's links with the country in which one's family has lived for generations are usually stronger than with a long-lost far-away notional 'homeland'.[18] Others point to instances where identities and attachments of this kind are culturally powerful and politically significant and speak of diaspora nationalism, or of 'transnational national communities'.[19] No one will seriously ascribe an Irish national identity to all the tens of millions of people of Irish ancestry in the United States. But neither can one deny that there have been, over time, numerous examples of active and passionate involvement in Irish affairs on the part of Irish-Americans that are best described as displays of Irish nationalism.

In the final analysis, neither official nor scholarly definitions are decisive when it comes to shaping and defining the identity of groups and individuals. Many of the Jews of the world will, in fact, define themselves as belonging to the Jewish people. This does not always mean that they will define their national identity as Jewish, or solely Jewish – or that they (or other diaspora communities), will always have an unambiguous definition at hand if asked to provide one. Just as it is clear that no Israeli law or official rhetoric can impose a Jewish national – or any other – identity on Jews living outside the country, so it is clear that there is a deep sense of identification with Israel on the part of many Jews around the world, regardless of the exact way in which they define their Jewishness (if they even choose to define it at all).

It matters little, therefore, whether Jewish communities around the world should be defined as actually belonging to the 'people' whose national independence is embodied by the State of Israel, or as merely being attached and affiliated to it. The Jewish State and the Law of Return can only be denied legitimacy if one denies the right of the Jewish people in Israel to a state of their own.

6 A 'neutral state' and a democratic nation-state

The neutrality principle and a typology of democratic systems

Two concepts popular in contemporary liberal discourse often feature in the debates about the Jewish character of Israel: the 'neutrality of the state' and 'civic (as opposed to ethnic) nationalism'. As Professor Ruth Gavison of the Hebrew University, one of Israel's leading experts on human rights law, puts it:

> Among the scholars of liberalism – supporters and critics alike – there has developed an approach which interprets liberalism as a form of 'neutrality' between different perceptions of 'the good'; a kind of granting precedence to the concept of rights, shared equally to all members of society, over the concept of 'the good', which can be variously interpreted by individuals and groups. The neutrality approach may be described as the 'privatization' of non-civic affiliations and preferences. Liberal-neutral democracy is, as it were, indifferent to these particularist affiliations and preferences.[1]

The principle of state neutrality can therefore be seen as an attempt to extend the principle of civil equality. Not only must there be no discrimination between citizens in terms of their rights; in addition, the state must also refrain from preferring a particular view of the world, cultural symbols or the historical narratives of a particular group of citizens, even if that group constitutes an overwhelming majority of the population. In Israel's case, it is obvious that any specifically Jewish characteristic of the state cannot apply to all of its inhabitants, and hence cannot be viewed as culturally 'neutral' in respect of the country's various groups of citizens. Hence it may be argued that these characteristics adversely affect those who are not Jewish, on the symbolic and emotional level at least. While the Israeli flag or the national anthem do not confer on Jewish citizens any rights which are not available to their non-Jewish counterparts, they are nevertheless clearly connected with the national and cultural identity of the country's Jewish citizens, and hence are not neutral. The same applies to the Law of Return: while it does not discriminate between one citizen and another in the state (as we have tried to show), it is undeniably a law which, from the national point of view, is not neutral. Indeed, it is a clear marker of the bond between the State and the Jewish people. Since liberal values occupy an important place in modern democracy, it is worth delving into the contradiction between Israel's Jewish character and the principle of neutrality.

As Gavison rightly points out, the strictly neutralist view of the state is incompatible not only with Israel's Jewish character, but also, more generally, with the very raison d'être of the nation-state. However, this radical liberal approach is far from being universally shared by the theoreticians of liberalism themselves. Surveying this debate, Ruth Gavison observes that 'the argument that liberalism does not demand neutrality, or even that it cannot demand neutrality, and that neutrality, if it is possible, is not necessarily desirable – is a very strong argument'.[2] The debate obviously has an impact on a number of areas, over and above the question of the relationship between the State and national and cultural identities which concerns us here.

In order to be 'neutral' in terms of national and cultural identity, a democratic state must either successfully foster an identity and culture common to all its citizens (not a realistic prospect in most countries), or become merely a legal mechanism devoid of any cultural content (and thus, indeed, neutral between the different cultures). Even a bi-national state is not truly 'neutral' if, as invariably happens, it includes citizens who belong to neither of the two main national groups on which the state is based. In theory, the principle of state neutrality is debatable: it can be argued that while rightly seeking to ensure that the minorities do not feel excluded and marginalized, it goes too far and ignores the legitimate needs and wishes of the majority, as well as what is needed to make a modern state function (if only because of the crucial importance of a national language). In practice, however, it is obvious that describing the typical real-life Western democracy as 'neutral' as regards culture and identity is wholly unrealistic. It is of course true that there are strict limits to the extent to which a modern liberal state can actually impose cultural contents and norms on its citizens. However, it is clear that a typical modern democracy not only promotes such contents and norms – first and foremost, national or state language – but also defines them as the bedrock of the country's national identity. There is no denying that the practice of democratic nation-states is a long way off the theory of the neutral state. One would be hard put to imagine any state-level symbol which does not, one way or the other, contradict the principle of neutrality. Hence Israel cannot be nationally neutral, if only because of its name – Israel, which is anything but neutral – and its primary state language, Hebrew. The same applies, naturally, to other countries. In fact, there is scarcely a significant formal aspect of a country's public life that does not infringe, at least to some extent, on the principle of neutrality. The country's flag, coat of arms and national anthem, its Declaration of Independence (or similar documents of historic and symbolic significance), the solemn preamble to its constitution, its public holidays and memorial days, the ritual of state ceremonies and the content of official rhetoric, the historical figures on its stamps and bank notes, the statues and monuments that adorn its towns and cities, the names of the central squares and streets in them, the national museums and the cultural mes-sages reflected in their exhibits and displays, the content of public broadcasting, the textbooks on history, civics and literature at its state schools – all these are typically non-neutral and in many ways cannot be neutral.

The existence of a national or official language, and the overwhelming pref-erence given to it in every sphere of public life, are a fundamental fact of life in the great majority of states. But language is not 'neutral'; it is widely, and rightly, considered the cornerstone of most modern national identities. A state with an official language is thus, by definition, fundamentally 'non-neutral' when it comes to national and cultural identity. This fact is well appreciated by every linguistic minority; though linguistic majorities tend to take the preference given to their language for granted as a banal fact of civic life.[3] Israel, which recognizes Arabic as the second official language, is in fact less 'non-neutral' in this field than most national states. The existence of an official language means that multiculturalism, where it has become a widely accepted doctrine in recent decades (mostly designed to accommodate immigrants), does not make a state culturally neutral. Moreover, in recent years multiculturalism, at least in its more radical versions, has become rather less popular, and there is a clear tendency towards greater insistence on immigrants' integration and on a common 'cultural core'. This core is variously defined, but it includes, above all, the need for immigrants to master the official or national language of the country. In various Western countries this has been made obligatory; in Netherlands, once renowned for its radical multiculturalism, the policy now is to insist on the knowledge of the Dutch language prior to immigration.

When the weekly day of rest has to be chosen, there is no 'neutral' way of deciding between Sunday, the standard day of rest in all Western countries, even the most secular, whose culture is influenced by Christianity, and the Jewish Sabbath, Saturday, as is the case in Israel (or the Muslim Friday). In fact, of course, Sunday as the official day of rest in a Western country is not deliberately and consciously 'chosen' – any more than its national language is; it is the natural product of the dominance of the majority culture (which often tends to regard itself as the culture of the country as a whole) As Will Kymlicka, a leading scholar of nationalism, puts it: 'Government decisions on languages, internal boundaries, public holidays, and state symbols unavoidably involve rec-ognizing, accommodating and supporting the needs and identities of particular ethnic and national groups. The state unavoidably promotes certain cultural identities, and thereby disadvantages others.'[4] Kymlicka's conclusion is that, since the majority necessarily determines the character of the state, the collective rights of minorities must be respected, primarily in the cultural and linguistic spheres, rather than simply making doing with the 'classical' individual rights. This approach seeks to combine traditional liberalism, which emphasizes indi-vidual rights, with recognition of the right of national and cultural groups to pre-serve their distinct identity, on the basis of the assumption that cultural identity and affiliation are a key element in many people's personalities.

The specific points raised in criticism about Israel's 'lack of neutrality' as a

Jewish state are the country's national emblems, constitutional definitions and the state's official ties with the Jewish Diaspora. But it is obvious that as regards these issues, many modern democracies are far from 'neutral'. The cross, which often appears on flags of democratic states (the United Kingdom, Australia and New Zealand, the Scandinavian countries, Switzerland, Greece, Hungary, Slovakia) and even more often on their coats of arms (including that of the liberal and secular Netherlands) is hardly more 'neutral' than the Star of David. In fact, in an important sense it is less neutral: the Star of David is indeed a traditional Jewish symbol, but it has no religious significance. No Christian or Muslim need, for example, feel any religious scruples saluting the Israeli flag bearing this symbol. Not so the cross.

Giving official status to a religion, or a Church, is clearly inconsistent with the principle of state neutrality. However, this is what happens, not only in Israel – where certain aspects of the status of religion (primarily, regarding the jurisdiction of religious courts in matters of personal status) do indeed deviate from proper democratic standards – but also in such well-established liberal democracies as the United Kingdom, Denmark and Norway, as well as Greece. Generally speaking, and especially given the centrality of the national language to modern national identity, the instances of cultural 'non-neutrality' in the contemporary democratic world are so numerous and significant that they cannot be described as mere exceptions; rather, they tend to be the rule.

Moreover, experience shows that there is not necessarily a correlation between adherence to the neutrality principle on the one hand and the extent to which citizens who belong to minorities feel equal and integrated on the other – even though the whole point of the theory of neutrality is precisely to ensure that this feeling should be maintained. The British example is a case in point. The Anglican Church is the Established Church in England – but not in the rest of the United Kingdom. The monarch – the head of State – must belong to this Church, and is also its head, as well as having to take an oath to defend it. Its representatives sit in the House of Lords, ceremonies of national importance take place in the churches and the bishops are appointed by the Crown. Hence there is no neutrality of the State in this instance. However, it is generally accepted that the status of the Anglican Church is not a source of frustration for non-Anglicans in England, nor does it make those who are not part of it feel discriminated or alienated from the State. Although there is sometimes talk of doing away with the official status of the Church of England, the likelihood of this happening is fairly low, although in the wake of House of Lords reforms, representatives of other faith groups may join the Anglican bishops there. The calls to disestablish the Church of England do not come from the leaders of the religious minorities: not from the Muslims, nor the Jews, nor the Hindus, nor England's large Catholic minority (even though in the distant past Catholics' rights were cruelly flouted in the struggles that followed the establishment of the Anglican Church). No one today can seriously claim that English Catholics feel second-class citizens.

Things are different, however, in Ulster. Since the Protestant population there is divided between a number of different Churches, it was decided in 1921, when Northern Ireland was separated from the south and set up as an autonomous province, that in this part of the United Kingdom, no one Church would have any official status. Legally speaking, Ulster is religiously neutral, and its Protestant character (the whole point of its original emergence as a distinct political entity) is not enshrined in any law. Nevertheless, it is clear to all that it was in Northern Ireland, rather than in England, that the Catholic minority was discriminated against for decades, against the background of a violent national and religious conflict, and was profoundly alienated from the State. In this instance, then, purely formal religious neutrality of the State did not give the Catholics either real equality or the feeling of being fully fledged citizens of Northern Ireland; just as the absence of neutrality does not lead to discrimination and alienation in England or in Scotland, which also has an official Church.

As regards neutrality in terms of giving expression to national identity, a state which is bi-national or multi-national is, in principle, bound to abide by this principle when it comes to its main national components. According to the logic on which this model rests, the state is not supposed to be identified with one national community – even if most of its citizens belong to it – more than with others. Because of the key importance of language to most national identities, states of this kind tend in fact to be punctilious about observing linguistic neutrality. In fact, bi-nationalism tends to be officially defined as bilingualism.

According to its Constitution, Canada is bilingual. However, since the French-speakers of Quebec consider themselves a nation, and the French language is a key element of their national identity, Canada is in fact a bi-national state. This is reflected in official terminology. When the Royal Commission on Bilingualism and Biculturalism was established in 1963, it was given a remit to recommend what steps should be taken to develop Canada 'on the basis of an equal partnership between the two founding races'.[5] However, in addition to the latter (where 'race' is to be understood in the sense of 'national group'), there are groups of citizens who do not belong to either of the country's two major linguistic communities. These are not just immigrants but also native or First Nations groups, in Quebec itself as well as in the rest of Canada. Their relations with Quebec's nationalist government (which is anything but 'neutral' when it comes to language and identity) are often tension-ridden. From these groups' vantage point, Canada's bi-national system is not neutral (although their interests and rights are supposed to be protected by the official concept of multiculturalism). In practice, the bilingual (bi-national) aspect of Canada has been primarily implemented in the shape of the special status conceded to Quebec, which has allowed its government to impose French language and culture in the province. Thus French has been promoted to the rank of the sole official language in this part of Canada, and laws have been enacted in order to ensure its pre-eminence in the entire public sphere, including signs in the private commercial sector. These laws have been strongly criticized, both in Canada and on an international level, for infringing the rights of non-Francophone minorities.[6] In practice, Quebec's minority groups have become subject to a quasi-sovereign political entity whose character is markedly lacking in national and cultural neutrality. This also applies to Anglo-Canadians, who represent the overwhelming majority of Quebec's 20 per cent of non-French-speaking residents.

Similarly, in Belgium, the complex constitutional arrangements which have turned the country, in recent decades, into a bi-national (officially, bilingual) federation have brought about a situation where both the Francophone minority of Flanders and the Flemish minority of Wallonia live under a system which is far from 'neutral'. Complaints are voiced about linguistic and cultural oppression, mostly by the French-speaking minority in Flanders. This situation results from the wide-ranging powers that have been conferred on the regional subdivisions of the State specifically in order to allow each community to foster its own identity and maintain the equal status of each of the two languages in Belgium as a whole. Only the inhabitants of the capital Brussels, which constitutes a separate bilingual region in the federation, are subject to a linguistically and culturally neutral system.

The bi-national state's name and emblems should logically be neutral, although sometimes this principle is not fully implemented. In Quebec, since the Francophone nationalists no longer define themselves as French-Canadians, but rather as Quebequois, the name 'Canada' has lost its neutrality and is now largely identified with English-speaking Canadians (although originally, the Canadian label applied specifically to the French-speakers in 'British North America'). In addition, there is a surviving symbolic link between Canada and the British Crown, which symbolically privileges the English-speaking Canadian identity. This takes the form of such institutions as the Governor General, who is formally appointed by the sovereign, the Royal Canadian Mounted Police, and the law courts, where the prosecution is referred to as 'the Crown'. However, these breaches of the neutrality principle are relatively insignificant. Over the last several decades, the tendency has been to underscore the equal status of Canada's two national-linguistic identities, the English-speaking and the French-speaking, on the practical and symbolic level alike. Unlike its Australian and New Zealand counterparts, in 1965 Canada adopted a new national (Maple Leaf) flag, which does not include the Union Jack as one of its elements (although Canada's coat of arms still includes the British crown).

A bi-national State is naturally apt to be 'non-neutral' towards minorities not belonging to either of the two main groups (as well as to the 'stranded' minorities like the French-speakers in Flanders). In Czechoslovakia, the State – in principle neutral towards the Czech and Slovak identities and giving an equal expression to both of them (although the former was in fact in a stronger position, which was the argument used by the Slovaks to sue for 'divorce') – was not neutral towards Slovakia's large Hungarian minority. In pre-Second World War democratic Czechoslovakia, the official view, anchored in the Constitution, regarded the State as giving expression to the identity of the 'Czechoslovak nation'. This state had large national minorities, both German and Hungarian.

Where the State is based on the perception of all its citizens sharing the same national identity (France being the clearest example), then by definition there can be no preference of one national identity over another within its citizen body. What is known as 'civic nationalism' is based on the assumption that citizenship and national identity are congruous. However, from the vantage point of any groups which do not share this perception, it is obvious that the state's national identity is in fact that of the majority and is neither neutral nor inclusive. For French citizens of Breton, Basque, Catalan, Corsican or Alsatian (German-speaking) origin, who see their origins as a national identity in the full sense of the word and not as a cultural–ethnic–regional identity in the framework of the French people, the markers and symbols of French nationhood – and first and foremost, the French language which dominates all walks of public life – are the markers and symbols of the majority only and do not express their own national identity.[7] Only the future will tell whether the descendants of Muslim immigrants (mainly from the Maghreb) will regard the French identity as fully 'theirs'. It should always be borne in mind that even a pronounced form of 'civic nationalism', French style, has been constructed, in historical terms, around a particular ethnic, cultural and linguistic nucleus. Even when this nucleus shows itself genuinely willing to integrate other groups on equal terms and to give them a 'feeling of being at home' within the shared state-level national identity, the latter will still, inevitably, be influenced by the identity of the nucleus much more than by that of the other groups – as long as these have not been entirely assimilated.[8] The French state can only be said to be ethnically neutral if what is meant by 'ethnic' is ethnic origin as such, and not ethnic identity which still retains its own cultural content, differing from mainstream French culture.

The French law banning the Muslim veil in public schools is a case in point. In many other Western democracies, such a law would be regarded as excessively interfering with individual freedom, and/or with the right of an ethnic and religious minority to preserve its distinct culture. From the viewpoint of the French Republic, however, there is only one legitimate culture in France: the French culture which is Republican, secular, modern and insists on gender equality according to contemporary French and Western norms. The report of the Stasi Commission, which recommended the ban, states that 'La laïcité est constitutive de notre histoire collective'. President Chirac, in his statement on the appointment of the commission, spoke of the principle of *laïcité* as being 'au coeur de notre identité républicaine', 'inscrite dans nos traditions', a basis of 'notre cohésion nationale'.[9] The report states that one of the values on which *laïcité*, as practised in France, is based is 'neutralité du pouvoir politique'. There is no room, in this discourse, for the possibility that some French citizens may regard themselves as belonging to another collective 'we', with a different history, culture and identity.

And indeed, many French citizens of North African origin – especially women – supported the law, and some of them actively campaigned for it. But for those French citizens, fairly numerous, who adhere to traditional Muslim and North African norms, and even for those who are less traditional but have adopted the veil as a badge of their distinct identity, this law is an extreme example of 'non-neutrality' on the part of the State, which is both cultural and, indirectly but very significantly, ethnic.

While the French Republic is 'non-neutral', from the standpoint of many of its Muslim citizens, because of its secular character (defended though it is by the rhetoric of neutrality), in some other West European countries the tension between Muslim immigrants and the prevailing culture is sometimes exemplified by an official acknowledgement of this culture's Christian roots. The Italian Republic, despite its officially secular character, has maintained the law, originally passed under Mussolini, requiring that the crucifix be displayed in State school classrooms, courts of law and hospitals. In 2002, in the wake of an application by a Muslim parent, a lower-court judge ruled that a crucifix in a public school violated the constitutional requirement for all religions to be equally respected. This caused a public outcry, in the course of which the president of the Republic stated that 'the crucifix has always been considered not only as a distinctive sign of a particular religious credo, but above all as a symbol of the values that are at the base of our Italian identity'. In 2004, Italy's Constitutional Court overturned the lower court's decision, and in 2006 the Italian Council of State ruled in a similar case that the crucifix was not just a religious symbol, but also a symbol of 'the values which underlie and inspire our constitution, our way of living together peacefully'. The Council's judges held that the notion of tolerance and individual rights originated with Christianity and 'in this sense the crucifix can have a highly educational symbolic function, regardless of the religion of the pupils'. They also noted that the concept of a secular state is variously interpreted in different states, depending on their history and culture.[10]

When it comes to the integration of immigrants in Western countries (a problem whose importance has increased greatly in recent decades), not just French-style civic nationalism but also the more flexible version which prevails in the United States, which allows for far greater cultural diversity within the common American nation, is non-neutral towards immigrants, their languages and cultures, as opposed to the 'host' country's language and culture. This is the reason why Kymlicka, commenting particularly on the cultural aspects of US integration policy, concludes that the belief that 'civic nations' are neutral between ethno-cultural identities is 'a myth'.[11]

A nation-state which includes a substantial minority insisting on its right to maintain its own identity, different from the national identity of the majority, cannot by definition be neutral between these two identities.

Partition and 'neutrality'

In the Israeli–Palestinian context, the principle of 'two states for two people' as a solution to the national conflict in the area between the Mediterranean and the Jordan obviously means that these two states cannot be neutral in terms of their national character. This is the logic that led to the 1947 UN Partition Plan. In the eyes of the international community, the need to give both peoples in the country, the Jews and the Arabs, a nation-state of their own outweighed the difficulty of partitioning a small country without clear ethnic dividing lines. The Israeli Declaration of Independence was worded in accordance with this logic. It also contained an expression of willingness to cooperate with the United Nations in implementing the partition plan. The Arab side's rejection of the latter and the ensuing war prevented the UN resolution from being implemented. However, the outcome of Israel's War of Independence meant that the Jewish state would come into existence only in part of Mandatory Palestine, and Israel would not determine the political future of the Palestinian Arabs in the West Bank and the Gaza Strip that were taken over by Jordan and Egypt, respectively. By accepting the armistice lines (and offering to sign a peace treaty with Jordan on the basis of those lines), Israel was accepting the principle of partition (though not the borders suggested by the 1947 plan). In the wake of Israel's victory in the Six Day War and the occupation of the West Bank and Gaza Strip, this partition was revoked de facto, and after the Israeli Right came to power in 1977, perpetuating Israeli control over the entire western part of the biblical and historical Land of Israel became an ideological goal of Israeli governments – up to the Oslo Accords in 1993, which started a new process of partition – this time with the Palestinian Authority as a (highly problematic) partner.

Had the principle of the 'Undivided Land of Israel', espoused by the ideological Right until Oslo, been implemented by annexing the territories to Israel, while observing the fundamental rules of modern democracy – in other words by granting full civil rights to the Palestinian Arabs living in these territories – then in practice, irrespective of any official definition, the result would have been a bi-national state. Even if this state had continued for some time to bear the name of Israel, this would not have changed its bi-national nature. Even had it been possible to maintain over time a stable, significant Jewish majority in a state of this kind (and in practice clearly this would not be feasible), there would have been no practical possibility nor democratic justification for such a state to function as a nation-state giving expression to the national identity of just one of the country's two peoples. Today, as opposed to the past, it is clear to most Israelis that a Palestinian-Arab state will come about, and most of the right-wing camp accepts this fact. Since Sharon's government officially accepted the 'Road Map' calling for the establishment of a viable independent Palestinian state, there is no longer a serious controversy over this question in the Israeli political mainstream. However, the other side of the coin – the legitimate existence of a state that gives expression to the Jewish people's right to national independence – is far from being self-evident and accepted by all.

The real alternative to Israel as a Jewish state is not some utopian state which has no national identity (yet to be seen anywhere in the world), nor a state all of whose citizens share the same national identity – a model of democracy which is possible and legitimate in principle, but is in complete contradiction to the culture, identity and aspirations of the Jews and Arabs alike. If the Jewish character of the state is done away with, it can only be replaced by a bi-national (Jewish–Arab) one. Generally speaking, the advocates of this approach avoid the explicit appellation 'bi-national state' – perhaps because an Arab-Palestinian state in one part of the country and a bi-national Jewish-Arab state alongside it (one-and-a-half states for one people and half a state for the other, rather 'than two states for two peoples') are too obviously not a fair deal.

Professor As'ad Ghanem of the Political Science Department at Haifa University, calling explicitly for a bi-national state within the 1967 borders, is a rare example of candour in this field.[12] Alternatively, As'ad Ghanem is willing to accept a single bi-national state between the Mediterranean and the Jordan. But there seems to be no good reason to assume that the Israeli Jews and the Palestinians from West Bank and Gaza are today more willing and able to co-exist within a single state than in 1947, when the international community opted for partition. Moreover, such a state, with an Arab and Muslim majority and in the heart of the Arab and Muslim Middle East, could not fail to become in practice, however it is defined on paper, an Arab and a Muslim state, rather than a bi-national democracy (a model very rare in the West and wholly non-existent in this region).

In 2007, a series of documents presenting the 'future vision' of Israel's Arab minority was adopted by leading public figures and civic organizations in the Arab community, and endorsed by the Arab parties in the Knesset. The documents reject the designation of Israel as a Jewish state and envisage a bi-national state in all but name. Among other things, they call for the adoption of a 'consociational democracy' on the model of Canada, Belgium and Switzerland, and for giving the representatives of the Arab community in the Knesset a power of veto over the decisions of the parliamentary majority on all important matters of state.[13] But even these documents shy away from calling the bi-national spade a spade.

Most of those who propose doing away with Israel's character as a Jewish state speak of turning Israel into a 'state of all its citizens'. In the civic-legal sense, any democracy is, and should be, a state of all its citizens. But in the national-cultural sense, this term can be properly applied to democracies in which all of a country's citizens are regarded as sharing the same national identity and there are, at least in theory, no minorities that belong to a people different from the one whose national independence is embodied by the State. This is not feasible in Israeli conditions, and is exactly the opposite of what is desired by most critics of the Jewish State, since they are usually the first to stress the Arab and Palestinian identity of Israel's Arab minority.

Those who suggest, explicitly or implicitly, that Israel should approximate the bi-national model (even if it does not fully adopt it), believe that, since the Arab minority in Israel is a large one, making up a considerable proportion (around 18 per cent) of the country's citizens, and in particular since this is a 'native' or 'indigenous' minority and not an immigrant community, the very definition of the state and its character must also give expression to the national identity of this minority (irrespective of the need to give independence to the Palestinians in the territories). It should be noted that in one important area – recognizing Arabic as a second official language – Israel has indeed followed this approach and provided an official expression of the importance of the Arab component of its civic community. This state of affairs is taken for granted in Israel and does not attract much attention, since it has never been disputed. In other countries, however, the question of the minority's language and its official recognition is one of the key issues – if not *the* key issue – in many national struggles. In the democratic world, the situation in which a nation-state fully recognizes the language of the minority as a second official language (and not just as a language recognized in those areas where members of the minority constitute a majority), and the minority's representatives are entitled to address parliament in this language, is far from self-evident. This arrangement reflects a far-reaching recognition of the collective identity of the minority. However, it is clear that in other areas, Israel manifestly functions as a national state which lays great stress on its Jewish identity. Is this justified?

Here it should be recalled that when the UN Special Committee on Palestine (UNSCOP) drafted the partition plan in 1947, there was supposed to be a very large Arab minority in the territory of the proposed Jewish state – more than 40 per cent of its total population (although it was assumed that the Jewish majority would grow as a result of Jewish migration). Under other circumstances, this ratio between two national communities within the borders of a single state might indeed have been thought to justify setting up a bi-national regime in it. However, since the UNSCOP members adopted the principle of partitioning the country between the two peoples in order to grant independence to both of them, the size of the Arab minority did not prevent them from recommending that a Jewish state – not a bi-national one – be established side by side with the Arab state. The authors of the UNSCOP report assumed that the two states would have a pronounced national character – so much so that they rhetorically identified the majority people with the state itself: the partition, in their words, is intended to 'qualify both peoples (Arab and Jewish) to take their places as independent nations in the international community'. They do not qualify this statement, with regard to the Jewish state, on the grounds of its future large Arab minority. Moreover, on one of the primary subjects of criticism over Israel's 'lack of neutrality' – immigration policy – the authors of the UNSCOP report assume, as we have seen, that the Jewish state will not be neutral, but will encourage Jewish immigration; in fact, they consider the Jewish insistence on opening the gates of the country to Jewish immigration as one of the main reasons for partition. They do not consider all of this to run counter to their insistence on complete civil equality for the Arab minority in the Jewish state.

The logic of partition is underscored by comparing it with the recent case of Macedonia, where a deliberate choice has been made to maintain the country's territorial integrity at the cost of attenuating its national character. Macedonia declared independence in 1991 after the break up of the Yugoslav Federation, as a national state of the (Slav)-Macedonian people speaking a Slav language called Macedonian. Among other things, the preamble to the 1992 Constitution stipulated that the Republic of Macedonia is 'the national state of the Macedonian people', which grants the various minority groups 'full equality as citizens and permanent co-existence with the Macedonian people'. The preamble referred to the Macedonian people's struggle to preserve their national identity and independence, and related to various historic events in this struggle. 'The Macedonian language, written using its Cyrillic alphabet', was declared the Republic's language (with a recognized status also for languages of minorities in areas where they constitute a majority). The Constitution provided for the state's ties with 'those persons belonging to the Macedonian people in neighbouring countries'. There was a special reference to the Macedonian Orthodox Church before 'other religious communities and groups'. This can be compared with an even stronger statement in the Constitution of one of Europe's 'new democracies': Bulgaria. Article 13 guarantees religious freedom to all: 'The religious institutions shall be separate from the state. Eastern Orthodox Christianity is considered the traditional religion in the Republic of Bulgaria'. This formula, which reflects the importance of Orthodox Christianity to Bulgarian national identity, is certainly not 'neutral' from the viewpoint of the country's large Turkish Muslim minority.[14]

A very large Albanian minority – more than one-quarter, or according to other estimates, up to one-third of the population – was included in the borders of the Republic of Macedonia, as well as a number of other minority communities. The Macedonian majority in Macedonia is therefore markedly smaller than the Jewish majority in Israel, although it is larger than the Jewish majority which was supposed to be in the Jewish state within the borders of the partition resolution immediately following its establishment.

The various European institutions, which went over the constitutions and laws of the states of the former Yugoslavia and the other Eastern European countries with a fine toothcomb, in order to make sure that they met European human rights standards, did not require Macedonia to change the national definitions in its Constitution (although they did criticize some practical aspects of the government's policy towards the Albanian minority). Macedonia's admission to the Council of Europe is a highly significant democratic 'stamp of approval'. In 1991 the European Union's Council of Ministers laid down the criteria for diplomatic recognition, by the Union's members, of the independence of the new countries which came into being following the break-up of Yugoslavia. One of the criteria was protecting the human rights of the ethnic minorities within each country, in accordance with European standards. Of the former Yugoslav republics, only Slovenia and Macedonia (under the 1992 Constitution) met the criteria stipulated.[15]

However, the Albanian minority did not accept its status as a national minority in a Macedonian nation-state. The more moderate Albanian leaders demanded a change to the constitutional definitions, so that the status of the Albanian language would be put on the same footing as Macedonian, wide-ranging self-rule would be given to the Albanian-majority areas and a mechanism would be introduced at the Macedonian parliament for decisions to be taken with the approval of the various ethnic groups. In practice, their demands amounted to a call to make Macedonia into a bi-national state. The extremists went further, demanding the secession of areas inhabited by Albanians. Eventually, armed groups of Albanian extremists from neighbouring Kosovo invaded Macedonia. Some local Albanians joined their ranks, and the state was faced with the danger of an all-out ethnic civil war. In order to avoid this, as well as to secure Western support, the Macedonian government was forced to accept the advice of West European countries and to negotiate a far-reaching constitutional reform with the Albanian parties. Talks between the parties took place with the active involvement of European representatives, who submitted compromise proposals, on which was based the final agreement which was signed on 13 August 2001. Its provisions were then enshrined in the country's new Constitution, adopted the same year.

Under these circumstances, it is not obvious that the content of the agreement necessarily reflects current European norms guaranteeing minority rights in a multi-ethnic society: this is a political compromise worked out under the pressure of armed violence directed against a country which had previously received European recognition as a democratic state. However, it must be assumed that current European norms did indeed influence the content of the arrangements made, and the agreement was praised by international human rights organizations as a good example of multiculturalism and multi-ethnicity. The agreement itself declares that it 'comports with the highest international standards [of democracy and human rights], which themselves continue to evolve' (Basic Principles, 1.4).

To a considerable extent the agreement waters down Macedonia's character as the nation-state of the Macedonian people, and introduces into its system of government elements of a bi-national state. The character of the state is not fully neutral between the various ethno-national identities within it, but it is considerably less 'non-neutral' than before. The preamble to the Constitution has been redrafted, with the expression 'the national state of the Macedonian people' deleted, and the references to the Macedonian national narrative substantially reduced. The new preamble speaks on behalf of the 'citizens of the Republic of Macedonia' and then lists the national groups which comprise the citizen body: 'the Macedonian people, as well as citizens living within its borders who are part of the Albanian people, the Turkish people, the Vlach people, the Serbian people, the Romany people, the Bosniac people and others'. Thus the expression 'the Macedonian people' still refers specifically to the Macedonian-speaking majority, but this people is merely the first in the list of 'peoples' comprising the state.

The powers of local authorities have been greatly expanded, which in practice means that Albanian-majority areas have been granted considerable local authority. The status of the Albanian language has been strengthened. Other religious groups – first and foremost the Islamic community – are now referred to in the Constitution together with the Macedonian Orthodox Church. Amendments to the Constitution, as well as new laws touching on culture, language, education, personal documentation and the use of symbols, must now be approved by a majority of members of parliament who belong to communities other than the country's majority (which basically means the Albanian deputies). This latter provision clearly brings Macedonia's new system of government close to the bi-national model.

However, the country's national character has not been entirely done away with in the new arrangements. First, the very name Macedonia expresses the national identity of the majority ('the Macedonian people'). The preamble to the Constitution still contains a number of historical references relating to the Macedonian national struggle. 'The Macedonian language, written using its Cyrillic alphabet, is the official language throughout the Republic of Macedonia and in the international relations of the Republic of Macedonia', while 'any other language spoken by at least 20 per cent of the population [i.e. Albanian] is also an official language' (Article 7). The country's flag and coat of arms, perceived as symbols of Macedonian national identity, remain unchanged (the minority communities are allowed to fly their own flags alongside the state flag), and the national anthem of the republic is still a distinctly national Macedonian song, extolling the heroes of the Macedonian national struggle. In addition, Article 49 of the 1991 Constitution regarding the ties between the state and the Macedonian ethnic diaspora appears in the new Constitution as well: 'The Republic cares for the status and rights of those persons belonging to the Macedonian people in neighbouring countries, as well as Macedonian expatriates, assists their cultural development and promotes links with them.' This point is particularly noteworthy: the state's official ties with the diaspora of the majority ('the Macedonian people') are acceptable under current European norms, even after its national character has deliberately been watered down as part of the compromise with the minority, creating a 'half-way house' between a national and a bi-national state. This minority, of course, has its own trans-national links beyond the country's borders (in fact the Constitution refers to it as 'citizens ... who are part of the Albanian people'), but it is with the diaspora of the majority that the state is officially connected. Hence the state is not 'neutral' in this respect. Another 'non-neutral' provision which remains in the Constitution is Article 36: 'The Republic provides specific social security rights [inter alia] to those imprisoned and expelled for supporting the ideas of the separate identity of the Macedonian people and of Macedonian statehood'.

If we try to compare the Macedonian case with the Israeli one, the point must first be made that the agreement in Macedonia is based on a logic which is the exact opposite of the logic of partitioning Mandatory Palestine between its two peoples. For the Slav-Macedonian side, the paramount consideration was to preserve Macedonia's territorial integrity. It ruled out not just secession by the Albanian-majority regions, but a federative solution as well, fearing that this would pave the way to secession. Hence the Macedonian leadership and the people whom it represents deliberately opted for the country's integrity over maintaining intact the national character of the state. Only time will tell whether this was the right decision for them. At all events, this decision enjoyed broad international support, since it maintained the stability of recognized international borders – a basic guiding principle of the international community. The second basic principle of the Framework Agreement signed in August 2001 (the first being the rejection of violence) reads: 'Macedonia's sovereignty and territorial integrity, and the unitary character of the State are inviolable and must be preserved. There are no territorial solutions to ethnic issues.'

In contrast, the partition of Mandatory Palestine between its two peoples endorsed by the international community in 1947 is exactly this: a distinctly territorial solution to an ethno-national problem involving a conflict between two peoples with conflicting national aspirations, living in a single country. To some extent, this applies to the UNSCOP minority proposal as well: establishing a bi-national federation in the territory of Mandatory Palestine, comprising two secondary entities – a 'Jewish state' and an 'Arab state'. As shown earlier, the Palestinian leadership rejected the second option as well, calling for a unitary Arab state in the entire country. The majority, in both UNSCOP and the United Nations, was convinced that given the situation prevailing in the country, the bitterness of the national conflict between the two peoples and the overall situation of the Jewish people, the need to give full national independence to the two peoples outweighed the aspiration to maintain the country's integrity – despite the accompanying problems of dividing the country up along ethno-national lines. The events since 1947 have fully vindicated this choice. Suggesting that an Arab-Palestinian state be set up alongside Israel and Israel itself be turned into a bi-national state, or one with bi-national characteristics, is equivalent to a (hypothetical) proposal to partition Macedonia and set up an Albanian state in the country's western areas with their dense Albanian population, and also to do away with the state's national Macedonian character in its remaining areas, which also contain a considerable Albanian minority. This would hardly have been a fair proposal.

Denying the Jewish people's right to maintain a democratic nation-state (alongside a Palestinian-Arab state which needs to be established) rides roughshod over the very moral principle which is supposed to be served by the theory of state neutrality: the value of equality, the duty to act even-handedly and fairly with regard to both sides – in this case, both sides of the national conflict. If we remember that the Jewish-Israeli public is a small minority within the large Arab-Muslim majority of the region (a minority which wishes to preserve its distinct identity); if we remember that each of the states which make up this regional majority expresses its Arab identity officially and explicitly, even when these states have considerable non-Arab minorities, and this does not arouse international criticism; and if we take account of the fear expressed, as we have seen, by the Palestinian intellectual Edward Said, at what the Jews can expect, if (or, as he put it, when), they give up their national independence and become a minority – if we take all of these considerations into account, it will be obvious that the rejection of Israel's Jewish identity in the name of equality amounts to nothing less than trampling the principle of equality underfoot in the guise of defending it.

It must of course be remembered that the principle of partitioning the country between its two peoples has not yet been realized, for all that it is quite clear today that the establishment of a Palestinian-Arab state is a question of time only. The process of its establishment actually began with the setting up of the Palestinian Authority in the wake of the Oslo Accords, when most of the Palestinian inhabitants of the territories came under PA rule. However, a series of separate Palestinian enclaves in the West Bank (Gaza was fully evacuated in 2006) cannot in any way be seen as constituting reasonable implementation of the Palestinian people's right to self-determination and dignified existence. This is indeed a situation where there is a lack of basic equality between the country's two peoples in terms of their national rights. The logical way of proceeding in order to set this right is to support the establishment of a viable Arab-Palestinian state which will recognize Israel and live with it in peace, without seeking to undermine its national character.

The neutrality principle, the Law of Return and the refugee problem

The principle of equal national rights for the country's two peoples should also apply specifically to one of the key and most controversial aspects of Israel's Jewish character: the issue of the Law of Return. There exists today, it must be admitted, a basic inequality between the two peoples in this field; not because there is a state which is prepared to take in and naturalize members of the Jewish diaspora, but rather because there is no state which is prepared to do the same for members of the Palestinian diaspora, many of whom live in dire conditions. The cliché that many Israelis (manipulatively adopting pan-Arabic rhetoric) have used in the past with regard to the national aspirations of the Palestinian Arabs – 'they have 20 states' – ignores the fact that there is in fact not a single state where Palestinian refugees are welcome, or which the Palestinians can call their national home; and such a state should exist.[16] What applies to the Jewish-Israeli case should apply similarly to its Arab-Palestinian counterpart: national independence for a diaspora people naturally entails a 'law of return', however worded; and no doubt the Palestinian state will adopt such a law when it comes into being.

Had Israel been the sole heir of Mandatory Palestine, rather than one of the two nation-states intended to exist within its boundaries, it would have been difficult to justify denying the Palestinian refugees and their descendants the right of repatriation conferred on Jews by the Law of Return (though this consideration does not seem to have concerned the supporters of the 'Undivided Land of Israel' from the Israeli Right). On the other hand, if the 'two states for two peoples' formula is accepted and account is taken of the fact that both peoples have their own diasporas, it goes without saying that these states will practise an immigration policy which will not be nationally neutral.

In order to assess Israel's rejection of any Palestinian right of return to its territory, note must be taken of the circumstances in which the refugee problem came about: a war which was waged by the Palestinian leadership and Arab countries with the stated goal of destroying Israel. By way of comparison, in 1947 British India was divided between India and Pakistan: the partition was accompanied by bloody clashes in various parts of the subcontinent. Estimates variously put the numbers of refugees at over ten million: Muslims displaced from India to Pakistan, and Hindus in the opposite direction. India's Constitution dwells at length on the issue of entitlement to citizenship, the guiding principle being continuity between British India and the Indian Union as its successor state. However, with regard to the millions of Muslim refugees who were born in the country's present-day territory, were subjects of British India and found themselves in Pakistan as a result of these bloody events, their right of return and citizenship (and consequently that of their descendants) was explicitly revoked under Article 7 of the Constitution: 'Notwithstanding anything in articles 5 and 6 [of this Constitution], a person who has after the first day of March, 1947, migrated from the territory of India to the territory now included in Pakistan shall not be deemed to be a citizen of India.' This provision was adopted despite the fact that the two countries were not, despite all the violence which accompanied the partition, engaged in a fully fledged war, that Pakistan was not officially defined as an enemy state when the Muslim refugees arrived from India, and that India's right to exist was never challenged, whether in 1947 or subsequently. It should be noted that these refugees did not become stateless, since Pakistan granted them citizenship (unlike the Arab countries in the case of Palestinian refugees). The comparison with the Indian example also indicates that the principle of equality is violated not by the existence of the Israeli Law of Return, and not by Israel's refusal to accept the Palestinian claim of a right to return to its territory, but by the fact that the Palestinian people has no national home of its own.

Another argument is that what is wrong with the Law of Return is that it is used by Israel as an instrument to impose its rule on the Palestinians in the territories. This argument has been advanced, inter alia, by Oren Yiftachel (Professor of Geography, Ben-Gurion University). He acknowledges that in fact Israel's Law of Return is not in breach of the norms accepted in the democratic world, but nevertheless opposes this law, because of the specific circumstances of the conflict:

> [I]n none of the European states in question has there in the last century taken place a process in which one ethnic group has gained control and expanded its hold over disputed territory, like the situation in Israel/ Palestine. Hence, the Law of Return, which allows only Jews to immigrate to Israeli-Palestinian territory, becomes part of the struggle for that territory, and therefore does not resemble the migration of the Bulgarians or the Germans to what is in any case their ethnic state.[17]

Yiftachel does not make it quite clear what the 'disputed territory' in question is – the State of Israel itself or the whole country between the Mediterranean and the Jordan. If what is disputed is the very existence of a Jewish nation-state in any part of the country, and hence doubt must be cast on the legitimacy of any law which helps Israel in its struggle on this matter, then the list of laws which are to be revoked according to this criterion is quite long: the budget laws are certainly 'part of the struggle', as is the law on compulsory military service, and perhaps also the law which regulates the functioning of Israel's universities. But if what is disputed is Israeli military rule over the Palestinians in the territories occupied in June 1967, then, clearly, this rule runs counter to fundamental democratic principles with or without the Law of Return, since it is by definition not based on 'consent of the governed'. Whatever the historical rights and wrongs of the prolonged conflict, and whoever should be thought to bear primary responsibility for its continuation, it is clear that the goal must be to put an end to the conflict and to the military occupation.

There is no real connection between the need to solve this conflict and the Law of Return, which was enacted in the early 1950s, long before the West Bank and Gaza fell into Israeli hands. It is a fact that despite Arab claims and fears to the contrary, since Israel's establishment there has never been any connection between immigration and the occupation of territory or unwillingness to evacuate territory: the mass immigration of the 1950s did not bring about any territorial expansion, the Six Day War took place when immigration was at a very low ebb, while most of the large-scale immigration from the former Soviet Union in the early 1990s took place on the eve of the Oslo Accords. Moreover, the idea of 'demographic competition' in a setting of the 'Undivided Land of Israel' (whereby supposedly the Palestinian population's birth rate would have to be offset by Jewish immigration, enabling Israel to maintain its rule over the occupied territories) has lost its relevance since the Palestinian Authority was established in part of the West Bank and Gaza, removing the bulk of the Palestinian population from direct Israeli rule. Israel's Right does wish to retain a large part of the West Bank and as many of the settlements as possible – something which will not enable the Palestinians to have a viable state. But there is no longer any question of retaining millions of Palestinians under Israeli sovereignty, and hence no question of trying to 'offset' their numbers with the help of Jewish immigration to Israel.

The conclusion, then, is that the Law of Return cannot be rejected on the basis of international human rights norms, and there is no basis for rejecting it on any 'local' grounds resulting from conditions that prevail in Israel. Denying the legitimacy of the Law of Return is merely yet another form of rejecting the principle of two states for two peoples.

Two examples of partition: India and Ireland

Above, we referred briefly to the Indian subcontinent's 1947 partition into two states, Pakistan for the Muslims and the Indian Union. Let us now look at how democratic India has developed since then. Under its Constitution, the Indian Union is a secular republic, containing a mosaic of ethnic and religious groups, including a large Muslim minority. It does not define itself as a Hindu state, and the Hindu religion has no official status in India, although Hindus make up the great majority of the country's population and Hindu culture overwhelmingly shapes the face of Indian society. It must, however, be remembered that the concept of nationhood prevailing in modern India – shaped by the Congress Party during the period of the struggle for independence and in the state's early years – regards all of India's ethnic, linguistic and religious groups as belonging to a single Indian people, as sharing the same national identity. Nothing could be further from the official, and widely accepted, view than to define India as a bi-national state (whether Hindu–Muslim, which would have meant accepting the view of Pakistan's founders who regarded the subcontinent's Muslims as a distinct nation, or in some other way). Rather, the state is based on an outlook which recognizes no distinct national identities within the ranks of its citizenry. This is a kind of 'civic nationalism' which differs from the French model in that it accepts far greater linguistic and cultural diversity (with various states having their own official languages), so that language is not central to the definition of national identity. India has managed to remain united and democratic (a very considerable feat) despite the separatist movements which in a number of areas reject the prevailing concept of Indian nationalism, fighting for secession and national independence. For these movements' supporters, Indian national identity and its symbols are neither 'neutral' nor 'inclusive', but simply alien.[18] It should, however, be noted that Indian democracy has managed to forge a strong sense of patriotism and belonging to the Indian nation among many members of ethnic groups with active secessionist movements.

The dominant concept of national identity in India is thus utterly different from that of the two peoples in the area between the Mediterranean and the Jordan. We have seen how, during the 1947 UN debate, the Indian representative, wishing to translate to the realities of Mandatory Palestine India's prevailing concept of nationhood, argued that there was no need to partition Palestine into two states because there were no two people there: the Jews and Arabs belonged a single nation, the 'people of Palestine'. Obviously, had this indeed been the case, there would have been no need for a 'Jewish state' or an 'Arab state', or for partition itself. But this view from India was completely out of touch with the realities in Mandatory Palestine.

India's 150 million Muslim minority is officially regarded, as are all of the country's religious or ethnic groups, as an inseparable part of the Indian people. This is also how its leaders define it. India does not accept the view which lay behind the founding of Pakistan, to the effect that the Muslims of the subcontinent constitute a distinct nation. Consequently, India's Muslim citizens are not considered a national minority – and certainly not a Pakistani national minority. If the Muslims in India were to see themselves as such, then clearly for them the national character of the Indian State and its symbols would not be 'neutral'. Calling for Israel to become a bi-national state, or one with bi-national characteristics, is analogous to calling for India to become an Indian–Pakistani state.

Although the definitions and symbols of Indian nationalism are, in principle, neutral and inclusive, the neutrality principle is not fully adhered to, primarily with regard to the national language. India's Constitution stipulates that Hindi shall be the official language of the Union.[19] However, Hindi is far from having the status enjoyed by the French language in France. Only one-third or so of India's inhabitants are Hindi speakers; however, they constitute by far the largest language group in the country. The Constitution allows each of the states which make up the Union to determine a local official language. In practice, English is widely used, on both the official and the unofficial levels. The Constitution allows for English to be used officially on a provisional basis, until Hindi gains a more commanding position. However, even after decades of independence, there has been no weakening in the status of English, the language of the colonial power and, to a large extent, of the Indian elite. It is precisely English, unlike Hindi, which enjoys the benefit of 'neutrality' between all of India's different linguistic groups; in this sense it is preferable to Hindi for many non-Hindi speakers. Understandably, however, the modern Indian state wishes to give a national status to an indigenous Indian language rather than to a foreign one. The natural candidate for this role is indeed Hindi, the most widely spoken Indian language, and one which represents a link between modern and ancient (Sanskrit-based) Indian culture. But a constitutional provision to this effect (however flexibly implemented) inevitably means that Indian nationalism is identified more with one particular linguistic-cultural group than with others. While this state of affairs runs counter to the neutrality principle, it nevertheless arises from the nature of the modern nation-state and the needs of nation-building.

Similarly, it is hard to view India's flag as neutral; particularly from the viewpoint of the Muslim minority. The dharma wheel which appears on the flag is an ancient symbol connected to Ashoka, the famous third-century Buddhist-convert emperor. This is a symbol with which both Buddhists and Hindus can identify, insofar as the dharma is a key concept with religious-normative connotations in both the Hindu and the Buddhist traditions. Not a few Muslims, however, probably have to make an effort not to see it as a symbol of idolatry. This example demonstrates how hard it is for a nation-state to meet the standards of cultural neutrality – even when it proclaims that all of its citizens constitute a single people and genuinely tries to find symbols and national expressions with which all population groups will be able to identify in equal measure. When a new state is founded, there is a natural desire to emphasize its historical roots and find symbols with which most of its population can identify. To this end, the historical and cultural heritage of the country is consulted. However, history and culture are not neutral, and what arouses emotional identification among some parts of the population does not necessarily do likewise among other parts. On the other hand, in the case of a long-established nation, generally speaking its array of national symbols will have emerged a long time ago under the influence of prevailing cultural traditions, such as the three crosses (St George's [England], St Andrew's [Scotland] and St Patrick's [Ireland]) on the British flag. Such powerful traditional symbols are not easily changed in the interests of 'neutrality'.

In recent decades, the Congress Party, which led the struggle for independence and went on to govern India for a long time after achieving it, has had to face a serious rival – the BJP with its notion of 'Hindu nationalism'. This idea now plays a prominent role in public life and in shaping the face of the country.[20] According to this outlook, known in Hindi as 'Hindutva', Hinduism is not a religious identity which exists alongside other religions in India, but a national one with broad cultural characteristics: India's original historical identity, on which the modern Indian state should also be based. Although the BJP's primary constituency is located in the Hindi-speaking north, the party also enjoys support in other parts of the country and does not limit its concept of Hindu nationalism to Hindi-speakers only. The BJP accepts the principle of India as a secular state as stipulated in the Constitution, but gives it a different interpretation from that of the Congress Party. Many of its representatives have claimed that, under the guise of secularism, the Muslim minority has obtained excessive rights. One of their major aims is to change school curricula, arguing that the education system must reflect the centrality of Hindu culture in India's identity.

As is usually the case with nationalisms, Hindu nationalism exists in different versions, more moderate and more radical, but they all share an emphasis on the bond between Hindu culture and Indian national identity. In an interview with Israel's *Ha'aretz* newspaper, the vice president of the World Hindu Council drew a parallel between the status of Jewish identity in Israel and that which he would like to see for Hindi identity in India:

> We want the Hindus to be a first-class nation, equal to all the great nations, and in order to do this they must be India's uncontested central element. Every country has its central element. In Israel this is the Jews, while India's central element is the Hindu culture.[21]

However, the notion of Hindu nationalism seems to imply that non-Hindu citizens of India have a national identity of their own, distinct from that of the Hindu majority, just as Israeli Arabs have an national identity distinct from that of the Jewish majority. In the circumstances of multi-ethnic and multilingual India, abandoning the idea of all-encompassing Indian nationalism and accepting that non-Hindu groups may have separate national identities would run the risk of providing grist to the mill of separatist ethnic movements. In particular, India's Muslims would then have to be regarded as a national minority, and arguably at least as a minority with a national bond to Pakistan. This might of course be very problematic from the viewpoint of the Indian state.

The version of 'Hindutva' officially espoused by the BJP (which as an actual or potential party of government has moved to the centre) retains the idea of a national identity common to all of India's citizens (and not just Hindus), but holds that Hindu culture should play a greater role in shaping this identity. This concept of nationhood is inclusive, but, inevitably, 'non-neutral' between the different religious communities that comprise the nation.

It can readily be seen that national identity is a complex issue. There can be no 'objective' determination of whether a given group constitutes 'a people' or 'a nation' – any more than there is a universally agreed-upon definition of 'people', 'nation', 'national minority' or 'national' (as opposed to merely 'ethnic') identity. Ethnic, cultural, linguistic, religious and historical character-istics may all play a role in shaping national identity, but ultimately, it is deter-mined by the self-awareness and self-definition of the group in question. Since national identities depend on how people see them, they often have fluid bound-aries, there may be some degree of overlap between them, and they may change over time. This applies not just to individuals but to whole groups. How then, one may wonder, is it possible to base political and legal claims on a concept which is so malleable, controversial and elusive? However, since the legitimacy of a democratic state is based on the consent of the governed, and since national identity is a vital component in the personality of many of those who are 'gov-erned', i.e. citizens, a democratic society cannot be constructed without taking account of issues of national identity. Ignoring the identity of the majority, or that of the minority (or minorities), is not an option. If the Hindu majority in India were to unequivocally adopt the notion that it constitutes 'a Hindu nation', such an outlook could not be invalidated 'from outside'. Under these circum-stances, the majority would also have to get to grips with the consequences, as far as India's minorities are concerned, of such a concept being adopted.

As for minority groups, the standard dilemma of such a group is how to pre-serve its special identity without giving up integration in general society. Various solutions and semantic definitions are possible in this field; one of them is to define the distinct identity in question as ethnic, linguistic or cultural rather than 'national'. A minority which exercises its right (widely, though not univer-sally, recognized in contemporary democratic and liberal thinking) to maintain and avow a national identity that differs from that of the majority is by definition a national minority; as far as it is concerned, the national identity of the state cannot be neutral. But, of course, defining a minority as 'merely' linguistic does not change the fact that a typical nation-state with an official national language cannot be culturally neutral on an issue of crucial importance for the minority. The same often applies to other areas where the culture of a minority (however defined) is significantly different from that of the majority.

Ireland provides another example of partition. This is closer to the Israeli situation insofar as, unlike the Indian mosaic, it consists of two communities with conflicting national and religious identities. On the one hand the Catholics, who form by far the majority of the entire island and constitute a large minority in the north, are Irish in their national identity; and on the other, the Protestants, who are in the majority in Northern Ireland (Ulster), adhere to British national identity and wish to remain part of the United Kingdom. In the south, partition gave rise to an Irish national state with a strong Catholic flavour, while the polit-ical entity which came into being in the north of the island was Protestant (though this was never enshrined in law) and British.

However, as part of the Ulster peace process in recent years, an effort has been made not only to guarantee full civil equality for the Catholics but actually to turn Northern Ireland into what may be termed a bi-communal entity – inter alia through power-sharing arrangements and institutions. One might claim that the lesson that should be drawn from the Irish case is that where there is a sufficiently large minority, it must be allowed to put its stamp on the identity of the state, even if the country had been divided in order to enable members of this minority's people to gain national independence in the other part. However, apart from the fact that the Catholic minority in Ulster is much larger than the Arab minority in Israel (more than 40 per cent), Northern Ireland is not an independent state, but together with Great Britain makes up part of the United Kingdom. Great Britain is largely Protestant, but above all it is British and not Irish. The British state is naturally not neutral between the identity of the Protestant majority in Northern Ireland, who see themselves as British, with Northern Irish local cultural overtones, (and do not define themselves as a distinct nation with aspirations to self-determination and independence), and that of the large Catholic minority, who see themselves, overwhelmingly, as part of the Irish nation.[22]

The Union with Britain, symbolically expressed in loyalty to the British Crown, is the bedrock of the Protestant community's identity – hence the use of the term 'unionists'. Even if all the reforms envisaged as part of the peace process are successfully implemented, Ulster's Irish-Catholic community will still not be subject to what it would regard as a 'neutral' system of government. The highest authority in the province will remain the Parliament in Westminster and, should the need arise, it will be possible to bring in British security forces. Traditionally, nationalist Irish-Catholic sentiment views the primary symbols of British rule – the Crown and the Union Flag – with profound hostility. The official designation of the state – 'the United Kingdom of Great Britain and Northern Ireland' – constitutes a comprehensive negation of the Irish nationalist narrative. For Northern Ireland's Catholics, the British label and its accompanying symbols define a national identity markedly different from theirs.[23]

The Good Friday Agreement (10 April 1998) provides that Northern Ireland will continue to remain part of the United Kingdom as long as most of its population so wish. It also states that if the majority so chooses, the province will have a right to secede and join the Irish Republic. Since the Catholics now comprise more than 40 per cent of the population, this is not an altogether unlikely scenario. Should this happen, around one million Protestants with British national identity – for whom this identity is of paramount importance precisely because of Northern Ireland's violently disputed 'Britishness' – would become a large minority in the Irish Republic. From their viewpoint, the latter would be hardly 'neutral', given its official name, its symbols (notably the flag, which, for generations, was the symbol of the Irish national struggle against Great Britain and, more recently, that of Ulster's Catholic nationalists against British rule and the Protestant majority), its holidays and its school syllabuses, in particular the teaching of history. The preamble to the Irish Republic's Constitution praises the 'heroic and unremitting struggle' for independence of the people of Ireland; the unionist view of Ireland's history is very different. According to the Constitution, 'the Irish language as the national language is the first official language', and the state invests great efforts in enhancing its status. This, in a country where English is spoken by a large majority of the population, reflects an ideological preference and a national narrative not shared by what would be a large Protestant minority in any future united Ireland. The Republic's national anthem is 'The Soldier's Song', and warns against 'the Saxon foe' waiting 'out yonder'. The Protestants of Ulster, were they to become Irish citizens, could no more identify with this anthem than can Ulster Catholics with 'God Save the Queen' – or Israel's Arab minority with 'Hatikva' ('The Hope' – the name of Israel's national anthem).

The only way to give effect to the principle of 'state neutrality' in the Irish context would be to make Ulster an entity independent of Great Britain and the Irish Republic alike, and to institute there a bi-national (or bi-communal) system. But this solution would run counter to both parties' national aspirations, which is why it has never been envisaged in the peace process. A future united Ireland would in all probability be much less 'neutral' from the viewpoint of its large Protestant minority than is the United Kingdom today from the viewpoint of its minorities (including the Catholics in Northern Ireland). The same would presumably apply to Scotland if it were to secede from the Union. A relatively recently created nation-state, such as the Irish Republic, which was set up by a national movement after a struggle for independence, is naturally inclined to stress its national character more than a country that has existed for hundreds of years (since before the era of modern nationalism). In assessing the extent to which the Jewish character of Israel finds official expression, the most appropriate comparison is with countries such as Ireland or Greece, and perhaps with the 'new democracies' in Central and Eastern Europe.

'Imperial' nations: the United Kingdom and Spain

The United Kingdom and Spain are what may be termed 'imperial nations': large and complex European states constructed, historically, around a core – England and Castile, respectively. In both cases this core has shaped, to a large extent, the character of the state as a whole, without becoming congruous with it and without erasing its other constituent identities. In the case of the United Kingdom, which is the outcome of a Union between the two historical kingdoms of England (including Wales) and Scotland, and which together with Northern Ireland forms the United Kingdom of Great Britain and Northern Ireland, there is no doubt that both factually and symbolically it is England which constitutes the nub of the British state. The Queen, as officially styled and as universally perceived, is first and foremost the Queen of England. 'God Save the Queen' is the national anthem of the United Kingdom, whose capital, London, is first and foremost the English capital. The Parliament sitting at the Palace of Westminster is, historically, the English parliament, joined, following the Union, by Scottish and Irish (now, Northern Irish) members. The history of the British state is mainly (though not exclusively) a history of England, its main heroes are England's heroes. Admiral Nelson's famous message to his sailors before the battle of Trafalgar was 'England expects that every man will do his duty'. The people of England are an overwhelming majority of the population of the United Kingdom, and the English language enjoys indisputable predominance throughout it.

Given this state of affairs, there is neither need nor room for official definitions proclaiming the United Kingdom's 'Englishness'. On the contrary, from an 'imperial' point of view, any such emphasis would be viewed as a threat to the Union between the kingdoms which make up the United Kingdom. British identity is not supposed to abolish the different historical identities throughout the kingdom; emphasising the latter is not viewed as necessarily negating the pre-eminent status of British identity. The terminology used in the United Kingdom with regard to national identity is not always consistent and systematic – in typical English (British?) fashion. The meaning of the term 'nation' is flexible: one can speak of the British nation as well as of the Scottish nation, without this necessarily been perceived as a contradiction. The widely accepted view – primarily of the English, but not just among them – is that British identity is an overarching supra-identity of all the constituent parts of the United Kingdom, without contradicting the existence of the secondary identities.

This concept of national identity is sufficiently 'inclusive' and flexible to enjoy wide-ranging support – even though it is not neutral, given the central position of the English component. However, not all parts of the population share this point of view. The nationalist (republican) community in Northern Ireland certainly does not. The Scottish nationalists, who wish to dissolve the Union, enjoy the support of a large part of the Scottish population (in May 2007 the Scottish National Party (SNP) received a plurality of votes in the Scottish elections and formed a government). They identify Britishness with Englishness, define the British state ('government by London') as the English majority's control of the Scots, and see British national symbols as foreign to them. As far as they are concerned, the Union between the two kingdoms signifies their country's loss of national independence. The Welsh nationalists have a similar view, although they are less influential than their counterparts in Scotland. They perceive the British state as a framework which guarantees the dominance of England (and of the English language) and contributes to obliterating the identity of the island's other peoples.

In contrast, for the English, the British label, in most contexts, fully expresses their national identity. Even England's extremist and xenophobic nationalist party calls itself the 'British National Party'. For the English, 'Englishness' and 'Britishness' are often more or less interchangeable, the latter perhaps regarded as an extension of the former[24] (although lately, the re-establishment of the Scottish parliament has prompted talk about English nationalism and calls for an English parliament). The English view Britain – the United Kingdom – not as a bi-national Anglo-Scottish state, but, basically, as an 'England plus'. Indeed, this view is shared throughout the world. Thus, the conflict with South Africa's Boers is known as the 'Anglo-Boer War', the agreement with the Irish Republic on Ulster is called the 'Anglo-Irish agreement' and the friendship with the

United States is referred to as Anglo-American. While this overlapping of Englishness and Britishness comes naturally to the English, official terminology nevertheless takes account of the sensitivities present elsewhere within the United Kingdom. Were Scotland to secede from the Union and establish an independent state, as called for by the SNP, this would be a classic nation-state with a clearly expressed national identity. There would be nothing neutral about its official name and symbols, its cultural policy and the vision of its historical past. Such a state would undoubtedly maintain ties with the Scottish diaspora. The status of large numbers of Scotland's English-origin residents would be affected; though their full civil equality would doubtless be guaranteed according to European standards. Those who would insist on the right to retain their English national identity would become a national minority.

Hence although an 'imperial nation', which has crystallized around a particular national and political nucleus and combines other more or less specific identity elements, is an inclusive model, it is not neutral in terms of national identity. The British nationhood, perceived as a supra-identity ('a nation of nations') and not solely as a matter of political and civil affiliation, is primarily though not exclusively identified with England. This state of affairs is symbolically represented by the Union Flag, which contains three flags – but England's St George's Cross is more prominent than those of St Andrew (for Scotland) and St Patrick (for Northern Ireland). There is no doubt that both in practice and symbolically, the United Kingdom guarantees to the non-English constituent peoples a high degree of participation and identification with the state. This is borne out by the long list of leading positions occupied by them, including that of Prime Minister. Nevertheless, significant groups of British citizens refuse to accept the British label as a definition of their national identity, and many of those favour secession.

It may be asked why Israel's Jews should not consider 'Israeliness' an adequate expression of their national identity, like the English with regard to 'Britishness'. The Israeli label would then be sufficient to define the identity of the state, and the Jewish definition of the state could be done away with without creating the feeling, among the Jewish majority, that it is sacrificing anything important. In this way the country's Arab minority could (if it so wished) be 'included' in the definition of the state's national identity without giving up its own (just as is the case with the Scots who consider themselves both British and Scottish in terms of national identity). In theory, this could be an attractive option for the Jewish majority, although not necessarily for the Arab minority, since the Israeli label, strongly associated with the history and culture of the Jewish people, is far less neutral than its British counterpart is for the inhabitants of the British Isles. However, the two countries' cases are very different. Israel is not a united kingdom that was formed round a 'kingdom of Judea'. Nor do Israel's Arab citizens consider their national identity a subdivision of an Israeli nation (of which Judea is the main component). Both the Jews and the Arabs in Israel regard themselves as belonging to two distinct peoples, each community having strong national ties outside the country's borders. There is no denying the widespread and strong attachment, among Israel's Jewish population, to the Jewish label. But any definition of its identity which Israel's Jewish majority might adopt – Jewish, Jewish-Israeli, Hebrew, or simply Israeli (as a national, as opposed to purely civic, definition) – would not be adopted by the Arab community, and hence could not establish a definition of national identity common to all of the country's citizens.

Spain is another example of an 'imperial nation' in the sense suggested here. Here the lack of neutrality of the state's national identity is more salient than in the British case. 'Spain', or officially 'the Spanish State', is the name given to the entire state. According to the Constitution, all citizens are defined as 'Spaniards', belonging to the 'Spanish nation', whose unity is inviolable. At the same time, this label, which refers to the whole country and its population, also refers specifically to the majority which speaks the language known as Spanish (although in Latin America it is more frequently referred to as 'Castilian'), as opposed to those Iberian peoples that speak different languages. Catalan and Basque nationalists sometimes complain that there is no Spanish parallel to the distinction between 'English' and 'British'.[25]

Although historically the name Spain is derived from the Romans' 'Hispania', it was the kingdom of Castile which formed the nub of the monarchy which, appropriating the Spanish label, extended its empire across the Iberian Peninsula. In the Catalan and the Basque nationalist narratives, the establishment of the united Spanish kingdom is viewed as Castile gaining control of the peninsula and depriving these peoples of their national independence. The name Castile survives today in the autonomous regions of Castilla–La Mancha and Castilla–León, but in Spain the majority define themselves as Spaniards and not as Castilians.[26]

Adopted in 1978, three years after the death of Franco, the Spanish democratic Constitution identifies the state first and foremost – although not exclusively – with its main, Spanish-(Castilian-)speaking component. Under Franco's dictatorship, there prevailed a hard-line nationalist approach which regarded all the population of the country as exclusively Spanish, proscribed any other national identity and imposed the exclusive use of the Spanish language in public life. The stated aim was to promote and guarantee the unity of the nation. The new Constitution – the outcome of arduous negotiations between the various political and national groups – is a compromise. On the one hand, it asserts the country's political unity and categorizes all citizens in the same Spanish nation (nación); on the other, it acknowledges the existing national identities as subdivisions of the Spanish nation, and gives autonomy to 'the nationalities (nacionalidades) and regions' of the state. According to Article 2:

> The Constitution is based on the indissoluble unity of the Spanish nation, the common and indivisible homeland of all Spaniards, and recognizes and guarantees the right to autonomy of the nationalities and regions which make it up and the solidarity among all of them.

According to Article 3 (1), 'Castilian is the official Spanish language of the state. All Spaniards have the duty to know it and the right to use it.' Article 3 (2) adds: 'The other languages of Spain will also be official in the respective autonomous communities, in accordance with their Statutes.'

As usual in the modern world (above all, in the West), national identity in Spain is expressed primarily through the national language, and the identity of the state is closely linked to the official status of a language, or languages. The status that the Constitution gives Castilian – as a language of the majority and, at the same time, the language of the entire 'nation' – underscores the key role that it plays in defining and shaping the nation's identity. The duty imposed on 'all Spaniards' to know this language goes beyond what it customary in democracies. Generally speaking, states limit themselves to declaring the national or official language, which signifies that this language is used by state institutions and is dominant in the public sphere. In the United Kingdom, where English is far more dominant than Castilian is in Spain, it has not been considered necessary to enshrine its official status in law – precisely because its pre-eminence is self-evident. Similarly, in the United States it was not, until recently, thought necessary to legislate on the status of English as the national language. It is only in recent years, with the steady growth of the Spanish-speaking population, especially in the south, that there arose a movement in favour of adopting such legislation, on both the national and the state levels, and laws to this effect were in fact passed in several states. The duty to know the state language, included in Spain's Constitution, can hardly be enforced by the government on individual citizens in a free country. The provision in question is largely symbolic, and is a strong statement on the nation's identity.

The national character of the Spanish State is also officially expressed in the flag and emblem of the state, in the Spanish Crown and in the status of Madrid as the Spanish capital; all of these characteristics, enshrined in the Constitution, identify the whole state chiefly with its primary component, Castilian Spanish. The marked emphasis that the constitution places on Spain's indissoluble unity constitutes official adoption of the Castilian Spanish national narrative, while the Catalan and Basque nationalists – even the moderate ones, who do not favour secession – profess their adherence to the principle of self-determination of Spain's peoples.

The official definition of the Spanish State's national identity is thus inclusive, but not neutral as between the majority and the minorities. But this inclusiveness depends on the extent to which the other national groups accept the Constitution's definition of their own identities as subdivisions of the Spanish nation. On this, the picture is complex. Many people outside the Spanish-speaking majority are doubtless quite comfortable with such a definition. But in both Catalonia and the Basque Country, moderate nationalist parties are in power which operate within the framework of the Spanish Constitution, but do not accept its national narrative. For the Catalan nationalists, Catalonia is in all respects a nation – rather than a subdivision of the Spanish nation – which has the right of self-determination. In 1989, a resolution passed by the parliament in

Barcelona noted that 'willingness to act within the framework of the Constitution does not imply that the Catalan people has renounced its right to self-determination'. The region's ruling nationalist party does not advocate actual secession from the Spanish state, but wishes to strengthen autonomy and to promote Catalan identity. In the Basque Country, nationalist tensions are more prominent and have a violent aspect in the shape of the nationalist terrorist movement, ETA, which demands national independence for the Basque Country. The moderate nationalists, who control the region's autonomous parliament and government, insist on the right of self-determination for the Basque people, including the right of secession. The attitude towards the idea of eventual secession and independence is ambiguous. In 1990, the regional parliament adopted an official resolution proclaiming the right of the Basque people to self-determination.[27] The Catalan and Basque nationalists thus regard themselves as citizens of Spain but not 'Spaniards' in the sense envisaged by the Constitution. The Spanish State, for them, is therefore by definition a state embodying a national identity other than their own.

When it comes to identity and language, Israeli Arabs are, in principle, in a similar position vis-à-vis the state to the Catalans and the Basques who insist on their distinct 'nationhood', except that that the name of the state is not identical with that of the majority (although of course the name 'Israel' is far from neutral). To draw a parallel, it would be necessary to imagine a 'State of Judea', in which the definition of 'Judean' (devoid of religious content) would apply to all citizens, where the Constitution would make Hebrew 'the official Judean language of the state' and where the Arabs would be recognized as a national community representing a component of the Judean (or Jewish, in Hebrew) nation. This is far from the way they regard themselves.

As might be expected, the question of majority–minority relations is very much present in Spain's autonomous regions. The national autonomies are not 'neutral', any more than is the central government. The linguistic and cultural policies pursued by the governments of the Basque Country and Catalonia sometimes trigger complaints on the part of the considerable Spanish-speaking minority in these regions. Catalan leaders maintain that their concept of Catalan identity is inclusive and civil, not ethnic. The definition provided by Jordi Pujol, President of the Generalitat de Catalunya from 1980 to 2003, has acquired almost official standing: 'Anyone who lives and works in Catalonia, and who feels connected to this country, is Catalan'. To this he added that 'sooner or later, the majority of people who live and work in Catalonia want to become Catalans'.[28] And in fact, many of those who live in the region but are of non-Catalan origin – immigrants from other parts of Spain and their descendants – integrate in Catalan society and adopt the language. What makes this easier is that, as long as Catalonia is part of Spain, people can regard themselves as both Spanish and Catalan without having to get into the precise relationship between the two labels. However, were Catalonia to secede, those who retain a Spanish identity will become a national minority in a Catalan nation-state. From the viewpoint of those who do not adopt Catalan identity, Catalonia as an autonomous region is 'non-neutral' in many respects, particularly its constitutional definitions, the flag, its historical narrative, its linguistic and cultural policy, and official ties with Catalan-speakers elsewhere in Spain, as well as in France and in Italy.

The structure of the autonomous region's institutions is governed by the 1979 Statute of Autonomy adopted by the Catalan parliament. Article 1 of this text explicitly defines the national character of the Catalan entity that is thereby established, using the term 'nationality' which appears in the Spanish Constitution: 'Catalonia, as a nationality and in order to accede to self government, is constituted as an Autonomous Community, in accordance with the Constitution and with this Statute, which provides its basic institutional rules.' On the face of it, spelling out Catalonia's national identity would appear superfluous, since its name attests to its identity. However, the reference to Catalan nationality is intended to emphasize that this is a fully fledged national self-government, as opposed to merely regional autonomies established in other parts of Spain that lack the status of a distinct nationality.[29] Article 6 of the Statute states that 'Catalan is the official language of Catalonia, together with Castilian, the official language of the Spanish State'. This form of words signifies a desire for Catalan to be given an advantage, within the limits allowed by the Spanish Constitution. Article 8 states that the official flag shall be the traditional flag of Catalonia.

In the Basque Country, the official flag is still less 'neutral'. The 1979 Statute on Autonomy confers this status on the Basque national flag. For many Spaniards living in this region, this flag is associated with separatist nationalism. The regional government is established by 'the Basque People or "Euskal Herria", as an expression of their nationality and in order to accede to self-government' (Article 1). Article 6 states: ' "Euskera", the language of the Basque people, shall, like Spanish, have the status of an official language in Euskadi'. Although this language is spoken by a minority of the population, its official promotion – both within and outside the region – enjoys the support of many Basques who do not speak it themselves, as the marker and symbol par excellence of their national identity.

Article 7 of the Statute guarantees all permanent residents of the region complete equality of rights with regard to the autonomous government:

> For the purposes of this Statute, the political status of Basque shall be accorded to all those who are officially resident, according to the general laws of the State, in any of the municipalities belonging to the territory of the Autonomous Community.

Thus the political and civic community of the Basque country comprises, according to democratic norms, all of its population, regardless of origin and identity. But when the Statute speaks of the Basque people whose national language is Euskera, and who cultivate their ties with the Basque diaspora, it is clear that these definitions do not apply to all the inhabitants of the region; and it is the existence of the Basque identity in the latter, national-cultural sense, that was the basis for granting self-government to 'the Basque people as an expression of their nationality'. A law adopted by the autonomous parliament in 1994 allocates budgets for activities to promote Basque cultural and linguistic identity outside the Basque country – naturally, at the expense of all the region's taxpayers. In the current situation, it may be said that the national autonomy's lack of neutrality to some extent counterbalances the lack of neutrality on the part of the Spanish Constitution. The latter, it should be remembered, rules out any possibility of secession. If, nevertheless, under the right to self-determination proclaimed by its parliament, the Basque Country were to opt for independence, this would result in establishing a distinctly Basque nation-state with a considerable Spanish minority.

Civic nationalism in a multi-ethnic society: the United States and other examples

The US brand of civic nationalism combines inclusiveness and a considerable degree of ethno-cultural pluralism. All US citizens are assumed to share the same national identity. Ethnic groups are not considered national minorities, nor as 'nationalities' within the same nation (on the Spanish model), nor as distinct peoples or 'nations within a (larger) nation', as it is sometimes said in Britain. In this, the US model is similar, in principle, to the French one, but it is far more tolerant and accepting of ethno-cultural specificities of minority groups within the common nation. This has come to include the acceptance of cultural ties with, and sometimes political support for, one's – or one's ancestors' – 'old country'. Such a bond with a foreign country is not confined to a particular minority, setting it apart from the American mainstream, but is common to many groups and is now accepted as a mainstream American characteristic. However, the American civic national identity is also based on the dominance of the English language in national institutions, the education system and society. The American identity is anything but 'neutral' from the linguistic and, in many other ways, cultural viewpoint.

For the immigrants coming to the United States, the transition to English has always been recognized as a crucial stage in their process of Americanization. As Kymlicka points out, historically the policy towards immigrants (in the United States as well as in Australia and English-speaking Canada) was openly based on the 'Anglo-conformity' principle, according to which the immigrant's successful integration in society requires the full adoption of the English-speaking majority's cultural norms. However, even after the emergence in the 1960s and 1970s of new approaches more inclined to accepting the different groups' sense of distinct identity (nowadays often associated with the notion of multiculturalism), the English language continued to maintain its central position in American national identity.

The desire to impose a common language is a constant in the history of American immigration policies. Gerald Johnson has observed appositely about the United States:

It is one of history's little ironies that no polyglot empire of the old world has dared to be so ruthless in imposing a single language upon its whole population as was the liberal republic 'dedicated to the proposition that all men are created equal'.

Citing Johnson, Kymlicka makes that point that for all the celebration of cultural diversity, there has been no weakening of the desire to make immigrants into English-speakers, something which is deemed vital for their participation in the country's social, economic, cultural and political mainstream.[30]

American civic nationality is therefore not solely political and legal, but has a strong cultural content. Of course, the cultural aspect is not confined to language. In fact, the very distinction between 'political' and 'cultural' in this context is particularly problematic, since the prevailing democratic political culture and 'civic religion' are considered in the United States, perhaps more than in any other country, as the most essential characteristic of the national identity, of what makes America American. Even the need to maintain the dominant position of the English language, in the face of massive Spanish-speaking immigration, is sometimes defended on the grounds that 'English is the language of liberty', rather than on the more down-to-earth and factual grounds (which might, in some ways, be actually easier for a non-English-speaker to accept) that English is the language of the United States of America. In such a context, liberty and American nationhood become rhetorically interchangeable. At all events, American liberty speaks English.

No American ethnic group originating in immigration – including the Jewish community, with its strong sense of Jewish peoplehood and, as part of it, attachment to Israel – claims the status of a national minority. In fact, one can hardly speak of a minority, or minorities, versus a majority, as the whole nation is often described as a mosaic of minorities (though with a strong cultural common ground). In practical terms, no such community is, or aspires to be, in a position comparable to that of Israel's Arab minority, which views the Arabic language as the central pillar of its national identity and sends its children to state schools where Arabic is the teaching language. Nor could a language other than English enjoy the status of a second official language in the United States. This is still true despite the huge increase in the numbers of Spanish-speakers in recent decades, and the resultant prominence of Spanish in some areas – sometimes to the point of de-facto bilingualism. The movement in favour of legislation proclaiming English as an official language is a reaction to this phenomenon; previously this has not been thought necessary precisely because its dominance was unchallenged (though knowledge of English has always been a formal condition for naturalization). It is obvious that the weight and influence of the Latinos will continue to increase. That this will bring about the demise of English as a defining cultural characteristic of the American nation as a whole seems, however, highly unlikely.

Kymlicka classifies the American Indians, the natives of Hawaii and the residents of Puerto Rico as genuine national minorities. Because these are small groups, they tend to be ignored in most discussions on American society and identity, which follow the premise that the country is made up of ethnic groups originating in immigration, and hence has no national minorities (since an immigrant community is generally not considered to 'qualify' as a national minority, on the assumption, not invariably justified, that immigrants adopt the national identity of the country to which they have immigrated). From the viewpoint of these native groups, American identity, with its language, its symbols, its holidays, its historical narrative, is far from neutral. Thanksgiving, one of the most important markers of American civic national identity, is a holiday that commemorates the arrival in North America of the first European settlers – the ancestors of the founding fathers of the American nation. Different groups of immigrants and the descendants of immigrants – not just from Europe – can identify with this holiday. But the prayer of thanksgiving to the Creator that was offered up by the European settlers for enabling them to survive and make a living in the New World is not a symbol with which all Native American citizens can readily identify. The Declaration of Independence enjoys a quasi-sacred status as part of the United States' 'civic religion'. The document enumerates the instances when King George III violated the rights of the American colonists; violations which led them to conclude that they must sever the tie with their 'English brethren' and found an independent nation. One of the grievances is the King's alleged support for 'merciless Indian savages' against 'us'. The Declaration, as a historical text (as distinct from the political principles which it proclaims), is neither neutral nor inclusive from the viewpoint of Native Americans as a group. The American national ethos of providing refuge to suffering and persecuted people from the Old World, so that they can make their dreams come true in the New World and be free – an ethos symbolized by the Statue of Liberty – is an ethos of immigrants from the Old World and their descendants.

All this does not mean that today's notion of American national identity is not inclusive in respect of Native American groups (as opposed to what was the case in the past). Despite the tormented historical background to the relationships between these groups and the American nation, and despite the fact that they did not get the vote until the 1920s (far later than when, at least in principle, the vote was given to the African-Americans who had been emancipated from slavery), in recent decades major efforts have been made to promote the inclusion of Native Americans in the nation's mainstream, as part of the American 'mosaic'. This inclusion has been combined with continued and, indeed, increased official acknowledgement of their specific collective identity, in a way which is utterly different from the normal model of integration in American civic nationhood that applies to immigrants. Today, in addition to civil rights, these groups enjoy a substantial measure of autonomy in specific areas of self-government (formerly known as 'reservations'). They are legally recognized as 'peoples' or 'nations'. Their self-administration in these areas involves not only fostering a special cultural identity and language and applying traditional methods of government and law that differ from mainstream practices elsewhere in the United States, but also, sometimes, a waiver from the application of certain provisions of the Bill of Rights which are deemed incompatible with their culture, including the separation between religion and state.[31] Such arrangements can of course be criticized on the grounds that they violate individual rights, as well as on the basis of a desire to maintain national unity and shared values – as is the case with any arrangement that involves recognizing collective rights, as opposed to classical liberal individual rights. On the other hand, there are arguments based on minority groups' attachment to their culture, which for many people is a vital part of their identity and personality. Here again there is tension between two positive values. Striking a balance between them is a legitimate subject for debate on the merits of each individual instance.

The official status of the groups of Native Americans who enjoy self-administration implies that they are regarded as subdivisions of the American nation – i.e. both sharing the common national identity and possessing, at a certain level, a national (rather than merely ethnic) identity of their own. However, the limited size of the phenomenon, the fact that these groups have no 'kin-states' outside the United States, the fact that a large part of Native Americans live outside the self-administration areas, and the fact that the subject is not at the centre of national consciousness – all of this helps explain why this exception does not change the overall perception of American civic nationality, whether in the United States or throughout the world.

When it comes to African-Americans, who did not immigrate to America but were brought there as slaves, the situation is more complex. They constitute a minority with its own cultural uniqueness, a tragic history and a widespread sense of solidarity and common destiny. But this minority does not have a language of its own, or a territorial centre in the United States, or a particular 'homeland' in Africa with which it can identity (beyond a sense of empathy with the entire 'Black Continent'). Although proposals have been put forward in the past for setting up a 'black state' in the southern United States, they failed to gain widespread support. Radical circles in the African-American community have adopted 'Black nationalism', which regards America's Blacks and Whites as belonging to two different nations. However it is clear that the great majority of African-Americans have not adopted this view, and their struggle for equal rights (which has resulted in major achievements in recent decades) has been conducted, overwhelmingly, in terms of an appeal to common nationhood and its shared democratic values, rather than in the name of a separate nationalism.

In Israeli terms, the notion of ethnic, or communal, pluralism within a shared national identity, on the American model, can be applied to the Hebrew-speaking Jewish population and the different communities (according to the country of origin) within it. It cannot be applied to the country's Arab population which has no desire to adopt the national identity of the majority, but wishes to maintain its own culture, national language and identity. The inclusion of this minority should therefore be civic rather than national. Any minority, however distinct, and whatever definition is applied to it, should of course be considered as part of the nation in the civic sense.

As for the criticism sometimes directed at the Jewish-Israeli identity, according to which it is 'closed' by nature and not accessible for people of non-Jewish origin who may wish to join it because of its 'ethno-religious' character, it should be noted that traditionally, Jewish identity can be acquired by conversion, which has always been regarded as joining both the Jewish faith and the Jewish people. The Jewish people have never been a closed ethnic group. However, this is not enough: it should be possible to join a modern democratic nation (as opposed to a diaspora community) without changing one's religion. In practice, such an option exists in Israel, and has in fact been realized on a wide scale, thanks to the provisions of the Law of Return which grants all the privileges of 'newcomers' (*olim*), including Israeli citizenship on arrival, not only to any Jew who immigrates to the country but also to his or her relatives, regardless of their origin and religion. Under this provision, large numbers of people who are not Jewish according to the restricted definition of the Halacha (Jewish religious law), and in many cases had no Jewish self-identification before their immigration, came to Israel and indeed 'joined the nation' in the classic sense envisaged by the model of civic nationalism: by immigrating, acquiring Israeli citizenship, adopting the Hebrew language and culture, integrating into Israeli society on various social levels (including military service[32]) and identifying with their adopted homeland. This situation differs somewhat from the phenomenon of immigration to Western countries, insofar as these are individuals who, from the outset, have a certain bond with the Jewish people as a result of their family ties, and in many cases this bond undoubtedly facilitates their integration into Israeli society. However, the decisive fact is that this is a process of naturalization and integration of people of whom many did not previously regard themselves as Jewish.[33] The excessive influence of the Orthodox establishment is an obstacle to the integration of these people – who came in especially large numbers as part of the massive immigration from the former Soviet Union in the early 1990s. Nevertheless it has not been able to prevent what is now widely conceded as its impressive success (among other things thanks to 'marriages in Cyprus' and other ways that have been devised over time in order to circumvent Orthodox Judaism's monopoly over matrimonial law). The Law of Return, which is often attacked as 'ethno-religious', has actually made a major contribution to rendering Israeli-Jewish national identity more civic and cultural and less ethnic (in the narrow sense of ethnic descent) and religious.

A decision taken by Sharon's government (and expanded under Olmert) opens a track for naturalization of foreign workers' children born in Israel, who, until now, have had no prospect of naturalization, though they receive their education in Israeli schools and are often well integrated, culturally and socially, in Israeli society. The procedure for naturalization of foreign citizens, in these and similar cases, has always existed under the Citizenship Law (apart from the Law of Return that applies to Jewish immigrants and members of their families), but remained largely dormant due to Interior Ministry policy. This has now been changed in an important field which has emerged in recent years as a result of the country's growing prosperity that has made Israel an attractive destination for foreign workers.

The term 'civic nationalism', popular in contemporary liberal discourse, is used in more than one sense. It may relate to a concept which regards all the citizens of a particular state as sharing the same national identity. This concept cannot be implemented in a state with a significant minority that has its own language and culture and insists on its right to maintain its national identity which is different from that of the majority. Where there are two national identities within a single state, they are both inevitably 'ethnic' rather than 'civic' in the sense that they do not comprise the whole of the citizen body of the country, and are thus not congruous with citizenship. In a different sense, a national identity may be defined as 'civic' if it is possible for persons of foreign birth to join it by using the legal – civic – mechanism of a modern state. This requires the existence of a track for immigrants to join the national collective through a legal process of naturalization, by adopting the language of the nation in question and integrating in its society. Every modern nation-state should have such a track, adapted to take account of its specific conditions and circumstances. In addition, the rhetoric of civic nationalism is sometimes intended to 'include' the minority (or minorities) in civic terms – to underscore their full membership of the nation as a community of citizens, with equal civil rights – without addressing the question of their distinct identity.

The insistence on 'civic' rather than 'ethnic' nationalism in much of the liberal discourse often reflects a negative or at best cautious attitude to nationalism as such, and a desire to see national identity 'swallowed', as far as possible, by citizenship. This attitude is understandable, given the horrors committed in the twentieth century in the name of extreme nationalism – especially one stressing race or ethnic descent. Perhaps it deserves some sympathy even when carried to an excess, provided that it keeps its distance from all nationalisms equally, rather than condemning some and privileging others (usually the more virulent ones). However, in the real world too many people care deeply about their culture and identity for any serious theory of liberal democracy to ignore the question of national identity – either that of a minority or that of a majority. While liberal anti-nationalists criticize nationalism as inherently collectivistic and thus hostile to individual autonomy, Kymlicka's acceptance of nationalism in terms of the liberal discourse,[34] focusing on the need to preserve the distinct identity of minorities, is justified by him precisely in the name of the centrality of the individual. Cultural belonging and identity are a key element of individuals' personalities, and hence, for many of them, there can be no guarantee of their real freedom and self-realization unless their needs in this area are taken into account. In addition, Kymlicka argues that the state is in any case not neutral in terms of national culture and necessarily favours that of the majority – if only because of the official and socially dominant status of the country's official language – so national minorities must be given tools that will enable them to preserve their distinct identity. This approach endorses in principle the possibility of separation between national identity and citizenship. It is disputed by many liberal scholars of nationalism, who fear that it may legitimize illiberal and discriminatory forms of 'ethnic nationalism'. Whatever the theoretical merits of the arguments on both sides of this debate, the approach adopted by Kymlicka's argument is undoubtedly an accurate reflection of what actually goes on in many modern democratic countries.

Another kind of civic nationalism, different from Western models, is to be found in former colonies in Africa and Asia. Most of these countries do not have a single language which unifies their populations, since colonial frontiers were set by the European powers, generally without taking into account ethnic and linguistic factors. Language, which in the West is widely considered as the main distinctive feature of national identity, could not therefore be a unifying force in those countries. Hence the process of nation-building there has sought, with varying degrees of success, to forge a common national identity for all the population, regardless of ethnicity and language. Apart from traditions about the distant past, factors that have contributed to this process include the shared experience of the colonial era, the struggle against foreign domination and, following independence, the common efforts invested in constructing a modern nation.

For example, the Indian national movement, represented chiefly by Congress, encountered, in its struggle for independence, a rival national movement – the All India Muslim League. Arguing that the Muslims of the Indian subcontinent constituted a separate nation, the League demanded the setting up of a separate state: Pakistan. This concept, though accepted by many Muslims, did not receive the unanimous support of the Muslim population in British India. A number of Muslims played an active role in the Indian national struggle, some of them holding senior positions in the Congress Party. Subsequently, this would help to facilitate the integration in the Indian nation of the large-scale Muslim population that stayed in India after the creation of Pakistan. Altogether, despite the trauma of partition and the large-scale bloodshed to which it gave rise (leading to the displacement of many millions of people on both sides), and although the Indian Union has continued to harbour a number of hotbeds of opposition and rebellion, the work of building the modern Indian nation, by whatever criteria it is judged, has been an impressive success. Everything indicates that the overwhelming majority of the citizens – including the majority of Muslims and the majority of non-Hindi speakers – regard themselves as belonging to the Indian nation. This is perhaps the most successful example of post-colonial nation-building in a multi-ethnic country. One of the contributory factors to this success – besides, of course, the Indian democracy, secularism and the flexible federal system – is the fact that in India, the ethnic, the linguistic and the religious do not coincide. The country consists of a complex mosaic of criss-crossing identities rather than two (or more) clearly defined identity groups confronting each other. Thus, in 2002 a Muslim could be elected as President of the Union – not the first such election, but for the first time one that came about with the support of the nationalist Hindu party, the BJP: a Muslim who defines himself as an Indian patriot and nationalist, who prides himself on being well-versed in ancient Sanskrit literature (the bedrock of Hindu culture), who is 'hawkish' on Pakistan, and one of the leading scientists who have helped to advance the Indian nuclear programme. As we have seen, back in 1947, during the UN debates about the partition of Palestine, the Indian delegate – incidentally, a Muslim, and, no doubt, a loyal Indian nationalist – argued that all of Palestine's inhabitants constituted one nation and one people, and that this people, as a whole, should obtain independence. But neither the Jews nor the Arabs thought then, nor do they think today, anything of the kind. If there is anything on which both the Jews and the Arabs in this country have unanimously agreed, throughout the history of the last 100 years, it is that they do not belong to the same people, but to two different ones. These two peoples have not experienced a common struggle against a colonial power. On the contrary, they were involved in a bitter national conflict under the Mandate, and when each of them, at different times, clashed with the British administration, they accused it of giving in to the national demands of the other side.

In South Africa, the African National Congress (ANC) waged its struggle against white hegemony not in the name of 'black nationalism' (the slogan adopted by more radical groups) but in the name of civil rights for the non-white population and a concept of civic nationalism encompassing all of the country's inhabitants, irrespective of ethnicity or language – including whites. All these people and communities, according to the ANC ideology, make up a single South African nation. In accordance with this concept, the leadership of the movement has always included white (as well as Asian) activists in prominent positions. Rejecting black nationalism allowed the ANC to reject white nationalism as well (in the shape of the claim, advanced by the white Nationalist Party, that white South Africans were a distinct nation entitled to statehood) – and hence, any idea of partition and 'white homeland'. It was this approach that was officially adopted by 'the new South Africa' after the end of apartheid. The inclusive civic nationalism appears in fact to be the only way to keep the country together, due to the high degree of ethnic and linguistic fragmentation within the black population, as well as among the population of Asian descent; it should be noted, moreover, that South Africa's white population comprises two language groups. As in many post-colonial countries, in South Africa too the real alternative to regarding all the ethnic communities as belonging to a single nation – and thus rejecting all secessionist claims – is not partitioning the country into two (or, say, three) independent states, but rather smashing it to smithereens. Among the Palestinians and many of their supporters there is a tendency to compare their movement to the ANC and its struggle against apartheid. The analogy with South Africa is often used to put forward the argument that the proper way to solve the Israeli–Palestinian conflict is by establishing a single 'bi-national state', allegedly on the model of the new South Africa. However, South Africa, while certainly multi-ethnic, is not a bi-(or multi-)national state: its official ideology rejects any notion that there can be more than one national identity within the territory of the country. As opposed to this, the Palestinian national movement has always prided itself on being Arab, sought to represent the Arab-Palestinian people, and never claimed to represent a national entity comprising all of the country's population, including the Jews. In other words, it stands for precisely the kind of 'ethnic' nationalism which is strongly rejected by the ANC-led South Africa. Of course, the notion that the Palestinians are an Arab people, an integral part of the Arab world ('the Arab nation'), is wholly legitimate and natural, given the history and culture of the people in question. The Palestinians could hardly be expected to define themselves in any other way; it is only the false analogy with South Africa, adopted for transparent propagandistic reasons, which is deplorable.

The Republic of Turkey, since the days of Mustafa Kemal (Atatürk), has been based on a form of strict civic nationalism which insists on the full 'Turkishness', cultural and linguistic as well as political, of all of the Republic's citizens. The 1982 Constitution proclaims, as a basic principle, 'the integrity of the eternal Turkish Nation and motherland' and pledges allegiance to the 'nationalism of Atatürk'. In the past this 'integrity of the Turkish nation' was understood as sanctioning not merely the denial of all national or ethnic specificity for the millions of the country's largest minority, the Kurds, but even making it a criminal offence to speak Kurdish in public. For many years, the official attitude was that there were no Kurds at all in Turkey; only 'mountain Turks'. Recent decades have witnessed a significant degree of liberalization – among other things, under the influence of European human rights norms. However, the official view is still that the national identity of all of Turkey's citizens is exclusively Turkish. The Kurds are not recognized as a minority, and the use of Kurdish in the public sphere is still restricted. Over time, a large number of citizens of Kurdish descent have adopted the Turkish language and culture and have integrated into the social and government establishment, sometimes reaching very senior positions; but many others remain attached to their distinct identity, which, among other things, connects them with Kurds from outside Turkey, even though there is no Kurdish nation-state. The guerrilla and terrorist warfare waged for many years by Kurdish separatists in areas of Eastern Turkey has practically ceased in recent years, which may make it easier for the Turkish government to relate to the Kurdish population's cultural demands as legitimate civic ones, and not as a threat to the unity of the country. It seems possible that eventually Turkey will accept, in the spirit of current European standards for the protection of national minorities and minority languages, that those people of Kurdish origin who so wish, have a right to regard themselves, and be regarded by the state, as a national minority. If this happens, Turkey will become a nation-state with an officially acknowledged large native national minority. But accepting that a minority has its own national identity, distinct from that of the majority, does not mean that the state (in this case, Turkey) becomes 'neutral' between those identities. One can safely assume that, even after recognizing the Kurdish minority, the Turkish state will still maintain a close official bond with the Turkish language, culture and national identity. Even today, Turkey's civic nationalism does not in fact mean that civic and national 'Turkishness' are fully congruous: as we have already seen in Chapter 5, Turkey's immigration and naturalization laws provide preferential treatment to foreign nationals of Turkish ethnic descent and with Turkish cultural identity. Moreover, Turkey regards the citizens of the 'Turkish Republic of Northern Cyprus' as Turks (while the Constitution of this entity proclaims that 'the Cypriot Turkish people are an integral part of the Turkish nation'). The Turkish-speaking minority in Greece is likewise considered as a 'kin-minority'. The state accepts, then, that there are Turks, by identity, outside its borders – but not that there can be any identity other than Turkish within them. If the latter attitude is changed, there will be a significant distinction between Turkish statehood and citizenship on the one hand, and Turkish national identity on the other – a distinction, but certainly not a separation.

Complex identities, national identity and citizenship

As we have seen, different national identities are not necessarily mutually exclusive. A particular national group may be perceived, by some of its members at least, as a component of a broader national identity. Such a view has a clear advantage: the minority can feel that it belongs to a national identity which brings together all of the country's citizens, without giving up its own distinctness. But this advantage comes at a price: the minority accepts what is an inevitably subordinate status in a 'composite' national entity whose overall character is shaped mainly, though not exclusively, by the majority. It can therefore be expected that not all of the members of the group in question will accept this perception, and some of them will insist on a fully fledged distinct national identity. This insistence, in a country like Spain, may or may not be accompanied by secessionist tendencies. Obviously, the decision on this issue lies with the people in question. Ultimately, the national identity of the Catalans and the Basques will be determined not by the Spanish Constitution but by the Catalans and the Basques, just as the relationship between the Scottish and British identities will be determined by the people of Scotland.

But it may be argued that the state ought not to be neutral in such a debate. Rather, it should generate conditions which will make it easier for minority groups to adopt a concept of nationhood that includes them as a subdivision of an all-encompassing national identity. To this end it must adopt official definitions, policy and rhetoric which will encourage integrationist tendencies. In this sense it may be argued that an 'inclusive' official definition of national identity has positive value regardless of whether most members of this or that group which is supposed to be included in this definition are prepared to accept it at a given time. Such a policy should, ideally, make it easier for minority groups to identify fully with the state and its culture while maintaining their cultural and linguistic distinctness. On the other hand, within these groups some will claim that this approach constitutes a refusal to recognize their identity on an equal footing with that of the majority. In the case of Spain, the statement that all of the country's citizens, irrespective of their 'nationality', are members of a single Spanish nation is closely related to the constitutional norm of the unity of the state – in other words, rejecting the right of secession. When Catalans or Basques insist on their right to self-determination, contrary to this provision in the Constitution, this is tantamount (and this applies also to those who do not support actual secession) to a declaration that their nationality is independent in all respects, and not just a component of Spanish nationality. The constitutional requirement for all of the country's citizens to know the Spanish language, which is meant to stress the unity of the nation, is perceived by Basque and Catalan nationalists as an attempt to impose inclusiveness on an unequal basis – with a lack of neutrality between the different components of the whole.

What can be learned from this dilemma for the case of Israel? It may be argued that the state should have adopted and fostered a definition of Israeli national identity inclusive of the Arab minority, regardless of whether most of them would be prepared to accept this definition and regard their own national identity as a subdivision of the larger Israeli one. Such a policy would, of course, have necessitated the abandonment of the notion of the Jewish state; the state would be defined simply as Israeli. But the situation in Israel differs in crucial ways from that in Spain or the United Kingdom. The different peoples that inhabit those countries have for centuries lived together in a single state, each having a territorial base of its own. In the course of their shared history they experienced tensions and antagonism, but also a great degree of coopera-tion and shared destiny. The notion of a 'composite' national identity (expressed directly in the Spanish Constitution, with its distinction between the single nation and the different nationalities, and implied in the British concept of a 'nation of nations') is closely linked to, and presumably, in the minds of many people, virtually indistinguishable from, the composite nature of the two states in question. Accepting that the Basque nationality is included in the definition of the Spanish nation seems natural for someone who accepts the inclusion of the Basque country in the Spanish State (although some people accept the latter while rejecting the former, and, moreover, there are people who regard them-selves as Basques, and are recognized as such by the Basque autonomous government, outside the autonomous region).

Israel is not a united kingdom, nor a state composed of regional subdivisions; the country's Arab citizens have no regional entity within Israel that could 'express their nationality' as in the case of the Basques and the Catalans, nor is the Arab population concentrated in a certain area which could conceivably serve such a purpose. While this group's identity lacks a territorial focus within the state, it is characterized by a significant affinity to people outside its borders: both Palestinians and the larger Arab world. The same, of course, is true for the Jewish majority and its affinity to the Jewish people outside of Israel. In both instances this is a strong bond, often involving family ties and playing a key role in the identity of the two groups. A Catalan from Spain can perhaps feel a national affinity to the small Catalan communities outside Spain while still accepting the notion of a Catalan 'nationality' as a subdivision of the Spanish nation: Catalonia, as an autonomous region in Spain, is overwhelmingly (though not totally) congruous with the Catalan identity. But in Israel, the Jews' ties with the Diaspora and the Arabs' ties with the Palestinians in the territories and the Arab countries, and their sense of belonging to the Arab world and its culture, greatly strengthen their sense of distinct national identity, despite being compatriots in the same state.

At the time when the State of Israel was established, the two national identities among its future citizenry – the Jewish identity and the Arab one – had already existed for considerable time, and were in conflict with each other. The process of nation-building in the first decades of Israel's independence was, above all, about absorbing huge waves of Jewish immigrants. The newcomers consisted mainly of two groups: Holocaust survivors from Europe and immigrants from Arab countries where Jewish life had become impossible; altogether, they numbered twice as many as the state's original Jewish population. The result could only be a stronger, not a weaker bond between the country and its population and the Jewish people outside its borders. The political circumstances in which the State of Israel came into being – the war between the two peoples of Mandatory Palestine and the tragedy of the Palestinian refugees – as well as the continuation of the Israeli–Arab conflict after its establishment, would certainly have militated against any attempt to forge a national identity common to Israel's Jews and Arabs. But the conflict is not the whole story, probably not even the most important part of it. Had the Palestinian-Arab state come into being peacefully side by side with Israel, according to the UN Partition Plan, the Arabs in Israel would, no doubt, maintain close ties with this state's Arab majority (and Israel's Jews with the Jewish minority of this state). If Palestine were, for generations, a region within Israel, just as Scotland is part of the United Kingdom and the Basque Country or Catalonia are part of Spain, this, in all probability, would have given rise to a notion that the Palestinian-Arab identity is a component of Israeli national identity. It would then make sense for Israel to adopt and foster this idea, even if not all of its Arab citizens accepted it. Given Israel's fundamental realities, any attempt on the part of the State to pursue such a policy would have been not merely pointless but harmful: it would undoubtedly have been regarded by the Arab minority as an attack on its culture and identity. In such a situation, trying to artificially forge or 'engineer' national identities and 'blend' peoples would be, at best, an exercise in futility. All of this does not mean that there are no grounds for criticizing the policy of successive Israeli governments towards the Arab minority. A more integrationist policy might well have resulted in a better civic inclusion of this community, but not in any fundamental change in its national identity.

It is sometimes argued that the traditional link between the Jewish religion and Jewish peoplehood is an obstacle to the emergence of an inclusive civic nationalism in Israel. But this obstacle is quite hypothetical: it would appear that while, in principle, it would not have prevented the emergence of a 'composite' Israeli national identity with an Arab component as its subdivision, it would have made impossible a complete national blend between the two groups (an option even more obviously unfeasible). In fact, during the early stages of the conflict, under the British Mandate, one of the favourite themes of anti-Zionist polemic on the part of the Arab-Palestinian spokesmen was precisely the secular and 'atheistic' character of the Zionist movement and of the Jewish society it was creating in Palestine. This was adduced as proof of the thesis that the Zionists were a foreign element, deeply alien to the country's and the region's traditional culture. Later, it became more fashionable – in the Middle East as well as beyond it – to reproach Israel with being 'a state based on religion'; not because anyone could plausibly claim that it is more religious than its neighbours (quite the opposite is true), but on the strength of the theory according to which the Jews are only a religious group, not a people. Within Israel, one of the salient cultural differences between the Jewish majority and the Arab minority is that the latter is, on the whole, considerably more religious than the former.

A majority often tends to identify itself with the country and its people as a whole. Members of the Hebrew-speaking majority in Israel often treat the terms Israeli and Jewish(-Israeli) as if they were interchangeable, and refer to themselves, or define their identity, as 'simply' Israeli. There is in principle no great difficulty in adopting the idea, suggested by some, of officially defining the national identity of this majority, and thus, that of the state itself, as 'simply' Israeli. The term 'Jewish state' would then indeed be discarded; the state would be defined 'simply' as Israeli. Contrary to what many people would assume, there is no reason either to welcome or to oppose such an idea on the grounds that the Israeli label is inherently more secular than the Jewish one. This feeling reflects no more than current Israeli usage, which would certainly not 'survive' if the change in question were introduced. The religion, which today is usually called Judaism, calls itself, its sources, the religion, or the Torah, of Israel, and regularly refers to the Jewish people as 'the people of Israel'. The term 'Israel' is infinitely more frequent in those sources than the term 'Jew' and its derivations. In current usage, religious people certainly make a point of using 'Jewish' terminology; on the other hand, they regularly use the term 'people of Israel', often with clear religious implications.

Everything that today makes the Jewish state Jewish could just as easily and logically be defined as an Israeli characteristic of the Israeli nation-state – including, of course, its official ties with the 'people of Israel' abroad. Moreover, it is a mere illusion to think that a semantic change of this kind can help resolve any of Israel's political and cultural controversies in favour of the more liberal side. Orthodox Jews who today would strongly oppose any idea of defining their national identity as Israeli rather than Jewish, would find no difficulty at all in appropriating the Israeli label for their demands – including the most far-reaching ones. Nor would any illiberal nationalist, religious or secular, who today claims that only Jews should have full rights in the Jewish state, have any difficulty in asserting that only those belonging to 'the people of Israel' are true legitimate masters of the Israeli state.

It would presumably be somewhat more difficult to attack Israel for being Israeli than to attack it for being Jewish – though ways would no doubt be devised, soon enough, to overcome this difficulty. But from the viewpoint of Israel's Arab minority, such a change would not signify any improvement in their status. In fact, it might well make things worse. In today's official usage, there are Jews and Arabs among the state's citizenry, and all of them are considered Israelis – i.e. citizens of Israel. A minority can thus be non-Jewish without the implication that it is non-Israeli. If, however, the national identity of the majority (but not of the whole citizen community) is defined as Israeli, then any national minority which does not share this identity and does not regard itself as a subdivision within it inevitably becomes, in an important sense, 'non-Israeli'. Even today the term 'Israeli' is not seldom used, by Jews and Arabs alike, in this sense: a mixed group of Jews and Arabs, all of them Israeli citizens, will often be described as a group of 'Israelis and Arabs'. Today this usage is 'politically (and officially) incorrect': all of the state's citizens are officially Israelis. But it is hard to see on what grounds it can be opposed if the Israeli label becomes a national definition which applies to the majority and not to the minority, rather than (or at least in addition too) an inclusive civic definition. In the Arab sector, many avoid or even expressly refuse to define themselves as Israelis, either because of the term's lack of national neutrality, or simply for political reasons (while in the Druze community this label is readily adopted). However, in this field the official definitions at any rate are inclusive.

The usual concurrence between the name of the state and that of its people (or majority people) may help explain certain countries' reluctance to recognize various ethnic and linguistic groups within their borders as 'national minorities'. When a group of citizens opts for a national definition other than that of the state, the latter may see this as weakening the tie between it and the group – especially, as if often the case, when this national definition links it to a foreign state. Greece is a case in point. It refuses to acknowledge the existence of both the Turkish and the (Slav-)Macedonian minorities in its territory. Officially, there is a Muslim minority in Greece, and it is acknowledged that it is 'Turkish-speaking' – but not Turkish. This sensitivity is undoubtedly related to Greece's strained relations with Turkey, despite the peace between the two countries, their common membership of NATO and their diplomatic ties. The Slav-Macedonians are not even recognized as a linguistic minority. Rejecting any identification of the Macedonian label with Slav-Macedonia, in the 1990s Athens brought major pressure to bear on the latter after it became independent, on the grounds that its name hinted at an intention to take over Greek Macedonia. The cumbersome official designation of this state – Former Yugoslav Republic of Macedonia – is a result of this pressure. In this context, it is easy to understand the refusal of Greece to acknowledge the existence of a Macedonian national minority in the northern part of the country.

All of Greece's citizens are presumed to be Greek and the State certainly looks askance at those who would define themselves otherwise. As formulated in the country's Constitution, the official definition of Greek identity has ethno-national connotations (with official bonds with the Greek diaspora worldwide) as well as religious ones (in the form of the official status of the Greek Orthodox Church). It goes without saying that both culturally and linguistically, this identity is that of the majority. In this situation it is clear that a group of citizens which does not share this national-cultural identity is in all respects a national minority: but the Greek State rejects this definition and sees it as an expression of disloyalty.[35] Thus a Greek citizen who declares that his or her national identity is Turkish or Macedonian is viewed by the authorities and most Greek public opinion as someone who has expressed allegiance to a foreign state, and not to Greece. The exchange which took place in November 1990 during a session of the Greek parliament, between an MP of Turkish origin, Ahmet Faikoglu, and the Speaker is an apt illustration of the Greek establishment's approach to the matter:

MP: We are Greek citizens, but we are part of a different people, we are Turks.
SPEAKER: You cannot say that you are Turks.
MP: We are Turks, Mr. Speaker, yes, this is what I am saying. I am saying that we are Turks, we are Turks with Greek citizenship.
SPEAKER: My dear colleague, sir, you are Greeks.

In 1989, a Greek citizen of Macedonian origin and human rights activist brought a defamation case against a nationalist Greek journalist who had called him a Macedonian government agent. During the proceedings, counsel for the journalist questioned the plaintiff, asking him, 'Are you Greek?' Whereupon the latter, brandishing his Greek identity card, asked whether the lawyer was questioning the authenticity of the official document. Of course this was a ruse on the part of the Macedonian activist in order to sidestep the question of his national identity. He decided on this strategy in advance, as advised by his barrister who anticipated this question and warned his client not to fall into the trap: the answer 'I am not Greek' might, at the time, have made him liable to criminal charges. In the 1990s, such expressions as 'I am Macedonian, not Greek' by representatives of minority groups in Greece were still considered crimes against the state and in a number of cases led to criminal prosecutions and convictions.[36] Under European norms, no such restriction on freedom of expression is acceptable, and the Greek government now refrains from taking legal steps which cannot meet the test of the European Court of Human Rights. In recent years, voices advocating a more liberal attitude to minorities have been increasingly heard, coming not only from activists who belong to Greek and international human rights organizations, but also from the ranks of the Greek political establishment.

However, even should a more liberal official line be adopted, allowing members of the Turkish minority in Greece to define themselves as Turks without fearing that this would be perceived as an expression of disloyalty to the State, their basic dilemma would still remain: how could this minority express its national and cultural identity, and its affinity to its 'kin' in Turkey, without undermining its civic status in Greece? The way the 'man in the street' sees things, irrespective of official policy and definitions, is that someone can be either Greek or Turkish, but not both: if he defines himself as a Turk, then he is not Greek, or at least not fully Greek. This is a typical dilemma of a fully fledged national minority, especially when its name links it to a foreign country.

In a situation like this, a distinction between the name of the state and the name of the majority people actually benefits the minority, by enabling it to accept the former while rejecting the latter. Members of the Turkish minority in Greece would have found it easer to express their identity had there existed, in the Greek language, a distinction between 'Greek' and 'Hellenic': they could then define themselves as Greeks but not Hellenes, a minority of Turkish Greeks alongside a majority of Hellenic Greeks. In Israel, the country's Arab citizens can certainly say that they are Israelis, but not Jews. In fact, there is nothing to prevent them from saying that they are Arabs, or Palestinians, with Israeli citizenship, and not Israelis. However, at least in terms of the accepted official definitions, there is no contradiction between Israeliness – in other words, Israeli citizenship – and Arab or Palestinian-Arab national identity. This being the case, the term 'Israeli Arab' has never been seen as posing an internal contradiction (unlike a 'Greek Turk'). In the past, the label 'Palestinian', as opposed to Arab, was indeed (and still is sometimes today) perceived as problematic for political reasons relating to the conflict with the Palestinian national movement; but in recent years there has been increasing recognition of the legitimacy of the affinity of the Arab minority in Israel to the Palestinian-Arab people.

Civic nationalism in the sense of full concurrence between peoplehood and citizenship has many advantages. It can be argued that in many respects, this is the optimum situation, although a price (sometimes a very high one) may have to be paid for it in terms of cultural pluralism. Where the situation can be realistically described (and not only officially defined) in such terms, this may well be a result of the fact that in the past, strong pressures were applied to minority groups – not merely immigrants, but native minorities as well – to assimilate. This certainly happened in France, as late as, and notably under, the Third Republic.[37] In today's world, such pressures would be clearly impermissible – though it is permissible to benefit from the results of their application in the past. In Israel, the facts on the ground call for official recognition of the Arab community as a national minority, rather than calling into question the legitimacy of Israel as the embodiment of the Jewish people's right to national independence. As for the conflict with the Palestinians in the territories – which cannot fail to overshadow relations between the Jews and Arabs in Israel – efforts must be made to solve this on the basis of a sincere and genuine acceptance, by both sides, of the principle of two states for two peoples. According to this principle, there must be two viable nation-states living side by side: a Palestinian-Arab state and an Israeli-Jewish state.

The above discussion is based on the fact that Israel's population comprises two main sub-groups: Jews and Arabs. There are of course Israeli citizens who do not fall into either of these categories, but this does not change the overall picture. The largest group of people who are neither Jews nor Arabs consists of people from the former Soviet Union who acquired Israeli citizenship under the Law of Return, which also, as we have already noted, applies to the non-Jewish relatives of Jews. Surveys show that the overwhelming majority of these immigrants identify with the State. There is no significant support for the idea of abolishing Israel's Jewish character among 'non-Jewish' immigrants. In many cases these are people who have only a Jewish father, and hence are not considered Jewish according to religious law. Many of them who have unmistakably Jewish surnames suffered from anti-Semitism in the countries where they grew up. However, the others also – the grandchildren of Jews or non-Jewish relatives of Jews – came to Israel with their families in the full knowledge that they were coming to a Jewish country called Israel. Regardless of halachic definitions, the vast majority of these people have integrated well into Hebrew-speaking Israeli-Jewish society. Their children speak Hebrew as their mother tongue. The cumulative experience since the beginning of the mass immigration from the former Soviet Union demonstrates that there is no such thing as an emerging 'Russian minority' in Israel which separates itself from the country's Hebrew-speaking Jewish majority. While this process of integration would undoubtedly be facilitated by an end to the current Orthodox monopoly over personal status issues (marriage and divorce), even as things currently stand it is progressing well.

Nevertheless, it must be said that there is one important respect in which the way the question of national identity is perceived and regulated in Israel merits criticism. While the de-facto recognition of more than one national identity is, in Israeli conditions, a good thing, the barriers between Israel's different national groups are set too high and should be lowered. The European Council's Framework Convention for the Protection of National Minorities lays down an important principle – according to Article 3:

> Every person belonging to a national minority shall have the right freely to choose to be treated or not to be treated as such and no disadvantage shall result from this choice or from the exercise of the rights which are connected to that choice.

Israel, however, has no such mechanism by which an Arab citizen can choose not to belong to his or her national minority. For a member of the Arab minority, in practice there is no equivalent to the procedure by which a new immigrant who is not considered Jewish can join Israel's majority people, by means of cultural and social integration. In theory, the conversion route to such affiliation is available, but as we have pointed out, in a modern nation-state this is not good enough. True, the Arab community as a whole does not manifest any tendency to assimilate in the majority society, and the same applies to most of the country's Arab citizens as individuals; but even under these circumstances, the individual's freedom of choice must be maintained. This is why the decision, taken in 2002, to eliminate the 'nationality' (national identity) category from Israeli ID cards must be seen as a positive step. Everything should be done to make it easier for any given individual to determine their own position relative to the majority society, and to decide to what extent they wish to integrate in that society – whether this is to be integration so complete as to amount to assimilation, or partial and selective integration.

For example, Israel's Arab citizens should have a recognized right to educate their children in Hebrew schools. Today, within the country's education system, there are a few mixed schools which teach in a combination of Hebrew and Arabic, and some Arab pupils (in mixed towns, notably Haifa) learn at Hebrew (Jewish) schools. Rules need to be laid down which will make such arrangements easier. The country's community-based marriage laws make it impossible for people from two different religious communities to wed in Israel. This contrasts with the situation in India, where, although marriage arrangements are similarly community-based, a special law makes it possible for people of different faiths to contract a civil marriage. While it is possible to get round this problem by getting married in Cyprus, for this as well as other reasons civil marriage should be made legally available in Israel.[38] Not requiring members of the Arab minority to perform compulsory army service is justified in the light of the Israeli–Arab conflict, but those interested in doing so should have an acknowledged right to volunteer and serve in the IDF. Some actually do so, and this should be actively encouraged – even though the leadership of the Arab community is strongly opposed to military service.

All of the changes which are called for in these areas should expand the individual's freedom of choice and facilitate the civic integration of the Arab minority. However, it is clear that they will not fundamentally change the map of national identities in Israel. This map also contains unique minority groups, and first and foremost the Druze and the Circassians, who have a particularly close relationship with the Jewish majority – notably expressed by the fact that they serve in the IDF – but do not wish to assimilate, nor to adopt Hebrew as their primary language. The definition of Israel as a Jewish nation-state with an Arab national minority is based on this social and cultural reality. Given this situation, the State must pursue a policy of civil equality and integration, but cannot be expected to demonstrate neutrality in terms of its national identity.

In conclusion: the theory of state neutrality, as regards national and cultural identity, does not meet the test of the realities in the modern democratic world. The manifestations of 'non-neutrality' in those fields that are customary in contemporary democracies are too wide-ranging, numerous and significant for it to be possible to define neutrality as a norm, and any deviation from it as an exception or an anomaly. Sometimes the term 'neutrality' is used when what is actually meant is that the state should ensure complete equality of civil rights. Naturally when it comes to the civil rights of the different groups of citizens, a democratic state must indeed be neutral. The same does not apply to the identity and character of the state.

The dividing line between the issue of civic rights and that of the state's character may, in certain cases, be blurred or in dispute. However, the majority's right to put its stamp on the character of public life in the country, subject to the need to guarantee the rights of minorities, must not be denied. Denying this right is not merely impractical and unrealistic, but runs counter to basic democratic principles. Usually, however, what happens is that this right is not denied but rather taken for granted (as in the case of an official language), often with the help of identifying the majority, explicitly or implicitly, with the whole. It is then possible to rely, more or less innocently, on the principle of neutrality while pursuing the most 'non-neutral' policies. This is eloquently demonstrated by the report of the French governmental commission which called for a law banning the Muslim veil in public schools in the name of, among other things, the neutrality of the state. Perfectly valid arguments can be advanced in support of this controversial law, but neutral it is certainly not.

Since a nation-state which has a national minority (or minorities) cannot have a 'nationally neutral' identity, the only way of doing away with this 'non-neutrality' is to eliminate the majority and minority categories by merging the different groups into a single national identity. However, despite its advantages, this blend, even if quite successful, is itself not 'neutral' in terms of what it asks the two sides to give up: what it basically means is that the minority will assimilate into the majority (in part, at least), while the majority shows itself willing for the minority to assimilate on 'easy terms'. The more a minority maintains an identity which differs from that of the majority, especially if this difference is defined in national terms, the greater the tendency for the state's identity to become less neutral. There are many ways in which this 'absence of neutrality' is expressed in contemporary democracies, from the name of the state, its official language and its symbols, all the way to its historical narrative.

All of these are normal and often inevitable characteristics of a modern nation-state. They should not be denounced in the name of the neutrality principle: the majority (where a more or less clearly defined majority exists) also has its own identity and a natural need to express it. The nation-state, its language, its culture, its symbols and its festive days are the natural setting for meeting this need.

In relatively new states which were established by national movements after a struggle for independence, this fact is naturally reflected in their symbols, their official holidays, their public culture and frequently in their constitutions. These characteristics do not always suit the entire population. We have seen such a situation in the case of Ireland. The preamble to the Macedonian Constitution, even after its specifically Macedonian cultural content was watered down, continues to refer to the Macedonian people's struggle for national independence – something with which many members of the Albanian minority in Macedonia will find it difficult to identify. While the Greek Constitution does not refer to the Greek struggle for independence in the early nineteenth century, it stresses emphatically the Greek-Orthodox religious tradition of the Greek people, and these clauses are certainly not neutral from the viewpoint of the country's Turkish-Muslim minority. The Indian Constitution, in addition to classical references to human rights, contains a list of fundamental duties of India's citizens (Article 51A). Among other things, every citizen is obliged 'to cherish and follow the noble ideas which inspired our national struggle for freedom'. Since India officially regards all of its citizens as sharing the same national identity, the authors of the Constitution did not consider that by making this ideological statement they were indicating a preference for one national narrative over another. But this view is far from enjoying unanimous support among the Muslims of Kashmir, or people in other parts of the country where there are separatist tendencies. This constitutional provision is therefore far from 'neutral' – which is not to say that there is necessarily anything wrong with it.

The struggle for Italy's national unification and independence is a piece of nineteenth-century history. The Constitution of the Italian Republic, adopted after the Second World War, does not refer to it, but Italy's national anthem is devoted to this story. The anthem, celebrating the liberation of Italy from the Austrian yoke, is neither neutral nor inclusive in respect of the German-speaking Italian citizens of South Tyrol who are in fact Austrians by origin (i.e. former German-speaking subjects of the Habsburg monarchy) and maintain cultural ties with Austria to this day. The Netherlands' War of Independence began in the sixteenth century: the national anthem speaks in the name of William of Orange, the hero of this war and the founder of the Dutch state, who justifies his struggle against Spain under Philip II. Since this was also a conflict between Protestants and Catholics, theoretically it might be said that this anthem lacks neutrality from the point of view of the Netherlands' large Catholic population – although this quarrel is, in all probability, subject to the statute of limitations and is no longer relevant. It is to be hoped that one day the Arab–Israeli conflict will meet the same fate; the symbols of Israeli statehood will then become considerably less controversial.

All of this does not, of course, rule out criticism of specific manifestations of 'non-neutrality' that are offensive to the minority. In this respect, what was considered acceptable in the past may not be acceptable today. The American Declaration of Independence accuses the King of Great Britain, among other things, of having 'endeavoured to bring on the inhabitants of our frontiers, the merciless Indian Savages, whose known rule of warfare, is an undistinguished destruction of all ages, sexes and conditions'. At the time, members of these groups were not considered citizens of the United States. According to today's norms, it would be obviously unacceptable for an official document of a civilized country – even if it reflects the history of a national struggle – to contain such a hostile reference to any ethnic group as such. In some Southern states there has been and continues to be a controversy on the subject of the Confederate flag – that flag of the Southern states which seceded from the Union and fought in the Civil War to preserve black slavery and prevent its restriction. This flag, to which many among the white population of the South had an emotional bond, was adopted by some of the states as part of their state flag and promoted by various public bodies as a symbol of patriotic Southern tradition. In this case, since it involves a symbol historically related to a terrible phenomenon like slavery (as well as to a rebellion against the Federal government), it is clearly wrong to adopt such a symbol, even if there is a majority that supports this for historical and emotional reasons.

Italy's national anthem, as explained above, glorifies the country's War of Independence against Austria. However, while the song lauds those who fought to liberate and unite Italy, its fifth and last verse decries the Austrian eagle which 'drank the blood of Italy' and refers to the loss of its plumes. Since Italy has a considerable German-speaking population with an affinity to Austria, it would have been inappropriate for such sentiments to be officially expressed as part of the nation's anthem. And indeed, the Austrian eagle is left alone when the anthem is played, since, as in the case with many national anthems, only the first verses are actually sung. The Israeli anthem, 'Hatikva', is a Jewish song, but it is not confrontational in its character (unlike many national anthems). Even if in some cases there may be controversy over where to draw the dividing line between a legitimate expression of the majority's identity and historical outlook and an affront to the minority, it can usually be defined without great difficulty with the use of common sense and a modicum of sensitivity.

Israel is a nation-state which was established in 1948 after a bitter struggle in order to implement the Jewish people's right to self-determination. As is only natural, this fact is expressed in the name of the state, in its system of symbols and in the official definitions of its character. There can be no ignoring the resultant difficulties from the point of view of the members of Israel's Arab minority – and not only because its national identity differs from that of the state. The fact that the national struggle which led to the establishment of the state was undertaken against the Palestinian-Arab national movement, and that the national struggle is still continuing, undoubtedly makes things difficult for them. However, anyone who accepts the principle of partition and two states for two peoples cannot demand of Israel neutrality in terms of national identity. Such a demand finds no support at all in the international democratic norms and practice. What it usually reflects is simply a rejection of the idea that the Jewish people have a right to national independence.

Epilogue
Nowhere else

Why did Zionism, this movement which would give birth to the State of Israel, appear at the end of the nineteenth century? After all, the Jews had been persecuted and had longed for Zion throughout the generations. So what was it that happened in Europe which gave rise to the demand for a Jewish state in the country of 'Zion and Jerusalem'? Much has been written on the topic, and we do not feel that we can add anything useful, other than to underscore and highlight the profound disappointment that was felt by the Jews – above all in the West, but in the East also – at the fact that both democratization and the Enlightenment, which began at the end of the eighteenth century, gave birth to a new form of anti-Semitism. For most Jews, the 'old' anti-Semitism was the result of old-style Christian religious hegemony in traditional, pre-Enlightenment European society. They thought that this unenlightened state of affairs must necessarily yield to the brightness of emancipation, human rights and liberal democracy.

But to the dismay of educated Jews who pinned their hopes on the Enlightenment, and especially those who sought to assimilate, these processes merely rekindled the embers of a fire which they thought had gone out. For example, in the Austro-Hungarian Empire the process of democratization led to parties whose platform primarily consisted of anti-Semitism, ultimately resulting in the election of a self-declared, extremist anti-Semite as mayor of Vienna. While many Jews were prepared to throw off the outward signs of Jewish religiosity so as to be 'like everyone else', 'everyone' did not think this a good idea. Among the Christian intelligentsia, who should have been allies of the Jews, many reacted with renewed and even more vehement hatred.

There were pre-Enlightenment precedents for this phenomenon. For example, Voltaire, as a liberal philosopher and a great humanist, issued protests against the persecution of the Jews, but at the same time was certainly not without strong anti-Jewish prejudices of his own. How could this contradiction be resolved? The fact is that it corresponded to a deep-rooted European preconception which conferred upon the Jews an inferior status in the family of nations. This renewed hatred culminated at the end of the nineteenth century in a series of pogroms in Russia, the expulsion of all the Jewish student members of German university fencing clubs, and massive anti-Semitic propaganda in

French publishing and the press, with anti-Jewish hatred peaking at the time of the Dreyfus Affair. Historian Arthur Herzberg observes:

> For all those Jews who stop short of conversion there must always remain a specifically Jewish sense of alienation, which is quite different from any momentary travail of Western man. It is the feeling of being not quite inside a culture even when one dominates much of its literature. It is, in short, not alienation, but exile, galut.[1]

Sure enough, the self-same outrage and frustration as were experienced by Theodor Herzl when he found that even an assimilated Jew like himself was unable to break down the walls of opposition and hostility, were channelled into formative experiences by many of Zionism's founders. Although Christian religious hostility to Jews was virulent, it could be understood in the context of a confrontation between the two faiths – and one might look forward to it weakening and eventually disappearing in more enlightened modern times. Moreover, it had the advantage, in a sense, of offering a way out, in the form of conversion. In the second half of the nineteenth century, this path was in fact taken by many in the young German-Jewish generation. In contrast, the new anti-Semitism, driven by an ideology rooted in the writings of Gobineau, Chamberlain and Wagner, could not be explained in traditional religious terms. It attacked Jews for their very ethnic descent, from which there was no escape. It was at this point that the idea arose of escaping Europe itself, and building a national home in the ancient homeland of the Jews. It came from people most of whom had, at best, fairly weak ties with the Jewish tradition. It was, for them, primarily a matter of self-respect; and for those, like Herzl, who saw the catastrophic potential of the new anti-Semitism, a matter of self-preservation as well, as far as the Jewish masses in Europe were concerned. The idea that national independence would be followed by a cultural renaissance, so central to other nineteenth-century national movements in Europe, was certainly adopted by the Zionist movement and played an important role in its activities in fostering Hebrew culture. But this was not the main original motivation of most of its founders.

In this sense, the Jews were truly unique. Many Jews wanted to integrate in the Christian majority but always remained suspect. Nothing worked – not even laying down their lives for their homeland, singing what were basically Christian hymns, saluting and marching to battle under standards adorned with a cross. It was simply impossible to pass through this 'invisible wall', as it is called by W. Michael Blumenthal, former US Treasury Secretary and director of the Jewish Museum, Berlin.[2] Modern Jews remained trapped between this obstacle and the walls of the ghetto which they had deserted. Zionism sought to take the Jews out of this no-man's-land and bring them to a national home of their own, where they would not be forced to divest themselves of the last vestiges of their national identity. It must be remembered that this was a traumatic process for the Jews of Western countries as well as those of the Russian Empire, profoundly disappointed by the attitude of the intelligentsia and the anti-Semitism of many writers and intellectuals. The new Jewish intelligentsia were shaken by the pogroms which erupted in 1881 and continued to 1884, not only because of their ferocity, but also because most of Russia's intellectuals failed to condemn them robustly, as they should have.

Today, after the Holocaust and in the light of the atrocities of the Nazi murder apparatus, it is difficult to imagine the panic that these pogroms sowed among Russian Jewry – at the time the world's largest Jewish community. As Arthur Herzberg observes, anti-Jewish violence was nothing new in the Russian Empire. What was shocking, however, was both its severity and the fact that educated people holding public office took part in it, and the pogromists were more or less openly supported by government elements.[3] Moreover, notoriously, the socialist revolutionary party *Narodnaia Volia* published a leaflet supporting the pogroms on the grounds that they were an explosion of popular rage against the Jewish capitalist exploiters, which would serve the cause of the revolution. This convinced many Russian Jews of the futility of assimilation. In the aftermath of the pogroms, Leon Pinsker, one of Zionism's earliest thinkers, left the 'Society for the Diffusion of Culture', declaring that there were 'new ways to solve the problem of the Jews' – meaning, bringing them together in what would be their own state, as he would later advocate in a book called *Auto-Emancipation*, published in 1882.

Moses Leib Lilienblum, another Zionist ideologist and a fellow traveller of Pinsker's, gives a moving account in his diary of the panic which the pogroms generated in his circle:

> We lie down to sleep fully clothed, terrified that the bandits will attack us, so that we can quickly grab the young children ... and flee wherever the wind takes us. But will we be able to? Will they spare the tiny tots who don't yet know that they're Jews? ... Terrible, how terrible! How long, Lord, God of Israel?

Like Pinsker, Lilienblum was forced to admit that 'it is not the lack of [modern secular] education which lies at the root of our misfortunes: strangers we are, strangers we will remain, even if we were soaked in science'. As a result, he resolved to abandon the idea of Russian education, leading to integration in Russian society, as a solution to the Jewish problem, and henceforth devoted himself to Zionism. Peretz Smolenskin, a novelist and essayist who wrote in Hebrew, rebuked Russia's Jews for thinking that Russian education 'would be their crowning glory'.

In Western countries where legal equality of rights had been achieved, there was another aspect to Jewish particularity. In addition to anti-Semitism and the resultant obstacles to integration, there was another difficulty as well. Emancipation may have given the Jews legal rights and opened the doors of education to them, but in many respects Christian society did not give up its Christian nature, first and foremost as regards the days of rest and the major holidays, nor did it allow the Jews to observe their own festivals. Hence even without hatred, points of friction remained in Western Europe; they have not wholly disappeared even today. Moses Hess embodied the classical educated Jew, completely integrated in European culture and the socialist movement. As far as is known, he never suffered any hostility personally as a Jew. But after discovering the strength of anti-Jewish sentiments in socialist circles, he reacted in a surprising fashion. In the preface to his 1882 *Rome and Jerusalem*, he made the following declaration:

> Here I stand again in the midst of my people, after being estranged from it for 20 years, and actively participate in its feasts and fasts, in its memories and hopes ... and in its contacts with the civilized nations of the world.[4]

In his book he describes anti-Jewish hatred in Germany and the failure of assimilation. He also calls for a national solution to the problem of the Jews. The case of Moshe Hess is not exceptional. The same path was taken by a number of Russian Jews who had initially been involved in revolutionary socialist organizations after the trauma of the 1881 pogroms and the failure of the 1905 Revolution. Yitzhak Ben-Zvi, who subsequently became president of the State of Israel, gives a fascinating account of the moment that he became converted to Zionism. As he was delivering, in Russian, a socialist address to an enthusiastic public, different thoughts came to his mind:

> At that very moment, I asked myself: whom am I addressing? Do the people here in Poltava understand me, do they believe me? Are we Jews really part of this revolution, of this triumph? Will this revolution, which presages salvation for the Russians, also bring us, the Jews, the hoped-for salvation? Why am I here and not there? Why are we all here and not there? Once I had thought of these questions, I could not shake them off, and when my speech was over, I thought not about this demonstration or about the success of the Russian revolution, but about our Jerusalem. At that point I took a definitive resolution: my place was in Eretz Israel, and I had to devote my life to building it up, as soon as possible.[5]

The memories of the Tsarist pogroms were still vivid for the Soviet Jews of the 1950s. Natan Sharansky relates how, when Stalin died, he saw his mother weeping, terrified that a pogrom would engulf the Jews of their town of Donetsk in 1953, nearly 40 years after the October Revolution. His mother had seen a Russian slap a crying Jewish woman on the face, saying: 'Your lot murdered Stalin, and now you're crying?' As a result of this incident, the Sharansky family barricaded themselves into their apartment, young Sharansky and his brother remaining at home for days on end.[6] Soviet anti-Semitism reached its peak during Stalin's last years, culminating in the blood libel of the 'doctors' plot'. The policy of discrimination against Jews continued, in more subtle ways, under his successors – never openly avowed, but always a very real fact of life. Another modern project – in this case, the Communist Revolution – that many Jews had hoped would make anti-Semitism a thing of the past, thus brought bitter disappointment, in this respect as well as in many others. This was yet another proof that integration and assimilation (strongly encouraged by an atheist state that suppressed Jewish culture) were no guarantee against anti-Semitism. The Jewish and Zionist revival in the Soviet Union came after the Six Day War, in the midst of the virulent Soviet campaign against Israel and Zionism that was widely regarded as having anti-Semitic overtones.

Jewish attempts at integration in the Arab countries met a similar fate. The Iraqi pogrom which took place in June 1941 during the pro-Nazi uprising of Rashid Ali al-Gaylani, resulted in some 200 deaths and 1,000 wounded among Baghdad Jews. Known as the Farhud, the Middle East's equivalent of the 1881 Russian pogroms, it contributed to the mass emigration to Israel, several years later, of practically the entire Jewish community of Iraq – including those who had tried to find a 'patriotic' Iraqi alternative to Zionism. This was not a random event. It had been preceded by an intense nationalist and religious anti-Jewish campaign, which refused to distinguish between Zionists and non-Zionists. The acts of violence perpetrated against Jews had put paid to the dream of the non-Zionist part of the community of being accepted by the Iraqi majority as an integral part of the nation. Just as in Europe, it was precisely the economic and social successes of Jews seeking integration, and the prominence achieved by some of them, that provoked resentment and hostility, expressed in both religious and nationalistic terms. This was naturally exacerbated by the Zionist–Arab conflict.

The question of Jewish particularity is still very much alive today, even when there is no violence against the Jews – apart from the activities of extremist Arab and Muslim groups and the fringes of the extreme Right – and when undisguised anti-Semitism appears to be out of fashion. But when the situation in the Middle East deteriorates, and Israel replies robustly to Palestinian terror, things also take a turn for the worse in terms of anti-Semitism, a topic which has received major coverage in the European media since the September 2000 outbreak of the 'second *intifada*'. For several years after 2000, attacks on Jews and their institutions in the European countries proliferated so greatly that it became difficult to decide whether loathing for Israel triggers hatred for the Jews, or the reverse. In a series of articles on 'the new anti-Semitism', Israeli journalist Yair Sheleg summarizes the situation as follows:

> The new anti-Semites are mainly Muslims, but they cooperate with the extreme Left and the neo-Nazi Right. The new outbreak of anti-Semitism would appear to be fuelled by the Europeans' ridding themselves of feelings of guilt for the Holocaust and by the struggle for the restitution of Jewish property.[7]

The Jewish Diaspora is not the only one, in our world, which is connected to a nation in conflict – but there is nothing that can be compared to attacks on Jews in Europe as a 'punishment' for Israel. We have not seen Indian temples in Europe bombed because of the bloody and prolonged conflict in Kashmir, or the

Armenian diaspora targeted because of the conflict with Azerbaijan. And yet even moderate and reasonable people, while condemning anti-Jewish violence in Europe, have sometimes been willing to show some understanding for the motives of the attackers. The total and unreserved condemnation with which every other type of racist violence is met in today's Europe is not always visited on those who target Jews: this is, after all, not pure racism but a regrettable 'spill-over' from the Arab–Israeli conflict. Interestingly, this conflict never 'spills over' in the opposite direction; nor can one imagine such a thing, if it were to happen in Europe, being treated as anything other than downright racism – and rightly so.

Perhaps the very belief that the establishment of a Jewish state would be sufficient to put an end all at once to such an ancient and deep-rooted hostility as that against the Jews – people who until modern times were not considered deserving of equality and dignity – was utterly unrealistic from the very beginning. In this sense, Herzl's Zionism did indeed disappoint. However – and, in fact, all the more so precisely because of what has been mentioned above – the idea of a Jewish national home has lost none of its validity.

Today, the beliefs and sentiments that move many of those who refuse to renounce Jewish particularity and wish to be part of the Jewish people – including completely acculturated and integrated Western Jews – are very different from the idea of divine choice. They do not necessarily imply any religious element or a desire to be considered a 'chosen people'. Even less so do they imply abandoning the ideals of enlightenment and equality, strongly supported by the Jews in modern times. Striving to realize these ideals in a Jewish state, under difficult and unfavourable conditions, is in every respect a worthy challenge.

Because of their history and culture, because of the way they regard themselves and are often regarded by others, the Jews are not merely a religious community, but a people who have their own distinct character and whose national existence focuses on the Jewish nation-state – Israel. This is no longer a matter for ideological debate, but a fact of modern history. Ultimately it is this that explains not only the establishment of the state, but also the strength of Jewish commitment to Israel, as well as the waves of immigration (*aliya*) that brought millions of Jews to the country. It must, however, be emphasized that Zionism did not seek simply to establish a 'safe haven' for Jews. The aim was rather for there to be an independent location where Jewish and Hebrew cultural creativity could develop and flourish unhampered by fear or worry about pleasing others. In this sense, Zionism is a remarkable success story. What appeared to be mission impossible – the renaissance of the Hebrew language, literature and culture – has become a reality. In addition, Israel's standard of living is today far higher than in those countries from which most of the Jews – Middle Eastern and European alike – came to the country. This gap is such that, for the first time in Jewish history, non-Jews pass themselves off as Jews so that they can immigrate to Israel and become citizens.

It is sometimes claimed that the creation of Israel put an end to the peaceful co-existence of Arabs and Jews in the Muslim countries, and that without Zionism, which fuelled Arab anti-Semitism, this harmony would have survived. The facts, however, do not support this argument. Earlier in this book, in Chapter 1, we quoted Tunisian-Jewish writer Albert Memmi on this subject. As early as the first Zionist Congress, which took place half a century before Israel's establishment, an Algerian delegate, Ya'acov Behar, reported on the Jews' distress in his country. The recent history of the Arab and Muslim countries in the Middle East shows that minorities which do not fall into either of these categories – even when they are not associated with a hostile foreign country or with any kind of hostility towards their state – continue to be discriminated against and sometimes persecuted. The treatment of the Baha'i in Iran, the Copts in Egypt, the Kurds in Iraq and Syria, or the Christians under the Palestinian Authority (for all their Arab nationalist credentials) does not suggest that the Jews, had Zionism not been invented and had they continued to 'provoke' the majority society by their sheer success and prominence, would have been able to experience security and equality in those countries.

In this book, we have presented the Jewish democratic state as a legitimate response, in terms of international law and democratic principles, to the problems facing the modern Jewish people – its national aspirations, common with many other peoples, and its particular predicament alike. The comparisons we have made between Israel and other contemporary democracies disprove the fashionable arguments that the Jewish State is quintessentially an exception to the norms of the democratic world. On what are these arguments based? Some of them, clearly, are based on anti-Zionist ideology. But a considerable degree of ignorance also plays its part. While Israeli and foreign academics who attack the idea of a Jewish state may be familiar with US and European campuses and influenced by the radical discourse prevalent in some of them, they often seem to be far less acquainted with the complicated world of the European nation-states. When they think of Europe, it is usually the Europe of 'post-national' rhetoric rather than contemporary Europe as it actually exists. The rhetoric sometimes speaks of Europe's nation-states as if their replacement by a single super-state in which they will become mere provinces were both inevitable and imminent. It is rather less obvious today than it seemed to many only several years ago that this is indeed the direction in which Europe is moving; nor is it by any means safe to assume that a future united Europe would be culturally neutral. At all events, no other people's desire for national independence – or unwillingness to renounce it, once achieved – is condemned in the name of a debatable speculation about where Europe might be heading. No such norm exists anywhere in the world, least of all in the Middle East.

Undeniably, national movements, nation-states and national identities (sometimes with an admixture of religion) have been a source of great evils in the twentieth century. In a utopian vision there is no place for anything other than pure universalism, devoid of any particular national attachments, as in John Lennon's song 'Imagine': which invites the listener to imagine a world without countries and without religion, with the resultant universal peace and brotherhood. Such a utopia is hardly around the corner. If, one day, the peoples of the world were to give up their identities and their respective states, the Jews and their state would also fall in line, but would not be at the head of the queue. But until these messianic times come, the record has to be set straight. This we have tried to do in this book.

In early November 1917, two events of historic importance took place a few days apart. On 2 November, the Balfour Declaration was issued. It expressed support for the Zionist movement in its aspiration to establish a Jewish national home in Palestine. A few days later, the Bolshevik Revolution broke out in St Petersburg. This would give rise to both the Soviet Union and a fervent hope of world revolution. At that time, the Zionist revolution looked like a mere trickle compared with the mighty torrent threatening to drown the Old World beneath its waves. By the end of the century, the picture was very different: the Soviet Union had been dismantled, taking with it the vision of a worldwide communist revolution, while the Jewish State had survived, preserved and developed its democracy, and will soon be home to most of the world's Jews. Only here can they live as a people in their homeland, speaking their language, celebrating their festivals and holidays, preserving their tradition and shaping their culture. In the fullest sense of the word, for the Jewish people in Israel there is nowhere else – no other country.

Appendix 1

Extracts from some contemporary democratic constitutions

This appendix contains extracts from the constitutions of a number of democratic states. Statements of a cultural, historical or ideological character, including issues of national identity, generally appear in the preamble to a constitution or in its opening articles. As these texts indicate, in many instances a modern democratic constitution is not a culturally 'neutral' document. It often goes beyond specifying the structure of the institutions of government and the rights of citizens. The distinct character of each state may be expressed in a variety of ways, including, regularly, relating to the status of the national language and sometimes the status of religion in the country, the character of state education or the state's ties with its national diaspora. The Irish Constitution specifies a national goal – the reunification of Ireland; a similar statement appears in South Korea's Constitution, and was to be found in the Constitution or Basic Law of the Federal Republic of Germany prior to the unification of West and East Germany. At the same time, modern constitutional texts lay great stress on universal values and on guaranteeing civil rights, and in particular on the principle of equality – not only in the preamble and the opening articles that state general principles, but also in detailed provisions regarding civil rights. Frequently, these sections constitute a considerable portion of the constitutional text. We will reproduce some of this material here, primarily in order to show how universal democratic principles and culturally specific provisions co-exist in contemporary constitutional texts. For the texts of the constitutions cited here, see International Constitutional Law, www.servat.unibe.ch/law/icl.

Ireland

The first example is the Constitution of the Republic of Ireland. The Constitution was adopted in 1937, but has since been amended on a number of occasions. These amendments include the revocation in the 1970s of an article which conferred official status on the Catholic Church. Nevertheless the Constitution retains its Christian character, as expressed emphatically in its opening paragraphs. Another amendment, introduced as part of the Irish peace process in the 1990s, accepted the principle that Irish unification can only come about if a majority of Northern Ireland's inhabitants agree to it. Article 8 of the Constitution stipulates that the Irish language, as the national language, is the first official language of the State. This, far from being a 'banal' statement of fact, is an ideological statement which expresses the country's national identity. In practice, only a relatively small minority of the Republic's citizens are Irish-speaking. The Constitution, in the name of 'the Irish nation' (Article 1), proclaims the island's unification as a national objective. This nation includes not only the Republic's citizens, but also, in principle, all of the island's inhabitants – although Article 2, according to which belonging to the Irish Nation is the 'birthright' of all of the island's inhabitants, can also be interpreted as implying recognition of the fact that in practice, many of them (the Protestant majority in the north) define their national identity differently. Article 2 includes a reference to 'people of Irish ancestry living abroad who share (the nation's) identity and heritage'.

Constitution of Ireland

Preamble

In the name of the Most Holy Trinity, from Whom is all authority and to Whom, as our final end, all actions both of men and States must be referred,
We, the people of Ireland, humbly acknowledging all our obligations to our Divine Lord, Jesus Christ, Who sustained our fathers through centuries of trial,
Gratefully remembering their heroic and unremitting struggle to regain the rightful independence of our Nation, and seeking to promote the common good, with due observance of Prudence, Justice and Charity, so that the dignity and freedom of the individual may be assured, true social order attained, the unity of our country restored, and concord established with other nations, Do hereby adopt, enact, and give to ourselves this Constitution.

ARTICLE 1

The Irish nation hereby affirms its inalienable, indefeasible, and sovereign right to choose its own form of Government, to determine its relations with other nations, and to develop its life, political, economic and cultural, in accordance with its own genius and traditions.

ARTICLE 2

It is the entitlement and birthright of every person born in the island of Ireland, which includes its islands and seas, to be part of the Irish Nation. That is also the entitlement of all persons otherwise qualified in accordance with law to be citizens of Ireland. Furthermore, the Irish nation cherishes its special affinity with people of Irish ancestry living abroad who share its cultural identity and heritage.

ARTICLE 3

It is the firm will of the Irish Nation, in harmony and friendship, to unite all the people who share the territory of the island of Ireland, in all the diversity of their identities and traditions, recognising that a united Ireland shall be brought about only by peaceful means with the consent of a majority of the people, democratically expressed, in both jurisdictions in the island.

ARTICLE 8

(1) The Irish language as the national language is the first official language.
(2) The English language is recognised as a second official language.
(3) Provision may, however, be made by law for the exclusive use of either of the said languages for any one or more official purposes, either throughout the State or in any part thereof.

Greece

The current Constitution of Greece was adopted in 1975, after the re-establishment of democracy following the fall of the 'regime of the colonels'. A number of amendments have been made to the original version, but these did not modify the official status of the Orthodox Church. This status, largely determined by the close historical ties between Orthodox Christianity and Greek national culture and identity, is expressed in the Constitution more emphatically, and in greater detail, than is customary in democratic constitutions adopted in recent decades. However, the official status of the Church is not in and of itself an exceptional phenomenon. The European Commission for Human Rights in Strasbourg has repeatedly ruled that the very fact that a particular Church enjoys the status of 'official Church' or 'state Church' does not breach European human rights norms, provided that all individuals are free not to belong to it without being adversely affected. It should be noted that the constitutional ban on proselytism – which is also translated into a corresponding article in the criminal law – has in recent years been applied very rarely, after the European Court of Human Rights ruled that the State could prohibit only 'improper' proselytism (i.e. a form which goes beyond legitimate persuasion).[1] Greece's Constitution is unique in conferring official status on a foreigner – the Patriarch of Constantinople ('the Oecumenical Patriarch'), who is a Turkish citizen. Unlike foreign citizens of Greek ethnic origin, who under the citizenship law enjoy preference in respect of naturalization, a foreign citizen who is admitted as a monk or novice to one of the monasteries of Mount Athos is, according to the Constitution, granted Greek citizenship automatically. This also is a symbolic expression of the strength of the ties between Orthodox Christianity and Greek identity.

Constitution of the Greek Republic

[Quasi-Preamble]

In the name of the Holy and Consubstantial and Indivisible Trinity, the Fifth Constitutional Assembly of Greece votes:

Part I Fundamental Provisions

ARTICLE 1 [PARLIAMENTARY DEMOCRACY]

(1) Greece is a Parliamentary Democracy with a President as Head of State.

(2) Popular sovereignty is the foundation on which the form of government rests.

(3) All powers are derived from the People, exist for the benefit of the People and the Nation, and are exercised in the manner determined by the Constitution.

ARTICLE 2 [HUMAN DIGNITY]

(1) Respect for and protection of human dignity constitute the primary obligation of the State.

Section II Relations between church and state

ARTICLE 3 [RELATIONS OF CHURCH AND STATE]

(1) The prevailing religion in Greece is that of the Eastern Orthodox Church of Christ. The Orthodox Church of Greece acknowledging as its head Our Lord Jesus Christ is indissolubly united in doctrine with the Great Church of Constantinople and every other Church of Christ of the same doctrine. It observes steadfastly, as they do, the holy apostolic and synodical canons and the holy tradition. It is autocephalous, exercising its sovereign rights independently of any other church, and is administered by the Holy Synod of Bishops and the Parliament Holy Synod which emanates from the former and is constituted in accordance with the Constitutional Chart of the Church and the provisions of the Patriarchal Document of 29 June 1850 and the Synodal Deed of 4 September 1928.

(2) The religious status prevailing in certain parts of the State is not contrary to the provisions of the foregoing paragraph.

(3) The text of the Holy Scriptures shall be maintained unaltered. The official translation thereof into any other linguistic form, without the sanction of the Autocephalous Church of Greece and the Great Church of Christ in Constantinople, is prohibited.

Part II Individual and Social Rights

ARTICLE 4 [CITIZENSHIP AND EQUALITY]

(1) All Greeks are equal before the law.
(2) Greek men and Greek women have equal rights and obligations.

ARTICLE 13 [RELIGION]

(1) The freedom of religious conscience is inviolable. The enjoyment of civil and individual rights does not depend on the religious conviction of each individual.
(2) Every known religion is free and the forms of worship thereof shall be practised without any hindrance by the State and under protection of the law. The exercise of worship shall not contravene public order or offend morals. Proselytizing is prohibited.

ARTICLE 16 [EDUCATION]

(1) Art and science, research, and teaching are free and their development and promotion constitutes a state obligation. Academic freedom and the freedom to teach do not override the duty to obey the Constitution.
(2) Education constitutes a fundamental state objective and aims at the moral, intellectual, professional, and physical instruction of the Greeks, the development of national and religious consciousness, and the formation of free and responsible citizens.

Section II The President of the Republic

Chapter I Election of the President

ARTICLE 33 [INSTALLATION]

(2) The President of the Republic shall take the following oath before Parliament, and prior to his taking office:

> I swear in the name of the Holy, Consubstantial, and Indivisible Trinity to observe the Constitution and the laws, to provide for the faithful observance thereof, to defend the national independence and territorial integrity of the country, to protect the rights and liberties of Greeks and to serve the public interest and the progress of the Greek People.

ARTICLE 108 [GREEKS LIVING ABROAD]

The State shall be concerned with those Greeks who live abroad and the maintenance of their links with the Motherland.

Scandinavian countries

In Scandinavian countries, the Lutheran Church traditionally enjoys the status of a national or state Church. In Sweden this status was rescinded in 2000; it still obtains in Denmark, Norway (despite calls to repeal or change it), Iceland and Finland (where the small Orthodox Church also enjoys official status). The current Norwegian Constitution was adopted in 1884. Although it has been amended several times since then, it still retains provisions which would not be considered acceptable in a constitution drafted today – such as the article requiring more than half the number of the Members of the Council of State (Norwegian government) to belong to the official Church. The provision to the effect that members of the Lutheran Church must bring up their children in the same religion is obviously unenforceable in a modern democracy. Retaining it in a constitution has symbolic value, further highlighting the connection between Lutheran Christianity and Norwegian culture and society. However, it should be noted that the official status of the Church affects the nature of religious instruction classes in the state education system. Most internal matters of the Church are now decided by democratically elected Church bodies, but the government still appoints the bishops.

Constitution of the Kingdom of Denmark

Part I [General Provisions]

SECTION 4 [STATE CHURCH]

The Evangelical Lutheran Church shall be the Established Church of Denmark, and, as such, it shall be supported by the State.

SECTION 6 [MEMBER OF THE STATE CHURCH]

The King shall be a member of the Evangelical Lutheran Church.

SECTION 66 [CHURCH CONSTITUTION]

The constitution of the Established Church shall be laid down by Statute.

SECTION 67 [RIGHT TO WORSHIP]

The citizens shall be entitled to form congregations for the worship of God in a manner consistent with their convictions, provided that nothing at variance with good morals or public order shall be taught or done.

SECTION 69 [REGULATION OF OTHER RELIGIOUS BODIES]

Rules for religious bodies dissenting from the Established Church shall be laid down by Statute.

SECTION 70 [FREEDOM OF RELIGION]

No person shall for reasons of his creed or descent be deprived of access to complete enjoyment of his civic and political rights, nor shall he for such reasons evade compliance with any common civic duty.

Constitution of the Kingdom of Norway

[Section] A. Form of government and religion

ARTICLE 1 [INTEGRITY OF THE KINGDOM]

The Kingdom of Norway is a free, independent, indivisible and inalienable Realm. Its form of government is a limited and hereditary monarchy.

ARTICLE 2 [RELIGION, STATE RELIGION]

(1) All inhabitants of the Realm shall have the right to free exercise of their religion.
(2) The Evangelical-Lutheran religion shall remain the official religion of the State. The inhabitants professing it are bound to bring up their children in the same.

ARTICLE 4 [RELIGION OF THE KING]

The King shall at all times profess the Evangelical-Lutheran religion, and uphold and protect the same.

ARTICLE 12 [COUNCIL OF STATE]

(1) The King himself chooses a Council from among Norwegian citizens who are entitled to vote. This Council shall consist of a Prime Minister and at least seven other Members.
(2) More than half the number of the Members of the Council of State shall profess the official religion of the State.

ARTICLE 16 [PUBLIC WORSHIP]

The King ordains all public church services and public worship, all meetings and assemblies dealing with religious matters, and ensures that public teachers of religion follow the norms prescribed for them.

ARTICLE 21 [APPOINTMENT OF OFFICIALS]

The King shall choose and appoint, after consultation with his Council of State, all senior civil, ecclesiastical and military officials.

Italy and Spain

Between the two extreme possibilities – the complete separation between religion and state, on the one hand, and the existence of an official Church, on the other – lies a wide range of intermediate possibilities in respect of arrangements for ties between religion and state. This applies to the symbolic and declarative area as well as practical matters, such as participation of state officials in church events, display of religious symbols (the cross or the crucifix) in public locations and institutions (sometimes including state schools, as in Austria and Italy), Sunday laws, government financing for religious institutions and religious schools (the latter receive government financing in France as well, despite the separation of church and state), property matters of the religious establishment (including tax exemptions), religious public broadcasting, as well as religious instruction classes at state schools. Issues involving moral and family matters are also sometimes influenced by the degree of the religious establishment's influence in the State, the most salient example being the abortion issue and, in recent years, the status of same-sex couples.

Italy and Spain are, historically, Catholic countries. They also share a strong anti-clerical tradition, precisely because the Church used to be very powerful in both countries. Today, neither gives official status to the Catholic Church, although both of their constitutions mention this Church in a way that gives it a certain symbolic advantage over other religious groups. The Spanish text, adopted in 1978 when democracy was restored after the death of Franco, is more secular than that of Italy. The Spanish Left in particular saw the Church as a conservative element which had collaborated with the Franco regime, and agreed to no more than a low-key reference to it in the Constitution.

We also reproduce here the articles which express the official view of the Spanish State on the question of national identity: a single Spanish nation containing different 'nationalities and regions' as a national supra-identity of all the country's citizens, and the key role of the Spanish-Castilian language in defining this identity. Article 11, on dual nationality, reflects the special relationship between Spain and the Spanish-speaking countries of Latin America (cf. Article 7.4 of the Constitution of Portugal: 'Portugal maintains special bonds of friendship and co-operation with the Portuguese speaking countries').

Constitution of the Italian Republic

Article 7 [Relation between State and Church]

(1) The State and the Catholic Church shall be, each within its own sphere, independent and sovereign.

(2) Their relations shall be regulated by the Lateran Pacts. Such amendments to these Pacts as are accepted by both parties shall not require the procedure for Constitutional amendment.

Article 8 [Religion]

(1) Religious denominations shall be equally free before the law.
(2) Denominations other than Catholicism shall have the right to organize themselves according to their own by-laws, provided they do not conflict with the Italian legal system.

Constitution of Spain

Article 2 [National Unity, Regional Autonomy]

The Constitution is based on the indissoluble unity of the Spanish nation, the common and indivisible homeland of all Spaniards, and recognizes and guarantees the right to autonomy of the nationalities and regions which make it up and the solidarity among all of them.

Article 3 [Official Language]

(1) Castilian is the official Spanish language of the State. All Spaniards have the duty to know it and the right to use it.
(2) The other languages of Spain will also be official in the respective autonomous communities, in accordance with their Statutes.
(3) The richness of the linguistic modalities of Spain is a cultural patrimony which will be the object of special respect and protection.

Article 16 [Religion, Belief, No State Church]

(1) Freedom of ideology, religion, and cult of individuals and communities is guaranteed without any limitation in their demonstrations other than that which is necessary for the maintenance of public order protected by law.
(2) No one may be obliged to make a declaration on his ideology, religion, or beliefs.
(3) No religion shall have a state character. The public powers shall take into account the religious beliefs of Spanish society and maintain the appropriate relations of cooperation, with the Catholic Church and other denominations.

Bulgaria

Bulgaria is one of the 'new democracies' which came into being in Eastern Europe following the fall of the Communist regime. It has been an EU member since January 2007. Its Constitution contains an interesting and original form of words with regard to the ties between religion and the state: the relevant article (13) stipulates both that the religious institutions shall be separate from the State's institutions and that Orthodox Christianity is the traditional religion of Bulgaria. The desire to emphasize the Orthodox Christian aspect of Bulgarian identity may well have to do, among other things, with the fact that the country has a large Muslim Turkish-speaking minority. The national status of the Bulgarian language is strongly emphasized: going beyond the standard formulations regarding the official language of the State, the Constitution stipulates that the study and use of the Bulgarian language is an obligation of every Bulgarian citizen. 'Autonomous territorial formations' are banned (Article 2), as well as 'parties based on ethnic, racial, or religious lines' (Article 11.4). 'A person of Bulgarian origin shall acquire Bulgarian citizenship through a facilitated procedure' (Article 25.2). The Constitution includes the usual provisions guaranteeing full equality of civil rights for all its citizens, irrespective of religion, race and national origin.

Constitution of the Republic of Bulgaria

Article 3 [Language]

Bulgarian is the official language of the Republic.

Article 6 [Human Dignity, Freedom, Equality]

(1) All persons are born free and equal in dignity and rights.
(2) All citizens shall be equal before the law. There shall be no privileges or restriction of rights on the grounds of race, nationality, ethnic self-identity, sex, origin, religion, education, opinion, political affiliation, personal or social status, or property status.

Article 36 [Language]

(1) The study and use of the Bulgarian language is a right and obligation of every Bulgarian citizen.
(2) Citizens whose mother tongue is not Bulgarian shall have the right to study and use their own language alongside the compulsory study of the Bulgarian language.
(3) The situations in which only the official language shall be used shall be established by law.

Poland

Traditionally, Poland is one of the most Catholic countries in the world. Following the Second World War, it had practically no national minorities left, and currently it has a few hundred thousand at most. In the period leading up to the eventual adoption of the democratic constitution in 1997, it became clear that the status of the Church in Poland following the fall of the Communist regime was highly controversial.[2] Among the authors of the Constitution there was a majority for those who feared that 'over-generous' formulations with regard to the Church might provide a basis for exaggerated claims on its part. As a result, the Constitution is, for Poland, a remarkably secular document. The Roman Catholic Church is mentioned by name, there is a statement that relations between it and the State will be determined by special arrangement concluded with the Holy See, and the preamble to the Constitution relates to the nation's 'Christian heritage'. However, not only is no official status conferred upon the Church, but the preamble to the Constitution adopts a posture of official neutrality between religious faith and the absence of faith.

This is a strong secular statement. While most democratic constitutions make no reference to God, in numerous other cases God is mentioned (even when no preference to a particular faith is expressed). The preamble to the German Constitution, for example, refers to the responsibility of the German people 'before God and men'; the new version of the Swiss Constitution, adopted in 1999, opens with the words: 'In the name of God Almighty!'; and the preamble to the new South African Constitution of 1996 finishes with 'May God protect our people', followed by a sentence asking God, in a number of languages, to 'bless South Africa'. The opening sentence of the Canadian Constitution Act, adopted in 1982, states: 'Whereas Canada is founded upon principles that recognize the supremacy of God and the rule of law'. In Poland, precisely because of the great power of the Catholic Church and its controversial demands, recognizing the 'supremacy of God' would not have been acceptable to secular forces, since this expression might be interpreted very differently than in Canada. For the same reason, such a formula would not be acceptable in Israel.

The preamble to the Constitution speaks in the name of the 'Polish Nation' (the original Polish – *Naród Polski* – can also be rendered as the 'Polish People'), which is synonymous with 'all citizens of the Republic'. Accordingly, 'the Nation' is declared in Article 4 to be the source of 'supreme power'. Nevertheless, the Constitution does not assume that Polish national identity is common to all citizens: it recognizes the existence and rights of 'national or ethnic minorities' whose language is not Polish. The national struggle throughout Polish history is, according to the preamble, the struggle of 'our ancestors', and these ancestors bequeathed the current generation 'our culture rooted in the Christian heritage of the Nation'. The preamble refers to the ties between the Nation and communities of Polish 'compatriots' dispersed throughout the world, and Articles 6 and 52 give expression to this affinity, including the right of anyone of Polish origin to settle permanently in Poland. While the Polish national-cultural identity does not entirely coincide with 'the Nation' as defined in the Constitution, it shapes the nation's character decisively.

Constitution of the Republic of Poland

[Preamble]

Having regard for the existence and future of our Homeland, Which recovered, in 1989, the possibility of a sovereign and democratic determination of its fate, We, the Polish Nation – all citizens of the Republic,
Both those who believe in God as the source of truth, justice, good and beauty, As well as those not sharing such faith but respecting those universal values as arising from other sources,
Equal in rights and obligations towards the common good – Poland,
Beholden to our ancestors for their labours, their struggle for independence achieved at great sacrifice, for our culture rooted in the Christian heritage of the Nation and in universal human values,
Recalling the best traditions of the First and the Second Republic,
Obliged to bequeath to future generations all that is valuable from our over one thousand years' heritage, Bound in community with our compatriots dispersed throughout the world,
Aware of the need for cooperation with all countries for the good of the Human Family,
Mindful of the bitter experiences of the times when fundamental freedoms and human rights were violated in our Homeland,
Desiring to guarantee the rights of the citizens for all time, and to ensure diligence and efficiency in the work of public bodies,
Recognizing our responsibility before God or our own consciences,
Hereby establish this Constitution of the Republic of Poland as the basic law for the State, based on respect for freedom and justice, cooperation between the public powers, social dialogue as well as on the principle of aiding in the strengthening the powers of citizens and their communities.

Article 4

(1) Supreme power in the Republic of Poland shall be vested in the Nation.
(2) The Nation shall exercise such power directly or through their representatives.

Article 6

(1) The Republic of Poland shall provide conditions for the people's equal access to cultural goods which are the source of the Nation's identity, continuity and development.
(2) The Republic of Poland shall provide assistance to Poles living abroad to maintain their links with the national cultural heritage.

Article 25

(1) Churches and other religious organizations shall have equal rights.
(2) Public authorities in the Republic of Poland shall be impartial in matters of personal conviction, whether religious or philosophical, or in relation to outlooks on life, and shall ensure their freedom of expression within public life.
(4) The relations between the Republic of Poland and the Roman Catholic Church shall be determined by international treaty concluded with the Holy See, and by statute.

Article 27

Polish shall be the official language in the Republic of Poland. This provision shall not infringe upon national minority rights resulting from ratified international agreements.

Article 52

(5) Anyone whose Polish origin has been confirmed in accordance with statute may settle permanently in Poland.

Slovakia

A different meaning is attached to the term 'nation' in the Constitution of Slovakia, a state with a sizeable Hungarian minority amounting to over 10 per cent of the population and an EU member since 2003. The 'Slovak nation', in whose name (and in the name of whose right to self-determination) the preamble speaks, is clearly the Slovak-speaking majority. The Constitution is adopted in the name of the Slovak nation, 'together with members of national minorities and ethnic groups living on the territory of the Slovak Republic'. Since not all of the country's citizens are included in the concept of 'the Slovak nation', the source of State power is, according to Article 2, defined as the country's citizens and not the 'nation'. Article 1 declares that the State is not linked to any ideology or religious belief. However, according to Article 9 the state emblem and flag include the cross. Article 7a of the Constitution, which refers to the Republic's links with Slovaks living abroad, was added in 2001.

Constitution of the Slovak Republic

Preamble

We, the Slovak nation,
mindful of the political and cultural heritage of our forebears, and of the centuries of experience from the struggle for national existence and our own statehood, in the sense of the spiritual heritage of Cyril and Methodius and the historical legacy of the Great Moravian Empire,

proceeding from the natural right of nations to self-determination, together with members of national minorities and ethnic groups living on the territory of the Slovak Republic, in the interest of lasting peaceful cooperation with other democratic states,

seeking the application of the democratic form of government and the guarantees of a free life and the development of spiritual culture and economic prosperity, that is, we, citizens of the Slovak Republic, adopt through our representatives the following Constitution:

Chapter I Basic Provisions

ARTICLE 1

The Slovak Republic is a sovereign, democratic, and law-governed state. It is not linked to any ideology or religious belief.

ARTICLE 2

(1) State power is derived from citizens, who execute it through their elected representatives or directly.

ARTICLE 6

(1) Slovak is the state language on the territory of the Slovak Republic.
(2) The use of other languages in dealings with the authorities will be regulated by law.

ARTICLE 9

(1) The state emblem of the Slovak Republic is represented by a red early Gothic shield featuring a silver double cross on the middle of three blue symbolic mountain peaks.
(2) The national flag of the Slovak Republic consists of three long bands – white, blue, and red. The front side of the national flag of the Slovak Republic features the state emblem of the Slovak Republic.

Slovenia

Earlier in this book (Chapter 5) we have discussed the Constitution of Slovenia and the delicate balance between the national and civic aspects in this text.

Constitution of the Republic of Slovenia

Preamble

Proceeding from the Basic Constitutional Charter on the Sovereignty and Independence of the Republic of Slovenia, and from fundamental human rights and freedoms, and the fundamental and permanent right of the Slovene nation to self-determination; and from the historical fact that in a centuries-long struggle for national liberation we Slovenes have established our national identity and asserted our statehood, the Assembly of the Republic of Slovenia hereby adopt the Constitution of the Republic of Slovenia.

ARTICLE 1 [DEMOCRATIC REPUBLIC]

Slovenia is a democratic republic.

ARTICLE 3 [SELF-DETERMINATION, SOVEREIGNTY]

(1) Slovenia is a state of all its citizens and is founded on the permanent and inalienable right of the Slovenian nation to self-determination.
(2) In Slovenia, supreme power is vested in the people. Citizens exercise this power directly and through elections.

ARTICLE 5 [STATE OBJECTIVES]

(1) Within its own territory, Slovenia shall protect human rights and fundamental freedoms. It shall protect and guarantee the rights of the autochthonous Italian and Hungarian national communities. It shall maintain concern for autochthonous Slovene national minorities in neighbouring countries and for Slovene emigrants and workers abroad and shall foster their contacts with the homeland. It shall provide for the preservation of the natural wealth and cultural heritage and create opportunities for the harmonious development of society and culture in Slovenia.
(2) Slovenes not holding Slovene citizenship may enjoy special rights and privileges in Slovenia. The nature and extent of such rights and privileges shall be regulated by law.

Constitution of Malta

The only European democracy where today the Roman Catholic Church has the status of a State Church is the tiny island of Malta. The Constitution of Malta was adopted in 1964, and it gives particular prominence to the official status of the Church:

Section 2 [State Religion]

(1) The religion of Malta is the Roman Catholic Apostolic Religion.

(2) The authorities of the Roman Catholic Apostolic Church have the duty and the right to teach which principles are right and which are wrong.

(3) Religious teaching of the Roman Catholic Apostolic Faith shall be provided in all State schools as part of compulsory education.

Constitutions of Latin American countries

The Roman Catholic Church has official- or quasi-official status in a number of Latin American countries. Thus the Constitution of Costa Rica, which is considered a model of stable democracy in Latin America, states in Article 75:

> The Roman Catholic and Apostolic Religion is the religion of the State, which contributes to its maintenance, without preventing the free exercise in the Republic of other forms of worship that are not opposed to universal morality or good customs.

According to Section 2 of the Constitution of Argentina, 'The Federal Government supports the Roman Catholic Apostolic religion'. In the past, the Constitution stipulated that the President of Argentina must be a Roman Catholic; this requirement has been revoked.

According to the Constitution of Peru (Article 59) 'the State recognises the Roman Catholic Church as an important element of the historical, cultural and moral development of Peru'.

The Autonomous Region of the Basque Country

For a discussion of the national character of the Basque autonomy, see Chapter 6 above (pp. 169–171).

The statute of autonomy of the Basque Country

Article 1

The Basque People or 'Euskal-Herria', as an expression of their nationality and in order to accede to self-government, constitute an Autonomous Community within the Spanish State under the name of 'Euskadi' or the Basque Country, in accordance with the Constitution and with this Statute, which lays down its basic institutional rules.

Article 2

(2) The territory of the Autonomous Community shall comprise the Historic Territories which coincide with the provinces of Alava, Guipúzcoa and Vizcaya,

respecting their present boundaries, and with the province of Navarra, should it decide to join, in accordance with the procedure laid down in Transitory Provision Four of the Constitution.

Article 5

(1) The flag of the Basque Country has two crosses, a green diagonal cross and a superimposed white perpendicular cross, on a red background.

Article 6

(1) 'Euskera', the language of the Basque People, shall, like Spanish, have the status of an official language in Euskadi. All its inhabitants have the right to know and use both languages.

(3) No one may suffer discrimination for reasons of language.

(4) The Royal Academy of the Basque Language is the official advisory institution in matters regarding 'Euskera'.

(5) Given that 'Euskera' is the heritage of other Basque territories and communities, the Autonomous Community of the Basque Country may request the Spanish Government, in addition to whatever ties and correspondence are maintained with academic and cultural institutions, to conclude and, where necessary, to submit to the Spanish State Parliament for authorization, those treaties or agreements that will make it possible to establish cultural relations with the States where such territories lie and communities reside, with a view to safeguarding and promoting 'Euskera'.

Article 7

(1) For the purposes of this Statute, the political status of Basque shall be accorded to all those who are officially resident, according to the General Laws of the State, in any of the municipalities belonging to the territory of the Autonomous Community.

Constitution of the French Republic

France's Constitution (adopted in 1958) most closely corresponds to the model of secular civic democracy which considers national identity and citizenship to coincide in full. This civic nationalism has a pronounced cultural content – the French language. It is not by chance that its status is stipulated as being the language of the Republic in a section entitled 'Sovereignty', together with the Republic's basic principles and national emblems. As we have seen, this constitutional provision has been interpreted as not allowing France to ratify the European Charter for Regional or Minority Languages. Similarly, we have seen the interpretation that France's Constitutional Council has given to the principle of indivisible national sovereignty, which lies with the entire French people. This interpretation limits the degree of regional autonomy that can be granted to a given part of the Republic (in this case, Corsica), and rules out the recognition of such a region's population as a distinct national group in the framework of the French people.

Title I Sovereignty

Article 2 [State Form and Symbols]

(1) France is an indivisible, secular, democratic, and social Republic. It ensures the equality of all citizens before the law, without distinction as to origin, race, or religion. It respects all beliefs.
(2) The language of the Republic is French.
(3) The national emblem is the blue, white, and red tricolour flag.
(4) The national anthem is the 'Marseillaise'.
(5) The Motto of the Republic is 'Liberty, Equality, Fraternity'.
(6) Its principle is government of the people, by the people, and for the people.

Article 3 [Electoral Rights]

(1) National sovereignty belongs to the people, who exercise it through their representatives and by means of referendums.
(2) No section of the people, nor any individual, may abrogate to themselves or to him or herself the exercise thereof.
(3) Suffrage may be direct or indirect under the terms stipulated by the Constitution. It shall always be universal, equal, and secret.

Appendix 2

Armenia and the Armenian diaspora – Nansen's address to the League of Nations

As we have seen, Armenian national identity is considered a classical example of 'diaspora nationalism'. There are numerous points of similarity between the Armenian and the Jewish cases – just as, of course, there are differences as well. Following the First World War and the Armenian genocide in Turkey, international public opinion manifested great sympathy for the Armenian people and its suffering. This sympathy, which was shared also in circles highly critical of the Soviet regime, benefited the Soviet Armenian Republic. The latter proclaimed itself the national home of the entire Armenian people and appealed to the Armenian diaspora (which comprised both ancient diaspora communities and those who had recently fled Turkish areas) in an attempt to enlist support for what it officially defined as repatriation to this national home. Altogether, over the years around a quarter of a million Armenians responded to these calls; today, the descendants of these 'returnees' make up a considerable proportion of Armenia's population.

Below we reproduce an excerpt from the address given by Fridtjof Nansen, a Norwegian diplomat and renowned humanitarian activist, to the League of Nations Assembly in 1927. In this speech, he calls upon the League of Nations to help settle these refugees in the Armenian Republic:

> I beg [you] to think for a moment what the history of the Armenian people has been. During the past twelve months I have spent a great part of my time in studying the history of the Armenian people, and I have been forced to the conviction that no people in recorded history have endured misery and maltreatment in any way comparable to that through which the Armenians have passed ... I would not dare to evoke again the picture of what happened to them in the years 1915 to 1918 ... I would not care to describe the nerve-shattering terror and the nameless infamy of the appalling pilgrimage of death which the historians will call deportations, when innocent victims – men, women, greybeards, tiny children – perished ... by hundreds of thousands, and with every circumstance of savage torture....
>
> Here was a people with immense national feeling, with a remarkable history of achievement in by-gone days, with the finest gifts of intellect and prac-

tical capacity, a people who had made – though few of us here may know it – a great contribution to the medieval culture from which our modern civilization is in so great a part derived – here was this people in a few years almost wiped out or scattered to the winds. And yet the surviving remnant of this people, with a tenacity and a national patriotism which no one can sufficiently admire, is now making with desperate courage another valiant attempt to build up a new national home.

The Republic of Erivan is nothing less than that to Armenians of every class and every party in whatever land they may now be.... [They] look not to Syria, not to Anatolia, not to South America, but to Erivan, the land at the foot of the eternal snows of Ararat, as the place where the destiny of their nation must in future lie. There, year after year, they are striving to build up a new community, a political and social system which is Armenian through and through.

Slowly they are gathering together ... their destitute brothers who had found a temporary refuge in foreign land, and they are sending them, with such funds as they can privately contribute, to the Armenian State in Erivan.

Notes

Introduction

1 R. Lapidoth and M. Hirsh (eds) (1948) *The Arab-Israel Conflict and its Resolution: Selected Documents*, Dordrecht: Martinus Nijhoff Publishers, p. 1.
2 The Law of Return refers to the principle that is reflected in two separate laws: the Law of Return itself, which that stipulates all Jews (and non-Jewish members of their families) are entitled to immigrate to the State of Israel; and the Citizenship Law, which determines that all immigrants under the Law of Return are entitled to Israeli citizenship.
3 Nevertheless, this is sometimes stated explicitly. For example, Dr Joseph Sadeh wrote in the *Ha'aretz* supplement on 27 July 2001, in the context of a debate over the definition of Israel as a Jewish state: 'Rubinstein maintains that there exists a Jewish people that has the right to self-determination, but this approach – which turns on a collective that lacks a common political culture and shared concrete practices – is pure mythology.'
4 T. Judt, 'Israel: the alternative', *The New York Review of Books* 50 (16), 23 October 2003, p. 8.

1 The establishment of the State of Israel: the UN debates in 1947

1 For the text of the Declaration of Independence, see R. Lapidoth and M. Hirsh (eds) (1992) *The Arab-Israel Conflict and its Resolution: Selected Documents*, Dordrecht: Martinus Nijhoff Publishers, pp. 61–63.
2 The term 'nation-state' may refer to a state that embodies the national independence of a particular 'nation' or people while acknowledging that some of its citizens have a different national identity; or a state that views all its citizens as sharing a single national identity and does not recognize national minorities within its borders. For more on this, see R. Gavison (1999) *Israel as a Jewish and Democratic State: Tensions and Chances*, Jerusalem: Van Leer Institute and Hakibbutz Hameuchad, p. 26 (Hebrew). We will use the term 'nation-state' here mainly in its first meaning.
3 From an interview with Ami Ayalon, *Ma'ariv*, 10 January 2003.
4 'United Nations Special Committee on Palestine, Report to the General Assembly', *Official Records of the Second Session of the General Assembly*, Volume 1, Supplement 11, New York, 1947, pp. 28–47. Quotations and references throughout this chapter to the UNSCOP report are based on this text.
5 For a similar view on the issue of Jewish immigration after the partition – the territorial restriction that would be created as a result of the very delimitation of the Jewish aspirations to part of the land – see Chapter VI of the commission's report, 'A Commentary on Partition' ('a self-operating control of immigration'). At the same time, the committee held that any solution to the Palestine problem could not be considered a solution of the Jewish problem in its entirety (Chapter V, Recommendation 12).

6 For this discussion and all quotations from UN meetings and debates on this issue in 1947, see *United Nations General Assembly, Plenary Meetings* (1947), Lake Success, NY.

7 J. Garcia-Granados (1948) *The Birth of Israel: the Drama as I Saw It*, New York: Alfred A. Knopf, p. 240.

8 Garcia-Granados: 206.

9 See, for example, the extensive discussion of this matter by the delegate of the Arab Higher Committee for Palestine in his speech to the Ad Hoc Committee of the members of the General Assembly on 18 October. In his speech to the General Assembly, the Syrian delegate based his remarks on 'two expert anthropologists from Columbia University' to prove this claim; see also the Lebanese delegate's remarks to the Ad Hoc Committee, 3 October.

10 Garcia-Granados 1948: 238.

11 The UNSCOP majority report sought to overcome the economic difficulty by means of an 'economic union' between the two countries.

12 Thus, for example, the Canadian delegate explained Canada's position to the Ad Hoc Committee on 14 October: The ideal solution for a situation in which two peoples with different cultures live in the same land was the federative solution like that of Canada; however, Canada's federation was based on agreement of the two groups; since the sides in Palestine rejected this solution, Canada had no choice but to support partition. It is not clear from these comments whether Canada would have been willing to support the federative solution if only the Arab side had accepted it, but it is clear that the rejection of that solution by the Arabs facilitated its decision to support partition. The comments made by the Dutch delegate in the plenary of the General Assembly on 26 November represent a view similar to that of the Canadian delegate.

13 The Egyptian delegate asked at the meeting of the Ad Hoc Committee of 8 October if the Nazi persecution still continued. 'If it continues, I cannot understand why 30,000 German Jews in Palestine have asked to be repatriated to Germany. It is not clear why these people are not being allowed to return.' The Lebanese delegate informed the Ad Hoc Committee on 3 October that 'Thousands of Austrian and German Jews [in Palestine] have asked to be repatriated to Austria and Germany'.

14 In the words of the Syrian delegate to the first committee of the General Assembly on 14 May:

> We understand that a great percentage of the Jews were massacred in Eastern Europe. Well, the survivors, who are a small percentage under the ruling democracies of Eastern Europe, could go back and take into their possession the properties of all the Jews who were there before, and each of them would be seven or eight times as rich as he used to be before.

15 The fact that Pakistan was established just a short time earlier in order to satisfy the aspirations of the subcontinent's Muslims, who maintained that they represented a separate nation, in complete opposition to the will of the majority of the population of British India, did not prevent the Pakistani delegate in the UN General Assembly from passionately arguing against the partition of Mandatory Palestine. He described, in a speech in the General Assembly on 28 November, partition as a cruel vivisection of the land:

> We shall first cut the body of Palestine into three parts of a Jewish State and three parts of an Arab State. We shall then have the Jaffa enclave; and Palestine's heart, Jerusalem, shall forever be an international city. That is the beginning of the shape Palestine shall have. Having cut Palestine up in that manner, we shall then put its bleeding body upon a cross forever.

16 For a discussion on the right to self-determination, the right of secession and dilem-

mas related to this issue, see, for example, W. Twining (ed.) (1991) *Issues of Self-Determination*, Aberdeen: Aberdeen University Press; A. Heraclides (1997) 'Ethnicity, secessionist conflict and the international society: towards normative paradigm shift', *Nations and Nationalism* 3 (4), pp. 493–520; M. Moore (ed.) (1998) *National Self-Determination and Secession*, Oxford: Oxford University Press; D. Philpott (1995) 'In defence of self-determination', *Ethics* 105 (2), 352–385.

17 Garcia-Granados 1948: 216.

18 Garcia-Granados 1948: 219.

19 Garcia-Granados 1948: 217.

20 Garcia-Granados 1948: 227.

21 Garcia-Granados 1948: 212.

22 R. Crossman (1946) *Palestine Mission: a Personal Record*, London: Hamish Hamilton, pp. 85–91. Crossman holds that while Zionist activity and propaganda did go on in the DP camps, 'even if there were not a single Zionist activist in the camps nor any trace of Zionist propaganda, these people would choose Palestine'.

23 On this matter, see the comments of the delegate of the Philippines before the plenary of the General Assembly on 26 November.

24 See, for example, R. Khalidi (1997) *Palestinian Identity: the Construction of Modern National Consciousness*, New York: Columbia University Press, pp. 145–175.

25 Cf. the remarks made by the delegate of the United States before the Ad Hoc Committee of the General Assembly on 11 October. He underscored his county's traditional stance since the end of the First World War: support both for the independence of the Arab nations and for the establishment of a national home for the Jews in Palestine.

26 The question of Zionism and colonialism will be discussed in the next chapter.

27 For a discussion of group rights and the problematic nature involved in this concept, see, for example, J. Stapleton (ed.) (1995) *Group Rights. Perspectives since 1990*, Bristol: Thoemmes Press.

28 On this matter, see, for example, W. Kymlicka (1989) *Liberalism, Community and Culture*, Oxford: Clarendon Press.

29 See Lapidoth and Hirsh: 25–32.

30 In fact, the minority report too recognized this historic connection.

> It is recognized that Palestine is the common country of both indigenous Arabs and Jews, that both these peoples have had an historic association with it, and that both play vital roles in the economic and cultural life of the country.
>
> (Chapter VII, Article 2)

Since the Jews, unlike the Arabs, were not 'indigenous', but rather mostly immigrants, it is clear that the 'historic association' in their case relates to the history of the Jewish people.

31 Garcia-Granados 1948: 63.

32 The brief speech of the Norwegian delegate before the Ad Hoc Committee on 16 October represents an exceptional instance of relying on the Jews' historical connection to the land of Israel as the primary (though not the sole) argument in support of a Jewish state:

> The delegation of Norway, in a spirit of compete impartiality and of equal amity for the two peoples, had finally decided to vote for the majority plan, in the first place because of the unchallengeable ties of the Jewish people to Palestine, secondly, because of the international undertakings with regard to the Jewish National Home and, finally, because of the wrongs which the Jews had suffered at the hands of mankind.

33 The delegate of Guatemala to UNSCOP also saw the problem in its broad regional context: 'I had heard enough to see that that the Middle East question was not only

one concerning the British, the Jews and the Arabs, but also involved the rights of non-Arab and non-Muslim groups in this region.' Garcia-Granados 1948: 201.

34 For text, see Lapidoth and Hirsh: 353–356.

35 Interview with Ari Shavit, *Ha'aretz* Weekend Supplement, 8 August 2000.

36 Interview with Ari Shavit, *Ha'aretz* Weekend Supplement, 3 January 2003.

37 Those who hold this view criticize the wording of the constitutions of some of the new democracies in Central and Eastern Europe that connect the state to the national self-determination of a certain people (a subject that will be discussed later in this book). However, it is noteworthy that the European institutions do not view such formulations as improper, and have not requested that they be abolished as a condition of these countries being accepted as members of the Council of Europe, and later of the EU, which requires them to meet European standards of democracy and human rights.

38 A proposal of this kind was presented to the Knesset by MK Amnon Rubinstein, but was voted down by a majority of 34 to 24 in a preliminary vote held on 23 October 2002.

39 *Knesset Minutes* I, p. 271; *Knesset Minutes* VIII, p. 1362.

40 A. Memmi (1975) *Jews and Arabs*, Chicago: J. Philip O'Hara, Inc., tr. Eleanor Levieux, p. 16. Memmi, who defined himself as a 'Jewish-Arab and a leftist Zionist', states that he does not regret his support for the Arab struggle against colonialism despite what happened to the Jews in the Arab countries after independence. He mentions

> the hangings in Baghdad, the prisons and burnings in Cairo the acts of robbery and economic strangulation in the Maghreb. ... Here another myth needs to be shattered: that this persecution is seemingly the result of Zionism – so reply the Arab-Muslim propagandists.... Historically, this is utter nonsense: It is not Zionism that was the source of Arab anti-Semitism, but just the opposite, exactly as in Europe. Israel is the answer to the oppression that the Jews experienced everywhere in the world, including our [oppression], that of the Jewish-Arabs.
>
> (Ibid.: 9–10)

37 M.H. Heikal (1996) *Secret Channels. The Inside Story of the Arab-Israeli Peace Negotiations*, London: HarperCollins, p. 114. See also pp. 13–14 and p. 68 on the Palestinian refugees and on the attitude of Egypt's Jews to the establishment of the Jewish State.

38 See Garcia-Granados 1948: 272.

39 The results of the vote were as follows:

> Supporting the partition: Australia, Belgium, Bolivia, Brazil, Byelorussia, Canada, Costa Rica, Czechoslovakia, Denmark, Dominican Republic, Ecuador, France, Guatemala, Haiti, Iceland, Liberia, Luxembourg, the Netherlands, New Zealand, Nicaragua, Norway, Panama, Paraguay, Peru, the Philippines, Poland, Sweden, Ukraine, Union of South Africa, USSR, USA, Uruguay, and Venezuela.
> Opposing partition: Afghanistan, Cuba, Egypt, Greece, India, Iran, Iraq, Lebanon, Pakistan, Saudi Arabia, Syria, Turkey, and Yemen.
> Abstaining: Argentina, Chile, China, Colombia, El Salvador, Ethiopia, Honduras, Mexico, Great Britain, and Yugoslavia.

40 See, for example, what Moshe Shertok said at the Security Council session in April 1948, Security Council (1948), *Official Records, The Third Year, Meetings 261–285*, Lake Success, NY, 277th Meeting, pp. 5–23.

41 Just how unfounded this claim is may be learned from the assessment made by Yigal Yadin, the acting Chief of Staff, to the 'people's executive' (the future provisional government) on 12 May 1948. The latter hesitated between declaring independence and giving in to massive American pressure to postpone this step and try to attain a

truce as part of the 'international trusteeship' plan. The decision was ultimately made by a majority of six to four. What Yadin had to say did little to encourage the Zionist leaders:

> The regular forces of our neighbouring countries at this time, with their equipment and weapons, have an advantage over us. We lack weapons and armoured vehicles. The question is the extent to which our people will manage to overcome such a force. ... It has been proved in certain cases that it is not the number and formation that count. ... If to sum up and to be cautious, I would say at this moment that the chances are quite even. If to be more candid, I would say that their advantage is great.
>
> (Naor and Giladi 1991: 402)

42 Security Council (1948), *Official Records, The Third Year, Meetings 261–285*, Lake Success, NY, 16 April, p. 19. The candour of the Palestinian representative on this occasion was unusual: most of the time, the Arab delegates made sure to place full responsibility for the violence in the land on the 'Zionist gangs' at the same time as they rejected the partition plan and declared their intent to forcibly prevent its implementation. However, they rejected any idea of a cease-fire that implied an agreement on their part to implement the partition plan. The Syrian delegate told the Security Council on 1 April 1948:

> I have just heard the representative of the Jewish Agency say that it would never agree to any truce if it impeded or interfered with the timetable of the implementation of the Plan of Partition. I know that the views of the Arabs of Palestine are just the contrary. They say, 'We will agree to a truce if it is not used as a screen to shield the activities for the continuation of the implementation of the Plan of Partition'.
>
> (Session 277, p. 28)

43 For a discussion of this subject, see A.R. Sureda (1973) *The Evolution of the Right of Self-Determination: a Study of United Nations Practice*, Leiden: A.W. Sijthoff, pp. 35–48.

44 For the position of the Jewish Agency, see Chapter IV, Articles 9 and 19 of the UNSCOP report. For Ben-Gurion's comments regarding the willingness to consider partition, see United Nations Special Committee on Palestine, Report to the General Assembly (1947) *Official Records of the Second Session of the General Assembly*, Volume 3, Annex A: Oral evidence presented at public meetings, New York, pp. 56, 62.

45 *Knesset Minutes* I, pp. 758–759.

46 The story of the relations between Abdullah and the Zionist leadership in the years 1947–1948 is a matter of controversy among scholars. For a 'collusion' theory, see A. Shlaim (1988) *Collusion across the Jordan: King Abdullah, the Zionist Movement and the Partition of Palestine*, Oxford: Clarendon Press. The claim of a 'collusion' leading to Transjordan taking over the West Bank assumes that the Zionist leadership was indeed willing to agree to have the country partitioned and did not aspire to take control of its whole territory. Since it was impossible to reach an agreement with the existing Palestinian leadership, there was, in fact, no one to partition the country with except Transjordan. However, there was considerable mistrust between the two sides. For arguments against the claim of a collusion, see Ephraim Karsh (1999), *Fabricating Israeli History; the 'New Historians'*, Tel Aviv: Hakibbutz Hameuhad, pp. 83–108. Dan Schueftan surveys the contacts between the two sides up to the proclamation of Israel's independence, when the Jewish side tried to make sure that Abdullah would not join forces with Israel's enemies. These contacts eventually failed and the Arab Legion engaged in a confrontation with Israel, although this confrontation was limited to the vicinity of Jerusalem. Schueftan underscores that the basic orienta-

tion towards a settlement with Jordan was adopted by the Zionist leadership after it despaired in the 1930s of a settlement with the Palestinian national movement, which rejected any possibility of such a settlement, see D. Schueftan (1986), *A Jordanian Option – Israel, Jordan and the Palestinians*, Tel Aviv: Hakibbutz Hameuhad (Hebrew).

47 For references regarding Sharett's cable, Ben-Gurion's remarks and the conversation in Amman, see Karsh 1999: 102–103. Schueftan (1986) maintains that Sharett's comments, at certain stages, in favour of the Palestinian option reflected his personal position not shared by Ben-Gurion. In his words, 'Sharett himself admitted that due to the 'Mufti-dominated' character of the Palestinian national movement, this was no more than a theoretical option, even if the alternative of Abdullah was not ideal, and to a certain extent, even dangerous.' Although Schueftan (1986: 89, 118) quotes an entry in Ben-Gurion's diary from December 1948, prior to the debate on the contacts with Transjordan: 'Annexation or an independent state' (as one of the questions on which Israel would have to determine its position), he ultimately attributes to Ben-Gurion an understanding, throughout the events of the War of Independence, that the only practical partner for partition and for a peace settlement was the king of Transjordan; consequently, Ben-Gurion also refrained from exploiting Israel's clear military advantage in late 1948 to occupy the West Bank.

48 The consensus that prevailed in the Arab world following the signing of the armistice agreements is described by Heikal: 'Peace was out of the question; the absence of war was the maximum that the Arab world was willing to consider, and even that was a matter of controversy', Heikal 1996: 8.

49 For more on this, see R. Pedatzur (1996) *The Triumph of Confusion: Israel and the Territories, 1967–1969*, Tel Aviv: Bitan (Hebrew).

2 Two arguments: Zionism as a colonialist phenomenon and the invention of Jewish nationalism

1 *Haaretz*, 20 May 2001 (letter to the editor in reply to an article by writer Yoram Kaniuk).

2 O. Yiftachel (1999) 'Ethnocracy: the politics of judaizing Israel/Palestine', *Constellations* 6 (3), pp. 369, 387.

3 M.H. Heikal (1978) *The Sphinx and the Commissar: the Rise and Fall of Soviet Influence in the Arab World*, London: Collins, p. 72.

4 Heikal 1996: 75.

5 For the text of the Balfour Declaration, see R. Lapidoth and M. Hirsh (eds) (1992) *The Arab–Israel Conflict and its Resolution: Selected Documents*, Dordrecht: Martinus Nijhoff Publishers, p. 20.

6 I. Pappe (1997) 'Zionism in the test of the theories of nationalism and the historiographic method' (Hebrew), in P. Ginossar and A. Bareli (eds), *Zionism: a Contemporary Controversy*, Sde Boker: The Ben-Gurion Research Center and the Institute for Research in the History of Zionism, Ben-Gurion University, pp. 252–257. The quotations from Pappe in the next passages come from those pages.

7 For quotations from UN meetings and debates in 1947, see *United Nations General Assembly, Plenary Meetings* (1947), Lake Success, NY.

8 G. Shafir (1989) *Land, Labour and the Origins of the Israeli-Palestinian Conflict, 1882–1914*, Cambridge: Cambridge University Press.

9 A. Rubinstein (2000) *Herzl to Rabin: the Changing Image of Zionism*, New York: Holmes & Meier, Chapter 4.

10 A. Koestler (1952) *Arrow in the Blue: an Autobiography*, New York: Macmillan, pp. 204–205; A. Koestler (1954) *The Invisible Writing*, New York: Macmillan, pp. 378–379.

11 D. Brown (2000) *Contemporary Nationalism: Civic, Ethnocultural and Multicultural*

Politics, London and New York: Routledge, p. 7 ff.; A.D. Smith (1986) *The Ethnic Origins of Nations*, Oxford: Blackwell, pp. 24–26.

12 E. Hobsbawm and T. Ranger (eds) (1983) *The Invention of Tradition*, Cambridge: Cambridge University Press; B. Anderson (1983) *Imagined Communities: Reflections on the Origins and Spread of Nationalism*, London: Verso. See also E. Gellner (1983) *Nations and Nationalism*, Oxford: Blackwell, pp. 55–57.

13 N. Masalha (2000) *Imperial Israel and the Palestinians: the Politics of Expansion*, London: Pluto Press.

14 E. Hobsbawm (1990) *Nations and Nationalism since 1780*, Cambridge: Cambridge University Press, pp. 47–48.

15 A.D. Smith (1998) *Nationalism and Modernism*, London: Routledge, pp. 190, 130–131, 137.

16 On Zionism as an example of diaspora nationalism, see also J. Rex (1996) *Ethnic Minorities in the Modern Nation State*, New York: St. Martin's Press.

17 A.D. Smith (1999) *Myths and Memories of the Nation*, Oxford: Oxford University Press, pp. 212–213.

18 For text of Mandate, see Lapidoth and Hirsh: 25–32.

3 Zionism and international norms

1 D. Ben-Gurion (1957) *Ba-ma'arkha*, Vol. IV, Tel Aviv: Am Oved, p. 259 (Hebrew). For more on this position, see Karsh 1999: 16 ff.

2 Theodor Herzl, *Der Judenstaat*. Translated from the German by Sylvie D'Avigdor. This edition was published in 1946 by the American Zionist Emergency Council.

3 A.D. Smith (1999) *Myths and Memories of the Nation*, Oxford: Oxford University Press, Chapter 8. See also G. Sheffer (ed.) (1986) *Modern Diasporas in International Politics*, London: St. Martin's Press.

4 Max Nordau (1849–1923), born in Budapest, the son of a Polish rabbi, was a physician, thinker and man of letters, and Herzl's right-hand man.

5 Originally published as *Old-New Land*, by Theodor Herzl. Translation by Lotta Levensohn, New York, Bloch Publishing Co. and Herzl Press, 1941.

6 G. Shimoni (2001) *The Zionist Ideology*, Jerusalem: Magnes (Hebrew), p. 55.

7 Shimoni 2001: 57.

8 Herzl, *The Jewish State* (Der Judenstaat), pp. 33, 49.

9 Avnery, U., *Tikun*, Vol. 16, No. 2, 2000, p. 19.

10 Unpublished letter, Zionist Archives, Jerusalem.

11 T. Herzl, *Igrot* (Letters), Vol. 3, Jerusalem: The Zionist Library and Publishing House, pp. 309–310 (Hebrew).

12 Herzl, *Old-New Land* (Altneuland), p. 253–254.

13 D. Ben-Gurion (1975) *Meetings with Arab Leaders*, Tel Aviv: Am Oved (Hebrew).

14 D. Ben-Gurion (1935) *Our Neighbours and Us*, Tel Aviv: Davar, pp. 32–39 (Hebrew).

15 See J. Nedava (ed.) (1985) *Jabotinsky's Reflections of an Era*, Tel Aviv: Jabotinsky Institute, p. 92 (Hebrew).

16 Ibid.

17 V. Jabotinsky (1941) *The War and the Jew*, Jerusalem: T. Kop, p. 86 (Hebrew).

18 Ibid.

19 Ben-Gurion 1957: 86.

20 Ben-Gurion 1975: 11.

21 Cited in S. Sofer (2001) *The Birth of Political Thought in Israel*, Jerusalem and Tel Aviv: Schocken, p. 134 (Hebrew).

22 The British Royal Commission under Lord Peel had proposed an initial partition plan which was rejected by the Arab leaders and opposed as insufficient by many in the Zionist movement – though accepted by Ben-Gurion.

4 The Jewish State and Israeli democracy

1 On this, see, for example, A.D. Smith (1998) *Nationalism and Modernism*, London: Routledge.
2 On the first day of the Suez War, 29 October 1956, 47 Israeli-Arab villagers from Kafr Qassem were gunned down as they returned from their fields. The village had been placed under curfew, of which the victims, returning from work, were unaware.
3 Y. Lahav (1980) *The Soviet Attitude Towards the Split in the Israel Communist Party 1964–67*, Jerusalem: The Hebrew University of Jerusalem, The Soviet and East European Research Centre, pp. 8–10, 15–16.
4 On this point, see D.H. Nahas (1976) *The Israeli Communist Party*, London: Portico Publications, pp. 39, 41, 72.
5 Lahav 1980: 29.
6 See A. Rubinstein (2006) 'Israeli Arabs and Jews: dispelling the myths, narrowing the gaps', online: www.ajc.org/site/apps/nl/content3.asp?c=ijITI2PHKoG&b=846725& ct=1043985.
7 In the spring of 2007, a scheme was launched by the government providing, for the first time, the opportunity to Arab citizens exempt from military service to volunteer for civilian 'national service' (mostly in their own communities). This is an important, though still limited, step in the right direction. Unfortunately, most Arab members of the Knesset have spoken out against it, opposing any kind of service for the State, even voluntary and non-military.
8 HC 6698/95, *Adel Kaadan and Imane Kaadan vs. the Israel Lands Authority*.
9 Ibid., Section 31.
10 HC 727/00, *The National Committee of Arab Mayors et al. vs. Minister of Construction and Housing*, judgment of 12 December 2001.
11 HC 1113/99, *Adallah et al. vs. Minister of Religious Affairs et al.*, P.D. 54 (2) 164 at 170, 172.
12 For the text of the Declaration of Independence, see R. Lapidoth and M. Hirsh (eds) (1992) *The Arab-Israel Conflict and its Resolution: Selected Documents*, Dordrecht: Martinus Nijhoff Publishers, pp. 61–63.
13 S. Smooha (2000) 'The regime of the State of Israel: civil democracy, non-democracy or ethnic democracy?', *Soziologia Israelit*, II (2), 593–594 (Hebrew).
12 For the text of the Convention and the Explanatory Report, see www.conventions.coe.int. See also, along similar lines, Venice Commision (European Commission for Democracy through Law), *Vademecum of Venice Commission Opinions and Reports Concerning the Protection of Minorities*, Strasbourg, 6 March 2007, online: www.venice.coe.int/docs/2007/CDL-MIN (2007)001-e.asp.
13 In July 2002, Israel's High Court of Justice handed down a major judgment which underpins the status of Arabic as a second official language (HC 4112/99). The court ruled in favour of petitions against the municipalities of Tel Aviv and some other cities, requiring that they provide information on municipal signposts in the Arabic language also. Justice Heshin, in a minority opinion, argued for rejecting the petitions. Inter alia, he held that such an arrangement was not obligatory as a result of Arabic's status as a second official language; moreover, this involves conferring collective rights on a minority and not defending individual rights, and hence in his opinion the arrangements relating to this matter should be left to the political system.
14 See H.J. Heintze (2000) 'Minority issues in Western Europe and the OSCE High Commissioner on National Minorities', *International Journal on Minority and Group Rights* 7, p. 384. The Convention itself does not define what a national minority is. The Explanatory Report stresses (Paragraph 12 in the General Considerations) that the:

> Framework Convention contains no definition of the notion of 'national minority.' This being the case, [I]t was decided to adopt a pragmatic approach, based on the

recognition that at this stage, it is impossible to arrive at a definition capable of mustering general support of all Council of Europe member States.

5 'Either Jewish or democratic'?

1 H. Bar'am, *Kol Ha'ir*, 25 April 2001.
2 B. Kimmerling (2001) *The End of the Rule of the Elite*, Jerusalem: Keter, pp. 100–101 (Hebrew).
3 Venice Commission (European Commission for Democracy through Law), *Report on the Preferential Treatment of National Minorities by their Kin-State*, adopted by the Venice Commission at its 48th Plenary Meeting, Venice, 19–20 October 2001, online: www.venice.coe.int/docs/2001/CDL-INF(2001) 019-e.html.
4 The Combined 13th and 14th Periodic Report of the Government of Finland on the International Convention on the Elimination of All Forms of Racial Discrimination (1997), online: www.formin.finland.fi/doc/fin/ihmisoik/ihmisoic.html.
5 The law lays down detailed criteria for the recognition of the immigrant as a Finn:

> A permit for residency may be granted 1. if the applicant himself, one of his parents or at least two of his four grandparents are or have been registered as having Finnish origin, or 2. if there is another tie that shows the applicant's affinity to Finland and Finnishness, but he has no documents to show that he meets the requirements mentioned in point 1.

6 See on this, and on similar cases, Anne de Tinguy (1999) 'Ethnic migrations from and to the new independent states following political changes in Eastern and Central Europe: 'repatriation' or privileged immigration?', 20–22 May 1999, p. 9, online: www.demographie.de/ethnic/papers/tinguy.pdf.
7 Similarly, Section 25 of the Bulgarian Law of Citizenship provides that a 'person of Bulgarian origin will receive citizenship through a facilitated procedure'.
8 See the Venice Commission, *Report on the Preferential Treatment of National Minorities by their Kin-State*, pp. 4–5, 9–10, 13–15. The most far-reaching example of an official connection with a national diaspora is Croatia, which allocates seats in its parliament to represent foreign Croats (particularly Bosnian Croats who are entitled to Croatian citizenship without the need to immigrate to Croatia). This arrangement has been widely criticized, but continues to be the law of Croatia, even after the passing of the highly nationalistic regime of President Franjo Tudjman and its replacement with a more liberal government.
9 Law 8, 27 May 1994 'On Relations with Basque Communities and Centres outside the Autonomous Community of the Basque Country'.
10 See P.J. Bolt (1996) 'Looking to the Diaspora: the overseas Chinese and China's economic development 1978–1994', *Diaspora* 5 (3), p. 467.
11 *Report of the High Level Committee on Indian Diaspora*, 8 January 2002, www.indiandiaspora.nic.in/contents.htm.
12 See J.T. Levy (2000) 'Three modes of incorporating indigenous law', in W. Kymlicka and W. Norman (eds), *Citizenship in Diverse Societies*, Oxford: Oxford University Press, pp. 312–316.
13 See, for example, Smooha 2000: 570 ('Israel declares about herself, and indeed is, the state of the Jewish people, and not the state of all of its citizens').
14 Civil Appeal 96/2316.
15 HC 6924/98, *Association for Civil Rights in Israel vs. Government of Israel*, p. 10.
16 MK Azmi Bishara in an interview with Ari Shavit, *Ha'aretz Weekend Supplement*, 29 May 1998.
17 See on this Y. Shain (1994) 'Ethnic diasporas and U.S. foreign policy', *Political Science Quarterly* 109, pp., 811–841; Y. Shain (1999) *Marketing the American*

Creed Abroad: Diasporas in the U.S. and Their Homelands, New York: Cambridge University Press.

18 See, for example, D. Miller (2001) 'Nationality in divided societies', in A.G. Gagnon and J. Tully (eds), *Multinational Democracies*, Cambridge: Cambridge University Press, pp. 302–303.

19 V. Roudometov (2000) 'Transnationalism and globalization: the Greek Orthodox diaspora between Orthodox universalism and transnational nationalism', *Diaspora* 9 (3), pp. 367–378.

6 A 'neutral state' and a democratic nation-state

1 R. Gavison (1999) *Israel as a Jewish and Democratic State: Tensions and Chances*, Jerusalem: Van Leer Institute and Hakibbutz Hameuchad (Hebrew), pp. 34–35.

2 Ibid., p. 35. On the different meanings of the principle of neutrality, see J. Rawls (1993) *Political Liberalism*, New York: Columbia University Press, p. 193 ff.

3 On 'banal nationalism' of long-established nations, see Michael Billig (1995) *Banal Nationalism*, London: Sage Publications.

4 W. Kymlicka (1995) *Multicultural Citizenship: a Liberal Theory of Minority Rights*, Oxford: Clarendon Press, p. 108.

5 D. Karmis and A.G. Gagnon (2001) 'Federalism, federation and collective identities in Canada and Belgium: different routes, similar fragmentation', in A.G. Gagnon and J. Tully (eds), *Multinational Democracies*, Cambridge: Cambridge University Press, p. 149.

6 M. Keating (1996) *Nations Against the State: the New Politics of Nationalism in Quebec, Catalonia and Scotland*, London: Macmillan, pp. 85–91.

7 On Breton nationalists who refuse to define themselves as French, see, for example, D.H. Fortier (1980) 'Brittany: "Brez Atao"', in C.R. Foster (ed.), *Nations without a State: Ethnic Minorities in Western Europe*, New York: Praeger Publishers, p. 151. These are clearly marginal phenomena in contemporary France. But the question of Muslim immigrants' integration is far from marginal.

8 On this issue, see, for example, A.D. Smith (1986) *The Ethnic Origins of Nations*, Oxford: Blackwell, pp. 138–139.

9 For the text of the report and the President's statement, see www.fil-info-france.com/-actualites-monde/rapport-stasi-commission-laicite.htm.

10 On this, see blogs.britannica.com/blog/main/2007/01/italys-crucifix-controversy-schools-the-state-and-the-sacred.

11 W. Kymlicka (2000) 'Modernity and national identity', in S. Ben-Ami, Y. Peled and A. Spektorowski (eds), *Ethnic Challenges to the Modern Nation State*, London: Macmillan, p. 17.

12 A. Ghanem (1998) 'State and minority in Israel: the case of ethnic state and the predicament of its minority', *Ethnic and Racial Studies* 21 (3), p. 444.

13 See The National Committee for the Heads of the Arab Local Authorities in Israel, *The Future Vision of the Palestinian Arabs in Israel*, online: www.adalah. org/newsletter/eng/dec06/tasawor-mostaqbali.pdf; www.adalah.org/eng/democratic_constitution-e.pdf.

14 Another provision which stresses the connection between the state and Bulgarian national identity is Article 36 relating to the Bulgarian language, formulated in an unusually emphatic way – precisely because, one may assume, Bulgaria contains a large Turkish-speaking minority:

> The study and use of the Bulgarian language is a right and obligation of every Bulgarian citizen. Citizens whose mother tongue is not Bulgarian shall have the right to study and use their own language alongside the compulsory study of the Bulgarian language.

15 L.M. Danforth (1995) *The Macedonian Conflict: Ethnic Nationalism in a Transnational World*, Princeton: Princeton University Press, p. 149.

16 Jordan's attitude to its long-established Palestinian population is an exception in the Arab world. This attitude, which included conferring citizenship and integration in the country's various walks of life, differs greatly and positively from that of the other Arab countries. However, Jordan also does not consider itself a potential national home for the population of the refugee camps living in difficult conditions in Lebanon, where the Lebanese government denies them the most basic rights. There is no doubt that the refusal of Arab countries to integrate Palestinian refugees and their descendants (born in those countries) can be explained by the desire to use their distress as a political weapon against Israel. In the case of Lebanon, however, there is another factor: the risk of undermining the fragile intercommunal equilibrium.

17 O. Yiftachel, 'On "Zionist enlightenment" and its enemies' (Hebrew), *Ma'ariv*, Books and Literature Supplement, 7 September 2001.

18 For an overview of India's ethnic composition and its problems in the area of nationalism, see R.L. Hardgrave (1994) 'India: the dilemmas of diversity', in L. Diamond and M.F. Platter (eds), *Nationalism, Ethnic Conflict and Democracy*, Baltimore and London: The Johns Hopkins University Press, pp. 71–85.

19 Article 343: '1. The official language of the Union shall be Hindi in Devanagari script.'

20 See O. Shani, 'The Resurgence of "Ethno-Hinduism" – a theoretical perspective', in S. Ben-Ami, Y. Peled and A. Spektorowski (eds), *Ethnic Challenges to the Modern Nation State*, London: Macmillan, pp. 267–293.

21 M. Odenheimer (2001) 'The tiger, the horse and the Indian problem', *Ha'aretz*, 16 November (Hebrew).

22 This is of course a schematic description which cannot do justice to all the nuances of the two rival identities. It should be noted that the two communities often prefer to define their identity in national and political terms rather than religious ones.

23 Although geographically speaking the island of Ireland, next to the British island itself, belongs to what is known collectively as 'the British Isles', the authors of the Good Friday Agreement used the term 'these islands', apparently in order to avoid offending the sensibilities of the Irish party to the agreement, for whom the British label traditionally represents foreign rule.

24 On this point see M. Canovan (1996) *Nationhood and Political Theory*, Cheltenham and Northampton, MA: Edward Elgar, pp. 75–80 ('English/British Nationhood').

25 See, for example, J. Estruch (1991) 'The social construction of national identities: the case of Catalonia as a nation in the Spanish state', in U. Ra'anan, M. Mesner, K. Armes and K. Martin (eds), *State and Nation in Multi-Ethnic Societies*, Manchester and New York: Manchester University Press, pp. 134–139. Estruch, Professor of Sociology at the University of Barcelona, defines himself as 'Catalan, not Spanish', rather than both Catalan and Spanish.

26 With the exception of certain radical left-wing circles who define their national identity as Castilian. In doing so they are giving expression to a view which maintains that Castilian identity is merely one of the national identities to be found in Spain. According to this approach, the label 'Spanish' should be a neutral civil definition shared equally by all the national groups in the state, and the state should become a multi-national federation.

27 A. Balcells (1996) *Catalan Nationalism: Past and Present*, London: Macmillan, tr. Jacqueline Hall, p. 193.

28 Keating 1996: 126.

29 Keating 1996: 128–129.

30 G. Johnson (1973) *Our English Heritage*, Westport, CT: Greenwood, p. 119; Kymlicka 1995: 15. Johnson is quoting President Lincoln's Gettysburg address.

31 Kymlicka 1995: 38–40. In this respect see also J.T. Levy (2000) 'Three modes of

incorporating indigenous law', in W. Kymlicka and W. Norman (eds), *Citizenship in Diverse Societies*, Oxford: Oxford University Press, pp. 305–311.

32 The military service performed by the Druze and other minority groups undoubtedly strengthens their Israeli civic identity and brings about a special feeling of closeness to the Jewish majority society; however, unlike the case of non-Jewish immigrant soldiers, this does not involve them adopting its language and cultural identity.

33 It must however be noted that in a fair number of cases, immigrants who are not defined as Jewish according to Halacha have a Jewish father (and a non-Jewish mother) and many of them identified themselves as Jews in their countries of origin.

34 See Kymlicka 1995; for a similar approach, see Y. Tamir (1993) *Liberal Nationalism*, Princeton: Princeton University Press. For a classic statement of strong opposition to nationalism, see E. Kedourie (1993) *Nationalism* (4th edn), Oxford: Blackwell; see also M. Seymour, J. Coutre and K. Nielsen (eds) (1996) *Rethinking Nationalism*, Calgary, Alberta: University of Calgary Press.

35 On Greek identity and the situation of national minorities in Greece, see A. Pollis (1992) 'Greek national identity: religious minorities, rights, and European norms', *Journal of Modern Greek Studies* 10, pp. 171–195; S. Stavros (1995) 'The legal status of minorities in Greece today: the adequacy of their protection in the light of current human rights perceptions', *Journal of Modern Greek Studies* 13, pp. 7–17; Danforth 1995: 108–141.

36 The examples are from Danforth 1995: 113–133.

37 See, for example, F. Weber (1976) *Peasants into Frenchmen: the Modernization of Rural France, 1870–1914*, Stanford, CA: Stanford University Press.

38 The Jewish religious establishment's opposition to civil marriage may actually encourage people to leave the majority society and join the minority. Thus there is today a phenomenon of Jewish women who marry Muslim men, convert to Islam, move to Arab localities with their husbands, and in practice assimilate in Muslim-Arab society.

Epilogue: nowhere else

1 A. Herzberg (1992) 'The American context of Galut', in G. Shimoni (ed.), *Zionist Thought Today*, Jerusalem: WZO, p. 45.

2 W.M. Blumenthal (1998) *The Invisible Wall*, Washington, DC: Counterpoint.

3 A. Herzberg (1970) *The Zionist Idea*, Jerusalem: Keter, p. 133 (Hebrew); see also G. Shimoni (2001) *The Zionist Ideology*, Hanover, NH and London: Brandeis University Press, p. 30.

4 M. Hess (1958) *Rome and Jerusalem*, translated by M.J. Bloom, New York: Philosophical Society.

5 Quoted by A. Elon (1971) *The Israelis: Founders and Sons*, Jerusalem and Tel Aviv: Schocken, p. 79 (Hebrew).

6 N. Sharansky (1998) *Fear No Evil*, New York: Vintage Books.

7 *Ha'aretz*, 5 May 2002.

Appendix 1: extracts from some contemporary democratic constitutions

1 On the case law of the European Commission and the European Court for Human Rights (in which the Commission was subsumed following its reorganization in the 1990s), see S. Stavros (1999) 'Human rights in Greece: twelve years of supervision from Strasbourg', *Journal of Modern Greek Studies*, 17 (1), pp. 7–9; N.C. Alivizatos (1999) 'A new role for the Greek Church?', *Journal of Modern Greek Studies*, 17 (1), pp. 26, 35, n. 14.

2 For a description of the 1990s struggles in Poland over matters relating to the status of

the Catholic Church, see Sabrina T. Ramet (1997) *Whose Democracy? Nationalism, Religion and the Doctrine of Collective Rights in Post-1989 Eastern Europe*, Oxford: Rowan and Littlefield, pp. 97–110. Inter alia, the issues included abortions, a law requiring public broadcasting 'to respect Christian values', the tax exemption given to Church property, and the struggle over the extent of the Church's control of religious instruction at state schools (including the appointment of priests as religious education teachers whose wages would be paid by the State).

Appendix 2: Armenia and the Armenian diaspora – Nansen's address to the League of Nations

1 Nansen's address is taken from E.E. Reynolds (1949) *Nansen*, Aylesbury and London: Penguin Books, pp. 265-266.

Bibliography

Documents

Council of Europe, Parliamentary Assembly (2006) *Recommendation 1735 (2006), 'The Concept of a nation'*, online: www.assembly.coe.int/main.asp?Link=/documents/adoptedtext/ta06/erec1735.htm.

International Convention on the Elimination of All Forms of Racial Discrimination, 4 January 1965, online: www.unhchr.ch/html/menu3/b/d_icerd.htm

Knesset Minutes, Jerusalem: Knesset.

La commission de réflexion sur l'application du principe de laïcité, Rapport au Président de la République, 11 December 2003, online: www.fil-info-france.com/actualites-monde/rapport-stasi-commission-laicite.htm.

Report of the High Level Committee on Indian Diaspora, 8 January 2002, online: www.indiandiaspora.nic.in/contents.htm.

The Combined 13th and 14th Periodic Report of the Government of Finland on the International Convention on the Elimination of All Forms of Racial Discrimination (1997), online: www.formin.finland.fi/doc/fin/ihmisoik/ihmisoic.html.

United Nations Ad Hoc Committee on the Palestinian Question (1947) *Official Records of the Second Session of the General Assembly*, Lake Success, NY.

United Nations General Assembly (1947) *Plenary Meetings*, Lake Success, NY.

United Nations Security Council (1948) *Official Records, The Third Year, Meetings 261–285*, Lake Success, NY.

United Nations Special Committee on Palestine (1947) 'Report to the General Assembly', *Official Records of the Second Session of the General Assembly*, Volume 1, Supplement n. 11, New York, pp. 28–47.

United Nations Special Committee on Palestine (1947) 'Report to the General Assembly', *Official Records of the Second Session of the General Assembly*, Volume 3, Annex A: Oral evidence presented at public meetings, New York.

Venice Commission (European Commission for Democracy through Law) (2001) *Report on the Preferential Treatment of National Minorities by their Kin-State*, adopted by the Venice Commission at its 48th Plenary Meeting, Venice, 19–20 October 2001, online: www.venice.coe.int/docs/2001/CDL-INF(2001)019-e.html.

Venice Commission (European Commission for Democracy through Law) (2007) *Vademecum of Venice Commission Opinions and Reports Concerning the Protection of Minorities*, Strasbourg, 6 March 2007, online: www.venice.coe.int/docs/2007/CDL-MIN (2007)001-e.asp.

For European conventions on minority rights, with explanatory documents, see www.conventions.coe.int.

For decisions of the Constitutional Council of the French Republic, see www.conseil-constitutional.fr.

For texts of Constitutions quoted here, see www.servat.unibe.ch/law/icl/.

For the law on Citizenship of the Hellenic Republic see, http://www.legislationline.org/legislation.php?tid=11&lid=1794

Books and articles

Alivizatos, N.C. (1999) 'A new role for the Greek Church?', *Journal of Modern Greek Studies* 17 (1): 23–40.

Anderson, B. (1983) *Imagined Communities: Reflections on the Origins and Spread of Nationalism*, London: Verso.

Avnery, U. (2000) *Tikun* 16 (2): 19.

Balcells, A. (1996) *Catalan Nationalism: Past and Present*, London: Macmillan, tr. Jacqueline Hall.

Bar'am, H. (2001) *Kol Ha'ir*, 25 April.

Ben-Gurion, D. (1935) *Our Neighbours and Us*, Tel Aviv: Davar.

Ben-Gurion, D. (1957) *Ba-ma'arkaha*, Vol. IV, Tel Aviv: Am Oved (Hebrew).

Ben-Gurion, D. (1975) *Meetings with Arab Leaders*, Tel Aviv: Am Oved (Hebrew).

Billig, M. (1995) *Banal Nationalism*, London: Sage Publications.

Blumenthal, W.M. (1998) *The Invisible Wall*, Washington, DC: Counterpoint.

Bolt, P.J. (1996) 'Looking to the Diaspora: the overseas Chinese and China's economic development 1978–1994', *Diaspora* 5 (3): 467–496.

Brown, D. (2000) *Contemporary Nationalism: Civic, Ethnocultural and Multicultural Politics*, London and New York: Routledge.

Canovan, M. (1996) *Nationhood and Political Theory*, Cheltenham and Northampton, MA: Edward Elgar.

Crossman, R. (1946) *Palestine Mission: a Personal Record*, London: Hamish Hamilton.

Danforth, L.M. (1995) *The Macedonian Conflict: Ethnic Nationalism in a Transnational World*, Princeton: Princeton University Press.

Elon, A. (1971) *The Israelis: Founders and Sons*, Jerusalem and Tel Aviv: Schocken.

Estruch, J. (1991) 'The social construction of national identities: the case of Catalonia as a nation in the Spanish state', in U. Ra'anan, M. Mesner, K. Armes and K. Martin (eds), *State and Nation in Multi-Ethnic Societies*, Manchester and New York: Manchester University Press.

Fortier, D.H. (1980) 'Brittany: "Brez Atao"', in C.R. Foster (ed.), *Nations without a State: Ethnic Minorities in Western Europe*, New York: Praeger Publishers, pp. 136–152.

Garcia-Granados, J. (1948) *The Birth of Israel: the Drama as I Saw It*, New York: Alfred A. Knopf.

Gavison, R. (1999) *Israel as a Jewish and Democratic State: Tensions and Chances*, Jerusalem: Van Leer Institute and Hakibbutz Hameuchad (Hebrew).

Gellner, E. (1983) *Nations and Nationalism*, Oxford: Blackwell.

Ghanem, A. (1998) 'State and minority in Israel: the case of ethnic state and the predicament of its minority', *Ethnic and Racial Studies* 21 (3): 428–448.

Hardgrave, R.L. (1994) 'India: the dilemmas of diversity', in L. Diamond and M.F. Platter (eds), *Nationalism, Ethnic Conflict and Democracy*, Baltimore and London: The Johns Hopkins University Press, pp. 54–68.

Heikal, M.H. (1978) *The Sphinx and the Commissar: the Rise and Fall of Soviet Influence in the Arab World*, London: Collins.

Heikal, M.H. (1996) *Secret Channels. The Inside Story of the Arab-Israeli Peace Negotiations*, London: HarperCollins Publishers.

Heintze, H.J. (2000) 'Minority issues in Western Europe and the OSCE High Commissioner on National Minorities', *International Journal on Minority and Group Rights* 7: 381–392.

Heraclides, A. (1997) 'Ethnicity, secessionist conflict and the international society: towards normative paradigm shift', *Nations and Nationalism* 3 (4): 493–520.

Herzberg, A. (1970) *The Zionist Idea*, Jerusalem: Keter.

Herzberg, A. (1992) 'The American context of Galut', in G. Shimoni (ed.), *Zionist Thought Today*, Jerusalem: WZO, pp. 44–47.

Herzl, T. *Old-New Land* (Altneuland) (1960) translated by Lotta Levensohn, New York: Bloch Publishing Co. and Herzl Press.

Herzl, T. *The Jewish State* (Der Judenstaat) (1970) translated by Harry Zohn, New York: Herzl Press.

Hobsbawm, E. (1990) *Nations and Nationalism since 1780*, Cambridge: Cambridge University Press.

Hobsbawm, E. and T. Ranger (eds) (1983) *The Invention of Tradition*, Cambridge: Cambridge University Press.

Jabotinsky, V. (1941) *The War and the Jew*, Jerusalem: T. Kop (Hebrew).

Johnson, G. (1973) *Our English Heritage*, Westport, CT: Greenwood.

Judt, T. (2003) 'Israel: the alternative', *The New York Review of Books* 50 (16), 23 October: 8–10.

Karmis, D. and A.G. Gagnon (2001) 'Federalism, federation and collective identities in Canada and Belgium: different routes, similar fragmentation', in A.G. Gagnon and J. Tully (eds), *Multinational Democracies*, Cambridge: Cambridge University Press, pp. 137–175.

Karsh, E. (1999) *Fabricating Israeli History; the 'New Historians'*, Tel Aviv: Hakibbutz Hameuhad.

Keating, M. (1996) *Nations Against the State: the New Politics of Nationalism in Quebec, Catalonia and Scotland*, London: Macmillan.

Kedourie, E. (1993) *Nationalism* (4th edition), Oxford: Blackwell.

Khalidi, R. (1997) *Palestinian Identity: the Construction of Modern National Consciousness*, New York: Columbia University Press.

Kimmerling, B. (2001) *The End of the Rule of the Elite*, Jerusalem: Keter.

Koestler, A. (1952) *Arrow in the Blue: an Autobiography*, New York: Macmillan.

Koestler, A. (1954) *The Invisible Writing*, New York: Macmillan.

Kymlicka, W. (1989) *Liberalism, Community and Culture*, Oxford: Clarendon Press.

Kymlicka, W. (1995) *Multicultural Citizenship: a Liberal Theory of Minority Rights*, Oxford: Clarendon Press.

Kymlicka, W. (2000) 'Modernity and national identity', in S. Ben-Ami, Y. Peled and A. Spektorowski (eds), *Ethnic Challenges to the Modern Nation State*, London: Macmillan, pp. 11–41.

Lahav, Y. (1980) *The Soviet Attitude Towards the Split in the Israel Communist Party 1964–67*, Jerusalem: The Hebrew University of Jerusalem, The Soviet and East European Research Centre.

Levy, J.T. (2000) 'Three modes of incorporating indigenous law', in W. Kymlicka and W. Norman (eds), *Citizenship in Diverse Societies*, Oxford: Oxford University Press, pp. 297–325.

Masalha, N. (2000) *Imperial Israel and the Palestinians: the Politics of Expansion*, London: Pluto Press.

Memmi, A. (1975) *Jews and Arabs*, Chicago: J. Philip O'Hara, Inc., tr. Eleanor Levieux.

Miller, D. (2001) 'Nationality in divided societies', in A.G. Gagnon and J. Tully (eds), *Multinational Democracies*, Cambridge: Cambridge University Press, pp. 299–318.

Moore, M. (ed.) (1998) *National Self-Determination and Secession*, Oxford: Oxford University Press.

Nahas, D.H. (1976) *The Israeli Communist Party*, London: Portico Publications.

Naor, M. and D. Giladi (1991) *Eretz Israel in the Twentieth Century: from Settlement to State, 1900–1950*, Tel Aviv: Ministry of Defence Publishing (Hebrew).

Nedava, J. (ed.) (1985) *Jabotinsky's Reflections of an Era*, Tel Aviv: Jabotinsky Institute (Hebrew).

Odenheimer, M. (2001) 'The tiger, the horse and the Indian problem', *Ha'aretz*, 16 November (Hebrew).

Pappe, I. (1997) 'Zionism in the test of the theories of nationalism and the historiographic method' (Hebrew), in P. Ginossar and A. Bareli (eds), *Zionism: a Contemporary Controversy*, Sde Boker: The Ben-Gurion Research Center and the Institute for Research in the History of Zionism, Ben-Gurion University, pp. 223–263.

Pedatzur, P. (1996) *The Triumph of Confusion: Israel and the Territories, 1967–1969*, Tel Aviv: Bitan (Hebrew).

Philpott, D. (1995) 'In defence of self-determination', *Ethics* 105 (2): 352–385.

Pollis, A. (1992) 'Greek national identity: religious minorities, rights, and European norms', *Journal of Modern Greek Studies* 10: 171–196.

Ramet, S.T. (1997) *Whose Democracy? Nationalism, Religion and the Doctrine of Collective Rights in Post-1989 Eastern Europe*, Oxford: Rowan and Littlefield.

Rawls, J. (1993) *Political Liberalism*, New York: Columbia University Press.

Rex, J. (1996) *Ethnic Minorities in the Modern Nation State*, New York: St. Martin's Press.

Roudometov, V. (2000) 'Transnationalism and globalization: the Greek Orthodox diaspora between Orthodox universalism and transnational nationalism', *Diaspora* 9, (3): 367–378.

Rubinstein, A. (2000) *Herzl to Rabin: the Changing Image of Zionism*, New York: Holmes & Meier.

Rubinstein, A. (2006) 'Israeli Arabs and Jews: dispelling the myths, narrowing the gaps', online: www.ajc.org/site/apps/nl/content3.asp?c=ijITI2PHKoG&b=846725&ct=1043985.

Schueftan, D. (1986) *A Jordanian Option – Israel, Jordan and the Palestinians*, Tel Aviv: Hakibbutz Hameuhad (Hebrew).

Seymour, M., J. Coutre and K. Nielsen (eds) (1996) *Rethinking Nationalism*, Calgary, Alberta: University of Calgary Press.

Shafir, G. (1989) *Land, Labour and the Origins of the Israeli–Palestinian Conflict, 1882–1914*, Cambridge: Cambridge University Press.

Shain, Y. (1994) 'Ethnic diasporas and U.S. foreign policy', *Political Science Quarterly* 109: 811–842.

Shain, Y. (1999) *Marketing the American Creed Abroad: Diasporas in the U.S. and Their Homelands*, New York: Cambridge University Press.

Shani, O. (2000) 'The resurgence of "Ethno-Hinduism" – a theoretical perspective', in S. Ben-Ami, Y. Peled and A. Spektorowski (eds), *Ethnic Challenges to the Modern Nation State*, London: Macmillan, pp. 267–293.

Sharansky, N. (1998) *Fear No Evil*, New York: Vintage Books.

Sheffer, G. (ed.) (1986) *Modern Diasporas in International Politics*, London: St. Martin's Press.

Shimoni, G. (2001) *The Zionist Ideology*, Hanover, NH and London: Brandeis University Press.

Shlaim, A. (1988) *Collusion across the Jordan: King Abdullah, the Zionist Movement and the Partition of Palestine*, Oxford: Clarendon Press.

Smith, A.D. (1986) *The Ethnic Origins of Nations*, Oxford: Blackwell.

Smith, A.D. (1998) *Nationalism and Modernism*, London: Routledge.

Smith, A.D. (1999) *Myths and Memories of the Nation*, Oxford: Oxford University Press.

Smooha, S. (2000) 'The regime of the State of Israel: civil democracy, non-democracy or ethnic democracy?', *Soziologia Israelit*, II (2): 565–630 (Hebrew).

Sofer, S. (2001) *The Birth of Political Thought in Israel*, Jerusalem and Tel Aviv: Schocken (Hebrew).

Stapleton, J. (ed.) (1995) *Group Rights. Perspectives since 1990*, Bristol: Thoemmes Press.

Stavros, S. (1995) 'The legal status of minorities in Greece today: the adequacy of their protection in the light of current human rights perceptions', *Journal of Modern Greek Studies* 13: 1–32

Stavros, S. (1999) 'Human rights in Greece: twelve years of supervision from Strasbourg', *Journal of Modern Greek Studies*, 17 (1), pp. 7–9.

Sureda, A.R. (1973) *The Evolution of the Right of Self-Determination: a Study of United Nations Practice*, Leiden: A.W. Sijthoff.

Tamir, Y. (1993) *Liberal Nationalism*, Princeton: Princeton University Press.

de Tinguy, A. (1999) 'Ethnic migrations from and to the new independent states following political changes in Eastern and Central Europe: 'repatriation' or privileged immigration?', online: www.demographie.de/ethnic/papers/tinguy.pdf.

Twining, W. (ed.) (1991) *Issues of Self-Determination*, Aberdeen: Aberdeen University Press.

Weber, F. (1976) *Peasants into Frenchmen: the Modernization of Rural France, 1870–1914*, Stanford: Stanford University Press.

Yiftachel, O. (1999) 'Ethnocracy: the politics of judaizing Israel/Palestine', *Constellations* 6, 3: 364–390.

Yiftachel, O. (2001) 'On "Zionist enlightenment" and its enemies', *Ma'ariv* Books and Literature Supplement, 7 September (Hebrew).

Index

Abdullah, King of Jordan 224n46; assassination of 62
Ad Hoc Committee of the UN General Assembly, partition debates in 1947 28, 30–3, 50, 52, 58
Administration of Rule and Justice Ordnance, Israel 119
affirmative action in Israel 114–15
African-American minority 173–4
African National Congress 178–9
Albanian minority in Macedonia 152, 189; extremists 153
Al-Husseini, Haj Amin 21, 33
Al-Khalidi, Yussef Diya'uddin 90
Altneuland 89–91
America, United States of 171–2, 174; Anglo-American committee 35; Declaration of Independence 173, 190; Japanese-origin citizens during the Second World War 105; *see also* United States
annexation (of the West Bank by Transjordan) 60–2
anti-colonialist national struggles 65
anti-Semitism 35–6, 50, 52, 72, 75, 85, 108, 111, 182, 187, 192–6, 198; Arab 223n40; in Germany 34
Arab citizens of Israel 8, 84, 108–11, 186; community 117, 167, 186–7
Arab countries 30, 53, 62, 182
Arab delegates to the UN, 1947–48 28, 31, 38, 44, 51, 57
Arab Higher Committee of Palestine 28, 30, 31, 33, 38, 43, 49, 68, 73, 77
Arab–Jewish relations 30, 51–2
Arab League 59, 62
Arab-majority Communist party of Israel Rakah 110–11
Arab majority in the Middle East 20, 45, 48, 55

Arab military forces in Israel's War of Independence 58, 95
Arab minority in Israel 5, 15, 18–21, 29, 91–3, 104, 107–8, 111, 114, 166, 181, 183, 188; civil rights 104, 119; in Israel 47–8, 51, 83–4, 163; status 94, 106, 117; under-representation 112, 120
Arab-Muslim countries 47, 56, 150
Arab-Muslim Middle East 45, 89, 155; Jewish minorities 23, 48–9, 51–3
Arab national homogeneity 45, 52
Arab national identity 9, 27, 45, 100, 166
Arab nationalism 1, 16, 37–9, 46, 49, 67, 71, 89, 100, 137; extremists 111, 196
Arab-Palestinian state 14, 149, 156; leadership 59
Arab population 16, 18, 27, 38, 63, 73, 94, 103, 106–7, 110–13, 115, 119–20, 174, 181; Arab homeland 29, 46; civic equality 105; public opinion 46, 55; status in Israel 7, 117
Arab representation in Israel 43, 76, 114, 117, 119; politicians 112; protest vote 108, 150; votes 108, 112
Arab state 15–16, 20, 23–4, 27–8, 30–1, 37, 41, 47, 50, 61, 67, 70, 159; Arab-Muslim state 10, 71; League of Arab States 45; unitary 155
Arab world 44, 51; struggle against colonialism 223n40
Arabic language 5, 93; second official language in Israel 8, 143, 150, 227n13
Arabs of Palestine 2, 10, 29–30, 37, 39, 51, 73, 83, 90, 179, 182; rising 70
Arafat, Yasser 64, 113
Argentinian constitution 215
Armenia 80–1, 86; Constitution 131; diaspora 87, 139, 197, 218; history 79, 218; national home 219

armistice (between Israel and Arab countries) 225n48; lines 110, 149
assimilation, Jewish 189, 192–4, 196; failure of 195
Australian immigration policy 126
Austro-Hungarian Empire 85, 192
Auto-Emancipation 194
Avnery, Uri 89
Ayalon, Ami 14

Balfour Declaration 11–13, 15–16, 18, 38, 42, 52, 68, 72, 88, 94, 199
Bangladesh 32
Barak, Ehud 112–13
Bar'am, Chaim 124
Basle Programme 1, 87, 88
Basque Country 32, 171, 180–1; Constitution 215–16; diaspora 170; nationalists 167–9; parliament legislation 132; people or Euskal-Herria 215
Begin, Menachem 104
Belgium 87; constitutional arrangements 146; delegate 36
Ben-Gurion, David 13, 59, 61–3, 83–4, 92, 94–5, 100, 225n47
Ben-Gurion University 66, 157
Ben-Zvi, Yitzhak 195
bi-national 93, 145, 164; state 10, 19–20, 22, 27–30, 47, 59, 142, 146, 149–50, 152–5, 178
Bishara, Azmi 137–8
Blumenthal, W. Michael 193
Boer Republics 72–3
border 13–14, 18, 33, 37, 42, 78, 133, 149, 180; administrative 122; changes 130; controls 106–7; Greece's with Turkey 107; Israeli 110–11; opening of 85, 87; recognized 154; shifting 29, 51, 128
British 165, 180; Ambassador to Amman 61; Anglican Church 144; citizens 166; Mandate 39, 59, 182; national flag 166; Peel Commission 16, 59, 94
British Empire 65, 67, 74; agent 62; colonialism 70, 72, 109; interests in the Middle East 69
British India 32, 156
British military 69; government 38
British state 72, 163, 166, 165; foreign policy 70; Government 59, 69; history 164; promises to Jewish people 37; promises to the Arabs 16, 38, 67
Bulgaria 152; Constitution 208–9; national identity 229n14

Bunche, Ralph 61
Bund 21, 85

Camp David talks 64
Canada 145, 210, 221n12; Anglo-Canadians 146; Quebec 32, 146
Capitalist states of West Europe and anti-Semitism 35; modernization 77
Castilian Spanish 168, 230n26
Catalonia 32, 169–70, 180–1; nationalists 167–8
Catholic 209; Church 232n2; minority in Ulster 163; official status 200, 207
Central and Eastern Europe 164; new democracies 223n37
Children of Israel 52, 76
Chinese 86; diasporas 132
chosen people 80, 197
Christianity 192, 209; attitudes hostile to Jews 193; Israel's Arab community 114; minority 100
citizenship 3, 95, 136–7, 147, 176; eligibility 128; of non-Jews 126
civic community 8, 151
civil marriage 102, 188
civil rights 43, 101, 103, 134, 149, 173, 200; for immigrants 129; lacking 63; for non-white population in South Africa 178; organizations 113, 115
civil service in Israel 119; appointments 114
coalition (governments in Israel) 98, 100, 101, 112–13; international (in favour of partitioning Palestine in 1947) 56; politics 101
Cold War 109
collective rights 121; of minorities 143
colonial rule 54; liberation from 33
colonialism 37, 40, 65–7, 70–2, 74–5, 177
communists 53, 69, 109, 195; fall of 208, 210; party 60, 110, 112
compromise 59; political 58, 153
conflict 6, 17–18, 29, 40, 45, 49, 72, 83, 88, 105–6, 125, 157–8, 186, 196; Arab-Israeli 53–4, 57, 69, 95, 102, 109, 190, 197; Arab-Zionist 93, 196; armed 111; Jewish–Arab 47, 51, 55, 58, 65; over Palestine 53; national and religious 145, 162
constitution 3–6, 49, 81–2, 86, 126, 153, 180, 223n37; Arab states 45–6; democratic 202; of the Italian Republic 190
Conversion to Judaism 175, 187, 193
Costa Rican Constitution 215

Council of Europe 123, 152; member
    states 137
Croatian diaspora connection 228n8
Cuban delegate to the UN, 1947 partition
    debate 37
cultural identity 142, 148, 173–4, 176, 179
cultural ties 80, 171–2, 190
'Cyprus marriage' in Israel 102, 188
Czech Republic 32
Czechoslovakia 32, 69; Constitution 146;
    Delegate to the UN, 1947 25

Dahle, Mohammed 47–8
declaration of independence 81, 142
democracies 7–8, 10, 20, 89, 98, 105,
    134–5, 168, 172, 175; civic 136, 216;
    consociational 150; contemporary 6,
    198; modern 111, 137, 142, 144, 149,
    188, 200, 208
democratic principles 29, 56, 64, 94, 101,
    124–5, 158, 188, 198
democratization 192
demographic balance 20, 121–2, 158
Denmark 205–6
Der Judenstaat 84
descendants of emigrants 130, 131, 147
diaspora 6, 80, 85, 128, 139, 156;
    communities 129, 140, 175; intellectuals
    81; Jewish communities 67, 87, 116; of
    the majority 154; national 3, 49, 200;
    nationalism 86, 218
discrimination 3–4, 66, 89, 95, 104, 107,
    113–18, 141, 195, 198; budgetary 117;
    forbidden 126, 134; racial 25, 50, 126,
    129
disloyalty to the State 185
displaced persons 19, 34, 35, 50, 177;
    camps 17, 30, 35, 56, 222n22; German
    127; Jewish 15, 26, 31, 34
disputed territory 110, 157
Dreyfus Affair 193
Druze community in Israel 112–13, 184,
    188, 231n32
Dutch delegate to the UN, 1947 32, 36

Eastern Europe 35, 85–6, 127, 128, 152,
    208; Jews 72–3, 85; new democracies
    135
Egypt 59–60, 62–3, 69, 149; Communist
    party 54; delegate to the UN, 1947 50,
    52; Jewish community 53; president 108
emancipation 192–4
England 164–6; Catholic minority 144;
    English language 171

equality 1–2, 11, 14, 20, 28, 74, 89, 115,
    117, 120, 124–5, 145, 200; of all
    citizens 13, 93, 134; civic 49, 56, 117,
    141, 166, 188; civil 3–4, 103; legal 113,
    194; on paper 10; of rights 13, 20, 29,
    45–7, 89, 92, 94–5, 103, 114, 118, 156,
    174, 176, 188; of status 119, 146; value
    of 155; violated 125, 157
Eretz Israel 61, 78, 195
Eshkol, Levy 107
ethnic groups 52, 126, 171, 173, 190;
    communities 139, 178; Germans 128;
    Hungarians 126; minorities 45, 210
ethno-national fracture 33
European Commission for Democracy
    through Law *see* Venice Commission
European Convention for the Protection of
    National Minorities 120, 123;
    Explanatory Report to the Convention
    121–2
European democracies 5, 99, 136–7, 152,
    164, 214; constitutions 131; languages
    75; migrating populations 128; minority
    languages 7, 216; nation-states 198
exile 130, 132
exploitation 66, 72, 137, 194
expropriation of land 95, 107–8, 122
expulsion 122, 154, 192; of Arabs 95

family allowances 114
Farhud 196
fascists 9, 22–3, 53, 108
Fatah 63, 64, 110
Federal Republic of Germany 109, 128;
    Constitution 200
Feisal, Emir 16
Finland 129; immigration laws 5;
    Orthodox Church 205; repatriation 130
First Nations groups 145
first official language 163, 201
First World War 16, 37–40, 67, 74, 80, 88,
    218
foreign workers in Israel 175–6
former Soviet Union 5, 130, 132, 158, 175,
    186, 187
French Republic 7, 85–6, 98–9, 147, 186;
    constitution 216–17; delegate to the UN,
    1947 36; national identity 76, 216;
    nationalism 139; war in Algeria 105

Garcia-Granados, Jorge 19–20, 34
Gavison, Ruth 141–2
Gaza Strip 59, 62–3, 102, 104, 106, 109,
    149–50, 156, 158

General Assembly of the United Nations 13, 21, 23, 30, 32, 43, 50, 56; debate 25, 28, 44; resolution 94

genocide 87, 139; Armenian 81, 218

Germany 68, 105, 193; constitution 127, 210

Ghanem, Professor As'ad 150

globalization 5, 101, 133

Good Friday Agreement 163

Great Arab Revolt 92, 94

Great Powers 70–1

Greece 80, 107, 189; citizenship 129, 202; Constitution 99, 139, 203–5; diaspora 99, 129, 184; Greek-Americans 139; independence 81; minority peoples 129, 184; national identity 185; national movement 86, 99; Orthodox Church 100, 189

Green Line 110–11

Gromyko, Andrei 21, 22, 23, 35, 36

Guatemalan delegate to the UN, 1947 19, 27, 33, 42

Haifa University 150

Halacha (the laws of Orthodox Judaism) 85, 97, 100, 175

Hashemite Kingdom of Jordan 59, 62

Hebrew language 86, 88, 116, 138, 169, 175, 197; Ashkenazi and Sephardi 74

Hebrew-speaking majority in Israel 183, 187–8

Hebrew University of Jerusalem 125, 141

Heikal, Muhammad Hassanein 55, 69

Herzl, Theodor 41, 68, 84–5, 87–91, 95, 193, 197

Hess, Moses 89, 95, 195

High Court of Justice in Israel 114, 117

historic connection to the land of Israel 17, 43, 65, 76, 81–2, 160, 222n32

Hobsbawm, Eric 78

Holocaust 12, 34–5, 56, 66–7, 71, 81, 84, 94–5, 194, 196; survivors 19, 31, 65, 182

homeland 2, 10, 29, 36, 174; adopted 175; return to 129

homeless people 12, 35, 42, 43, 56

human rights 1–2, 20, 28, 90, 99, 100–1, 105, 114, 152–3, 189, 192; abuses 6, 40, 105; European Court 5, 99–100, 128, 179, 185, 202, 231n1; international 134, 158; law 141

Hungarian minorities 87, 212; economic privileges 126

Husseini, Jamal 28

Idische Kolonizatsie Organizatsie 75

immigrants 48, 73, 101, 186; from Arab countries 54; defined as Jewish 231n33; illegal 30; Muslim minority 114; to United States 171

immigration 3, 13, 16–19, 20, 29–30, 33, 39, 61, 68, 83–4, 89, 107, 125, 129–33, 143, 151, 158, 173, 175, 187, 197, 220n5; of ethnic Finns 129; laws 6, 126, 133, 134; to Palestine 34–5, 67; preference 127

imperial nation 164, 166–7

inclusiveness 171, 174, 178, 181–2, 184

independence 9, 23, 31–3, 43, 151; diplomatic recognition 152; right to 8, 14, 88

India 32, 86; Constitution 134, 189; delegate 26, 27; diaspora 132; Hindu religion and nationalism 159–61, 177; partition 158; refugees 157

individual rights 148; violated 174

injustice 51, 118

integration 143, 148, 175–6, 180, 182, 187–8, 196; obstacles to 194

international community 20–1, 37, 43–4, 56–9, 75, 82, 84, 88, 148, 154–5

international law 126, 198

intifada 64, 111, 196

Iraq 53, 62; delegate to the UN, 1947 44, 50, 52, 68; Jewish community 106; Kurd minority 45

Ireland 162, 189, 230n23; citizenship 130–1; Constitution 99, 139, 200–2; Irish language 163, 201; nationalism 99, 139; peace process 200

Irish Republic 164; Constitution 163

Islam 46, 111, 153; political influence 100; state religion in Muslim countries 46

Israel 64, 88, 106, 122–3, 181–4, 191, 197, 220n3; allocated territory 29; anthem 191; Arab minority 48, 113, 120, 123, 150, 169, 183, 191; Basic Laws 135; Cabinets 112; Citizenship Law 175; Constitution 123; democracy 8, 108, 115, 125; draft constitution 93; education system 121, 188; growing prosperity 176; High Court of Justice 227n13; independence 57; Jewish population 47, 54, 133, 138, 142, 150, 166–7, 174, 187; lack of neutrality 143; Lands Authority 114–15; right to exist 108–9; standard of living 197; state of emergency 105–6; Supreme Court 97, 101, 114, 116–17, 135

Israeli 104, 175, 186; academics 124; civic
community 135; communism 109, 134;
conflict 5, 178, 182, 188; Declaration of
Independence 10, 12, 14, 18, 43, 49, 70,
79, 88–9, 94–7, 117–18, 122–3, 134,
149; government 61–3, 108, 111; ID
cards 187; leaders 60, 63; Left 2;
military administration 107, 158; people
183; political divide 63, 102, 112; Right
149; right of suffrage 135; settlement
14, 133; ties with diaspora 182;
universities 158; War of Independence
59
Italy 105, 207–8; Constitution 207–8;
German-speaking population 191;
national unification 190; Republic of 148

Jabotinsky, Zeev 92–3
Japanese national identity 86
Jerusalem 88, 102; Jewish Quarter 96;
Mayor of 90
Jewish Agency 31, 56–9, 88, 115
Jewish community 52, 66, 88, 94, 95, 100;
in Egypt 55; in Palestine 16, 19, 24, 83,
91, 106; in Tunisia 54
Jewish diaspora 3–4, 9, 12, 30, 86, 89, 92,
133, 138, 144, 156, 196
Jewish homeland 9, 29, 41, 74, 80, 86, 96,
103; return to 116, 182
Jewish majority 7, 48, 71, 90, 92, 103,
107, 114, 149, 151, 166–7, 183
Jewish minority 23, 28, 39, 45, 46, 47,
118, 133
Jewish nation-state 11, 98, 133–4, 157,
188, 197
Jewish National Fund 3–4, 115
Jewish National Home 18, 24, 38–40, 42,
52, 65, 67, 71–3, 75, 82, 84, 88, 126,
193, 197–9
Jewish national identity 9, 21, 27, 41,
78–80, 85–6, 137; in Israel 14, 138, 140,
164, 175, 197
Jewish national independence 2, 22, 29,
42, 104, 149, 186
Jewish national movement 71, 75, 86, 89,
98, 104
Jewish people 9, 12–17, 21, 24–7, 30,
34–7, 40–2, 45–9, 56, 63–5, 71, 79, 87,
97, 135, 138–42, 166, 191, 198;
aspirations 31, 36, 40, 43, 66, 68, 75,
198; capitalists 194; citizens 66, 141;
communists 108; historic roots 41–3,
52, 55, 74, 77, 80, 84, 94, 144; hostages
53; refugees 34, 66; rights 23, 33, 125

Jewish peoplehood 7–8, 25, 52, 78, 84,
172, 182; denial of 31, 53; working
class 73
Jewish population 35, 54, 113; of
Mandatory Palestine 88–9, 107
Jewish problem 194–5
Jewish property 53; struggle for restitution
196
Jewish religion 25, 46, 134, 182; religious
community 197; religious courts 135;
religious establishment 231n38;
religious law 175
Jewish settlement 63–6, 72–5, 90, 103–4;
Arab opposition 45, 91; Birobidzhan
22
Jewish State 1, 2, 4, 7, 10, 12–29, 33–5,
41–8, 52, 55–7, 64–5, 68–71, 84, 88–9,
92–8, 102–5, 113, 120, 123–4, 128,
135–7, 140–4, 149–51, 159, 181–3,
197–9; democratic 83, 198; international
recognition 87; legitimacy denied 59;
opponents 8; territory allotted 18–19
Jews 75, 79, 81, 192; in Arab countries
51–2, 223n40; of Eastern Europe 24;
European 31, 76; Orthodox 183; of
Palestine 37, 62, 92; Russian 194–5
Jordan 60, 62–4, 149, 230n16; army 95
Judaism 137, 183

Kaadan case 3; ruling 115
Kemal, Mustafa 179
Khazars 31, 76
Kimmerling, Baruch 125
kin-minorities 128–9, 180; abroad 131–2,
138–9; protection of rights 127
kin-states 126–7, 138
Knesset 53, 60, 95, 109, 111, 113–14, 119;
allotment of seats 122; Arab members
102, 135, 150; member 137; records 108
Koestler, Arthur 74
Kurd minority in Iraq 45, 179; diaspora 87
Kymlicka, W. 148, 171–2, 176–7

Labour Party in Israel 63, 101, 112;
government 103; movement 58;
Zionism 100
Land of Israel 12–13, 41, 58, 65, 67, 78,
82, 92–3, 149; Arab part 60
landmark decision (by Israel's Supreme
Court, on non-discrimination) 115–16
language 7, 21, 44, 49, 86–7, 119, 120,
153, 169, 177; bilingualism 121, 145,
172; Castilian 207; diversity 137, 159;
groups 178; Hindi 159–60; key

importance 145; of the majority 121; of minorities 143, 152; multilingual India 161; national 6, 142–3, 200; official 160; oppression 146; rights 20, 127; Sanskrit 178; Spanish 167–8, 181; Turkish 179

Latin America 65; constitutions 215; Spanish-speaking 207

Law of Return, Israel's 1–3, 19, 81, 102, 116, 125–6, 128–9, 133–5, 138, 140–1, 156–8, 175, 186, 220n2; legitimacy denied 158

laws to revoke 157

League of Nations 9, 15–16, 30, 37, 58, 88; Assembly 218; Mandate 25, 41, 82

Lebanon 46; Hizbollah movement 111; Lebanese delegate 37; refugee camps 230n16

legitimacy 4–6, 8–9, 19–20, 31, 40, 49, 58, 74, 87, 103, 122, 133, 138, 140, 149, 157, 162; called in question 186; democratic 124; denial of 2, 97; international 9, 12, 37, 57, 85, 88, 103, 124; lacking 65

liberal democracy 1, 4–6, 88, 98, 101, 113, 118–19, 124–5, 128, 130, 144, 176, 192

liberalism 100–1, 141–3

liberalization 99, 107, 179

Likud Party 103, 112

Lilienblum, Moses Leib 194

Macedonia 153, 185; Albanian minority 152; Constitution 151, 189; ethnic diaspora 154; national minority 184; territorial integrity 155

Majadele, Raleb 112

majority 125, 142, 186; culture 3, 143; language 121

majority–minority relations 169

Maki Israeli Communist Party 108, 110

Malta 214–15

Mandatory Palestine 9, 12, 15–19, 28, 36–7, 39, 42, 58, 95, 100, 138, 149, 154–6, 159, 182

Mapai Labour Party 100, 107

Mapam Party 108, 134

Masalha, Nur 78

massacre 105, 221n14; Kafr Qassem 107

Meir, Golda 8, 62, 101, 103

Memmi, Albert 54

military 58, 63, 110; administration 95, 103–4, 107–9; armed forces 70; confrontation 67; government in

Germany 34; international force 57; occupation 63, 158; permits 106; restrictions 107

military service 158, 175, 231n32; compulsory 188; evasion 101; exemption 113–14; right to volunteer 188

minorities 2–7, 37, 144, 154, 180, 198; affront to 191; effective participation 120; ethnic and cultural 127; indigenous 150; native 186; marginalized 122; non-marginalized 142; protection of 53, 123; recognized 151

minority groups 20, 162, 171, 174; Berbers in North Africa 45; Circassian community in Israel 188; dilemma 7; French-speaking in Belgium 146; in Greece 185; inclusion 176; in Israel 116; in Palestine 31; unique 188

minority language 120, 151, 176; teaching in 121

minority rights 21, 28, 56, 119, 120–1, 125, 133, 153; restricted 122

modernization 98, 101

Mufti of Jerusalem 21, 28, 33, 52, 62, 72, 77, 94, 108

multiculturalism 92, 143, 153, 161

Muslim 70, 100, 196; All India Muslim League 27, 177; Arabs 89, 231n38; collective identity 79; countries 50, 198; extremist groups 196; immigrants 148; Kashmiri 190; minorities 152, 158–61, 209; refugees 157

Nasser, Gamal Abdul 44, 63, 108–9

nation state 4–5, 9, 127, 128, 148, 198; democratic 3, 6, 155; modern 87, 176, 189; in Palestine 78; ties with kin 126

nation-building 77, 160, 182; post-colonial 177

national aspirations 27–9, 33, 39, 58, 65, 68, 137, 156, 164; Arab 93; conflicting 37, 155

national community 19, 127, 136, 145

national conflict 8, 32, 37, 51, 55, 58, 74, 117, 148, 155, 178

national emblems and flags 142, 144, 146, 160, 168, 189, 191, 216

national identity 6–9, 28, 49, 58, 76, 78, 81, 85–7, 105, 118, 128, 130, 134–40, 142–7, 150, 162, 165–7, 171, 174–7, 180, 183–4, 187, 191, 193, 198, 201, 207; composite 181; in conflict 182

national independence 2, 8, 10, 14, 19, 22, 24, 40, 43, 46, 47, 48, 65, 66, 81, 118, 150, 155, 163, 167, 169, 193, 198; denial of right 125
national minority 6, 13, 14, 49, 118, 120–2, 128, 133, 146, 152, 159, 162, 166, 171, 173, 179, 184–5, 189, 209; collective rights 115; in Greece 231n35; official recognition 123; protection of 119, 122–3, 127, 187, 227n14
national movements 17, 68, 70, 78–9, 81, 92, 164, 189, 198
national rights 17, 41, 52, 93
national unity 174; governments 104
nationalism 77–9, 82, 138, 143, 161, 183; black 174, 178; civic 7, 141, 147, 159, 176–8, 182, 186, 216; ethnic 177, 179; modern nationalism 9, 81, 85–7, 98–9
Native Americans 173–4
naturalization 127, 129–30, 172, 175–6, 202; laws 6, 126, 133–4
Nazis 9, 12, 22, 33, 35, 66, 72, 77, 194, 221n13; Nazi Germany 28, 66
neutrality 142, 159–60, 162–3, 180, 188–9, 191, 210; lack of 145, 171, 181, 184, 190
non-Arab minorities in Arab countries 45, 155
non-Jews 89–91, 97; immigrants 187; minority 89, 184; political rights 103; relatives of Jews 186
non-neutral 143, 148, 153–4, 161, 163, 165–70, 176, 188–90; to immigrants 148; to minorities 146
Nordau, Max 87, 89, 95
North American colonies 72–3
Northern Ireland 144–5, 163, 200; nationalist community 165; peace process 162; sectarian violence 105
Norway 205–7
Nusseibeh, Sari 14

occupied territories 59, 103, 104–5, 111, 149
official language 116, 121, 136, 154, 162, 168, 188, 189
Orthodox establishment in Israel 97, 101–2, 134, 175
Orthodox Judaism *see* Halacha
Oslo Accords 64, 102, 149, 156, 158
Ottoman Empire 37–8, 68, 88

Pakistan 32, 100, 157–9, 221n15
Palestine 21–8, 38–9, 65, 67–70, 78; autonomy 104; Basic Law 46; British administration 88, 178; economic development 73; Government 62; independence 31, 36, 60, 63–4, 104, 149; Jews presented as 'alien element' 44–5, 47–8, 55; liberation 109; minorities 31, 72, 119; national home 156–7; state 45, 60
Palestine Liberation Organization 45, 63–4, 110
Palestinian Arabs 13, 17, 30, 38–9, 45, 50, 52, 55, 60, 62, 66, 75, 83, 94, 103, 106, 149; aspirations 31, 156; leadership 21, 33; national identity 63, 186; national movement 92, 191; representatives 57; state 133, 149, 155, 182
Palestinian Authority 113, 149, 156
Palestinian Declaration of Independence 45
Palestinians 63–4, 103, 110, 120, 133, 150, 157–9, 178–9, 230n16; diaspora 156; intellectuals 39, 47; leadership 62–3; national movement 104, 178, 186; nationalism 38–9; paramilitary groups 106; refugees 55, 156, 182; right of repatriation 64, 156
Pappe, Ilan 65–6, 70, 73–4
Parliamentary Assembly of the Council of Europe 136–7
partition 14–17, 19–25, 28–9, 31, 36, 40, 44, 49, 50, 53, 64, 82, 88, 91, 92, 94, 103–4, 108, 126, 133, 149–55, 159, 162, 177–8, 191, 221n15; along armistice lines 59; debates 45, 77; implementation 58; of India 27, 32; opposition 28–9, 36–7, 43, 56, 62, 92; recommendation 56–7; resolution 62, 65
partition plan 15, 18, 21, 30, 33, 46, 58, 68, 69, 88; international trusteeship 58, 68, 224n41; legal validity 57; rejected 224n42, 226n22; support 43, 76, 221n12
peace 16, 45, 50, 60–1, 64, 88; process 113, 163; settlement 63, 109–10
persecution 80, 198; Armenian 81; of Jews 23–6, 53, 56, 66
personal status 97–8, 135, 187; law 102, 134; marriage for people of different faiths 188; matrimonial law 175
Peru 215; delegate to the UN, 1947 36
Pinsker, Leon 194
pluralism 100, 174
pogroms 66, 192, 194–5; Iraqi 196
Poland 35, 209; Church status 210; Constitution 211–12; Polish delegate 24;

Polish diaspora 130; repatriation 130; Republic 66, 80
political freedom 79, 108–9
political ideologies 37, 85, 137, 167
property confiscation 53
Protestant community in Ulster 163; majority 201; minority in Ireland 99

Rabin government 114, 117
'racial homogeneity' 44–5, 52
reactionary regimes 53, 108
refugees 34–5, 50, 67, 218; camps 106; German 127; illegal 56; Indian 32; Jewish 26; Palestinian 95; problem 57, 83, 108; of Turkish descent 132
religion 86, 134, 209; status 102, 144, 200
religion and state 102, 202, 205; separation of 98–100, 134, 148; ties between 207, 209–10
religious 99; coercion 1, 4, 101–2, 105, 118; community 15–16, 25–8, 51, 76, 137, 161, 183; establishment 98, 207; freedom 98, 134, 152; instruction 205; minorities 144; political parties 98, 100–2; rights 20; scholarship 80; symbols 3, 207
repatriation 3, 6, 130, 156, 210, 218; Finnish 129; laws 128, 131
Revisionist Right 92, 103; Zionism 104
right of return 14, 41, 67, 110, 127, 133, 138
right wing in Israel 98, 102, 103
rights 50, 89, 110–11, 136, 141, 188; clash 41; of minorities 20; of non-Jews 92; political 27, 51; violated 145, 173
Roman Catholic Church 99, 210, 214–15
Romania 126–7
Rome and Jerusalem 195

Scandinavian countries 205–7
Scotland 32, 164; diaspora 166; identity 180; Scottish parliament 165
secession 36–7, 152, 166, 168–9, 180–1, 190; of Belgium 32; right of 32, 163; ruled out 154
second official language (status of Arabic in Israel) 3, 5, 120, 151
Second World War 15, 22, 28, 35, 71, 85, 86, 91, 105, 190, 209
self-determination 2, 8, 12, 14, 22, 31, 33, 36, 39–41, 48–9, 56, 60, 88, 94, 97, 103, 110, 136–8, 156, 163, 168–9, 173, 181, 191
Sharon, Ariel 64, 113; government 149

Shertok, Moshe (Sharett) 52, 60, 76–7
Six Day War 43, 59, 63, 102, 110–11, 149, 158, 196
Slav-Macedonians in Greece 184
slavery 174, 190; emancipation 173
Slovakia 32, 212–13; Hungarian minority 146
Slovenia 152; Constitution 135–6, 213–14
Smith, Anthony 79–80, 86
Smolenskin, Peretz 194
Smooha, Professor Sammy 119
socialist 99, 195; socialist-Zionist 89
South Africa 72, 179; apartheid 178
South Korea 200; diaspora 132
Soviet Union 21–3, 26, 31–2, 35, 53, 56–7, 68–9, 75, 86–7, 109–10, 127, 199; Armenian Republic 131, 218; Bolsheviks 21, 85, 199; campaign against Israel 196; collapse of 128–9; delegate to the UN, 1947 24, 59; foreign policy 108; support for Israel 62
Spain 32, 87, 105, 164, 180, 207–8; Constitution 7, 169, 171, 180–1, 207–8; national identity 167–8, 172
Stalin, Joseph 68, 108, 132, 195
state 186; of all its citizens 135–6, 150; democratic 48, 96–7, 103, 106, 135, 142; education 119, 121, 188, 200, 205; emblem and flag 144, 212; land use 117; national character 49, 188; neutrality 141, 155, 164
State of Israel 40, 64, 69, 81, 84, 95, 97, 108, 114–15, 118, 138, 182; recognition of 61; values 116
struggle for independence 160, 164, 177
Suez crisis 106, 108
Swiss Constitution 210
Syria 45; Ba'ath Party regime 110; delegate 24–6, 38, 44, 68

territorial claim 43, 181; compromise 63, 92; concessions 64
territorial integrity 31, 33, 36–7, 85, 151, 154–5
terrorism 64, 105–6, 109–12, 169, 179, 196
Toubi, Tawfiq 53
traditional Judaism 86, 98, 101, 175
Transjordan 37, 59, 61
Tsarist Russia 66, 75
Turkey 68, 87, 107, 184; civic nationalism 132; Constitution 179; national identity 180; Settlement law 132
Turkish minority in Greece 184–6

Turkish-Muslim minority 189; Greece
209; Bulgaria 152
Turkish Republic 100; of Northern Cyprus
180
two states for two peoples 2, 23, 38, 41,
46, 64, 133, 148, 150, 156, 158, 191

Uganda 41
United Kingdom 32, 37, 61–2, 71, 87, 88,
163–5, 166; abstention on the UN
partition vote in 1947 56; colonies 72;
Jewish refugees 71; majority population
165; Welsh nationalists 165
United Nations 14–15, 23, 26, 37, 49, 50,
58–9, 129; Charter 30, 33, 52, 56, 58,
95; committee 19, 39; General
Assembly 2, 4, 18, 22, 53, 64, 68;
International Organization for Refugee
Affairs 34; partition plan 9, 12–13, 15,
56, 59, 67, 76, 83, 92, 97, 148–9, 182;
Security Council 57
United Nations Special Committee on
Palestine 15, 19, 20, 27, 29, 30, 44, 59,
69, 88, 151; majority report 31;
members 34, 42; minority report 33, 56,
155; report 18, 25, 38, 39, 41, 43, 58,
76, 83
United States 31, 57, 59, 65, 168;
administration 68; Bill of Rights 174;
civic nationalism 148, 171; Communist
Party 109; Confederate flag 190;
English national language 168;
integration policy 148; national
minorities 172; non-neutral 171;
Presidents 40, 59, 133; State
Department 56, 68; war on terror 105
Uruguayan delegate to the UN, 1947 24,
37

values 9; competing 124; shared 174

Venice Commission 126–7, 131
Vilner, Meir 110
violence 22, 32–3, 64, 105, 113, 157, 196;
racial 53, 197; rejection of 155;
threatened 52

war 13, 40, 53, 55, 57–62, 88, 105–6,
110–11, 156, 182; Arab launched 14;
arms via Czechoslovakia 68–9; civil
153; zones 83
War of Independence: Israel 60, 62, 68,
83, 95, 105–6, 108, 119, 149, 225n47;
Netherlands 190
Weizmann, Chaim 58–9
Weizmann-Feisal Agreement 16
West Bank 59–60, 62–4, 102, 104, 106,
149–50, 156, 158
West European 22–3, 74, 148; colonialism
54; democracies 56, 128, 147

Yemeni delegate to the UN, 1947 31
Yiddish culture 22, 85–6
Yiftachel, Oren 66–7, 157
Yom Kippur War 54, 111
Yugoslavia 32, 152; Yugoslav delegate to
the UN, 1947 28–30

Zionism 1–2, 8, 12, 36, 39–41, 66, 74, 75,
78–80, 83–5, 91, 96, 99, 100, 103, 138,
192, 193, 197, 198; foreign support 68,
88; non-Jewish support 84; opponents
21, 54, 65, 95, 108, 133
Zionist 36, 51, 63, 87, 94, 109; activity 22,
71, 196, 222n22; aspirations 30, 104;
and colonialism 65–7, 70, 73, 75, 91;
Congress 1, 84, 87, 88, 198; leaders 57,
62, 83, 224n46, 225n46; movement 3–4,
10, 13, 39, 55, 58–9, 67–8, 72–4, 85, 88,
98, 137, 183, 199